HARVARD STUDIES IN BUSINESS HISTORY · 48

Published with the support of the Harvard Business School
Edited by Thomas K. McCraw
Isidor Straus Professor of Business History
Graduate School of Business Administration
George F. Baker Foundation
Harvard University

PULL

Networking and Success
since Benjamin Franklin

PAMELA WALKER LAIRD

Harvard University Press
Cambridge, Massachusetts
London, England
2006

Library of Congress Cataloging-in-Publication Data

Laird, Pamela Walker, 1947–
Pull : networking and success since Benjamin Franklin /
Pamela Walker Laird.
p.   cm.—(Harvard studies in business history ; 48)
Includes bibliographical references and index.
ISBN 0-674-01907-5 (alk. paper)
1. Business networks—United States—History. 2. Success in
business—United States—History. 3. Businesspeople—United
States—History. 4. Social networks—United States—History.
5. Social capital (Sociology)—United States.
I. Title: Networking and success since Benjamin Franklin.
II. Title.   III. Series.

HD69.S8L35 2005
650.1′3—dc22   2005050247

For Frank

Contents

Illustrations

Acknowledgments

Everybody has stories of social capital, whether they call it favoritism, nepotism, office politics, connections, or pull. Embedded in each of these stories are advantages unevenly distributed, so some people's stories express resentment, while others express gratitude. Moral judgments and differential material benefits intensify the tellings because of Americans' tendency to associate workplace success and failure with character.

Because of people's desire to tell their stories, writing this book felt to me like being in the middle of a parade. I started this project intending to write about the famous men in America before 1900 whom popular culture hails as self-made. I wanted to explain how each of them had benefited from mentoring and access to influential networks. Each of them had advantages from pull—a product of social capital—that others lacked. This initial phase of my study demonstrated how business operates through social processes and, therefore, that self-made business success is impossible. The parade began when other people—scholars, friends and family, people I just happened to be chatting with—asked me about the present. Didn't that still happen? Didn't it still hurt one's career not to have any contacts, not to be connectable?

In expanding my project to tie the past to the present, I realized that we needed the words of the social capital lexicon—mentoring, networking, role models, gatekeeping—to understand how and why some people succeed and others do not. These words have only recently come into our everyday language, and they make it possible to explain how individual merits balance against social assets. So, thanks to those challenging questions, my parade turned a corner as I began to assess the effects of social capital in the workplace and how we learned about them.

In American history workplace discrimination has most obviously targeted race and gender. Therefore, as advocates for equality addressed occupational inequities regarding race and gender, they generated the insights that revealed how social capital works in the United States. It could have been otherwise. Class has always been and remains a potent determinant of social capital, even though the nation's dominant culture has tried to render class invisible, pretending that its manifestations simply reflect individual merit.

Like any parade, this one has been lively and sometimes overwhelming. The route took years to figure out, but the many intriguing detours and sidetracks have educated and engaged me. Because my parade moved through so many disparate territories, I am especially grateful for the remarkable scholarship that had already explored some of the terrain and made my journey easier.

Every time I mentioned this project, people offered encouragement and shared their stories. My project and its goals beckoned to them; it helped them put their stories into perspective. Were I a sociologist instead of a historian, I would have enjoyed writing a book about all those stories.

Many have encouraged me and given substantive guidance; my deep thanks go to Lindy Biggs, Regina Lee Blaszczyk, John K. Brown, Colleen Dunlavy, Wendy Gamber, Roger Horowitz, Leonard Johnson, Angel Kwolek-Folland, Naomi Lamoreaux, Susan Warren Lanman, Susan Ingalls Lewis, Roland Owens, Mark H. Rose, Eugene L. Schwaab Jr., and John M. Staudenmaier, SJ. For other friends and family, I am also and always grateful.

Mark S. Foster, Walter A. Friedman, and Daniel Horowitz joined the effort early and energetically. Not only have I benefited from the unusual care with which they read the entire manuscript, but I have also had the good fortune to tap their insights and be buoyed by their encouragement time and again. Others who have generously read and commented on versions of some or all of the manuscript include Mansel Blackford, Lori Breslow, Myra Hart, Richard R. John, Terri Lonier, Walter S. Rosenberry III, and Heather Thorwald. I have benefited greatly from their suggestions and encouragement. I also appreciated the opportunity to present a portion of my work, and receive comments on it, at the Business History Seminar at the Harvard Business School, led by Geoffrey Jones and Walter A. Friedman.

Thomas K. McCraw's early and ongoing faith in this project has mattered more than I could have foreseen. His investment began when he accepted it for the Harvard Studies in Business History series at Harvard University Press. Since then, his careful but forceful editing and advice have sharpened the manuscript. I cannot thank him enough for his kindness, insight, and generosity.

Working with Harvard University Press has been a very positive experience. Jeff Kehoe did me the great favor of recruiting the project. Kathleen McDermott then took it on and has provided encouragement, plus answers to my endless questions, ever since, ably guiding me through the publishing process. I also very much appreciate Donna Bouvier's skillful and energetic editorial work.

Archives and their caretakers earn historians' debts every day. The Hagley Museum and Library offers a wealth of resources in business and technology history, which in turn pertain to every aspect of life. Researching there is a privilege and a pleasure. I especially appreciate the helpfulness and knowledge of Lynn Catanese, Marjorie G. McNinch, and Michael Nash. I also used to great advantage the American Association of University Women Library and the Library of Congress Manuscripts Room, plus many other Library of Congress resources.

Lois K. Herr gave me a key boost. I had decided early on not to conduct interviews for this project because I found people's memories of the relevant events and attitudes too colored by the intervening years to be reliable. Lois, however, had built a rich personal document collection from her years as a feminist within corporate America. It surpasses any archive I could find on that subject. Just as she was finishing her own book on the 1973 AT&T and EEOC settlement, Lois gave me two full days of her time. She energetically guided me through rich material that addressed many of the issues with which I was struggling. She not only assured me that I was on the right track, but she also provided hard evidence to prove it.

For financial assistance that allowed me to take time for research and to travel to archives, I profoundly thank the American Association of University Women Educational Foundation for its Postdoctoral Research Leave Fellowship and the Hagley Museum and Library for its Business History Grant-in-Aid. For funding support I also thank Dean W. James Smith of the College of Liberal Arts and Sciences at the University of Colorado at Denver and the Walter S. Rosenberry III Fund for the History Department of the University of Colorado at Denver.

The History Department within the University of Colorado at Denver is a great place to be a historian. Over the years of this project Myra Rich has chaired the department, building and deepening its capacities for scholarship and outreach and nurturing everyone who enters, whether student or faculty. My gratitude to her and to the department as a whole is boundless.

The luxury of research assistants! Each of these women contributed according to her substantial abilities, and all with initiative and enthusiasm: Sarah Marino Fischler, Tracey Limbaugh, Anne Steffens, and Heather Thorwald. I learned a lot from each of them, and I am grateful to them for all that they contributed.

Networking can enhance more than our vocational lives. Friends have connected me with friends, and one of them—to whom I remain ever grateful—introduced me to Frank N. Laird. Our partnership as spouses and colleagues enriches every aspect of my life and work.

PULL

Connections at Work

The chief glory of America is that it is the country in which genius and industry find their speediest and surest reward. Fame and fortune are here open to all who are willing to work for them. . . . We are emphatically a nation of self-made men, and it is to the labors of this worthy class that our marvelous national prosperity is due.

— Walter R. Houghton, *Kings of Fortune; or, the Triumphs and Achievements of Noble, Self-Made Men,* 1888

The America of our ideals rewards merit, and only merit. In our imagined land, self-made men and women triumph by applying their talents to difficult tasks. In the meritocracy that is this ideal America, the denizens of every rank earn their places. Worldly success, we like to think, handily and fairly gauges individual worth.[1]

In the *real* America, however, opportunities have never been distributed evenly. Even in the nineteenth-century heyday of new industrial and financial fortunes and so-called rugged individualism, most business leaders came from privileged origins. America's business heroes have not routinely pulled themselves up by their own ragged bootstraps. Yet in the national imagination, exhilarating individual exceptions overwhelm the staid statistical record. We retell these sagas with relish, as if they somehow prove the rule of equal opportunity. Instead, what the rare rags-to-riches story and *all* success stories prove is another rule, one to which there is no exception: that of the necessity for connections and connectability—the rule of social capital.

Social capital makes connections and connectability possible. A chauffeur, a secretary, a waiter, or a clerk may all have contact with a CEO who is searching for a successor or a colleague. But a contact is not necessarily a connection. Rarely will a CEO regard anyone in those positions as *connectable*—as someone with whom to dine or negotiate a business deal.

What determines who gets invited into the networks of business opportunity, that is, who has pull? What does an unacceptable candidate for such an invitation lack? The short answer is *social capital*—all those social assets that enable one to attract respect, generate confidence, evoke affection, and draw on loyalty in a specific setting. Social capital exists in and flows through personal connections and individuals' potential for making connections. Shared expectations and goals bind together networks, which can be made up of groups as informal as golfing buddies or as formal as incorporated institutions. Social capital operates through such networks, as well as through mentors, gatekeepers, and role models, to inspire as well as advance the ambitious.

Like the other assets that people try to grow in order to prosper, social capital is distributed unevenly through populations. This matters because networks and their gatekeepers control opportunities, training, and information, so individuals and groups can thrive by inclusion or suffer by exclusion. As political scientist Robert Putnam explained in *Bowling Alone: The Collapse and Revival of American Community*, social capital embraces the "connections among individuals—social networks and the norms of reciprocity and trustworthiness that arise from them." Although Putnam urged the regeneration of social capital in order to renew community-building, he also acknowledged its "dark side." "Social inequalities may be embedded in social capital," he wrote. "Norms and networks that serve some groups may obstruct others, particularly if the norms are discriminatory or the networks socially segregated." Putnam popularized this century-old but previously little-known phrase "social capital," and ideas about it continue to grow. Increasingly we recognize its powerful but mixed consequences for individuals, groups, and societies.[2]

Business enterprise pulls individuals' abilities and ambitions into webs of interaction and exchange with other people and institutions. The idea that social assets are relevant to achievement and that they provide opportunities, however, need not obscure individual abilities, hard work, and perseverance. Despite the importance of social factors, personal traits and efforts do matter greatly for success in work-related activities, as in any other arena. Social capital helps those who help themselves. Individuals can override their initial social capital allotments. They can propel themselves upward or squander their allotment and spiral downward. Someone who begins with no connections, but who is connectable because of characteristics—including hard work or personal charm—that appeal to network gatekeepers, may gain entry to relevant networks. It is important to note this because popular narratives that point solely to family background, ethnicity,[3] class, or sex as prevailing variables would diminish the promise of individual agency and, therefore, responsibility. If we assume that a forward-looking culture and political economy *should* instill ambitions and fuel personal efforts, how can we find an honest and useful balance of social and individual variables? Can we apply historical evidence more fully than we have to rebuild Americans' narratives of success and failure?

Neglecting social capital when studying success and failure has distorted our historical memory. Screening out this evidence in evaluating individuals and groups has also perpetuated and legitimated a stream of injustices, damaging material well-being and self-esteem for some while enhancing them for others. Disregarding social evidence in explaining success has denied often overwhelming causes of unequal opportunity. It has compounded the force of our long history of linking virtue with worldly success that has all but ranked individuals' souls along with their fortunes. By asserting that people make their own success, with luck and pluck the only variables, the American success ethos has rewarded almost all advantage with praise and affluence and punished almost all disadvantage with blame and hardship.

By contrast, looking at business achievement through the lens of social capital enables us to expand our ideas about what positive and negative workplace discrimination entails and how it operates. Comparing what becomes of people with social capital to what becomes of those without it makes clear that discrimination actually moves in two directions. It can push out, and it can pull in. Pushing out is what we typically mean by discrimination: excluding or abusing people because of their membership in some group that engulfs their individuality. Only after the worst practices of "push" discrimination diminished did "pull" discrimination—inclusion because of advantageous social capital—become fully apparent.

In 1957, Gary S. Becker published *The Economics of Discrimination,* a sophisticated analysis of ethnicity-based discrimination. His book received little attention initially, but as the momentum for civil rights rose, interest in his analysis grew, and a second edition was published in 1971. With numbers, formulae, and graphs, Becker sought objective measures of the economic impact from various "non-pecuniary motives" for discrimination. In summarizing his conclusions, Becker offered a startling insight. He observed that discussions about the differences between races were typically framed "in terms of discrimination against non-whites," yet "a theory based on nepotism in favor of whites would have almost exactly the same empirical implications." A "theory based on 'hatred'"—that is, push—"of one group is not easily distinguished empirically from one based on 'love,'"—that is, pull—"of the other

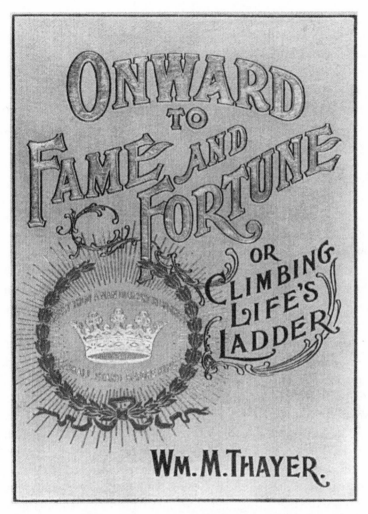

"Seest Thou a Man Diligent in Business, He Shall Stand before Kings."
This biblical expression (Proverbs 22:29) circles the crown on this 1893
book cover. It appeared widely, quoted most famously by Benjamin Franklin in his *Autobiography* and by John D. Rockefeller. The notion that diligence alone sufficed for one to climb "life's ladder" helped to legitimate
the myth of the self-made man, linking work, honor, fame, and fortune.

group." Although "push" discrimination seems more morally re-
pugnant than "pull," the objective consequences may be the same.
Becker's insight points to a core dilemma with social capital: as it
benefits one group, it disadvantages others.[4]

Prior to the mid-1960s, American norms of law and culture allowed certain groups to be excluded from most workplace opportunities other than low-level jobs. But today employers can no longer
turn away an otherwise qualified candidate by saying simply, "You
are a Negro," or claiming to one person that a job is filled, only
to hand an application to the next person in line.[5] Decades of
enforcing civil rights reduced, if not eliminated, the frequency of
exclusionary bias, and it gradually lost most of its legal and moral
standing. Yet frustrations continued as so-called glass ceilings to
ambition became visible. Efforts to discover ways to break or crash
through them initially assumed that "push" discrimination had
alone created the ceilings. By the late 1980s, however, it became
clear that *nobody* can penetrate a workplace ceiling without pull
from above. That pull requires social capital.

Terms such as "glass ceiling," "networking," "mentor," "gatekeeper," and "role model" have become buzz words in the social
capital lexicon over the past four decades. One of my concerns in
this book is how and why this vocabulary evolved and diffused.
Words are tools, and the ways people invent, alter, construct, use,
and accredit them offer potent evidence of cultures, perceptions,
and values. Language reflects habits of mind, as we develop words
and phrases to describe and facilitate our understanding of how
and why the world works as it does. New words, or new meanings
for old words, challenge habits of mind and can even help us see
our world differently.

With the words and meanings in the social capital lexicon as han-
dles, we can grasp processes that affect not only individual success
and failure, but also the societies and workplaces within which people function. Lacking words to point to how restricted social assets

affect business dynamics has crimped our view of the richness of business interactions. The social capital lexicon makes possible a larger perspective on the present and, when applied retrospectively as I have in this book, the past. Its words point to the fluid mix of individual and social factors that move people through their life's work. With these words, we can reweave business history into the fabric of its host cultures and societies—where business itself always resides.

Social resources have long influenced access to training and opportunities, so using power from above to assist someone else's career is not unique to business. Mentoring has always been common in music and art, medicine, politics, the military, and education. The word "mentor" itself dates back to ancient Greek mythology, from the name of the trusted counselor whose shape the goddess Athena took to care for Odysseus's son. Socrates, Plato, Aristotle, and Alexander belonged to one of the most illustrious mentoring lineages. Haydn mentored Mozart and Beethoven.

Medicine, law, science, art, and education are openly social in how they develop novices. Each of these fields has long-standing traditions—including apprenticeships, internships, and standards—for recruiting and training newcomers. Through these mechanisms, practitioners come to know, evaluate, and interact with each other. In the best cases, gatekeepers recognize youthful ability and ambition in order to identify, guide, and develop individuals who are most likely to contribute to a community's future. In the worst cases, gatekeepers exploit aspirants, such as on Hollywood's infamous casting couches.

Networks, like mentors, are social resources. "Networking" is the new umbrella term for the sharing of information, tools, skills, funds, and opportunities—the kind of cooperation in business that has always happened, and must happen. Sometimes, of course, "corruption" is a more apt term for this cooperation, depending on how legally and ethically networks conduct their affairs.[6] Varieties of favoritism, nepotism, and cooperation are nothing new, and typically they have only been concealed when they are illegal or politically dangerous. Thus, no one is outraged, or perhaps even annoyed, to observe nepotism in a small business, where it is expected and often necessary. In personnel systems that have no pretensions to meritocracy or objectivity, discrimination based on family, club, or religion can be open and straightforward. But in large and ostensibly meritocratic organizations, favoritism and discrimination based on anything other than performance violate proclaimed principles of equal opportunity.

In 1963, social scientist Seymour Martin Lipset challenged beliefs that the United States was and had always been exceptionally meritocratic. Lipset argued that Americans spoke of their country as a "classless society" because the "focus on the ideology of equal opportunity for each individual has made Americans relatively insensitive to gross inequalities of income and wealth in their country." But what if opportunity has never been equally distributed? If people with ability and ambition could not find opportunities in America, especially in its major employers, national and corporate belief systems were at risk.[7]

Neither Lipset nor any other scholarly critic of America's meritocratic pretensions reached a mass audience. But Shepherd Mead's satire *How to Succeed in Business without Really Trying: A Dastard's Guide to Fame and Fortune* did. First in a book (1952), then in a Broadway play (1961), and especially in a film (1967), Mead portrayed how the clever polishing of executive egos enabled a winsome youth's nimble climb from window washer to chairman of the corporate board.[8] The resounding popularity of Mead's assault on corporations' supposedly objective recruiting, hiring, and promotion practices hinted at widespread public awareness of the gap between corporate pretensions and their realities. Yet until the civil rights and women's movements of the 1960s and 1970s, policy-focused challenges to gatekeeping practices in business rarely gained a national forum. With those movements came broad-based demands for change, beginning at the margins of business, where the system's failings were most apparent.

Contrasting how we Americans have prospered—or not—with how we have talked about prospering exposes rich insights about how business really operates and where it fits within American culture.

The story of social capital in American business success begins with small colonial shops and continues to firms of all sizes in the twenty-first century. Rather than offer a definition of success for all situations, I have simply honored actors' notions of success, recognizing that they are contingent on historical, cultural, and social contexts. Thus, for many people, work at a respected trade counts as a success every bit as much as climbing a corporate ladder or building a profitable enterprise.

The power of social capital in American enterprise jumps out from the very stories that are usually held up as evidence of the archetypal American hero, the self-made man. Social capital was central to the achievements of Benjamin Franklin, Andrew Carnegie, Jay Gould, and J. P. Morgan alike, and that fact points to its ubiquity. Between the Civil War and World War I, Americans tirelessly formed trade and other associations to benefit members and exclude others. Organizations as different as corporations, unions, and professional associations flourished, despite growing praise of individualism. Marginalized groups organized to compensate for their social capital disadvantages; they recognized that self-help required collective effort. In the twentieth century, as corporations grew, business managers struggled to build new, formalized sets of practices to recruit, hire, and promote people. Despite vigorous attempts to build merit-based objectivity into these systems, social capital still determined access to opportunity.

After World War II, disadvantaged men and women began to expand their expectations for participating in the nation's working life. The GI Bill and postwar economic expansion, followed by the Civil Rights Act of 1964, helped to uncover the mechanisms of social capital. Peeling away each layer of exclusionary discrimination within firms and labor unions exposed the social dynamics that pulled some people into place and pushed others away. As previously marginalized groups gained entry to American business in numbers never before possible, laws and cultural values haltingly moved toward national meritocratic ideals. Yet, despite real progress in reducing exclusionary discrimination, many aspirants remained trapped under a glass ceiling. Activists, social scientists, and business analysts discovered how social capital had always aided those who most resembled the already powerful. They pinpointed the primary mechanisms of social capital—mentors, networks, and role models—and identified them as tools that could be used to redistribute opportunity and fracture the glass ceiling. The tools of social capital thus moved to the foreground of management training and public discourse. By the twenty-first century, the social bootstraps that are so much a part of individuals' success in business had changed from being what successful people used but did not talk about to what everyone talks about and what successful people still use best.

CHAPTER 1

Social Capital and the Mechanisms of Success

How would Benjamin Franklin's story look if we were to consider his social capital as well as his oft-praised individual efforts and abilities? This patron saint of self-made men, this renowned artisan, entrepreneur, inventor, and diplomat, flourished within several influential networks, even as a youth. His remarkable talents and energy have blinded us to other factors—social factors—that contributed to his success. To be sure, Franklin himself artfully constructed his *Autobiography* as dazzling lessons in self-making. Even though he detailed his social advantages, he deliberately set the eternal model for the self-made man, beginning the *Autobiography* with a letter to his son that framed the story and the lessons he wished to immortalize: "From the poverty and obscurity in which I was born and in which I passed my earliest years, I have raised myself to a state of affluence and some degree of celebrity in the world." Biographies of the successful still follow this pattern, replete with details of social factors, but crediting individual factors nonetheless.[1]

As a young man, Franklin took charge of shaping his life's course. He had only two years of schooling, but he educated himself assiduously. He ran away from an abusive apprenticeship and constructed a remarkable career as a printer, author, and publisher before moving on to spectacular public service in science and nation building, earning both pride and praise for his accomplishments. Nonetheless, to appreciate fully Franklin's dual success in self-creation—once in living his life and then in retelling it—we must remember that he was *not* poor as a child. Overall material conditions in the colonies had improved enough that his childhood circumstances were poor compared to those of the readers of his *Autobiography,* although Franklin as a boy had not been poor relative to most of his contemporaries. His artisanal roots in Boston did require hard work, but they also gave him respectability, training in a core trade, literacy, and self-esteem, plus access to men of influence. His greatest struggles occurred briefly in 1723 when, as a seventeen-year-old youth, he sought independence from apprenticeship to his brother and escaped from Boston to Philadelphia. He described his adventures and arrival, truly rugged and ragged, in great detail— "that you may in your mind compare such unlikely beginnings with the figure I have since made there." Yet this runaway had a trunk of clothing and books on the way, and money enough to feed and lodge himself in the meantime. Most important, he could readily form a connection through which he quickly gained work.[2] Soon his outstanding printing skills, combined with his superb business and political intuitions, launched him on his way toward affluence and prominence.

Community size mattered a good bit in making possible this bright young artisan's access to influential circles. In 1720, three years before Franklin ran away from Boston, that city's population numbered about 12,000, while the population of Philadelphia, where Franklin would find success, was somewhere between 7,000 and 8,000. Calculating from percentages in Boston's 1764 Provincial Census, white, male adults in Boston's 1720 population totaled less than 3,000; there were fewer than half that many in Philadelphia.[3] Given such small numbers for the relevant populations, it must have been easy for the members of the community's elite to notice a bright young fellow, especially one who worked in a core trade like printing, as he ran errands, met influential customers, and delivered finished goods. In contrast, a century later, growing population centers exacerbated the effects of the working classes' descent into the factories that displaced small shops. Classes lost contact with each other as larger, homogeneous neighborhoods replaced mixed settings. By the end of the nineteenth century, ongoing industrialization and bureaucratization had made even middle-class employees lose easy access to upper-level decision makers.

Franklin gained entrance to top networks also by virtue of his good breeding, in both senses of the term. His ethnicity, sex, and Protestant origins resembled those of the prominent, substantial, and authoritative people of his world. His family background had given him the pride and bearing that identified him as a proper and well-mannered citizen, despite his humble clothing. Franklin gained the opportunities to polish his innate brilliance because his well-respected artisan family in early eighteenth-century Boston could and did entertain all but the highest ranks of society. His father was well regarded in Boston, Franklin remembered, and influential citizens often consulted him "for his opinion in affairs of the town or of the church he belonged to." The senior Franklin often invited to dinner "some sensible friend or neighbour to converse with, and always took care to start some ingenious or useful topic for discourse which might tend to improve the minds of his children. By this means he turned our attention to what was good, just, and prudent in the conduct of life." Not a bad education, and excellent networking to boot. Franklin's education advanced further when "a merchant, an ingenious, sensible man, Mr. Matthew Adams, who had a pretty collection of books and who frequented our printing house, took notice of me, invited me to see his library, and very kindly proposed to lend me such books as I chose to read."[4] Although Franklin was poorer as a child than he was as an adult, his words do not describe a life of grinding and isolated poverty from which children working in mines and mills in the next century could rarely emerge.

During his adventurous journey from Boston to Philadelphia,

Franklin found assistance, both practical and professional, from strangers. Friendless though he was along the way, he was welcomed in houses and shops and did not meet with the wariness an alien might have faced. In New York City, he introduced himself to printer William Bradford, who soon introduced him to Philadelphia's two printers, one of whom was Bradford's son. Franklin's network soon expanded to include the governor of Pennsylvania, Sir William Keith, when one of Franklin's brothers-in-law, Robert Homes, showed the governor a letter that Franklin had written to Homes. As impressive as the letter might have been, a relative's "happening to be in company" with a governor was much more likely in the 1720s than now; and it was more likely still if that relative was a ship's captain, as was Franklin's brother-in-law. Later the "finely dressed" Governor Keith called on the young apprentice, surprising both him and his master by inviting him to "taste . . . some excellent Madeira." The governor lamented the lack of a fine printer in Philadelphia, disparaging both Franklin's master and the city's second printer. Recognizing Franklin's literary skills and intelligence, Keith offered what appeared to be a remarkable opportunity: encouragement and apparent backing to set Franklin up in his own shop. As it turned out, Keith did not have the wherewithal to fund Franklin, but he did open doors and also sent the young man to England in good comfort and company. Franklin's adventures and social achievements continued throughout his business career; he met and charmed many people who had the potential to improve his circumstances. As he said of one gentleman he met in England, "he became my friend, greatly to my advantage afterwards on many occasions."[5]

Franklin proved a consummate network builder. He thrived in his trade at the nexus of business, politics, and culture. Once back in the colonies, he "acquired friends" who "were afterwards of great use to me, as I occasionally was to some of them." One "acquaintance" brought Franklin's newly opened printing shop its first customer, a "country man . . . whom he had met in the street enquiring for a printer." Franklin later formed the Junto, a "club for mutual improvement," among some of his "ingenious acquaintance." Although the group conducted its "debates . . . in the sincere spirit of enquiry after truth" and became "the best school of philosophy, and politics that existed in the province," it also brought Franklin business. In the end his "industry visible to our neighbors" likely brought him more trade than the Junto, but together they built his presence as a productive and esteemed citizen.[6] In short, Franklin's social capital served him well, and he made the most of it. Alone, neither his abilities and ambitions on the one hand, nor his connections and connectability on the other, would have sufficed to win him success. Astutely combining all these features, Franklin became a model for enterprising Americans.

New Words for Old Stories

Was nineteenth-century America any more a land of the rugged, self-made individual than the eighteenth century had been for Benjamin Franklin? Not within the business sphere. Historian Judith McGaw coined the term "mutually-made men" to describe the clusters of businessmen who shared knowledge and capital to mutual advantage, because the claim that America was a land of the self-made man was no more true then than it is now. Rarely have successful businessmen pulled themselves up from truly disadvantaged beginnings: prior to 1900, business leaders, with few exceptions, came from yeoman farmer stock, the small-town gentry, or the urban bourgeoisie.[7] They benefited from the education, ambition, nutrition, ethnicity, and mutual respect that their middling— or better—status provided. Taking advantage of these strengths, they were able to participate in building the remarkable increases in wealth that marked the nation's growth and their own rising fortunes.

Yet questions remain. How did the fortunate benefit from their advantages? By what mechanisms did they gain opportunities to use their education, health, and personal attributes in service of their ambitions? Terms and concepts from a much later America can help us answer these questions. When we apply "role models," "mentors," and "networks" to earlier Americans' success stories, it becomes clear that social capital is the only indispensable resource for business success. This late-twentieth-century social capital lexicon can help us reinterpret the genre of heroic success stories and reduce the distortions from romantic rhetoric.

Role Models

Looking back over more than two centuries, how can we best describe the profound influence that Benjamin Franklin had on generations of ambitious young Americans? Using a term sociologists developed in the mid-twentieth century, we can say that Franklin served as nineteenth-century America's most popular *role model,* superceding George Washington as business rose as a respected road for the ambitious. Advice literature has always applied what we now call "human interest" stories, both fictional and biographical, to help "the young discover a secret of power, and learn the value of the virtues by seeing the men who practiced them," according to a popular 1893 text.[8] The impact of any role model follows from one person's seeing a benefit in following another's example. Such a linkage requires that one perceive some commonality with the admired model. The function of the role model is to raise hopes and move the witness to action, and the degree of commonality sets the limits of those who might benefit. If the differences between the two parties are too great, the model might instead depress one's hopes and ambitions by representing unattainable goals. Such models may also inspire unrealizable fantasies that distract their admirers from aiming for more realistic goals or from taking any action at all.

Widely read and cited, Franklin's example energized and guided countless careers. Among the best known was Thomas Mellon, founder of a vast fortune that still controls huge assets in banking, petroleum, and industry. As a lad, Mellon found a heavily used, "dilapidated" copy of Franklin's *Autobiography* with popular excerpts from *Poor Richard's Almanac*. According to his own autobiography, Mellon read Franklin "again and again, and wondered if I might not do something in the same line by similar means." This "turning point" of his life introduced Mellon to the possibilities that a young man, "so poor and friendless," could nonetheless thrive at a business or profession "by industry, thrift, and frugality." Confident that he had at least "the will and energy equal to the occasion, and could exercise the same degree of industry and perseverance," this farmer's son worried that he lacked talent. He determined, however, to make the effort, and thereafter improved his schoolwork and increased the time he spent reading. So strongly did young Mellon esteem Franklin that he even duplicated some of his role model's electrical experiments. As a prospering adult, Mellon placed a statue of his hero above the entrance to his bank, and he later distributed Franklin's texts and sayings to his family. A grandson confirmed that Mellon "revered Benjamin Franklin above all men and Franklin's name frequently was on his lips. The boys in our family literally were brought up on Franklin. . . . Franklin became a sort of genie of the Mellon family. I cannot exaggerate the influence."[9]

The settings in which Franklin had operated a century earlier were not so alien to the youthful Thomas Mellon. Their common Calvinist roots, British ancestry, and respectable "middling-class" backgrounds in a preindustrial country made it easy for Mellon to identify with the object of his admiration. In a sense, therefore,

Franklin's legacy provided two important functions of social capital: inspiration and instruction. With these at the ready, Mellon could pursue the connections available to him and make good use of their possibilities. Throughout the nineteenth century, parents and grandparents, like Mellon, showered their offspring with copies of Franklin's writings, including his famous aphorisms. The founder of B. F. Goodrich Company was named for Franklin in 1841, and his mother followed up her faith in the power of Franklin's lessons by reading the *Autobiography* and *Poor Richard's Almanac* to the future rubber entrepreneur as a child. Another devotee was Frederick Weyerhaeuser, most famous for building vast forest holdings and developing a lumber products industry. Not long after emigrating from Germany as a teenager he discovered Franklin and soon gained a reputation for citing *Poor Richard's Almanac*. In 1912, sixty years after coming to the United States, Weyerhaeuser wrote into at least one of the copies of excerpts from *Poor Richard's Almanac* that he gave to his ten grandchildren, "Please read, remember and practice the best of the within."[10] Franklin's prescription likely had more impact on children of modest means than it did on wealthy grandchildren, for whom frugality and industry had little to offer and for whom ambition often meant something quite different than it did to the youthful Franklin, Mellon, and Weyerhaeuser. Conversely, Franklin's prescription may have served precious few children working hard days in mines or mills.

Mentors

Not quite thirty years old, Thomas A. Scott became superintendent of the Pennsylvania Railroad's expanding western division in late 1852. When Scott decided to bring a telegraph line directly into his Pittsburgh office, he hired a seventeen-year-old boy whom he had noticed at a local telegraph office to be telegrapher and personal secretary. This young man had begun work at the O'Reilly Telegraph Office three years earlier, hired when the boy's uncle recommended him to the manager during a game of draughts (checkers). Scott and nearly everyone else could see this lad's extraordinary energy and ability. Having started as a messenger, the boy quickly learned Pittsburgh's business scene, and he became one of the earliest operators anywhere to "read" telegrams by ear. He also helped manage his coworkers and took night classes in accounting.[11]

Tom Scott also very much liked the youth's bright personality. As Scott moved up in the Pennsylvania Railroad, then one of the nation's largest and most important corporations, he brought his favored apprentice along. At each step, he introduced his protégé to business leaders, teaching him what were then modern management principles as only a railroad executive could know them. Scott even loaned the young man $600—twice a year's income in 1856 for many Americans—to invest in a speculation that Scott recommended. This began a series of speculations, often based on insider information (legal and customary then), that resulted in fortunes for both men, far exceeding their salaries.[12]

Without question, Andrew Carnegie possessed remarkable talent and ambition, and he pushed himself relentlessly. But also without question, Carnegie's rise as America's most notable rags-to-riches champion rested on Tom Scott's having noticed and then taken a shine to him. The Pennsylvania Railroad operated at the center of modernizing business practices and power in the mid-nineteenth century. Scott's links to the top of the railroad were strong, and he was on the move, becoming the railroad's vice president in 1859. Scott's pulling Carnegie into the heart of their century's core industry gave the ambitious young man an edge on fortune through both speculation and corporate management. It also gave Carnegie a compelling advantage when he elected to move into production, making steel for which the primary customers were railroads.

Does this description of Andrew Carnegie's beginnings in any way diminish his famous climb to fabulous wealth? Does it diminish his hard work or diligence or brilliance? Not at all. It does make clear, however, that Carnegie's rise cannot be understood without a consideration of the social processes involved in gaining opportunities, then learning about and doing business. In fact, Tom Scott was only the most important of many men, older and younger, who fostered Carnegie's career. Social capital unlocked his opportunities. Talented and ambitious youths who lacked the appropriate social assets for that time and place were, instead, locked out of opportunities to develop and prove their merit.

Without opportunity, the greatest genius withers. When young Andrew Carnegie suffered long hours of smothering, smoldering heat at a dead-end job, his genius and ambition could do nothing but keep him awake at night with visions of gauges gone awry and boilers exploding.[13] Had no other opportunity knocked, a slow

Victorian-era games and books often simulated Andrew Carnegie's legendary rise from telegraph messenger to tycoon in order to inspire boys to emulate his success. The winners in such games avoided traps into which boys with weaker characters fell, such as the temptations of cigarette smoking or sidewalk scuffles.

climb out of the boiler room might have led only to other mechanized nightmares. Yet opportunity knocked repeatedly for this lad; each occasion gave him a chance to prove his mettle, and he did so splendidly. Was Carnegie's personal magnetism irresistible, even through the steam? Was he the brightest seventeen-year-old boy in Pittsburgh in 1852? Perhaps. However, no boy without appeal to the men who did the hiring, and no girl at all, could have entered into the competition. In Carnegie's case, as always, opportunity came through the mechanisms of social capital—the connections, identities, and cultural styles that attract the gatekeepers who guard the doors to opportunity.

What can we call Tom Scott's lifting up of his brilliant and ambitious, but propertyless, clerk? Until recent decades business discourse was thin on the subject of support and guidance to junior colleagues. More to the point, storytellers and advisors to the ambitious have slighted or completely overlooked Scott's necessary assistance to Carnegie, instead lauding the apprentice's apparent rise on his own. Despite the ubiquity of pull from above in determining who succeeded, the mechanism of *mentoring* had no widely used name prior to the 1970s. Indeed, mentoring in U.S. business seems to have flourished under cultural and ideological cover, obscured by personal affection as well as genuine belief in individual talent- and character-based accomplishment. The word "protégé" identified beneficiaries of an influential person's support, but it has no verb closer than "to protect," and that appeared rarely in a positive sense. To "groom" and "prepare" were perhaps adequate, but vague; "patron," "patronage," and "patronize" carried too much the tone of charity and hierarchy to describe most such relationships to their participants' tastes. Apprentice-master relationships prepared shrinking portions of working-class laborers as industrialization proceeded, and these terms rarely appeared in white-collar situations, which lacked the legally binding and reciprocal obligations of true apprentices and masters. "Coaching" came into business use in the 1940s as a sports metaphor for team building and developing executives; "sponsoring" entered the field in the 1960s with limited usage. What words *did* businessmen use before the mid-twentieth century?

Instead of explicitly professional or managerial terms for what we now call business mentoring, the prevailing language prior to the 1970s featured personal, affectional relationships. Andrew Carnegie called Tom Scott "my great man," his "hero"; Scott, in turn, called his protégé "my boy, Andy." Similarly, Roy G. Munroe, a major figure in Colorado's utility industry during the early decades of the twentieth century, benefited from having a mentor and, in turn, he mentored young men. A letter to Munroe near the end of his career described four generations of mentoring in this fashion: "Pope says I am the best friend he has in the world, I think you are the best friend I have in the world and you say Mr. Stannard is the best friend you have in the world." As stories and words show, personal feelings defined both business and personal relationships, because the culture of business did not distinguish between them.[14]

Networks

The possibilities for personal relationships also set the boundaries of *networks*—chains and webs of contacts and communication channels. As with mentoring, prior to the mid-twentieth century no business-oriented words described the networks that provided the contexts and made possible the dramatic lives and fortunes of Carnegie, as well as of Benjamin Franklin, Thomas Mellon, Jay Cooke, Jay Gould, Henry Ford, John D. Rockefeller, and every other renowned business success. Instead, the language of family and friendship prevailed.[15] Personal connections—networks—determine who might come to mind should an opportunity arise or help be needed, whether that be finding a job, forming alliances, or raising credit. When no other considerations constrain selections, those whose names come favorably to one's own mind or those of one's acquaintances constitute a preferred subset of the acceptable population. Networks also distribute opportunities in the form of information, working capital, and authority—for corruption and graft just as for legitimate enterprises.

Families typically build the most resilient, loyal, and reliable networks, hence the constancy and strength of nepotism throughout the ages. Other commonalties that can forge relationships are ethnicity, religion, hometown, childhood or school years, vacations, or club membership—anything that can generate the common expectations and effective communications that generate connectability. In contrast, people insiders consider powerless, strange, ignorant, unpredictable, or otherwise unattractive are unlikely to gain access to a network and its assets. Membership in, or even just access to, a consequential network can nurture an individual of talent and ambition, whereas lack of access can defeat any hope. Not coincidentally, the American mobility stars of the eighteenth and nineteenth centuries, Benjamin Franklin and Andrew Carnegie, both flourished in state-of-the-art communication trades through which they formed vital networks to great effect.

A powerful gatekeeping mechanism, especially in the days before telephones, was the letter of introduction. "When it is desired to bring one friend into acquaintance with another at a distance," one guidebook explained, such letters could "answer the purpose" as a form of personal introduction. Another manual cautioned that letters of introduction "should not be given except to persons with whom you are well acquainted, and for whom you are entirely willing to vouch." In essence, written introductions, like spoken ones, asked friends and associates to admit the bearer into their networks, with access to the privileges, trust, and opportunities therein. Hence, a positive letter would "pledge your own character for his, . . . and any misconduct on his part will damage you." Anyone who harbored doubts should refuse to write—"and let nothing induce you to alter your decision." A sample letter from the mid-1880s concluded with the sentence "You can rely upon his statements, as he is a gentleman of high character; and should you be able to render him any assistance, it will be gratefully appreciated." Introducing someone to one's own networks carried serious risks, so one was wise to "leave nothing to uncertainty." Thus, when Henry Clews came to New York from England, his letters of introduction gained him employment with "possibilities." He had access to "people of culture and refinement" and the "good fortune to meet the great men of those days." His social capital thereby cleared his path into Wall Street's temple of opportunity, where he prospered.[16]

The intensely personal nature of mentoring and networking limits access to the mechanisms of social capital to those with whom gatekeepers feel comfortable and safe, or at least obligated. Benjamin Franklin charmed potential beneficiaries; he did not alarm them. Tom Scott liked Andy Carnegie and felt akin to his roots. Role models, in contrast to mentors, can aid admirers at a distance, without the cooperation or even awareness of the benefactor. Even so, alikeness enhances the benefits from role models. All in all, these three social capital mechanisms—mentors, networks, and role models—have always operated to distribute unevenly opportunities, inspirations, and the abilities to exploit them. The use of personal and familial words to describe business relationships and interactions reflected common sense about the intimacy of business. People develop words as tools to grab onto concepts they wish to share and use, so the dearth of business-specific words to describe mechanisms for distributing opportunity prior to the mid-twentieth century is significant. It indicates a parallel failure to imagine the mechanisms of social capital outside of the personal and familial domains. Within those domains, strangers had no place.

Andrew Carnegie's Networks

How did the youthful Andrew Carnegie acquire what made him fit into the Pittsburgh business community? Refining the idea of networks can provide deeper insight into the nineteenth century's most famous rags-to-riches epic. Before anyone in Pittsburgh could notice Carnegie's exceptional energies and abilities, he had to gain acceptance as a potential member of that city's business community by avoiding notice; he could not appear out of place. As a Scottish youth among Scotsmen, his ethnicity served him well; a German immigrant or an African American, or even a Catholic Irishman, could have expected no such welcome. His sex allowed him entrance denied to half of the population. In Carnegie's neighborhood, as in any other, one's getting noticed first as exceptional in the sense of alien would have thwarted getting noticed as exceptional in the sense of praiseworthy. Carnegie's ascribed identity within his *background networks* was thus a necessary, if not a sufficient, factor for his initial access.

Other necessary factors for young Carnegie's connectability included all the skills, presumptions, hopes, role expectations, language, style, humor, etiquette, mannerisms, and so on that each of us learns in our background networks. Families, neighbors, schools, and others who teach fundamental practical and social skills and expectations prepare us for presenting ourselves to various publics. They can provide or point to role models from whom we can learn both hopes and behaviors by example. If a person's background network prepares him or her to resemble the people who hold occupational opportunities, as did Carnegie's, then that person's individual qualities, such as intelligence, integrity, and energy, can shine. Otherwise, stereotypes, unpredictability, and discomfort can prevent gatekeepers from noticing an individual's unique qualities. In addition, norms of reciprocity within a shared background network can produce community-wide gains: by aiding each other, members of a network not only build trust and loyalty, they can also act as scouts who bring information, seasoned judgment, and opportunity into the community, increasing the community's effectiveness and ability to flourish.[17]

From their background networks children learn self-confidence and expectations regarding what the world offers and expects of them, along with the skills that are available to them. Antebellum family life fostered the rising middle class in part by seeing to it that sons received whatever education they needed—apprenticeships early on, schools later. Families dedicated financial resources as needed to prepare and nurture sons, investing heavily in them. Consequently, the much-praised individualism of nineteenth-century American men did not follow from genuine self-sufficiency, but rather was the product of widespread patterns of home life that nurtured boys and bestowed families' resources on them. True to this pattern, Carnegie's mother, Margaret, vehemently refused a suggestion that her young sons peddle trinkets; her immigrant family was not so desperate as to require abject toil that held no prospects for its sons. Nostalgia surely gilded Carnegie's memories, but he consistently recalled abundant details of family support. His *Autobiography* summarized his parents' efforts: "There was nothing that heroine [his mother] did not do in the struggle for elbow room in the western world. Father's long factory hours tried his strength, but he, too, fought the good fight like a hero and never failed to encourage me."[18] Will Carnegie's failure as a skilled artisan displaced by new technologies, first in Scotland and then in Pittsburgh, poignantly taught Andrew the value of staying ahead of the times.

Information, options, and warnings rank high among the benefits of effective networks. Carnegie's mother's sisters in western Pennsylvania first cautioned against migration, then, in 1847, encouraged it. The family left Scotland early in 1848, stayed briefly in New York City with an affluent girlhood friend of Margaret's, then pushed off to Pittsburgh. Having spent almost all they had on the trip to Pittsburgh and finding themselves in the slums of a rough frontier town, they turned to family and Scottish neighbors. For a while they lived rent-free in a house owned by Margaret's widowed sister. Andrew and his father learned of and obtained work at a factory owned by a "respectable" Scotsman who favored fellow Scots in hiring. A second Scotsman, a "dear old man . . . was moved by good feeling toward the white-haired boy," according to Carnegie's telling, and offered Carnegie a better-paying job, soon moving him out of the boiler room of his nightmares into the light of part-time office work. His five years as a star pupil—and teacher's pet—back in Dunfermline had already provided him with the reading, penmanship, and arithmetic skills he needed to qualify for this promotion.[19]

About a year after the Carnegies' departure from Scotland, a second aunt's husband, Thomas Hogan, earned his place in history as the checker-playing conduit of news about the telegraph office's opening. After a family discussion, Will accompanied Andrew to the interview at the O'Reilly Telegraph Office, which was managed by Uncle Hogan's friend, a Yankee for whom Carnegie minimized his brogue. As a measure of young Carnegie's eagerness to jump at opportunity's bait, he accepted a trial and began work immediately, forgetting to dismiss his "good old Scotch father," who had been left patiently waiting outside, lest he embarrass his son. Carnegie recorded his uncle's bearing the news of this opportunity to the family as one of life's "trifles" upon which "do the most momentous consequences hang," for without such a trifle, he would have had no such opportunity. This was, in his words, "my first real start in life," a "paradise, yes, heaven, as it seemed to me, with newspapers, pens, pencils, and sunshine about me." He remembers feeling "that my foot was upon the ladder and that I was bound to climb." All this progress in one short adolescent year fostered optimism. Instead of dreading exploding boilers, the lad's active mind could spend nights on new, more productive activity by memorizing and reciting all of Pittsburgh's firms and their locations.[20]

So it was that Carnegie continued to benefit from the opportunities that his background network supplied to his energies and talents. The "dear old man" who brought Andy out of the boiler room and the telegraph office manager who opened the gates of paradise belonged to a second type of network, an *authority network*. Participants enter these networks deliberately, rather than by birth, in order to pursue a livelihood or other ambitions. Although all networks have hierarchies and conflicts of interest, authority networks always operate on differential power and with lesser presumptions of direct reciprocal advantage. More important, not everyone who is subject to an authority network can hope to enter it or climb its ranks. Workers report to the authority networks of supervisors who can aid or damage their working conditions and prospects, but they are not necessarily connectable. Authorities may, by whim or policy, loyalty or self-interest, pick out some underlings from the lowest ranks and pull them up.

Andrew Carnegie, like Benjamin Franklin before him, had no talent more important than his ability to charm and impress authorities, and he had no greater insight than that he should do so. As a telegraph messenger working out of one of the two telegraph offices in the city, Carnegie quickly learned the advantages of getting to know those he called the "great men" of Pittsburgh. Recognizing such men gave him the immediate benefit of being able to deliver a message speedily, should he happen to bump into the recipient on his way; in addition, young Carnegie found within this group "models," as he put it. Much to his gratification, even the "leading men" of both civil and business affairs in this still small city "took notice" of him. Beginning when he first entered into the sunshine of telegraphy, Andrew Carnegie's fortunes grew along with Pittsburgh's, which became an important hub of the industrializing Midwest during his career.[21]

"Wise men are always looking for clever boys," Carnegie declared as an adult. As a youth, he self-consciously angled to get the attention of such men, for, as he wrote much later, "The battle of life is already half won by the young man who is brought personally in contact with high officials; and the great aim of every boy should be to do something beyond the sphere of his duties—something which attracts the attention of those over him." To attract attention, he took telegraph messages before he was authorized to do so and learned to read telegraph signals by ear before other operators in town did; and he was always eager. His rewards were rapid promotion from messenger to operator, plus attention and opportunities that served him well. Within this lively and invigorating setting, Andrew "made the acquaintance of an extraordinary man": Thomas Scott. Each instantly recognized the other's abilities, and they liked each other. Scott quickly became the center of Carnegie's professional world and remained there for years to come; he was, in other words, at the heart of Carnegie's authority network—his mentor.[22]

Thus did several men exercise valuable and helpful authority over young Carnegie. They transformed a series of mere jobs into a career. Each of them was attracted to Carnegie's cheerfulness and wit, his neat appearance and social graces, as well as to his quickness and efficiency in carrying out his duties. None of them noticed his ethnicity or sex as reason not to invite him into the networks within which they had authority. Their decisions as gatekeepers served Carnegie well. Each of his mentors taught Carnegie skills and, just as important, provided opportunities in the form of challenges through which the youth could learn and prove himself. They monitored and rewarded his accomplishments, enjoying the process and their protégé's progress, which reflected favorably on them.

Andrew Carnegie also flourished within yet a third sort of social system: *peer networks*. His background networks prepared him and his authority networks nurtured him, but Carnegie also required assistance, or at least cooperation, from peers in order to prosper. Sometimes, of course, peer cooperation comes grudgingly as one moves from being a peer to an authority. As a rule, Carnegie mastered the art of eliciting cooperation from peers early on and employed it very well, if not unfailingly. When he took accounting lessons at night, for example, he convinced his friends to go along with him. During his tenure at the telegraph office, he recruited, trained, and disciplined other messengers, and many of those young men rose with him into prominent positions as the region and its industries grew. As adults, they and many others worked with Carnegie at operating railroads, then at producing steel. As remarkable as Andrew Carnegie was, he of course could not be everywhere, do everything, and control everything at once. Various members of his network brought different insights, sometimes moving the group into different directions than a lone Carnegie might have done. Among those who helped make Carnegie's fortune, and whose cooperation with him made their own fortune, were his brother, Tom; brother Tom's childhood friend, Henry Phipps, Jr.; and two of his fellow messenger boys, Henry Oliver and Robert Pitcairn. A 1911 article in the *New York Times* listed forty-seven millionaires whom Carnegie "made"—four more than he claimed for himself.[23]

Tensions can arise between members of various networks, especially when the roles within them are unclear and personal and business relationships are entangled. For instance, Henry Clay Frick joined with Carnegie in business as an adult, and the notorious friction between these men resulted from more than their mismatched personalities. Their relationship did not fit neatly into either an authority or a peer network; as a result, their positions relative to each other were uncertain and constantly subject to negotiation. Similarly muddied network relationships ruined "Mr. Scott's" relationship after his "boy Andy" grew up. After twenty years of benefiting from their association, Carnegie refused to help Scott out of an unwise speculation during the panic of 1873. The former mentor's claim to loyalty was not enough to reverse the direction of authority and support with which the two had begun.

Accusations of disloyalty also came from J. Edgar Thomson, another member of Carnegie's former authority network. Although Carnegie could not have saved Scott and Thomson from their bad investments, he expressed guilt for the rest of his life for "refusing to stand by my friends." Carnegie's ensuing crusade against speculation and note endorsing may have been evidence of his sense of guilt. But in his failure to assist his former mentors, he expressed his sense of differing obligations to different networks. He justified his difficult, but deliberate, decision because of his loyalties to others—people who depended on him for leadership and livelihood, as Scott never should have done. Carnegie was also concerned about losing credibility with the bankers Junius and J. Pierpont Morgan, for he made his decision about Scott as he was preparing a momentous move from speculation to production.[24] Carnegie would have preferred to make this move without breaking ties to people at the core of his old authority network, but he clearly wanted to move on, and doing so required making new ties. The story of Carnegie Steel is, in no small part, that of Carnegie's construction of a new peer network.

Rugged Individualism on Wall Street

Two more dissimilar personalities could hardly be found than Andrew Carnegie and Jay Gould. The former was sociable and often animated; the latter was withdrawn and reserved. Almost everyone's favorite robber baron to disparage, in his own time and in ours, Gould seems an unlikely prospect for grand success in business's social world. Yet he mastered speculation, railroads, and communications with small bands of confederates operating around, and sometimes within, the most elite financial circles. Despite the abundant contrasts between them, however, neither Carnegie nor Gould could have conquered their worlds without applying charm or artifice, or both, as occasions warranted. Despite common nine-

teenth-century presumptions about enduring and steadfast character being the basis for true success, these two examples of a person's
acquiring vast wealth hinged on each man's personality and sensitivity to the perceptions, vanities, and wishes of others.[25] The business world has always been intensely social, and social skills of various sorts are important in general, but especially to win the favor of
mentors or peers. Jay Gould's eccentric and often cantankerous
path to financial glory does not disprove this fundamental rule of
business success.

Gould got his first big lift by an unequal partnership with a much
older businessman, Zadock Pratt, who later rued the relationship.
Gould shamelessly flattered Pratt's vanity, practicing a talent for social artifice that helped him win alliances time and again—at least
until his reputation for secrecy and self-serving precluded such
practices among all but the most armored or adventurous. Gould
continuously moved into and through other business relationships;
one early joint venture ended in litigation—and gunfire! Starting on
Wall Street as a lone outsider, in 1860 Gould found his entry into
railroading through a former colleague. He then became an associate and soon a son-in-law of a socially and financially prominent
New York businessman, who had experience and connections in
both railroads and finance.[26]

Throughout his controversial career on Wall Street and in railroading, Gould worked with and through other people, including
his father-in-law. Nothing could reconcile his reserved nature with
his ambition, however, and the strain of constant tension wore
heavily on him. Still, he refused to forego his ambition for the sake
of peace, knowing that he could not engage in the challenges of
business without engaging in its social dynamics. He understood
the importance of gaining information and influence through connections, even as he detested the process. Described as "on his own
in every sense of the word" by 1867, Gould could not call on his
background network for aid. Yet he had by then joined a peer net-

work far more influential and helpful than his parents and uncles could ever have been. With Daniel Drew and James Fisk Jr., he belonged to a group that one newspaper called "a batch of nobodies," but that was powerful enough to scandalize the nation over their control and exploitation of the Erie Railroad. Suddenly an insider, in part through his curious relationship and battles with none other than Cornelius Vanderbilt, Gould became party to some of the most important financial transactions in the United States between then and his death in 1892.[27]

A wild scheme to corner the gold market in 1869 demonstrated Gould's calculated pattern of soliciting, forming, and abandoning alliances. For this misadventure, Gould tried to gain inside information by taking advantage of his acquaintance with a brother-in-law to President Ulysses S. Grant. Through his connections, Gould was even in a position to meet with Grant himself once, when he attempted to read the president's intentions. Gould worked with Fisk on this project initially, then recruited others in what became a bizarre drama of speculative misjudgments that served no one in the end. For the intended coup, Gould even spun a team of brokers into a confusing web of accomplices. Despite these ties, Gould felt "all alone, so to speak, in what I did, and I did not let any of those people know exactly how I stood." Alliances might be necessary, but he did not fuse with people as much as use them. As the scheme fell apart, Gould needed bodyguards to assure his safety, although no one fired gunshots at him, as in his previous escapade. As in an earlier scheme, Gould required litigation to end the attempt at gold fixing, including twelve injunctions from judges suspiciously favorable to him.[28] He had cynically formed coalitions, weak and temporary peer networks, the members of which felt no more loyalty to each other than did he. So the group fell apart, leaving each conspirator to fend for himself and the U.S. gold market in shambles.

In a rare interview in 1877, Gould affirmed that he operated under "the disadvantage of not being sociable." Instead of enjoying "company and sport," his "tastes" were "domestic. They are not calculated to make me particularly popular in Wall Street, and I cannot help that." According to a family source, he called social functions "unescapables." Never admitted into what biographer Maury Klein called the "'old boys' network' that dominated the conservative banking houses," Gould built coalitions outside it. He formed his closest alliance and a true friendship with Russell Sage, and the two often worked boards of directors as a team. In Klein's words, Gould and Sage made "the perfect mating of misfits, men who had few other friends and cared nothing for the ordinary rituals of society or the approval of its arbiters." Sage had a generation of experience more than Gould, but no consensus prevails about which of the two was in control. Sage's biographer, Paul Sarnoff, described Gould as "predacious" and an "abject failure" before he came to Sage with the gold cornering scheme. Although Sage declined that initial invitation, he and Gould soon began to work together. Sarnoff presented Gould's position in this alliance as that of an "interest-paying customer" and protégé. He also concluded that it was the genuine friendship between the men's two wives that persuaded Sage to assist the younger man. From the perspective of social capital, the question of who built the other's fortunes matters much less than that they operated together at the core of a small and shifting peer network. From this core both Gould and Sage built huge fortunes, each landing in the U.S. all-time top twenty. Sometimes they worked as a team; always they sought each other's advice and introduced each other to opportunities.[29] Though each was more of a "rugged individualist" than most of the gentlemen on Wall Street, Gould and Sage still gained access to elite chambers and formed and shifted alliances between themselves and others. No financier is an island. Climbing social and corporate ladders was quite another thing, however, and Gould's personality would have ill fit him for the coming age of corporate management and bureaucracy. He was buried before it arrived.

Thus, while affection can build and lubricate a network, Jay Gould's career proves that participation in an effective network requires only respect enough to be eligible for entrance into negotiations. Fear and a grudging respect will do. Thus could Gould interact within and around the most powerful U.S. financial networks of the nineteenth century. Decades-long feuds between Gould and Commodore Cornelius Vanderbilt, William H. Vanderbilt, and J. P. Morgan roiled the communication and transportation investment markets, livening up the financial news, making and breaking both fortunes and spirits. Yet, to conclude one such feud, William Vanderbilt invited Gould and Sage to his Fifth Avenue mansion. This was not a venue for crossing race, sex, or class divides; the invitation recognized the combatants' membership in a common realm, even if they occupied different plateaus within that realm. Likewise, attendees at Gould's 1892 funeral included Morgan and any number of others with whom he had either joined battle or made deals, or both. According to a newspaper account of the time, attendees had "never loved the man, and the dead man never loved them, as he had never loved any of his kind, save those of his blood; so it is the cold truth that there was no sorrow by his bier. There was decent respect—nothing more."[30] But respect was all that Jay Gould had required to enter the arena wherein he could build and destroy coalitions and fortunes.

To benefit from social capital, especially mentoring, ambitious youths had to be willing to submit to the personal supervision and company of older men. This setting aside of masculine independence while seeking manhood was easier for some to do than others. At first Andrew Carnegie gloried in the attention and confidence Tom Scott gave him. But before long he became so eager to be his own man that he cared little for a raise in salary—having "a department to myself," he said, was "glory enough for me."[31] Being given this promotion marked Carnegie's passage from "Mr. Scott's Andy" into manhood. Nonetheless, throughout his career, Carnegie could readily use his charm when he needed to win an ally. In contrast, Gould champed at the bit of enforced contacts and dependencies, and was rarely able to keep alliances from going sour. Clichés to the contrary, any man too much the rugged individualist to work with others, at least temporarily, stood little chance of improving his lot. Jay Gould could only climb by compromising his misanthropy to garner the benefits of social capital.

Horatio Alger: Not So Rugged or Ragged

Tales of ragged city urchins conquering great obstacles as rugged individualists who achieve success fill our collective imagination about the triumphs of nineteenth-century American capitalism. Horatio Alger Jr. became famous as a symbol for describing and celebrating such idealized self-made paragons. The fabled "Horatio Alger hero" possesses personal character and abilities that, along with cheerful determination, take him from rags to riches solely on his own merit and effort—pluck helped along by a bit of luck. To be sure, luck in the sense of winning a lottery never brought such a champion success; luck instead gave him an opportunity to prove his merit.

Paradoxically, however, the currently popular profile of the Horatio Alger hero that evolved after 1920, unlike the portraits Alger created between the mid-1860s and his death in 1899, reflects an ideological individualism that Alger never intended. Whether or not Alger's hero began in rags or merely modest circumstances, he rarely got richer than the prosperous middle class. And, most important of all, he never climbed in isolation. A loving and upright (if often lost) home, friendships with other boys, and influential adult patrons always provided Alger's protagonist both opportunities and the means for fulfilling them. Within his background, peer, and authority networks, the hero's energetic, optimistic, honest, and generous responses to his opportunities shaped his fate. His sterling character was necessary, but not sufficient, for success.

For instance, Grant Thornton, a young man of requisite good character and breeding, does very well in Alger's *Helping Himself*, but only with the aid of several mature men. The young hero worked hard and honestly, turned down improper offers, and aided those in need. But Grant did not make it on his own. A solid family upbringing provided him with "an excellent training," and an esteemed gentleman of casual acquaintance saved him from a false arrest. A wise Wall Street broker then gave Grant a job at more pay than he could have earned at market rates and took him in "as a member of my family"—because of his charm and good character (even before Grant rescued the broker's weak son). Unlike Carnegie and Gould, Alger's protagonists do not seek entrepreneurial careers, or anything other than serving their employers or partners "faithfully." In fact, Ragged Dick, Alger's first and most famous hero, left his rough but profitable boot-blacking entrepreneurship to seek "respectability" as a lower-paid white-collar employee.[32] Alger's heroics are all profoundly social—boys and men moving and interacting within webs of social relationships that override market competition.

A passage in *Ragged Dick* summarizes Alger's balance of community and individual responsibilities. The father of Dick's first respectable friend, Frank, tells the lad, "Remember that your future position depends mainly upon yourself, and that it will be high or low as you choose to make it." Alger, along with almost all advice literature and sermons before and since, repeated this refrain endlessly: take responsibility for your life, and do your best. "You may not become rich," young Frank wisely advises his friend, "—it isn't everybody that becomes rich, you know,—but you can obtain a good position, and be respected." Alger immediately then balances this message of individual responsibility with his communal design for fostering hope and opportunity. Frank's father gives Dick a five-dollar bill, several days' wages for many adults at the time, saying, "I remember my own friendless youth. . . . Sometime when you are a prosperous man, you can repay it in the form of aid to some poor boy, who is struggling upward as you are now."[33] The social web, Alger believed, must provide opportunity, hope, and support, and we repay our debts by passing on our good fortune. This is not the same thing as legitimating wealth through philanthropy in the Carnegie or Rockefeller molds. This is Alger's recognizing the mutuality and reciprocity of needs and benefits that go into building a community's social capital.

Alger's heroes earn their modest success and greater happiness by virtue and generosity, never by business shrewdness. Money rewards their virtues; money measures—but does not constitute—success. In fact, Alger objected to individualism and competition as the guiding principles in properly run businesses. Despite this, long after the audience for Alger's stories faded, his name became iconic, appropriated for a very different message. At least 17 million copies of over one hundred novels of Alger's once circulated, plus newspaper and magazine articles. Yet by the late 1920s, the cultural memories of his encouragement to gentle ambition had morphed into a popular joke, then into a distorted cliché. People who never read Alger's social recipes for success tagged him the evangelist for rugged individualism, contradicting his very words and taking his name in vain.[34] So powerful became the appeal of the concept of the self-made man within twentieth-century American culture that the need for a standard bearer somehow overrode the symbol's true origins. Thus, Andrew Carnegie and Jay Gould, and most others to whom we now carelessly apply the Horatio Alger label, achieved their fortunes in competitive styles that sometimes entailed cynical exploitation of networks, profoundly violating the spirit of Alger's social messages. We have blurred the stories of such men, attributing to them the boyhoods and virtues of Alger's modest heroes but neglecting their social debts and privileges in order to legitimate their riches.

Success without Heroic Mobility

America's most high-profile legends about heroic, steep climbs from rags to riches are actually about movement through layers of social networks.[35] But what about other people in business, such as the already rich, the stable middle class, and pre–industrial-era artisans? They too have used social networks to maintain and improve their lot; but there are differences between the way the already rich and the never-to-be-rich generally operate within their networks and the way the highly mobile do. Whereas those who successfully seek upward mobility continually, even aggressively, nurture old authority and peer networks and develop new ones, the others rely more on their background networks. Most people, of course, fall in between these extremes, relying on background networks and building authority and peer networks to varying degrees.

Triumph over Wealth

If a climb to worldly success can be heroic, the longer and harder the road, the more admirable—hence the oft-cited notion of the "blessings of poverty." According to nineteenth-century cultural authorities, the key elements for rising into a valued adulthood for both men and women were self-control, self-improvement, and self-reliance. Untold numbers of sermons, speeches, articles, and books explained again and again the value of youthful poverty for teaching such virtues. Advice books, reminiscences (such as Franklin's *Autobiography*), and optimistic fiction (such as Horatio Alger Jr.'s stories) popularized the message throughout the nineteenth century, especially after the Civil War. This massive outpouring of counsel ostensibly offered hope. In 1885 Sarah K. Bolton wrote

Lives of Poor Boys Who Became Famous to show "that poverty is no barrier to success." To the contrary, it "usually develops ambition, and nerves people to action." Readers of Bolton's profiles of twenty-eight "careers of those who have overcome obstacles" should be "cheered and stimulated" to action in life's "struggles." The stories of Presidents Lincoln and Garfield proved that "there is a chance for other farmer-boys," just as the biography of Ezra Cornell proved that "other mechanics can come to fame." She hoped that even "toilers in factories" could find "encouragement and inspiration" in her tales.[36]

None other than P. T. Barnum rendered a parable to explain how "the poor boys get rich and the rich boys get poor" in *Dollars and Sense: or, How to Get On*. Imagine, he suggested, that a wealthy man dies, leaving elder sons who helped him with his business and younger sons who did not. The former "know the value of money" and have the skills to improve their inheritance. The younger boys, however, have had all their wants met, are flattered constantly, and grow "arrogant and self-conceited." They play as children and continue playing as "fast" college students, only to lose their health and their wealth in the end. In America, Barnum assured his ambitious audiences, such a generational cycle kept wealth moving from the privileged to those fortified by need. Unlike his sideshows, Barnum's recipes for success were standard fare. Nothing, it seemed, formed solid character like poverty. Moreover, struggle sanctified the material ends. As Russell H. Conwell's "Acres of Diamonds" oration proclaimed before thousands of cheering audiences for half a century beginning in 1861, "the number of poor who are to be sympathized with is very small." Only a few had not ruined their own character and, thereby, made their sorry fate. The rich, however, could well be pitied, for the temptations of abundance were so much more, well, tempting.[37]

According to this logic, the 1912 book *Men Who Made Good* could include those "reared in homes of comfort or even wealth."

The author contrasted the "poor boy who rises by his own exertions to a strong and useful life" with the "son of rich and indulgent parents." This rich young man earned "even higher praise," it seems, for, without the "stimulus" of poverty, he had shaken off "the soft chains of luxury [making] his life hard with self-denying toil." Thus could rich men's camels fit through the eye of heaven's needle. As the *New York Tribune* explained on J. Pierpont Morgan's death in 1913, even though Morgan had "no traditions of the steerage," he possessed "the qualities of the self-made man." Other

"The Pampered Child of Wealth." As the nation's affluent became more visible in the Gilded Age and the Progressive Era, the self-made man ethos had to assert downward mobility for undeserving inheritors of wealth. The nineteenth century's most famous entertainer, P. T. Barnum, provided this example in 1890 of how the temptations of riches could seduce and ruin young men. Sports, sporting women, alcohol, tobacco, and narcotics, plus a servant to open the champagne, deprived the wealthy of the character best built by poverty.

(From P. T. Barnum, *Dollars and Sense; or, How to Get On.* New York: Henry S. Allen, 1890.)

papers' obituaries pointed out that Morgan had purchased his way out of the Civil War, had come under congressional scrutiny for exercising undue influence on the nation's finances, and had crushed competitors and workers alike without apparent scruple or remorse.[38] To all, Morgan symbolized the economic power of the industrializing capitalist elite; granting him the sanctity of "self-made" either glorified or defiled the term, according to one's perspective.

To dismiss the favorable comments on Morgan as pandering to the powerful, however, misses an important point about how mainstream nineteenth-century and early twentieth-century Americans thought about self-construction and the choices that each individual had to make along the way. Self-control lit the road to manhood within this bourgeois culture, and allowed one to exercise constraint over dark passions of all sorts. The temperance movement, like other cultural trends of that era, presumed adults' obligations to control themselves and their dependents, whether those be spouses, children, or employees. Urbanization and immigration created enormous demands for self-control because they vastly expanded the number, variety, and strangeness of people one encountered during the course of the day. Young men in pursuit of livelihoods in this newly strange, newly urban world needed to gain the trust of people who had not known them from childhood. Advice literature admonished them to build a visibly honorable character through constant vigilance against temptation and poor judgment. Such self-made character would reassure acquaintances, reflecting the honest homes wherein youth had learned the finest of principles.[39]

In this vein, *New York Times* readers in 1910 were treated to "Sons of Millionaires Who Have Made Successes," an article that examined thirteen young men of favored circumstances. These "sons by birth" or "by business training and adoption" had no claim on poverty. Yet by all appearances they had earned their positions by the same recipe: self-control and self-reliance. Some of them had lived through a wild youth, as, for example, had William Kissam Vanderbilt Jr., son of William Henry Vanderbilt, who in turn was the son of "Commodore" Cornelius Vanderbilt. Known as a "speed maniac" for his youthful racing exploits, "Willie" had even gotten arrested in Europe. "But when everyone had made up his mind" about this apparent ne'er-do-well, so said the newspaper, "he surprised them by becoming a toiler." After acquiring a Harvard degree, he left the academy for "practical training," working "like a ten-dollar-a-week clerk, with this difference, that he didn't have to do it, and didn't get a cent for it." While admitting that young Vanderbilt "wasn't worrying much about the rent and coal," the article pointed out that "he kept the same hours as a clerk" in order to learn the trade. Likewise, J. P. Morgan Jr., scion of several generations of wealthy Yankees, "had to work harder than any one else in the place" once he joined his father's firm after apprenticing in an associated firm. He earned his manhood, and railroad magnate James J. Hill's high praise as "a chip off the old block," meeting all challenges ably and "always with precision and directness." When Hill prepared his own son, Louis W. Hill, for adulthood, he regretted that he could not give his son what he called the "richest heritage that a young man can have . . . stern necessity." But "he did what he could to make up for it. He gave him quite as valuable an asset—stern responsibility." Hill allegedly said of his sons that "they had done fairly well considering their lack of advantages." As an earlier *New York Times* article had observed, the "American theory of opportunity" should apply to "the rich man's son" just as to those without "exceptional advantages." Scions of such powerful families as Rockefeller, Vanderbilt, Guggenheim, Hill, and Morgan could fairly be judged, therefore, by "survival of the fittest" standards according to whether and how well they applied their "exceptional advantages" and "financial affiliations."[40] They, too, deserved the plaudits of "self-made" that were accorded the heroically mobile.

Keeping It in the Family

The rich and the powerful—correlated, but not identical, groups—have always fascinated the rest of us. Fascination has led to studies, as well as gossip, about how the rich and powerful try to maintain their position for themselves and their children. Some of those mechanisms are of course financial, such as setting up trust funds with assorted restrictions, building interlocking partnerships or corporate directorates, and so on. Many of the mechanisms, however, are social. These mechanisms reflect conservative approaches to maintaining both social and financial assets across generations, because keeping a tight rein on the one helps to control the other. Restrictive social measures include intraclass marriages, limited-membership clubs, exclusive schools, discriminating neighborhoods, and the like.[41] For those who prefer maintenance of wealth over growth, their authority and peer networks would derive entirely from their background networks, at most one step removed from a relative or someone known to their family or to themselves prior to adulthood. Nothing ever works perfectly, however, so complications arise when the young try to stretch their wings or adults err in their efforts to increase their assets rather than merely hold on. The resulting entanglements, including inappropriate marriages and poor investment partnerships, threaten one's ability to maintain wealth as much as the most glorious overspending, and have inspired memorable works of fiction by, for instance, Edith Wharton and Henry James.

Nineteenth-century advice literature thrived on stories of profligate heirs who allegedly had less chance at business success than frugal country boys. Although these parables were generally aimed at ambitious youths of modest backgrounds rather than at heirs, some wealthy parents took such concerns to heart. Junius Morgan, for instance, closely supervised the upbringing and business apprenticeship that his son, J. Pierpont Morgan, received. Junius was a master of stern Victorian warnings about character. He warned his young son to be "very careful with what boys you associate not to get intimate with any but such as are of the right stamp & whose influence over you will be good. You must bear in mind that *now* is the time for you to form your character & as it is formed now so it will be likely to remain. You cannot have this too strongly impressed upon you." Just as he worried about his son's adolescent peer networks, Junius created and fine-tuned first an authority network for his son and then a multilevel apprenticeship within it. Junius supervised, scolded, and rewarded Pierpont constantly, raising him as the fourth generation to build the family fortunes. (Pierpont's paternal great-grandfather had prospered in farming and real estate, and his grandfather had left a million-dollar estate in 1847.) He included the boy on trips with professional colleagues and investors, gave him tasks in one of the family firms, assigned suitable readings, and enrolled him in schools in New England and Europe to learn math, French, and German, as well as apt cultural arts. Pierpont traveled in powerful circles from the start.[42]

His schooling completed, Pierpont's formal apprenticeship began. He was first given a position as an unpaid clerk (with a $200 monthly allowance from his father, when an average working-class income was about $300 a year) in one of New York City's top investment firms, after having sailed from London with one of the firm's partners. (Junius's final message before his son set sail was "*Be true to yourself* & all is well. Kind regards to Mr. & Mrs. Sherman.") The young man's connections took him straight into the key networks of American and international finance. Junius was pleased when his son took his initial position in the correspondence department, which was at the nexus of the firm's operations. Pierpont resided in New York with a relative of his father's London partner, and his neighbors included August Belmont, the Rothschilds' American representative. Even so, Junius cautioned his son, "*slow & sure* should be the motto of every young man." When Pierpont received a promotion the following year, Junius exhorted him to "be true to those responsibilities and to yourself. . . . Never under any circumstances do an act which could be called in question if known to the whole world. Remember that there is an Eye above that is ever upon you & for *every act—word & deed* you will one day be called to give account." No preacher or essayist of the era could have phrased it more gravely. Later, when Pierpont angered his father for overly aggressive market manipulation during the Civil War, Junius scolded him, then placed a senior partner over him. After a time, Pierpont stepped into a firm his father created for him, Drexel, Morgan and Co., as senior partner with a member of another powerful banking family.[43] Even as Pierpont spread his reach and constructed his own peer networks, Junius never let up.

Taking the Family to Macy's

The story of Margaret Swain Getchell refutes the generally held notion that women could not gain high positions in business in the nineteenth century. At the same time it reinforces the principle that access to the gatekeepers of opportunity sets the limits for business advancement. Getchell became a top executive at R. H. Macy and Company in the days when women had little access to such positions, but when women's business activities were not entirely constrained.[44]

Margaret Getchell's modest New England upbringing afforded her an education solid enough to prepare her to teach school. In 1860, however, she lost an eye to injury and decided that she could no longer teach. Getchell was a distant cousin of Rowland H. Macy, who had established a fancy dry goods store in Manhattan in

1858, and that connection sufficed to gain her an interview. Macy's business had done well in its first two years, and he needed a cashier. He was sufficiently impressed with his young relative's poise and mathematical skills to hire her on the spot. Soon Getchell's managerial abilities came to the fore, and Macy recognized and appreciated her contributions. She became head bookkeeper in three years; and three years after that, her superb advice on expanding the store's lines and other aspects of the trade prompted Macy to make her store superintendent, the top executive position. Getchell oversaw the store's rapid expansion, as Macy's took over an entire city block during her first two years as superintendent, carrying ever more profitable lines of goods.[45]

The family ties at Macy's became further entwined. Rowland Macy's errant son never matured into an heir apparent. Instead, his misbehavior opened truly Horatio Alger–like opportunities for Major Abiel T. La Forge. La Forge had befriended Macy's wayward son during the Civil War, and this kindness pulled La Forge into Macy's authority network—a bit of "luck" that gave La Forge the chance to prove his "pluck." The grateful Macy lifted La Forge above the multitude of ex-soldiers seeking employment in 1865 and introduced him to potential employers. Before long, however, Macy pulled La Forge even deeper into his network. He courted La Forge for his store, and Mr. and Mrs. Macy's matchmaking abetted the young man's courting of Margaret Getchell. After La Forge accepted Macy's offer of employment, the couple announced their engagement. Mrs. La Forge continued in her position at Macy's until she became pregnant; thereafter she worked in a variety of important capacities in the establishment, albeit without pay. With Margaret La Forge's astute services, Macy's improved its position, even during the panic of 1873 and the ensuing depression. Nonetheless, as Macy planned for the future leadership of his store, he offered the major, not Mrs. La Forge, a partnership on generous terms as a surrogate son. Sadly, both La Forges died young, he of tuberculosis exacerbated by overwork, and she two years later of peritonitis, complicated by a broken heart.[46]

The thicket of family entanglements in R. H. Macy and Company's management and ownership continued to demonstrate how important family connections can be. In 1875 Rowland Macy took on a third partner, Robert Macy Valentine, a sister's son. After Macy's death in 1877, La Forge and Valentine formed a new partnership, which lasted only until the former's death in 1878. Valentine's next partner, Charles B. Webster, was a distant cousin to both Macy and Valentine. When Valentine himself died soon thereafter, Webster brought in his deceased partner's brother-in-law, Jerome B. Wheeler, who had married Macy's niece, and Webster later married Valentine's widow. Nonetheless, by 1888, the Webster-Wheeler partnership dissolved, and Webster took on as partners two brothers, Nathan and Isidor Straus. In 1896, Webster gave up his interest, and the store continued under Straus family ownership until 1994.[47] This intricate web of social connections was exceptional only in that the company's founder, Rowland Macy, opened the gate wider than most businessmen of his era to allow his female cousin, Margaret Getchell, to enter.

Artisanal Networks

People with fewer family assets than the Morgans, or even than Margaret Getchell, exploited those assets as best they could, according to their circumstances and abilities. Though more modestly than those of the great tycoons, social connections and connectability also influenced opportunity for the less mobile. In the Philadelphia of the early decades of the nineteenth century, almost one quarter of the male workers participated in construction and related occupations. When skilled workers could muster the credit or contracts, they often operated as businessmen, not employees. Many of these, like Benjamin Franklin's family in Boston, num-

bered among the city's respected citizens, their financial status ranging from moderately wealthy to insolvent. The most successful had
several advantages, including good timing. Their most potent advantage, however, came from their personal connections, based on
a variety of networks, which enabled them to initiate and grow
solid trades. Through both formal and informal connections, these
men had access to information, credit, clients, reputation, and
skilled workers.[48]

Master builder Moses Lancaster moved to Philadelphia from rural Pennsylvania in 1802 at the age of nineteen. Once he arrived, his
Quaker background connected him immediately to the city's craftsmen, and he relied on these networks for both labor and credit
throughout his career. Local meetings of the Society of Friends considered business as well as moral conduct to fall under their purview, so members in good standing held their community's trust.
This eased Lancaster's obtaining credit, finding apprentices, hiring
journeymen, and buying property. Lancaster was also a good citizen, contributing to charity, education, and various reform efforts.
He carefully built relationships with journeymen, assisting them in
gaining their own economic independence. He thereby forged reliable alliances with younger artisans, who assisted him on large
projects and formed a small market for his properties and unfinished projects. When these men gained their independence, Lancaster would then take on younger and less expensive workers to train
as apprentices and journeymen. In sum, Lancaster nurtured a set of
complex networks for trading in materials as well as labor, credit,
and markets.[49]

Like other entrepreneurs, artisans in Philadelphia extended themselves and took risks despite the vicissitudes of engaging in a vola-
tile trade because, within this community of artisans, all could see
the others' condition. Many suffered setbacks; but sufficient numbers, including Moses Lancaster, achieved prosperity and its comforts to serve as role models.[50] Thus did preindustrial novices learn

that networks of social and financial ties and apprenticeships within them offered the mechanisms by which they could prosper.

In the small, often intimate, settings within which business was conducted prior to the ascendance of corporations, individual actors held center stage in success dramas, moving within clusters of connections or confronting barriers to connectability. Focusing on social interactions makes it clear that success, like failure, depends greatly on the match—or mismatch—of personal traits and social capital. This rule of social capital kept its potency even as the stages for business interactions grew larger, more complex, and more formal in the later decades of the nineteenth century. As institutional backdrops and businesses' bureaucratic props seemed to engulf individual actors, efforts at organization spiraled upward, as if in defense against anonymity and weakness as individuals. As always, people needed others to succeed, but they increasingly recognized that their ties needed to be more formal, more specifically directed to vocations than when career-nurturing networks existed primarily for other purposes, as with Franklin's Junto, Carnegie's uncle's games of checkers, or Lancaster's affiliation with Philadelphia's Quakers. To augment their informal networks, Americans increasingly built organizations to advance their ambitions. Although rhetorical appeals to individualism swelled, organizations grew, facilitating and governing connections and connectability.

CHAPTER 2

Organizing and Synthesizing
Social Capital

Mrs. I. Tisdale Talbot worried a good bit about how her daughters might apply their education. Residents of Boston's wealthy Back Bay, they did not need to work for a living, but they wanted to engage the world usefully. Early exemplars of the so-called Progressive Era, the Talbot women believed in education as the beginning of every problem's solution and organization as its means. After Mrs. Talbot had joined others in an unsuccessful attempt to gain entrance for their daughters to the venerable Boston Latin School, she helped open the Latin School for Girls in 1878. Later, Mrs. Talbot's elder daughter, Marion, was unable to find a challenging use for her university degree outside of teaching because of prevailing "difficulties and uncertainties" for women seeking careers. According to legend, Mrs. Talbot conceived the Association of Collegiate Alumnae, precursor to the American Association of University Women (AAUW), in 1881 when a young woman came to her for help in finding some gainful application of her education and ambitions. Realizing that her daughter and this visitor shared the same frustration, and that they were part of a growing cohort of educated women, Mrs. Talbot suggested that they join forces.[1]

Marion Talbot reported that her mother thought that a "conventional social life seemed lacking in purpose or even in providing friendships on any such basis as college provided and was inadequate as a satisfying end in itself to this new generation." Although women developed acquaintances with their classmates, they could not easily meet or work with women from other colleges who lived outside of their immediate social circles. This lack of connections, they knew, limited their ability to solve mutual problems and to exchange information about vocational opportunities. Mrs. Talbot believed that "only through coöperation and united action" could women overcome the limitations imposed on them and also enhance the opportunity for girls to get an education. From its beginnings, the AAUW has committed itself to equalizing education for women and promoting professional contacts among educated women.[2] Founders and members understood that reaching their personal, professional, and organizational goals requires cooperation between capable women who share those goals. Thus, a century before the term "social capital" came into common currency, the AAUW's founders set out to promote women's professional lives through what we now call mentors, networks, and role models, helping women form and achieve their goals.

Since the eighteenth century, Benjamin Franklin and others who shaped what it meant to be Americans had formed voluntary associations to address any number of needs, both individual and communal, from fire protection to library resources. The tradition of voluntary associations became a national hallmark, and attracted early attention, most famously from Alexis de Tocqueville, who noted that "Americans of all ages, all stations in life, and all types of disposition are forever forming associations." The nation he observed had been busy for decades dividing itself up into voluntary associations that used class and other criteria to distinguish between people. The aims of these various associations included such things as promoting religious, civil, or commercial ends; managing money; saving lives; improving oneself or one's children; beautifying homes or communities; finding a life partner; participating in or promoting athletics; and, of course, simply socializing. One effect of such associations, however, was building walls between people who had previously expected regular, if not egalitarian, contacts with each other.[3] Looking back on the decades around the turn of the twentieth century, it appears that almost every adult, and even many children, succumbed to the organizing impulse. Associations formed at every turn and for every purpose throughout the United States.

In the course of all this organizing, mainstream American business culture moved in contradictory ways. On the one hand, expressions of faith in competition, self-reliance, individualism, and self-made success came to dominate popular praise for men's achievements. On the other hand, businessmen formed and participated in professional and social associations at an intense pace as they pursued advancement and recognition. As rhetoric moved in one way and actions moved in the other, the more powerful a group perceived itself to be, the more it lacked the candidness to admit to its goal of mutual assistance. The dominant explanations for individual, family, community, national, and racial differences in prosperity insisted that competition, not cooperation, determined (and *should* determine) success. Yet more and more Americans pursued goals collectively, even those who praised only individualism.

The Progressive Era

In the decades leading to the 1920s, the politics of class, ethnicity, and gender intensified the impacts of social capital. Massive and unprecedented waves of non-English-speaking immigrants, plus increasing numbers of poor and ill-prepared migrants from rural areas, accompanied the expansion of towns into cities and cities into metropolises. The walking cities within which the young Benjamin Franklin and Andrew Carnegie easily encountered men of influence disappeared; in their place grew ethnic and class-based neighborhoods and specialized zones of business activity. Urbanization resulted in strangers confronting strangers with unprecedented frequency. Men and women ranked each person they met according to the degree of apparent risk the stranger posed to safety, propriety, and comfort. While some reacted to strangers by urging assimilation and fair treatment, others tried to seal off entryways and contacts. Men defended themselves against perceived threats to their masculine prerogatives with fraternal and professional organizations that featured camaraderie in familiar, and wholly masculine, settings.[4] Nativism, which had roared through America in the 1850s, surged again in the 1880s and beyond. In 1882 Boston-area elites formed "The" Country Club in Brookline, Massachusetts, to restrict contact with people whose social assets failed specific tests. As its official history explained in 1932, the club's membership "was 100% recruited from a single and sharply defined social stratum." The club's services to "Boston Society" included hosting business meetings, both formal and informal, but always exclusive.[5] The National Society of the Sons of the American Revolution formed in 1889, the Daughters of the American Revolution in 1890, and the Mayflower Society tried to trump them all in 1897. The Ku Klux Klan began its resurgence in 1915.

In contrast, some organizations were formed to provide *synthetic* social capital for populations without useful assets of their own, often in order to promote assimilation. Institutionalized through an organization's formal activities, synthetic social capital can produce connections and connectability by setting up mentors, networks, and role models. Big Brothers/Big Sisters of America, for instance, exemplified the best of the Progressive Era's underlying faith in education and voluntary association to solve individual and community problems. Although the current association identifies its origins with a young Cincinnati businessman's compassion for a hungry boy in 1903, earlier groups had formed with the express purpose of pairing young people with adult mentors. For instance, a New York Children's Court judge in 1902 recruited ninety "influential men" from the New York Educational Alliance to accept responsibility for guiding one errant child each. The judge himself later joined the Jewish Big Brothers of New York City. The Ladies of Charity of that same city, in the same year, paired women with troubled girls; they became the Catholic Big Sisters of New York. Two years later, almost forty recruits from the Men's Club of New York's Central Presbyterian Church each promised to befriend one boy from the courts. Many city and religious groups joined together to form what is still a vibrant national institution. It has declared success each time a young person in trouble received attention, guidance, sometimes a bit of financial aid, then managed to achieve an education and become a contributing member of society. The first boy befriended under the auspices of the formal Big Brothers organization, according to official records, was an orphan whose brother was in prison and who was himself arrested for vandalism. To everyone's gratification, Michael Hennessy became "a promising young businessman," a worthy recipient of synthesized social capital.[6]

Each time an organization formed networks to assist business ambitions, it created social capital. Sometimes organizations, like Big Brothers/Big Sisters, aimed their efforts toward the casualties of the political economy, recognizing that at-risk children could only grow into solid citizens "one to one." They provided the mechanisms of social capital—mentoring, networking, and role models—for their charges, but in traditional terms of family and friendship. Other organizations also forged relationships to substitute for or augment background networks. Junior Achievement, for instance, quickly spread nationally after its founding in 1919 to teach youngsters business practices and to help them make connections with businesspeople. Other establishments, such as country clubs, served those already advantaged, raising class, sex, and/or ethnic boundaries. There, members and guests fostered social capital as well, but usually without formalizing its mechanisms. By the 1920s, one could find any number of ways to organize social capital between the extremes of Big Brothers/Big Sisters and country clubs—some for mobility, some for exclusion.

Organizing the Working Nation

The organizing impulse struck nineteenth-century working people just as it did everyone else. The term "labor organization" typically adheres to working-class institutions, yet only the most lowly of the working populations did not participate in voluntary associations to advance success at their vocations. Between 1870 and 1890, for example, over two hundred "learned societies" formed, ranging from the American Historical Association to the American Ornithologists' Union, to improve various fields and their participants' positions.[7] The Chamber of Commerce of the United States formed in 1912, although analogous state and local boards had operated throughout the previous century. The American Association of Public Accountants began in 1887; in 1916 that group formed the core of what became the American Institute of Accountants in 1917. In 1899 the American Association of Industrial Management began, followed in twenty years by the Administrative Management Association, and then in 1925 by the American Management Association. Advertising practitioners wrestled mightily with identity and credentials, forming several organizations in the 1890s and their most influential one, the American Association of Advertising Agencies, in 1917. Labor unions organized sometimes by beliefs, the Knights of Labor most notably, and sometimes by trade, such as the specialist trade unions making up the American Federation of Labor. Some groups drew together people who were excluded from dominant organizations or occupations. To titles containing the ever-popular words "national" or "American," these groups frequently added the reason for their marginalization, as did the AAUW and the Colored Farmers' National Alliance (1888).

As a preeminent case in point of organizing professional labor, a half century's struggle to establish medicine's professional identity and goals made the American Medical Association (AMA) the model for promoting a trade through formal and informal restrictive standards. In its founding year, 1847, the AMA tried to set standards for what qualified as a preliminary medical education and degree. That the AMA invested decades of lobbying and public relations work to achieve quasi-legal status for its standards through licensing indicates the importance the field's practitioners and advocates placed on self-regulation through exclusion. Even so, the gates only narrowed to the group's satisfaction after the AMA reorganized in 1901 and then gained licensing control over medical schools after 1906, buttressed by state licensing boards. Increasing costs of medical education and discriminatory admissions resulted in a more homogeneous profession than before, limited for decades to affluent or well-connected white males. Severe discrimination in hospital internships and residencies, which replaced individualized training through apprenticeships, further reduced women's and African Americans' opportunities.[8]

Professional organizations have always included in their mission statements and founding literature declarations of intent to improve their fields. Business and professional organizations to which only middle- and upper-class men had access typically set out the improvement of their field as their top priority. Often they mentioned nothing else. Self-appointed guardians of their vocations, members of these organizations set standards and codes of ethics to raise the stature and effectiveness of practitioners, firms, and whole fields. For example, the first words of the first article in the *Journal of Accountancy* declared in 1905, "Two problems confront the accounting profession to-day—legal recognition and professional education." This organ of the American Association of Public Accountants made clear that its goal was to develop "a profession comparable with law and medicine." Twenty-one years later, the first issue of the *Accounting Review* included a "Message" from the American Society of Certified Public Accountants that challenged the field to continue developing educational standards and methods. Only by formalizing education could accounting practitioners "justify our claims of being a profession," as law and medicine had succeeded in doing.[9]

Thus it was that major segments of working men—of all classes and trades—responded to the social, economic, and political disruptions after 1870 by closing ranks. The most successful of the resulting organizations, such as the AMA and the state and national bar associations, set standards for admission that approached legal stature. Social clubs and colleges also flourished as never before among elites, while fraternal associations, unions, churches, and service organizations became the focus of social activities throughout ranks and ethnicities. With the rarest of exceptions, such as the Knights of Labor, which admitted anyone, the glue that held each institution together was its promise to fortify its members' identity and worth by excluding someone else. Most developed formal rules for recruitment, admission, and promotion. Whatever balance between social and practical benefit that any particular group struck, each strove to provide its members a safe place within an alienating environment. Inside these enclaves—even if they were as informal as the neighborhood tavern—those who belonged could relax and build bonds along networks of familiarity. As insiders talked about what mattered to them, they easily exchanged information and ideas about their work and opportunities for advancement. Whatever vocational advantages accrued as a result reduced opportunity for anyone barred from admission.

Reasons abound for the deliberately exclusionary membership policies these organizations fostered. Given the degree of demographic, economic, technological, and cultural upheaval that adults of this era experienced, retreat into insularity was an all too human reaction. Anywhere people gathered, they calibrated others, admitting some into their networks and rejecting others. People can feel discomfort in others' company if they do not appear to share values or communication systems, including physical appearance and nonverbal signals. Strangers may be unpredictable, untrustworthy, and hard to hold accountable. Thus, individuals have traditionally favored forming business alliances with family and close acquaintances. They fulfill old and foster new obligations within the familiar, secure interactions that build relationships and communities— and that generate considerable advantages, both psychological and practical, to those inside the gates.[10] Whether one is doing business with someone in a labor union hall, a corporate boardroom, a loan office, or a downtown gentlemen's club, social perceptions determine confidence levels, thereby setting limits for business relationships.

Men's gathering places typically had high walls and strong gates that prevented strangers from entering as peers. Traditions and presumptions set men's social and work places off limits to women and girls, at least of the proper sort, and to men of other ethnicities and classes. Proper women risked their credentials as such if they dared invade; strange men risked more. Given the general understandings about gender roles and rules, men and women had their separate places in the nineteenth century outside their homes. Physiological differences between men and women were taken to indicate mental differences, justifying gatekeepers' belief that women's education and careers ought to be restricted because of their supposedly limited energy or other deficiencies. Even when women began to gain entrance to workplaces that had, by default and considerable enforcement, been male domains, the extracurricular associations through which novices became trained, certified, employed, and competent remained off limits. The numbers of women practicing professions like medicine or advertising thus declined with the rise of professional associations in the Progressive Era.[11] To stimulate opportunities, women and other marginalized groups responded by forming parallel organizations.

"For the Purpose of Mutual Advancement"

Throughout the nineteenth century, women built their management skills and their confidence by participating in organizations founded for all sorts of purposes. Many women's associations focused on reforms, such as temperance, abolition, public health, women's suffrage, and child labor regulations. Others focused on arts, literature, or prayer. Some groups, such as the famous Sorosis, combined literary, philanthropic, and reform goals. In joining these and other groups, women also gratified their need for active engagement in the community. They gained opportunities for developing themselves and for creating networks. A few even earned a livelihood through service within their organizations.[12] Of course, throughout history almost all women have worked, outside the home as well as in it, so the so-called cult of domesticity was a cultural standard not always connected to individuals' realities or to their ideals. As increasing numbers of women gained formal educations, they expanded the range of occupations they wished to pursue, whether or not from economic necessity. Though they may have been insiders within their own organizations, they were outsiders relative to their classes' well-paying and prestigious vocations.

Nineteenth-century literary clubs provided settings for women's intellectual and professional development. Sorosis and the New England Woman's Club, both founded in 1868, brought together women whose personal ambitions combined with various notions of feminism to explore and develop women's rights and options. Many of these women, and almost all of their leaders, sought to earn their living through writing, including journalism. Their active participation in this business arena taught them the value of encouraging women's practical education, freedom of movement, and social capital. To these ends, Jane Cunningham Croly founded Sorosis, then in 1889 she helped start the Woman's Press Club of New York City. She was also active in a number of other clubs and professional women's organizations. The precipitant for Sorosis was Croly's exclusion from Charles Dickens's lecture to the New York Press Club, even though her husband chaired its executive committee. Organizing sessions began among Croly's acquaintances and took place at her home. Nonetheless, the first *official* meeting of Sorosis took place at Delmonico's restaurant to make it clear that the organization was to be a public institution that was prepared to challenge restrictions against women's movements.[13]

Business and professional women from publishing, retailing, medicine, law, science, education, religion, and architecture joined their artistic sisters in Sorosis. Its constitution placed what we now call the functions of social capital as its top priorities: "to promote agreeable and useful relations among women of literary and artistic tastes . . . particularly when these qualities have found expression in outward life and work." They intended "to establish a kind of freemasonry among women of similar pursuits, to render them helpful to each other, and bridge over the barrier which custom and social etiquette place in the way of friendly intercourse." Such opportunities would, they asserted, "exert an important influence on the future of women and the welfare of society." Alice Cary, the organization's first president, hoped that the club would foster women's confidence. She wanted Sorosis to "open out new avenues of employment to women, to make them less dependent." Members provided markets for each other's work, helped each other explore opportunities, discussed protections for businesswomen, and fostered education through scholarships. The founding members agreed that self-growth, confidence, and professional assistance should be the group's top priorities, rather than altruistic reforms of the more traditional female sort. As with any trade organization, the members' lofty goals did not preclude exclusion; to the contrary, they believed that their aims required certain exclusions. Men were excluded for fear of "overpower[ing]" the proceedings; female aspirants had to submit applications, and race or class alone could determine their fate.[14]

Women often applied their experience and networks from nonprofit projects to profitable ones. The Women's Educational and Industrial Union (WEIU) evolved as one such opportunity-rich organization. In 1877, affluent reforming women in Boston founded the WEIU to improve the ranges of opportunities for themselves and their less fortunate sisters who had to earn a living. The organization augmented the traditional range of philanthropic projects to include educating, protecting, and, most of all, training women in marketable skills. Besides being concerned with typical women's trades, such as millinery, the WEIU's training included such innovations as a school of salesmanship, established in 1905 in response to the growing opportunities for women in department stores. A home economics program for college graduates was another of WEIU's fresh approaches to women's occupational needs, pointing its students toward economic independence through jobs in consumer product development and promotion, as well as in teaching. Some of these programs formed the core of a new women's college, Simmons, which opened in 1902.[15]

As part of the WEIU's general goal of preparing women for better jobs, whether vocational or avocational, after World War I the organization sponsored *Women Professional Workers*, a study of women's work options and conditions, accompanied by recommendations. Its author, Elizabeth Kemper Adams, Ph.D., identified "professional" work as typically requiring a formal education, preferably college level, plus "experience, judgment, [and] advice" beyond that education. Adams advised that women's full professional development therefore required participation in professional associations "as a means of fostering professional spirit and maintaining and raising professional standards." Although she pointed out that some "men's associations" may "encourage the spirit of exclusiveness and prestige," Adams recommended that women join them when allowed to do so. However, too many women accepted "mere membership" in such organizations. They have, she wrote, "timorously and uncomfortably attended meetings in which they have taken no part and in which they have been ignored and sometimes discriminated against, intentionally or unintentionally." Even though the "modern professional woman is not timorous," Adams recommended that women organize a "separate association and thus to gain confidence and experience that will win a hearing in later joint associations." She expressed confidence that this "stage" would pass; in the meantime, separate organizations offered women a "means of education in managing affairs."[16]

In 1912 Christine Frederick was a highly regarded home efficiency expert who consulted for many large firms and held a high-profile position as an editor at the *Ladies' Home Journal.* She shared her interests in shaping American consumer culture with her husband, J. George Frederick, who was an editor at the leading advertising trade journal of the day, *Printers' Ink,* and a member of the Advertising Men's League of New York. When Mrs. Frederick wanted to attend a lecture at her husband's organization, she learned that she could do so only by sitting behind a curtain in a balcony. Her husband as well as she objected to this constraint, and as a result of this incident the Fredericks invited all of New York's female advertising professionals to a meeting, out of which arose the League of Advertising Women, since 1934 known as the Advertising Women of New York (AWNY). Like most women's professional groups, the AWNY began as a means for women to compensate for their exclusion from the dominant men's groups. As

AWNY's historian wrote in the 1940s, if these women "couldn't share in the meetings and speakers of the men's group, they would form one of their own!"[17]

The league's founders defined their mission as enabling "women doing constructive advertising in an executive capacity to co-operate for the purpose of mutual advancement." Such an explicit, pre-eminent goal of mutual advancement set women's professional groups apart from their counterpart men's groups. Women's organizations proclaimed the priority of fostering their members' business success and pledging "to emphasize the work that woman is doing and is especially qualified to do." In contrast, elite male associations' mission statements typically emphasized what was just one component of the women's statement: "to further the study of advertising."[18] Like the AAUW and most other women's vocational groups, the League of Advertising Women fostered women's education, funding girls' and young women's education and supplementing the functions of women's background networks.

Similarly, in 1915 the Medical Women's National Association, forerunner of the American Medical Women's Association, set as its purpose "to bring Medical Women into communication with each other for their mutual advantage." Among its first projects was a Committee on Internship (later the Committee on Medical Opportunities for Women), which surveyed and publicized hospital internships and postgraduate training opportunities open to women, recognizing that informal networks were not sufficient. Likewise, the Association of Bank Women (ABW), founded in 1921 and renamed Financial Women International in 1991, stated as its primary purpose "to encourage mutual helpfulness and cooperation among its members with the end in view of making themselves increasingly valuable to the institutions with which they are associated." The ABW also sought to help "other women" interested in banking to "take advantage of opportunities" and, in a suggestion of the sense of siege female bank officers felt, pledged "at all times, to uphold the dignity and integrity of women associated with or employed by banks." A 1927 speaker acknowledged ABW members' sense of marginality in a talk entitled "Woman's Adaptability in a Man's World."[19]

The National Federation of Business and Professional Women Clubs (NFBPWC) appeared among the organizations mentioned by Adams in *Women Professional Workers.* The NFBPWC (now known as the BPW/USA) grew out of a 1918 assembly sponsored by the Young Women's Christian Association to develop communication among women in a variety of fields. Adams noted in 1921 that the federation had already held two "enthusiastic and largely attended annual conferences." Enthusiasm did characterize NFBPWC meetings and publications, enthusiasm both for opportunities and for maximizing those opportunities through social processes. "In the business woman's world of 1918," an official history explained decades later, "it was primarily 'every woman for herself.'" Circumstances rather than adequate training or networks determined where and how women entered and pursued business careers. "Each found her job unaided." The NFBPWC intended to remedy that.[20]

Over two hundred women from forty-five states attended the NFBPWC's first conference in 1919. A newsletter published during the conference summarized the proceedings and cheered on the participants and their colleagues at home. Its title, *Can Happen,* expressed the conference's optimism. The first editorial breathlessly described the excitement as akin to "standing on the ground watching a great, new, panting, breathing air-ship, about to take flight across a sea of difficulties and uncertainties to a land called 'Opportunity.'" A sense that NFBPWC truly could develop women's opportunities pervaded its publications. The next day's editorial banner proclaimed that "Handicaps Are Out of Date," and the president's column a few months later headlined "Illimitable Opportunities." Optimists are not necessarily fools, however, and these women knew that neither suffrage nor their best efforts would brush aside the serious challenges ahead, such as "lesser pay for equal service and . . . restricted opportunities."[21]

A 1919 *Can Happen* article, "Every Woman for Herself or Federation," challenged working women to learn suffragism's lesson of "team work" as "responsible members of the community." Similarly, women's success in the workplace depended on the same caliber of "efficient organization" as the nation had achieved in wartime production and "military prowess." Organizing for better pay and working conditions did not suffice. Women needed to organize to gain "the support of a body of their own kind to stand behind them at many critical junctures." Without this support, "cowardice and suppressions are bound to prevail in the unequal struggle of one woman against a group of organized employers, and the injustice of such a situation is essential." The NFBPWC identified with professionals and was conservative on nonfeminist issues, so these were strikingly bold words. Indeed, the article's final sentences read as if they had lost their way from an old Knights of Labor speech: "Unorganized we may gain as the world gains, always dragging a little upon its progress; but organized we can be a vital factor in helping it along. It is ours to choose."[22]

With the NFBPWC's rapid progress, *Can Happen* quickly seemed a "bit stale," and the newsletter soon grew into a journal that needed a different title. *Independent Woman* expressed an intriguing tension in title and content between independence and calls for cooperation. Right under the publication's new masthead lay a statement of the organization's mission, which included promoting business and professional women's interests through "combined action," gathering and distributing information about "vocational opportunity," and encouraging the establishment of state and local chapters and cooperation between them. As the organization's

1944 official history explained, "independent" meant self-support-ing. The independence these women sought carried a gendered sig-nificance, as reflected in their membership rules: only women could be conference delegates from member clubs, and only women within those clubs could vote on the delegates. The men who ob-jected to the publication's new name were not members, and the "criticism of non-members should not carry much weight." In an-other show of independence, the federation early on sponsored a study to "offset" the notion that women worked "for pin money." Instead, 85 percent of the women surveyed lived on their earnings alone, and many supported dependents.[23]

In addition to the NFBPWC's many general calls for collective ac-tion, support, and exchange of information, its practices and publi-cations during its first five years promoted the synthesis of social capital in specific ways. Conferences, for instance, featured events sponsored by local specialists for their peers. At the very first such meeting, in 1919, St. Louis's female lawyers and advertising practi-tioners set this precedent, scheduling events intended to bring to-gether their colleagues from across the nation. "Education, prepa-ration, co-operation" received much attention as a theme in the group's conferences and publications. Its journal worried that women in business suffered more than their sisters in law or medi-cine from "a low standard of efficiency" because they lacked the schooling that prepared professionals, both male and female. A woman in business too often lacked "precedent for her guidance," "adequate training," and even "comprehension of the relationship of her own particular 'job' to the vast business cosmos." Absent what we now call role models, mentors, and networks, a woman could only watch as "men who once were her juniors advance to greater responsibility." Moreover, as outsiders, all women were judged by a single failure. The solution? "Each one of us *must* be her sister's keeper." President Gail Laughlin declared that "per-haps" the main rationale for NFBPWC's existence was that "business and professional women may meet together and take counsel together"—that is, network. Together they could "come to wiser conclusions." The next president, Lena Lake Forrest, insisted that successful businesswomen guide junior women, telling a West Coast audience in 1921 that they share responsibility when a "business girl fails, from inexperience or inefficient training" if they have made "no effort to pave the way for the girl."[24]

Shortly after the NFBPWC's fourth convention in 1922, an article in the widely read *American Review of Reviews* emphasized its activities in mentoring and providing role models. Through the federation's activities, successful women put "their experience at the command of newcomers in business." Beyond practicalities, they also teach "their own spirit of work to younger women." With loans, scholarships, and curriculum improvement, plus the "friendly interest of the business women in the young girls," the federation worked to reform business education and make it more accessible. Through education, both institutional and informal, President Forrest declared that "we must spare the younger women the toil and waste and heartache with which we have won our way."[25]

The Beauty of Social Capital

Many female entrepreneurs, locked out of leadership careers and even jobs in mainstream business, built remarkable enterprises by making background, peer, and authority networks the basis of their business operations. Among the first American women to achieve millionaire status through firms that they started and operated were Martha Matilda Harper, Annie Turnbo Malone, and Madame C. J. Walker, who very deliberately built networks among both clients and agents. Presaging their twentieth-century counterpart, Mary Kay Ash, these three successful women produced and sold women's beauty products and techniques, training other women to be agents and businesswomen. Each created national, sometimes international, business empires by developing and mobilizing social capital among people with few other resources. Their achievements were all the more remarkable because their social capital had no value in mainstream business arenas.

Martha Matilda Harper opened her hair and skin care salon in Rochester, New York, in 1888 with her life savings of $360. Using her personal connections through church and former employers, particularly a prominent lawyer, Harper managed to persuade the owner of Rochester's most prestigious business address to lease her a room, over his objections that her then-unusual craft would attract improper women. She built her trade over the next half century not merely by producing hair products for a highly competitive market. Her success came from building a franchise system that at its peak included approximately five hundred U.S. and international salons, run by women to whom Harper licensed products and techniques for hair and skin treatment as well as business management procedures. In 1926, she reflected back on having built her business "brick by brick, woman by woman." Harper Shop owners and operators became Harperites, whom the founder called "my dear girls." She taught the art of pleasing elites, which she had learned working as a servant since the age of seven. She structured her franchise system to create opportunities for women who had little financial capital, developing their ability through extensive training. She gave business value to their social connections with other working-class women and to their connectability as white women trained as servants to the affluent. Many Harperites achieved business success and, thereby, a measure of independence.[26]

Harper's franchise system functioned as the best authority networks do, spreading opportunity, information, and training from the center, with reciprocal benefits accruing to all parties. She built it around herself, providing guidance in ethics and behavior, as well as in business and services. Harper started her first franchises by sending her sisters and closest assistants out to other cities. To develop and maintain the network, Harper trained recruits in her Rochester shop. She traveled to maintain cohesion and inspiration among the outlying franchise shops, and she published newsletters and handbooks. She urged shop owners to shape their own workers into loyal teams by setting a good personal example and by practicing solid management techniques, including holding regular staff meetings, rewarding achievement, and gently correcting errors. Harper continuously spoke and wrote in terms of the value of personal independence through entrepreneurship for women who were willing and able to take on responsibilities, but who lacked opportunities. Still, she discriminated in a manner no less powerful and constraining for its being idiosyncratic. White women who had worked as servants were the people with whom she identified and felt most comfortable. She recruited them almost exclusively, contending that their experience and lack of other business options would ensure their loyalty to her and compliance to her standards. She in turn offered them training, confidence, connections, housing while in training, and even start-up capital. Harperites vindicated her investment in them when they drew in recruits from their own background networks of family and friends.[27]

Harper built networks among potential clients as well, especially among suffragists, society leaders, and fellow Christian Scientists. Suffragist leader Susan B. Anthony became a Harper client while she lived in Rochester, often referring to Harper enthusiastically as a model for women seeking control over their own lives. Like many of Harper's clients, Anthony also brought out-of-town guests to Harper's shop and encouraged Harper to open shops to give opportunities to women in other cities, as both clients and businesswomen. When visitors urged her to expand to their town, Harper astutely asked them to collect signatures that assured patronage there. One such petitioner and client was another notable female activist, Chicago social leader Bertha Honoré Palmer. Daughter and wife of wealthy Chicago businessmen, Palmer presided over the Board of Lady Managers of the World's Columbian Exposition of 1891–1893 and held numerous other leadership positions over the years. With Palmer's signature on Harper's petition and, according to Harper legend, Anthony's encouragement, a Harper Shop opened in Chicago near the Exposition. This shop expanded her reputation, attracted a clientele, and demonstrated a successful woman-run business, square in the public eye. After the Exposition closed, the shop moved into Chicago's renowned Marshall Field's emporium, owned by a former partner of Palmer's deceased husband.[28] Harper made exquisite use of her connections.

Many twentieth-century entrepreneurs with few financial reserves managed, through abundant social networks, to profit with door-to-door selling and other low-overhead marketing strategies, selling everything from brushes to life insurance. Within that context, two women to whom Martha Harper would have denied opportunity built fortunes. Annie Turnbo Malone and Madame C. J. Walker offered beauty and business options for African-American women as both customers and agents in ways strikingly similar to Harper's, beginning in 1900 and 1905, respectively. All three women, from deprived backgrounds, expanded female roles, teaching women to enhance their beauty while improving health, self-confidence, and self-reliance with every increment in economic independence. Malone and Walker, however, did not have Harper's option of serving white elites. Instead, they targeted women with harder lives than Harper had ever known, even as a servant girl. As Walker announced to the 1913 assembly of the National Negro Business League, in full, self-made glory, "I am not ashamed of my past; I am not ashamed of my humble beginning. Don't think because you have to go down in the wash-tub that you are any less a lady!" Both Malone and Walker took their roles seriously as developers of African-American women's skills and networks. They established schools to train agents and taught their agents to train others at home; tens of thousands of women responded. Malone and Walker deliberately set themselves up as role models, urging women to expand their horizons as they built and used networks to move ahead. Walker well understood the business value of organized social capital, promoting her goods and her training opportunities through African-American fraternal organizations, churches, and colleges. As the Walker Company advised agents, the key to success was to "be a mixer."[29]

Banking on Social Capital

When people deposit, borrow, or manage money, their confidence in those with whom they interact matters greatly. So social capital invariably plays a part in such transactions. Perhaps the most famous statement confirming the centrality of social capital in finance came from J. P. Morgan's testimony in 1912 during hearings in the House of Representatives. When the committee's lawyer, Samuel Untermyer, asked whether "the big New York banks" gave credit to supplicants according to "the money back of them," Morgan replied "No, sir. It is because people believe in the man." After a follow-up question, Morgan reinforced this pure statement of the value of social capital by insisting that the successful loan applicant "might not have anything. I have known a man to come into my office, and I have given him a check for a million dollars when I knew they [sic] had not a cent in the world." Untermyer, perhaps a little incredulous, pushed the point further, asking, "Is not commercial credit based primarily upon money or property?" Exemplar of the old school that he was, Morgan responded, "No sir; the first thing is character." Untermyer: "Before money or property?" Morgan: "Before money or property or any thing else. Money cannot buy it . . . because a man I do not trust could not get money from me on all the bonds in Christendom."[30]

Morgan got it right: voluntarily giving someone our money really does require trust, in one form or another. But whom do we trust? Collateral helps reduce the need for judging a stranger's trustworthiness; a lifetime of experience, however, can form personal and community bonds based on predictability and reciprocal obligations. Imagine having no personal connections on which to base a judgment in a system with no regulatory protections and no standardized criteria for gauging collateral or references. In such a circumstance, a banker might well rely on a primitive screen—the appearance and mannerisms of a shared background—for which the word "character" was code among Morgan's class. Of course, rigid bonding between members of any group endangers the fair treatment of others. We neither loan them money nor deposit our own funds in their banks. If we accept their deposits, we do so only to gain access to their funds, not to reinvest in jobs for them or in their communities.

Prior to the institutionalization of financial systems, family and other social capital connections originating within background networks provided businesses' presumptive sources of human, political, and financial capital. Pooling of resources in community-based banks moved individuals' savings, often in small increments, into community or regional development. "Insider" business dealings were standard and accepted practice throughout the nineteenth century, and these collective actions built and applied funds for investment and entrepreneurship. Investors and borrowers necessarily shared important, identifying commonalties, sometimes political activities, previous business ties, proximity, or, most typically, kinship. Community banks helped poor people to gain some measure of financial security by pooling their resources. Even some of the most destitute of Irish refugees, for instance, adapted to their new environs and built impressive savings. One particular cohort came with their families and stayed in close proximity to their first homes in New York's impoverished Five Points, even when they could have afforded to leave. Within their community, they generated complex networks for those seeking jobs, as well as for banking.[31]

In 1904, when Amadeo Peter Giannini started the Bank of Italy in San Francisco, ethnicity mattered when people chose a place to deposit their savings. The largest two savings banks west of Chicago were the Hibernia Savings and Loan Society and the German Savings and Loan Society; California banks also included the Anglo-Californian. Through a wide variety of innovations, Giannini developed his San Francisco bank into one of the largest banks in the nation, and in 1930 he renamed it the Bank of America. According to legend, he used a social standard just like J. P. Morgan's, but applied at the other end of the socioeconomic scale: "with no better security than the calluses on the borrower's hands." His reputation and the personal contacts Giannini made as he walked around his community—starting at the age of fifteen in his stepfather's business—made the bank an immediate success among people who had not been welcome elsewhere and likewise had not trusted the existing banks with their savings. When he opened branches, he made sure that the tellers spoke the languages of their neighborhoods and did not wait inside, as did traditional bankers, for customers to appear.[32]

Many banks during these same decades developed sex-segregated divisions that attracted clients not accepted within traditional banking establishments. In order to inspire these clients' confidence and trust, banks sometimes hired from the marginalized but targeted groups. This double-edged sword of segregation offered limited career opportunities to a few. As one banker explained the benefits of segregating respectable women, "they do not have to come in contact with the general customers and business of the bank." Perceiving even affluent women as aliens of a sort, albeit aliens with attractive assets, the "general customers" and staff may too have appreciated the walls of segregation. Beginning in the last

As bankers and other professionals began to organize into formal, professional networks, their group portraits, like this one from 1921, made the primary qualification for membership unambiguously apparent.

(From *Journal of the American Bankers Association*, November 1921.)

quarter of the 1800s with male staffs, women's departments peaked in the 1920s, when they employed professional female staffs, including executives. In 1922 the NFBPWC reported that banking was the only business "profession" in which women served as long as men. Not surprisingly, banks preferred to hire affluent females who were engaged in women's voluntary and reform associations. Not only could such staff attract the deposits of similar women, but they could attract their associations' accounts as well. The positive and negative business implications of networking could not be more evident than here, both in banks' hiring strategies and in why a "Chinese wall" of gendered segregation had been "erected by the bankers themselves," in the language of *Independent Woman*.[33]

"Behind the Walls of Segregation"

How could African Americans best participate in the postemancipation economy? With too little capital in the South, tenant farming and sharecropping, overwhelming racism, and multiple agricultural crises, more people were concerned about subsistence than riches. Under such harsh and discouraging circumstances, African Americans evolved strategies that allowed them to meet challenges with remarkable fortitude and creativity.[34] Their greatest successes resulted from their pooling of financial, human, and social capital.

The great African-American banking and insurance projects between Reconstruction and 1929 derived from traditions of benevolent and burial societies that had provided community mutual assistance dating back to the 1600s. Despite emancipation, the barriers against African Americans' assimilation into the mainstream political economy remained insurmountable, so their churches and fraternal societies became pivotal to much of their social and economic life. Mutual aid societies formed to help members with expenses related to sickness and death. As a Tuskegee professor explained in 1918 about the postbellum era, these "local organizations, formed by the hundreds . . . , brought the people together and established friendly intercourse." In his estimation, the "chief value" of these organizations was to function as "schools in which the masses were taught the value and the methods of coöperation." National organizations began to grow in the 1880s, one of the most important moving outward from Virginia. Established in 1881, the Grand Fountain of the United Order of True Reformers claimed over fifty thousand members by 1900. In 1888, after a deposit of the order's substantial funds with white bankers had raised "race feeling" resulting in a lynching, the group chartered a bank. In its day it operated a mercantile and industrial association, a newspaper, a hotel, a retirement home, a building and loan association, and a real estate division.[35]

The notable success of African-American mutual aid societies in founding and operating financial institutions followed the painful lesson of the fall of the National Freedmen's Savings Bank and Trust Company. Because it was established with a federal charter in 1865, many African Americans thought the bank was an institution of the federal government, prompting them to trust their savings to it. In fact, however, the Freedmen's Savings Bank was operated by white businessmen; and although some of the bank's managers had philanthropic intentions, others intended to use the collected assets as venture capital. Worse yet, the bank was based in New York City and Washington, D.C., so it removed funds from their origins and never returned investments to the community. Moreover, no African Americans held managerial or executive positions. All of these policies reflected the founders' lack of connection to African-American clients and communities. Fourteen years after the bank's 1874 collapse, African Americans began to open their own chartered banks, and, although few were long lived (few banks lasted very long in those preregulated times), almost all did at least reinvest in their communities. Instead of being run at a distance by strangers, these new banks were either local or founded by fraternal and benevolent societies as depositories, pooling assets and contributing to economic development. Moreover, as historian Carter G. Woodson explained in 1929, fraternal associations' business endeavors, including both banks and insurance companies, "offered unusual opportunities for community effort, the promotion of racial consciousness, and the development of leadership."[36] In other words, they built human capital through social capital while consolidating financial capital.

Prior to World War II, African Americans developed institutions "behind the walls of segregation," in economist Abram L. Harris's 1936 words, through which they could work together in "defensive enterprises" to pool resources. In 1940, M. S. Stuart, whose positions included that of historian of the National Negro Insurance Association, decried the "high, invisible wall of commercial obstruction," which "policy" kept "in a state of repair." This "invisible barrier" to development required an "economic detour," confinement of African Americans to small, isolated businesses that were forced to compete economically though "caged behind the bars of racial prejudice." The main intellectual figures who guided the African-American culture of the preceding era, Booker T. Washington, W. E. B. Du Bois, and Marcus Garvey, as well as countless religious and community leaders, understood this necessity. They blended calls for collective action and personal responsibility into a self-help ethos that placed individual action in a community context; individuals could not succeed without their community. On this, if little else, Washington, Du Bois, and Garvey agreed.[37]

African Americans' experiences in venturing into the business world—in the North as well as in the South—challenged the credibility of typical success formulas that encouraged individualist ambitions. Instead, often devastating experiences made the relationship between individual agency and social capital crystal clear. African Americans' world was dominated by people who perceived them to be aliens and who, more often than not, regarded them as

cheap labor and powerless customers rather than as equal participants in market activities. The resulting political and economic burdens upon any enterprise initiated by African Americans constrained every individual's range of movement and possibilities,
however talented and ambitious he or she may have been. Within
that circumscribed range, of course, individual agency mattered,
and this is what prompted people like Booker T. Washington and
others to emphasize individual responsibility. Over and over they
praised the character, energy, and education of the achievers they
set up as role models. Yet too often, unbalanced statutes, even
mobs and arsonists, targeted African-American men who, despite
all odds, managed to do well in business. The odds against any African American acting alone were too great for them to see individual
effort as sufficient; and this reality fostered an appreciation for the
power of social capital.

As J. H. Harmon Jr. put it in 1929, "the exercise of civil rights"
after emancipation had failed African Americans, precluding success on an individual basis. Instead, success would have to come
through "the cooperative spirit," that is, pooling all forms of capital, including social. As Woodson explained, "Negroes in the final
analysis had to learn to look out for themselves." Harmon and
Woodson, with Arnett G. Lindsay, published these conclusions in a
1929 study sponsored by the Association for the Study of Negro
Life and History. They described how African-American businessmen learned the "value of co-operation" after failing as individuals
under conditions that challenged even less "handicapped" entrepreneurs. They contrasted individual and cooperative forms of business, counting corporations among the latter, along with partnerships, fraternal orders, and banks. Corporations, they believed,
could solve problems of financing, risk, managerial succession, and
efficiencies of scale and so could overrun "individualist" firms.
World War I home-front drives and the successes of white cooperation through associations and corporate structures—despite their

language of individualism—demonstrated the merits of "co-operative schemes." Not by coincidence, cooperation within churches, schools, fraternal orders, and neighborhoods had by then developed most strongly where oppression was the most severe, resulting in enterprises that could help "avoid any contact with whites." Because of prevailing conditions, "as long as Negroes remain individualists so long will they remain weak and helpless in business."[38]

Summarizing the needs of African-American businessmen as "cooperation, capital, credit, buying power, labor, and therefore more intelligent management," Harmon called for "the Negro public" to patronize businesses within their own communities, and for "cooperation between fellow merchants" in business practice "that each may benefit by the experience of the other." He noted how difficult it was for African Americans to learn so-called scientific business approaches because of "the disinclination of white business houses to take them into their establishments to learn their techniques." Harmon also remarked on a paradox of social dynamics that resulted from the small scale of African-American businesses and their dependence on social resources. On the one hand, it was unfortunate that African Americans had to deal "with people who have been so influenced by the procedure of churches and lodges that they require Negro business men to deal with them on the basis of friendship rather than according to strict up-to-date methods." Yet on the other, "it must be admitted that a large number of Negro business enterprises have been developed because they have had the support of churches and lodges." Harmon, like many others, rued African Americans' having to trade with white firms that could offer better prices because of whites' advantages within the larger economy. Only adequate training in business methods and building confidence in "race" businesses and "racial consciousness" could begin to resolve the problem. Du Bois called the solution a "group economy" through which African Americans would patronize and employ each other. Decades of campaigns exhorted African Americans, "Don't Buy Where You Can't Work."[39]

African Americans built their banking and insurance operations, in Woodson's words, through the "deep-seated idea of solving a social and economic problem through benevolent societies." In an unregulated field, where better to deposit one's money than through an organization based on community loyalties? Even if the institutions failed, deposits were spent within the community. Maggie Lena Walker founded one of the strongest of all mutual aid society banks on behalf of the United Order of St. Luke in Richmond, Virginia. Both Walker and the United Order were born in 1867. Walker began participating in the organization as a teenager, and in 1899 she became its Grand Secretary–Treasurer. Walker started the St. Luke Penny Savings Bank in 1903 to have a safe depository for the order's insurance funds and to provide jobs for African-American women. Her success with the St. Luke Bank resulted in her becoming regarded as the first female bank president in the United States—even though she earned half of what the bank's male cashier did. Urging participation in the bank in 1905, Walker contended it would be a means of "raising our pride of race." Other ethnicities deposited loyally, she lamented, but "the Negro is so wedded to those who oppress him that he carries to their bank every dollar he can get his hands upon and then goes back the next day, borrows and pays the white man to lend him his own money."[40] Walker had no patience for taking financial capital to people who disdained the value of one's social capital.

The Social Side of Social Capital

"The business and professional women all over the country have begun to feel the need of clubs where they may come in contact with other women of like interests and derive the helpfulness which comes with the interchange of ideas." In this way an article in *Independent Woman* began in 1920, just over a year after the founding of the National Federation of Business and Professional Women's Clubs (NFBPWC). The article noted that men had "always appreciated the help and stimulus so derived" from their many in-town clubs and public gathering places. More to the point, much "business is accomplished over the lunch table and new business acquired." Middle- and upper-class women had watched from the outside and noted the benefits of men's gathering together in a social environment with people of related interests. Women were therefore "merely following along well proven lines." Just about a year later, the president of the Philadelphia chapter of the NFBPWC worried that women were "not as good mixers as men are." Their "opportunities to mingle have been less frequent. . . . This is bad for the woman as well as for her work." Philadelphia required a "place to meet the needs of business women in a social way." In this spirit, *Independent Woman* carried an article or commentary each month through its early years with suggestions about designing and operating clubs and their advantages to business and professional women.[41]

How could anyone worry that women mixed and mingled less comfortably than men? The key to that riddle lies in prevailing assumptions that women's "socializing" was fundamentally different from men's "mixing and mingling." Thus, the words "social" and "society" applied to the networks that women built in their traditional roles in home and community—including religious and benevolent associations. "Socializing" described what women did in their circles, restricted to background networks or people with whom they had regular contact, even when they worked outside their own homes. Men, in contrast, "mixed" and "mingled" with other men in their networks, often among colleagues whose homes and families they might not know, even by reputation. Such acquaintances might be out-of-town or cross-town customers or salesmen. They might be associates in the same workplace or in the same trade. Men might or might not discuss business as they mixed, but should a problem or an opportunity arise, they knew how to find each other. Thus, one mixed to get to know people with shared interests, whereas one socialized with people one already knew through background connections. Women needed places outside their homes to meet, mix, and mingle comfortably with other women and possibly even with men through whom they could advance their vocational goals.

Gatekeeping for Fun and Profit

Protecting members and their interests has always ranked at the top of organizations' priorities. Within vocational associations, discriminating between worthy and unworthy practitioners can nurture a field's prestige and public authority. Discrimination likewise can benefit avocational associations. And of course there is always the sheer comfort of sharing company with people whose appearance, behavior, language, background, and values resemble one's own. In order to attain these benefits, organizations engage in various gatekeeping practices. Formalized membership criteria, as well as unspoken presumptive criteria, admissions committees, recruiting, and initiation processes characterize both vocational and avocational associations. Sex, ethnicity, religion, finances, residency, interests, education, skills, and so on are among the possible criteria for admission. The more exclusive a group, the more likely that joining it requires some personal recommendation as evidence of adequate social capital.

Social, service, and recreational purposes rank high among the primary stated missions of such groups as country clubs, downtown men's clubs, service clubs, religious groups, and elite athletic clubs. The balance of vocational and avocational benefits in any organization has been notoriously hard to ascertain. Although a club's bylaws may discourage "business talk," members can and do engage in networking and exchange business-related information. Employers have often paid employees' club dues as a way for them to build contacts and bring in business.[42] When income taxes entered into business calculations in 1916, deductions for such memberships and related expenses became part of the "ordinary and necessary" costs of doing business—whatever other pleasures such memberships offered.

During the Progressive Era, when the organizing impulse drove so much in American culture, the richest and most powerful Americans expended significant resources to build social institutions wherein they could exercise their political and economic power in safe, predictable venues. Membership in exclusive institutions not only measured status but also created platforms for exercising and even enhancing social capital, benefiting individual members and the membership communities collectively. As a founder proposed for New York City's Union League Club, its core members should be "men of substance and established high position socially." A second group should be "clever men" with a high reputation in literature and the arts. A third category should comprise "promising young men . . . ," especially "rich young men . . . who don't understand what their place can be in American society." Unlike Europe, America had no presumed role for a "leisure" class, so these young men must be "nourished with care." To prepare them for leadership, "older and abler established men ought to fraternize with them, to welcome and hold every true man of them in fraternity."[43]

Businessmen often congregated in clubs by industry or trade, or even sometimes by firm. Clubs assimilated newer elites into regional and even national elites, and once a family with the "proper" sort of religious and ethnic background achieved elite status, that status held for generations. Even if playing cards and eating looked to be an elite club's primary activities, frequent and exclusive contact improved members' abilities to protect and develop their interests and those of future generations. Businessmen founded and governed Chicago's most prestigious clubs, beginning with the Dearborn Club in 1861. Until the 1970s, these clubs almost always excluded women from their expensive settings for business deals. Many, such as Pittsburgh's Duquesne Club, were overtly business oriented, providing congenial, secure settings for business conversations and negotiations. In the 1940s, this club defended its dues as business expenses for tax purposes, making clear its mission as a social setting for consummating business connections.[44]

Although J. P. Morgan belonged to almost two dozen clubs by the end of his life, most of these memberships of his served primarily to boost the clubs' stature by demonstrating some connection to the great financier. Morgan, however, mainly used the Union Club, the Union League Club, and the Metropolitan Club, three of the most elite clubs in New York City (and therefore the country). In these sanctuaries he met with his peers and the nation's presidents, setting policies and making arrangements that shaped the nation's political economy. As another measure of his social capital, in 1911, even though retired from "active business," Morgan sat on sixty-three corporate boards of directors and exercised considerable influence. Sociologist C. Wright Mills placed at the pinnacle of what he termed the "power elite" men who, like Morgan, belonged to the top clubs and gained authority and credibility by conducting business at their clubs. These informal, yet exclusive, opportunities for making and deepening connections reinforced the elites in the interlocking corporate directorates that formed during the so-called Progressive Era.[45]

Organizing down the Ladder

Business and fraternal associations operated on all rungs of the socioeconomic ladder. The passion for such institutions as fraternal organizations, amateur sports, mutual aid societies, unions, and

temperance associations that blazed through the middle and working classes in the nineteenth century brought men together for mixing and mingling. In the process of sharing a beer or engaging in a
fraternal ritual, members might relay news of a job opening. Sundry
organized networks helped to provide social insurance and joint
support for times of need. Devout religious or deep political beliefs
also attracted men to each other's company. One working-class dia-
rist, Charles Snow (1831–1889), left a complete record of his engagement in a host of organizations and activities. Snow's diaries
document his attendance and dedicated participation at meetings
four or more nights a week. He was a member of fraternal organizations, such as the Temple of Honor, the Good Templars, and the
Odd Fellows, as well as the Moulders Union, the Sons of Temperance, and the Republican Party. Every imaginable combination of
interests and activities could satisfy a man's organizing impulses.[46]

The course of American unionization between the Civil War and
the Great War has caused analysts to question the impact of labor
organizations' trading breadth for inclusiveness in order to gain solidarity within their ranks. Unceasing migration and potent repres-
sion in the courts and in the streets combined to foster association
across groups whose members easily identified with each other and
shared interests. Building and maintaining solidarity ranked high
among people with minimal power as individuals, as many examples of labor activism have shown over the years. Diverse populations and organizations formed between strangers have had great
difficulties in cooperating or in staying together. If a group did not
share a certain outlook and loyalty—for instance, if one cohort was
too desperate for work to withhold its labor strategically—strike-
breaking, low wages, and poor working conditions resulted. Thus,
in the South, the Knights of Labor could not override whites' insistence on segregated locals. The decline of the Knights of Labor by
1890 crippled inclusive labor organizing for decades, and in 1919
the American Federation of Labor proclaimed the Chinese exclu-

sion acts as among its "greatest victories" in the interest of "self-preservation." This policy represented on the national level the regional and trade-specific practices of the federation's constituent unions, excluding strangers despite high-sounding national policy statements against prohibiting anyone's membership.[47]

Networking Services: Rotary

Within Chicago's intense whirlwind of growth a century ago, Paul P. Harris was unsure of how to build either a successful law practice or a community. He had grown up in small-town Vermont where, according to a biographer, he "learned the eternal verities from two elderly people of old New England stock. There, if he had but known it, was the very essence of Americanism. There he learned a matchless something called self-reliance." As a young adult, this paragon of self-reliance founded the first Rotary Club in 1905 because he believed that getting better acquainted with men from other businesses and professions could be mutually beneficial. Although Harris was both adventurous and well traveled, through his weekly meetings he tried to recreate in Chicago the small-town atmosphere that he and so many other young people had left behind in their ambitious forays into burgeoning cities. To Harris's surprise, over two hundred men joined Rotary within four years. By 1911, Rotary Clubs were thriving in all major U.S. cities; in 1917 there were 356 of them. Kiwanis (1915) and Lions Club (1917) soon rose to the top of the list of Rotary's imitators, and by 1920 U.S. service club memberships topped 300,000.[48]

Harris and other early Rotarians described themselves as having been lonely in their adopted cities, as well as frustrated in their ambitions. So, in the spirit of the times, they organized to aid their careers while curing their loneliness. To minimize competition between its members, Rotary limited membership within each club to one man per vocation (Kiwanis and Lions allowed two each). Harris later explained that "mutual assistance was very practicable." During its first years, Rotary openly fostered a lively mix of business and fellowship among its members. From 1907 to around 1912, members had to record "the amount of business transacted between members," according to the directions on a card that members were supposed to send weekly to their local clubs. The meetings themselves included singing, talking, storytelling—and sales pitches. As a promotional circular explained in 1907, "What is done sub-rosa in other clubs is here done openly." The early Rotary declared "frankly and plainly" that members were to "cultivate your fellow members," for the "spirit of reciprocity is strong." Thirty years later, Harris admitted that the original purposes of Rotary were "selfish," but insisted that members were always more interested in friendship and cohesiveness than profit. As the organizer of the New York City Rotary wrote in a 1910 recruiting letter, "This is an age of organization and cooperation, and the Rotary spirit is . . . bringing together those who would remain strangers, and turning the business of members and their friends into honest and brotherly channels." To avoid backsliding into formality, even when large clubs required name tags, members could be fined for using surnames and titles in addressing one another, even such egalitarian ones as "Mister."[49] Fraternal pretense trumped the realities of institutional size and business motives.

Explanations vary for Rotary's transition from a fellowship-and-profits club to a fellowship-and-service club that aided personal profit only obliquely. By some reports, Rotarians soon realized that legitimacy and public appeal required contributions to the community. In any case, the 1911 national convention heartily adopted as the organization's slogan "He Profits Most Who Serves Best." With more difficulty, Harris and others succeeded in expunging the phrase "to advance the business interests of the individual members" from the club's mission statement. In the enthusiasm of the age, declarations that cooperation had triumphed over individualism filled Rotary rhetoric through the 1910s. Although shameless self-promotion faded from the Rotary ethos within a decade of its founding, boosterism continued to burn brightly. Rotary evolved into a hybrid organization, combining the goals and activities of professional and community associations. Its leaders hoped to improve both vocational efficiency and business's public profile by trying to identify "business" as a profession with high ethical norms, which included community service. Within this framework, individuals could still benefit from contacts made at lunch, or while serving on committees or projects. The resulting tensions have compelled advocates for Rotary—officially and otherwise—to protest continuously that service to both vocation and community forms its bedrock. For instance, one devotee insisted that once "the backscratching policy" ended, the "back scratching" itself ended, and he explained the organization's explosive growth as being due solely to the pleasures of fellowship and service. How, then, can busy businesspeople afford to give two hours a week to Rotary? The quick reply remains that "they can't afford *not* to belong."[50] Missing too many meetings results in one's forfeiting club membership and the accompanying opportunities for high-quality business-related contacts.

In its first few years as a fledgling organization of businessmen in an age of mixed public attitudes regarding business, Rotary's sense of mission resembled more that of the American Association of University Women or the Advertising Women of New York than the National Association of Manufacturers or chambers of commerce, which presumed their members' elite status in business affairs. As long as Rotarians felt themselves to be operating at the margins of American enterprise—shut out, for instance, from the exclusive Chicago Club and Chicago Commercial Club—they did not hesitate to band together for mutual advancement in business as well as for social pleasure. Almost immediately, however, the organization's rapid growth made it clear that its members were neither alone nor at the margin. Bolstered by that realization, Rotarians shifted their self-image and came to see themselves, if not at the center of business power, then in the mainstream. This new self-image, of course, never precluded individuals from benefiting from the social capital that their Rotarian networks built. But, like other mainstream business and professional groups, Rotary's mission statements came to place vocational and community service front and center, emphasizing fellowship and professional standards while keeping the practical networking benefits from public view. Rotary thus joined the American Society of Certified Public Accountants and the American Medical Association in improving conditions and opportunities for those already within the mainstream. In contrast, the AAUW, labor organizations, and African-American mutual benefit societies continued to bring in people left out of the mainstream of opportunity.

In the Progressive Era, it seemed that everyone organized. Some associations set up standards to keep people out; others aimed to draw in those excluded elsewhere, although they often excluded others. In whatever way vocational and avocational associations defined their admission criteria, they followed one of two naming strategies. If members' sex or ethnicity were restricted but not specified in the name, the default gender was male, and the ethnicity most likely northern European Protestant. Unless challenged, such groups simply presumed the appropriateness of admitting only "our kind of people." In contrast, an association's mentioning its members' sex or ethnicity in its name acknowledged the marginality that precluded its members from joining dominant groups.

Marginalized populations realized early on that they had to band together to accomplish their goals. They explicitly recognized the value of organizing to develop social capital—"mutual advancement"—and their organizations' mission statements, unlike mainstream organizations', acknowledged this. Developing members' contacts or communications or skills were explicit goals. By contrast, when members of dominant groups gathered together for mutual advancement, they selected names for their organizations that contained no demographic markers: Rotary, the New York Press Club, the American Association of Public Accountants. The farther from the core of mainstream business, the more likely organizations and their advocates would be to state their goal of pooling and synthesizing social capital. Thus, Rotary's founders initially formed to institutionalize reciprocal business relationships. Once they realized their centrality within the nation's business world, they reframed their official mission to emphasize service, but the clubs continued to prosper as venues for building social capital.

As corporations (also products of that organizing era) grew throughout the twentieth century, their culture was influenced by individualist rhetoric no more appropriate to the new workplace environments than it had been to earlier ones. Managers struggled to reinvent personnel practices in workplaces where they could no longer know all their employees, much less their backgrounds. How could they balance the all-too-human dynamics of social capital with their organizations' goals for impersonal efficiency and objectivity?

CHAPTER 3

Social Rungs on Corporate Ladders

"What do you do for the young men who come into your office and ask you how to find a job that offers a future?" Edward L. Bernays asked a friend. A prominent pioneer in American public relations, Bernays recounted in 1927 that he and his associate had agreed that the best they could do for these hopefuls was "send them to friends with notes of introduction." Applicants hoped to parlay one acquaintance—one unit of social capital, so to speak—into a job with a "future." Bernays noted that "six or seven young men and women a day come to my office in an unorganized effort to learn something about this working world."[1] Neither Bernays nor anyone else knew quite how to operate within a business world that had dramatically changed working conditions by the mid-1920s. Bernays, other successful men, and the multitude of young people who turned to them were cobbling together connections at a time when traditional background networks were stretched often beyond usefulness within massive corporate job markets. Because initiates had always relied on traditional sorts of connections for finding their place in the working world, they continued the practice almost reflexively. Who knew any better? Even if a youth approached Bernays as the second cousin of his hometown neighbor's brother-in-law, any connection offered more hope than none at all.

It created a claim on the established businessman's time and professional networks.

Bernays mused that these young people "have no one to whom to go for any valuable, disinterested information, men who have no uncles, brothers or cousins who can send them to successful authors, doctors or meat packers for inside information."[2] Distressed at how little preparation most youths had, how inefficient this process was, and how many of his acquaintances in varied professions and industries shared his experiences and concerns, Bernays framed the problem as one of inadequate social capital. Too many young people had few or no claims to either traditional guidance or connections as they entered the vast bureaucratic workplace. In trying to understand, systematize, and contend with developing conditions, Bernays joined countless others through most of the twentieth century who attempted to "rationalize" and make more efficient the complex and vast personnel processes that individuals and institutions faced. Some, like Bernays, addressed the loss of personal contacts as the foremost problem to be solved. Others hoped that the rising tide of workplace anonymity would prove a boon to efficient, standardized personnel operations. While small businesses and their unabashedly social personnel practices continued, managers of the growing private- and public-sector bureaucracies struggled to balance impersonal, rationalist, and meritocratic goals with the complexities of human interactions.

Whatever a business's size, each individual within it—other than its owners—gains and holds status and appointments according to someone else's assessment. The characteristics that spark a superior's interest may be personal and unpredictable, or they may be quantitative, such as a test score. Matching one's profile to a superior's standards was, and remains, the core of employees' hope and opportunity. In a small, face-to-face operation, the path to the top is personal, paved with a mix of social and idiosyncratic criteria, which may include objective skills, but frequently includes obligations between members of background networks. Here, if one's profile cannot by any stretch match gatekeepers' criteria for hiring or promotion, hope might well lead to nothing more than a humiliating fool's errand.

In contrast, the growing bureaucracies of the twentieth century evolved personnel practices that aimed to reduce social and idiosyncratic criteria for mobility. Although many people have continued to work outside large firms, corporations have employed increasing portions of the population and have become the dominant cultural icon for the American private-sector workplace, its challenges, and its possible rewards. In these larger firms, owners and bosses could no longer know all their employees, much less all aspirants, so managers, their advisors, and authors of the burgeoning business literature worked to reinvent the processes of recruitment, hiring, and promotion. But after years of their touting the virtues of modern objective methods, at the start of the 1960s the employees who were considered promising, who had potential for management, still looked and behaved very much like their bosses. Upward mobility still required, more than anything else, personal endorsement from someone in authority. Neither a company's size nor its attempts to rationalize its personnel processes ever eliminated the role of the human gatekeepers, especially for positions higher than entry level.

Building Corporate Ladders

As the size of regional and national firms grew, beginning with railroads in the mid-nineteenth century, bureaucratization accelerated to distribute information, along with authority and responsibility, up and down layers of manual workers, supervisors, and middle and top managers. The Metropolitan Life Insurance Company, for instance, began with six men in 1867 and by 1929 totaled over forty thousand people. Owners and even managers could no longer know most of their employees. Moreover, almost none of those employees could expect ever to become owners, partners, or top management. In place of traditional hopes for "independence" through proprietorship, corporations presented ambitious youths with what came to be called a ladder, drawing on that metaphor's long spiritual and worldly traditions. Between 1870 and 1920, the portion of middle-class men who were self-employed fell from roughly two thirds to one third. From 1880 to 1920, the absolute numbers of employed people more than tripled, from about 9.6 million to 30.4 million; meanwhile, the numbers of non-farm self-employed people doubled, from 1.4 million to under 3 million.[3] Climbing to the top of any given ladder was beyond most people's imagination, but they could hope to rise several rungs.

Career ladders multiplied, lengthened, and were even transformed into mazes in the decades after 1900. Companies' employment offices or personnel departments took over front-line gatekeeping duties, aided by schools and professional associations. (I will use "personnel departments" throughout for referring to the offices that hired, trained, oversaw, and fired employees, even though different companies used different terms.) Attempts to systematize the selection process did little, however, to relieve the constraints on those who lacked appropriate social capital. If anything, existing social standards ossified, forming stiffer barriers against those who did not "fit." Authorities with the power to override rigid preferences operated further and further from the first layers of gatekeepers, the specialized personnel workers who had nothing to gain by risking their superiors' displeasure. Their own positions might be in jeopardy were they to deny entry to people with connections or allow entry to those without "potential"—that is, the right characteristics (including hue and sex) that made aspirants connectable. Despite the forests sacrificed to publish ideas about systematizing and rationalizing personnel procedures, the outcomes had more an aura than a core of objectivity, especially at the higher rungs of the ladder, where tight circles of connections continued to dominate.

Much ado about how true men behaved on the corporate ladder made competition on it a powerful new challenge to ambition. Steady promotions and salary raises measured achievement rather than an independent "interest" in a firm, as in the noncorporate world. In order to compensate for most men's lost hopes of a future as their own boss, competition and compensation had to appear real, objective, and fair. Yet standardized and formalized personnel practices never could eliminate social dynamics, what came to be known as office politics, for differentially distributing opportunities. Tensions between the explicit and the implicit rules of conduct often inspired cynical warnings about office politics as "the most hush-hush subject in business" and satires such as the popular book and musical *How to Succeed in Business without Really Trying*.[4] Those tensions also prompted earnest attempts to reform personnel policies, with reformers seeking a system that would operate strictly on merit. Meanwhile, discrepancies between explicit and implicit rules for success inspired ambitious men to devote much of their social lives and their own as well as their wives' efforts to forming and nurturing social connections that might induce patronage in high places.

Managing Personnel Complexities

What happened when size and distance made personal relationships between most people within a firm impossible? How could a company function with thousands of employees distributed over scores of job categories? How could it manage the fundamental personnel processes of recruiting, hiring, training, and promoting? Charts with layers and boxes within those layers were developed to clarify the modern bureaucracy, with supervisors in each box overseeing the processes and people assigned therein, and the system increasingly aided after 1900 by separate personnel offices. Supervisors report to, and are in turn managed by, people in the layers above them. The lower the layer, the more mechanistically theorists have portrayed the optimal personnel processes. "Workers," those at the lowest rungs performing manual labor, inspired little more from owners, top managers, and analysts than attempts to conceptualize and control them as cogs in the machinery these employees operated, whether that be drill presses or typewriters. According to

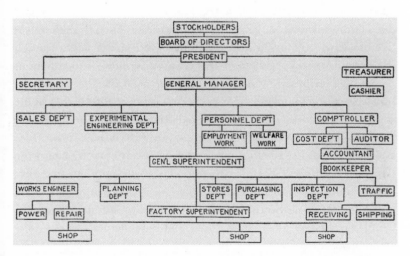

Organizational charts, like this generic one from 1919, visualized the formal, bureaucratic structures into which corporations and other modern organizations molded themselves. Although designed to clarify lines of communication and authority, these diagrams also laid out paths and barriers to promotion.

(From Enoch Burton Gowin, *Developing Executive Ability.* New York: Ronald Press Co., 1919, p. 425.)

a company president, "Only by a system—that is, by something that will work automatically, precisely, accurately—can one secure the fullest returns from his striving."[5]

During the 1920s, however, experiments and extensive interviewing at Western Electric Company's Hawthorne Works near Chicago yielded powerful evidence for the efficacy of treating workers like the human beings they were. These Hawthorne experiments helped to lay the foundations of "human relations" approaches to management by demonstrating the social nature of all working communities, however mechanistic their tasks. "Too often it is assumed," the analysis concluded, "that the organization of a company corresponds to a blueprint plan or organization chart. Actually, it never does." Everyone suffered, because "in the formal organization of most companies little explicit recognition is given to many social distinctions residing in the social organization." Even though objective measures for hiring and promotion were increasingly touted, the Hawthorne experiments exposed how foremen and others in authority distributed favors. One component of the studies, for instance, investigated "invisible authority" and reported that some supervisors blamed others' "personal friendships with superiors" for their own lack of career progress. Despite bureaucratic rules and procedures for advancement, interviewers frequently heard the phrase "It is not what you know but whom you know around here that counts." Socializing across levels of the organization chart had long raised concerns within the company about favoritism. Conflicts between social inclinations and bureaucratic codes generated constant tension.[6]

Personnel policies and strategies for managing managers were slower to develop than those for managing "workers." After all, the theorists belonged to the same classes and sex as did managers; many were or had been business managers or even company officers. The idea that men and assignments might be interchangeable thus had less appeal when they thought about managers than when they thought about assembly-line workers. The authors of the report on the Hawthorne experiments made this very distinction in their title, *Management and the Worker*. Even in the heyday of management's intrigue with industrial efficiency, those who were managers remained individuals, and were evaluated and trained as such. The social prerogatives and needs of managers were widely acknowledged. Thus, for example, prophets of scientific management at the System Company in Chicago distinguished between the various types of people in organizations in their volume *Employer and Employee* in 1907. The chapter on hiring factory workers lays out a set of criteria and indicators, including body strength and marital status, but no chapter says anything about preparing such men for any positions beyond the jobs for which they are hired.[7]

The authors of *Employer and Employee* wrote quite differently about office positions, holding out the promise of promotion for the ambitious. The lowly office boy, for instance, might become "the general manager of tomorrow." One chief always had new boys deliver a package to him so that he could have them "undergo a moment's scrutiny." He believed he could predict the "boy who makes good in business" by his class, national origin, cleanliness, and education—all factors that reflected back on the firm as well, in this manager's estimation. Informing each new boy that the firm expected him "to fit himself for something better," then giving the young man "encouragement and help" drew out the newcomers' best efforts. Such a policy also provided firms with the men who would fill "many of the most important desks"—or at least that was so in 1907, when firms still hired fourteen-year-olds with executive potential to run errands. Likewise, clerks allegedly worked best when a firm promoted "from the ranks." A stern-looking general manager pictured in *Employer and Employee* asserted that if the "selection of employees follows carefully tested principles," the business will operate as "a smoothly running, precise machine." And yet, in the midst of all this exhortation for systems in business, another contributor to *Employer and Employee* admitted that no "formula" existed for selecting a man to train for top executive positions.[8] Rarely did business writers admit that only a tiny percentage of office boys and clerks could climb up the ladder sufficient distances to move from office worker to top manager.

Strategies for Rising Men

Where one starts on a business ladder has always mattered. It matters even more on which ladder one starts. For some, the lowliest rung on a long ladder can hold promise. In the decades before Bernays wrote his "practical guide to achievement," real and fictional office boys inspired popular narratives by making good because their superiors noticed and developed them. For instance, in 1927, the *New York Times* noted the pleasure expressed by Western Electric Company's chairman of the board in notifying a man of his promotion to director and vice president, thirty-five years after the chairman had hired him as an office boy.[9] Within complex bureaucracies, however, each layer of the organization chart contained more dead-ends than paths that could span levels. Social factors, including connections as well as sex, ethnicity, and class, determined one's access to ladders, to the rules of the game, and to the masters of promotion. Merit came into play only as a second-order determinant of success.

All opportunity requires that one be noticed by a superior as being a candidate with "potential" for climbing a career ladder. Consistently noted distinctions between "workers" and decision makers, between people with potential and those without, across a century of business writing reinforced perceived differences. Changing paths—moving from one ladder to another—grew increasingly difficult as companies and their bureaucracies grew. Socially based constraints meant that some people could never move from one ladder to another. A forceful 1928 warning to female lawyers never to take a secretarial position applied to any ambitious woman. Only if starvation loomed should a female lawyer accept such a position, because by doing so she risked being forever typecast as a secretary. Yet at that same time senior lawyers interpreted a young man's taking a secretarial position as a sign of ambition and good attitude. Business advisors agreed: a young man's becoming "secretary to an important officer" could lead to substantial "opportunities."[10] For women, it led nowhere.

Despite the vastly changed environments in which more and more people worked, advice to the ambitious in the early twentieth century still sounded very much as it had when Benjamin Franklin was writing. Individualism remained the overriding theme of this literature. Of course, in any circumstances, doing one's best always offers the greatest chance for success. But what is the "best"? Hundreds of helpful souls offered their suggestions, some, like Norman Vincent Peale and Dale Carnegie, making their own fortunes by doing so.[11] In 1919, a successful businessman told a group of boys that "health, honesty, education, and industry" would enable them to succeed, although too many successful men lacked one or more of these qualities, and too many failures had them all. A 1925 radio broadcast offered ten "rules for success" that included honesty, hard work, imagination, education, and the exhortations "Never stop smiling" and "Never give up." A college graduation speaker in 1938 told his audience to like and take pride in their work, to compete with associates for challenges and victories, to have confidence in themselves, and to cooperate with both superiors and peers. A 1948 survey titled "The Way to Success," published in a popular magazine, received 202 responses. The top three factors for success were held to be "assuming responsibility and leadership," education, and "new ideas." Almost two decades later, a management journal featured "effort" and "drive" as keys.[12] And so on. Countless parables and analyses failed to take into account real-world limits on mobility. Not even Benjamin Franklin or Andrew Carnegie could have had their talents spotted for anything higher than a foreman's position if they had found themselves working on a twentieth-century assembly line. They would not have met a governor or encountered a man on his way to the company vice presidency.

No matter what the century, the main way for a person to gain access to and climb high on the most promising business ladders has always been to have social connections or at least connectability. Some hopefuls could win gatekeepers' support through the gatekeepers' sense of obligation to background networks of family and community. Others succeeded by attracting the favorable attention of someone influential within an authority or peer network. The language of "potential" and "promise" evolved to describe who got pulled in and who got pushed away with what seemed like objective gauges. Who had potential? Might ambitious youths enhance their initial promise? The realities belied the individualistic, optimistic responses. Yet because managers genuinely felt challenged by selecting individuals for grooming from within the restricted pool of socially acceptable candidates, they could actually believe that the system was truly a meritocracy. It allowed them to ignore entire groups of people, rejecting the notion that any member of these groups might have potential. The only ones left to see, to praise, and to manage were members of a subset of the whole population. It was their competitiveness and their individual efforts that gave participants their sense of an open contest.

What could an aspiring executive do? In 1950, a volume titled *Climbing the Executive Ladder: A Self-Training Course for People Who Want to Succeed* offered typical answers that mixed vocational and social activities. Success, according to this recipe, required substantial sacrifice by both the aspirant and his wife, and involved "*desire, determination,* and *a plan of action.*" The recommended methods were thoroughly social, requiring a "self-training course in human relations." In order to create the obligatory "good impression," developing a "good executive personality" was most important: "You should learn to look like an executive, think like an executive, act like an executive." An arduous course of study included classes and independent reading, but subject number one had to be close scrutiny of "the most nearly perfect executive you can find"—someone we now call a role model. The authors included an inspirational parable about a young man who was long on native talent and fervor but short on education and good grammar. Following the advice of his supervisor, he vowed to "let nothing stand in his way," working hard to develop the requisite poise and knowledge. But what if *nothing* could have made him look like or act like a "nearly perfect executive," according to mid-twentieth-century models?[13] Square pegs might as well not apply for jobs intended for round holes. They have no potential there.

Strategies for Raising Men

Succession crises have toppled kingdoms, and they can threaten firms as well. When people care about what they have built, they care about who follows them to look after it, whether they be owners, top executives, or kings. Like kings, business owners and executives have felt comforted when they could envision their fiefdoms ruled after them by people whom they could trust and understand. Thus, as corporate heads recognized the need for multileveled administrative decision making, their concerns about finding and holding onto talented and committed managers multiplied, as did their ideas about how to develop the right sort of successors. Against this background, a 1930s corporate president declared that the "most critical time in the development of a business is during the period when it ceases to be a one-man venture."[14] At this, or any stage of a firm's evolution, spotting promising candidates ranks as the first step to successful succession.

Founders, close associates, and their heirs manage noncorporate firms. The many national corporations that formed during the decades that straddled the turn of the last century, however, required coordination across distances and operations. As founders and owners gave up active control, layers of professional managers evolved at the top of most corporate ladders. Even so, distributing authority did not come easily for many founders and owners, and prospering firms died along with owners who had not developed successors. One of the three leading nineteenth-century advertising agencies, for example, ended when founder George P. Rowell retired, betrayed by his traditionalist maxim: "He who by the plough would thrive, / Himself must either hold or drive." He had failed to see the advantage of hiring a worthy successor, not even J. Walter Thompson when that young man applied for a position. Thompson proved Rowell's error and built a leading agency of his own after apprenticing under another agent's more welcoming wing. Thompson developed capable junior partners, as did F. Wayland Ayer of N. W. Ayer & Son; both of those firms left prominent legacies that continue today.[15]

Retailer Frank Woolworth learned a similar lesson, but only after he had lost his health in trying to supervise his early chain stores by himself. Later, calling his insistence that only he could make sound decisions "a conceit," Woolworth admitted that his company's major expansion began *after* he had delegated to others all but the "important matters, [especially] looking ahead." A "business is like a snowball," he said. "One man can easily push it along for a while, but the snowball becomes so large if pushed ahead that help must be obtained to roll it—and if you don't keep it rolling, it will soon melt." Decades later, the business trade literature still reinforced this point. In 1962 *Business Management* featured an interview with Don G. Mitchell, a longtime officer of several corporations and of the American Management Association, who insisted that the first basic rule of management was selecting other managers. If "the old man at the top" failed to delegate authority to well-selected and trained subordinates, not only would the firm suffer, but, as Woolworth had long ago discovered, he "goes to the hospital with ulcers or a heart attack."[16]

The selection and development of managers pervaded businessmen's concerns. In 1910 Richard W. Sears advised against the "one-man organization." Instead, he asserted, "it is the men you choose as subordinates who make your successes." Others agreed, over and over: the "success of every business man hinges on one thing—ability to select men. . . . It all depends on the selection and management of men to carry out the plans of the chief." John Wanamaker similarly addressed the changing needs of modernizing firms: "A good executive finds, develops and leans upon those who can carry forward for him the increasing divisions of his single great work." J. P. Morgan, himself the product of intense paternal and professional mentoring, understood full well the importance of building a line of succession. He developed his own son to lead the next generation of Morgans in finance. He also groomed other young men, building a firm that he expected to continue "for all time and for all generations . . . under the direction of men as yet unborn who will be trained to conduct it—we are an institution."[17]

Ladders to Manhood

Daniel Willard earned a reputation as a self-made man, rising from "financially secure but not wealthy" Vermont roots, according to a biographer, to become president of the Baltimore and Ohio railroad and a major figure in railroading for decades. Willard's climb to success points to the personal, affective, nature of the mentoring process that could move a promising youth onto and up mighty ladders. Born in 1861, Willard began his railroad work wearing a blue shirt, working on the tracks, in the locomotives, in routing towers, and as a conductor. He came under the eye of Frederick Douglass Underwood, general manager of the Minneapolis, St. Paul, and Sault Ste. Marie line. Twice Underwood tried to move Willard out of the engineering ranks into management—that is, from one ladder onto another. Willard rejected Underwood's first offer to move into the ranks of the white-collar; he was satisfied where he was. Willard accepted Underwood's second offer, however, as the opportunity to become trainmaster would keep him in touch with the rails. Willard realized that accepting the job as trainmaster amounted to "his first real step upon a long upward ladder," according to one biographer. Twice thereafter Underwood moved onto different railroads, and twice Willard moved up the ranks, following his "big boss—his friend and his advisor."[18]

Once Underwood had climbed as far as he could go himself, as president of the Erie, he artfully made a match between Willard and a more powerful railroad man, James J. Hill, often called the Empire Builder. Underwood's strong and positive recommendation carried a personal tone—"You will like Willard." He saw to it that Willard accompanied Hill on business and social occasions. Although Willard's loyalty to Underwood compelled him to turn down Hill's first offer, Underwood insisted that he accept the second, and grander, offer, or else "the whole railroad world will talk of it." Hill and Willard became close, sharing long trips and leisure time discussing railroading and violins, and singing together. Hill admitted that "Danny" could always have his way in decisions; Hill appeared to be willing to "do anything in this world" for Danny, whose company gave him great pleasure. When Underwood brokered another match for Willard, a return to the B&O as president, Hill did what he could to keep Willard. Failing that, he promised Willard that "there's always a desk waiting for you up here with me."[19]

Mentoring has always operated as businessmen's means of recruiting and training successors. But what else did business mentors gain? What about mentors who moved their protégés onto others' ladders, as Underwood did with Willard? In practical terms, a man's influence could extend as far as his protégés could move into other departments, other firms, other industries, carrying their debts to him as they progressed. Beyond the practical gains that might ensue, established men also gained pleasure and honor from assisting youths, as Franklin's and Carnegie's many benefactors did. Traditions in America that stretched back to the first European immigrants held that a major component of men's success entailed "settling" their adult sons or other male dependents on farms, in parishes, or in trades. Such legacies gave status and worth to their own lives.

As industrialization and urbanization proceeded, settling sons either on farms or in trade apprenticeships—traditional signs of success—became increasingly difficult, and often economically unrewarding. Yet the power to confer manhood in this way on a dependent continued to reflect a man's stature. Mentoring could also gratify frustrated paternalistic ambitions as family dynamics evolved.[20] Urban men were most likely to be out of their homes on business when their own children were young. This separation exacerbated the cultural tendencies of the nineteenth century to distance even loving men from their families. Bourgeois homes came under the sway of women, and schools became feminized as well. These factors could combine to alienate men from their sons, especially if fathers perceived sons as lacking in manly character. As a result, men often expressed strong paternal feelings toward their protégés, as did Tom Scott toward Andrew Carnegie, and both Underwood and Hill toward Willard. Horatio Alger's protagonists, contrary to popular legend, achieved both manhood and livelihood through the caring paternalism of mature men other than their fathers, who placed them on upright ladders and nurtured their climb. In all socioeconomic strata, men sought and satisfied needs for intimate social relationships and affection within their vocational lives. Such affective needs and desires resulted in their erecting durable barriers that limited eligibility.

A young man's willingness to accept a patron's leadership could gratify the patron, especially when the youth was bright and admired by others. From the youths' perspective, this setting aside of masculine independence as they approached manhood was easier for some than others; it was, for example, easier for Daniel Willard than it was for Jay Gould. In an era of unsettling cultural fluidity and uncertainty, traditional rites of manhood, such as completing apprenticeships or possessing land, served fewer and fewer young men. Achieving financial independence or authority over other men, however, remained a mark of masculine maturity. After Willard had accepted Underwood's second offer to move into management, their conversation wound its way to Henry Dana's *Two Years before the Mast,* a favorite book of the era and a classic narrative of emerging manhood. Underwood asked Willard if he remembered "that fine young man going out to sea as a common sailor and coming back on the return voyage as second mate, with the crew addressing him as 'Mister'? From this time on, you will be *Mister* Willard."[21] With this promotion, Underwood conferred manhood on Willard.

The symbolic power of promotion explains much of why gatekeepers selected whom they did. In part, it tested a man's ability to judge talent and character in a visible and competitive arena. Moreover, finding and placing a worthy person on a promising ladder reflected and promoted one's own success—both practically and symbolically. Because being selected in this way carried such symbolic weight, no one deemed inappropriate for such regard on a personal level could qualify for support on an occupational level. No woman could qualify. For instance, as highly as Rowland Macy regarded his protégé Margaret Getchell La Forge, he made her husband his partner and successor. Compared to her husband, Getchell—both before and after her marriage—had by far the greater impact on R. H. Macy and Company's robust growth. But she was not allowed to climb the same ladder as her husband; she could not replace Macy's profligate son. In this vein, a homily in a popular magazine of 1948 explained that a boy was "a bank where you may deposit your most precious treasures—the hard-won wisdom, the dreams for a better world." In the end, your boy "will inherit your world. All your work will be judged by him."[22]

A man of undesirable ethnicity or social class had no better chance than a woman to set foot on a ladder with white-collar potential in a white-run firm. In 1951, for example, a California accounting firm unwittingly hired an African-American man on the basis of his credentials alone. When Tallmadge C. Tillman, Jr., arrived to take the position, the chief gruffly asked him, "Boy, what can I do for you?" Tillman identified himself as the person hired over the telephone the previous day, only to be told, "You are a Negro, I cannot give you the job." After working at another firm for almost a year, Tillman was fired when the office's managing partner returned from "fighting for democracy" in Korea and declared, "It doesn't look good to have Negroes in the office." Refused other positions for which his skills should have qualified him, Tillman turned to teaching and became the sixth African American to hold both a CPA and an accounting Ph.D.[23] Such a "boy" had no potential for white manhood, so he had no business potential, regardless of his occupational merits.

In the midst of telling a powerful tale of mentorship, Daniel Willard's biographer asserted that Willard "was making himself an executive." In one sense, by virtue of hard labor, earnest study, and astute decisions, he was. But to exercise these virtues Willard required opportunities. Those opportunities resulted in part from a recognition of Willard's talents and efforts, but also in part from the appeal of his personal charm and his resemblance to the prevailing ideal of what a man should be. "Secure" Yankee roots, complete with violin lessons, had helped provide this appeal. Powerful men were delighted to see themselves reflected in Willard. His companionability and business ability drew men to him and attracted their support, and Willard's success brought his mentors paternalistic pleasure and pride.[24]

So imbued with the culture of man-to-man networks was Willard's biographer that he saw neither irony nor hypocrisy in concluding his admiring portrait of social nurturing with a rousing apologia for individualist self-sufficiency. In his mind, Willard embodied "the spirit of the old America—that spirit that today seems everywhere to be struggling for its very existence. It is the spirit of courage, of self-reliance, of independence, the spirit of a man standing squarely upon his own two feet." Disdainful of the New Deal, this author in 1938 told Willard's tale of social capital as if it were the story of a self-made man: "the good blood of his ancestry, the thoroughness of his self-education, the dignity of his character—all these and more have gone into the making of it, into the making of a man."[25] That powerful mentors had discerned and developed Willard's potential as a railroad man only enhanced his stature. That Willard could fulfill his promise only through the opportunities his elders gave him reduced his own manly individualism not in the least. Willard's life story was simply a reflection of how men developed men for business leadership while providing companionship and continuity for themselves and their work.

Developing Executives Professionally

The first step in developing a business manager involves identifying candidates likely to be capable of performing the required duties within the firm, many of which are social in nature. Because decision makers invest time, money, effort, and a good deal of personal resources and reputation in selected candidates, such decisions can never be taken lightly. So how might leaders find promising candidates? Some fortunate youths were easy to spot: they were the sons and nephews of existing leaders. Their background and authority networks gave them high visibility. In some cases, the opportunities they had to climb gilded ladders exceeded their merits, but social capital could trump individual merit. Through most of the past century, however, owners' and managers' families were unable to fill all the managerial vacancies of growing corporations. As a result, many pages of business writing and endless hours of deliberation explored strategies for recruiting ideal candidates. The 1957 work *Selection of Management Personnel* speculated that "no nation . . . has sufficient persons with the all-around characteristics needed to fill all executive positions"; therefore, firms without "systematic programs for the identification of those with executive aptitude" risked overlooking possible candidates.[26]

Once promising candidates were found, how could companies develop and retain them? Expert opinion through the 1960s held that internal promotion was the key. Most agreed with meatpacker Gustavus F. Swift, who asserted, "I can raise better men than I can hire." Also using familial language, Richard Sears advised chiefs to "Let your employees grow up with you." Once selected, the "right kind" of employees required opportunities to prove themselves fit or unfit. Transplanting a man trained elsewhere and placing him "over the heads of old employees" could impair loyalty and commitment, said Sears and countless other authorities. Some firms even required that managers develop their own successors before they could be considered for promotion themselves.[27]

Professional methods of developing executives descended directly from noncorporate owners' intuitive understanding of how to groom their sons, nephews, and other favorites for succession. Just as owner-managers have prided themselves for following their firms' every detail, preparing their crown princes—whether relatives or not—for leadership entails building a similar grasp in the anointed. Therefore, owners rotate potential successors through the firm. This type of on-the-job training serves ideological as well as practical purposes, legitimating ascendancy to executive thrones. For instance, Jay Hormel—obvious heir to his father's meatpacking firm—chose to leave college to begin working, in overalls, in the packinghouse. Then he moved through every department over two years before becoming first vice president. Thus, he *did* work his way up a ladder, albeit a gilded one, satisfying his father's desires for an able successor in every sense. Likewise, during its first century, the DuPont Company recruited its managers from the du Pont family. Tested initially in low-level positions, including manual jobs, they would climb the family ladder quickly, receiving stock and responsibility as older relatives retired. "Training the Owner's Son," an article reprinted at least six times in various trade journals in 1926 and 1927, urged a rotation plan under supervision of either the father or "a man who knows how to train men." Even though parents might "dread putting the young man through the hard experience," the harsh competition and difficult challenges of the business world required deliberate and demanding leadership development.[28]

As corporations grew in size and became more removed from their founders' generations, owners and officers found themselves having to look beyond scions for managerial reproduction. Between 1900 and 1950 chief executives who had inherited their office fell from 30 to 15 percent among firms that were at least twenty years old. In a model transition away from family operation, du Pont family and DuPont Company leaders selected and groomed Walter S. Carpenter Jr., who eventually headed the firm. From a prosperous business family, Carpenter followed an uncle and a brother into DuPont, and through them he had access to owners and top managers from the start. His background, personality, Ivy League education, work ethic, and remarkable managerial capabilities so strongly attracted powerful mentors to him that the links approached filial. A top executive and close friend of Pierre du Pont considered himself Walter's deputy uncle; Irénée du Pont ushered at Walter's wedding; Walter named sons for his mentors; and Walter's children called Irénée "Uncle Bus." Carpenter's intertwining of personal and business ties combined to make him a comfortable surrogate heir, who was assigned challenging opportunities that forged his leadership capabilities. Carpenter's combination of connections, talent, and eagerness eased the transition to professional top management for the DuPont Company.[29]

In the 1950s, economist Mabel Newcomer summarized why corporations had typically promoted from within, and every one of her points relates to the social capital insiders accrued. Newcomer noted that existing employees are "better known, and to that extent safer, than outside talent." Such individuals knew their companies, and they had likely been selected and groomed by leaders. Their longevity testified to their loyalty to both the firm and its officers, and promoting them earned the loyalty of other ambitious and talented staff farther down the ladder, who hoped to follow. Despite all these reasons in favor of promoting from within, Newcomer questioned the merits of the practice in all but the most rapidly growing firms. Inbred top executives may not provide the most dynamic talent pool, she noted.[30] Nevertheless, promotion from within persevered as the favored practice until at least the 1960s, for both the practical and social reasons Newcomer itemized. What was most prized was one's fit into a firm's subculture and knowledge of its idiosyncrasies, both human and procedural. The reluctance to look outside for candidates reflected all the comforts to be found with the familiar and predictable, as well as the discomforts of testing and integrating the unfamiliar.

As firms set up formal programs to recruit and develop promising midlevel managerial candidates from within, they expected to make the processes more objective as they became more structured. Such formal processes could also overcome what concerned a DuPont executive in 1913, the difficulties of "knowing that such best men exist" from department to department within the company. A firm benefited through formal and fair programs that "fill capably all key positions" and recognize each employee's "experience and potential" in doing so, according to Standard Oil Company of California's Office of Executive Development in midcentury. As one authority expressed the problem in 1950, corporate complexity and size had made the "'normal' emergence" of corporate leaders uncertain. Traditional reliance on a (presumably) natural survival of the fittest, he worried, could no longer assure that the best clerks would reach the top. Requirements that managers first specialize, then generalize their training and activities intensified the importance of planned managerial development.[31]

Formalization commonly included following patterns initially developed for heirs, such as rotating select men through various departments. In the mid-1950s, *Fortune* magazine emphasized rotation as a way of developing "well-rounded" managers, taking them out of specialized jobs into more general positions to "widen their experience."[32] Once spotted and tagged, such elites gained access to truncated, if still strenuous, ladders. So the successful *did* compete on their way to the top, but they competed only among others who, like they, had access to the right ladders. The stronger the candidate's resemblance and ties to people at the top—the more he could be taken for family—the better his chance to climb. In an important sense, such candidates *were* heirs to treasured realms; and, like any aristocracy, business elites rule by profoundly social means.

Building Objective Rungs on Subjective Ladders

Charles P. McCormick's frustration with his protracted seventeen-year apprenticeship in his uncle's condiment company inspired him in the 1920s to institute a "multiple management" system through junior boards of directors. This structured, planned development process for young men "who appeared to be promising" gave them opportunities to contribute to policy and to raise their profiles by exercising leadership. Acclaimed as a valuable method for both training and testing candidates for upper management, by the late 1950s over five hundred firms were using some version of McCormick's program. Participation in these junior boards provided senior managers with evidence of who among the promising young men could serve best in executive capacities. Charles McCormick also claimed that the junior boards had "entirely eliminated" office politics, since "nothing but merit counts" in getting onto the junior board or progressing from there. As underlings with the privilege of proposing policy, McCormick's 1934 junior board devised the firm's "sponsorship plan" to help "detect" the best in new employees and provide them with developmental opportunities. In the name of "building men to build the business," McCormick's junior managers formalized an early mentoring program.[33]

Early twentieth-century managers built their corporations and cultures with "system" as their watchword. Many avidly read the Chicago journal of that name founded in 1900, talked of scientific management, and pursued any and all measures that promised to further "system" and its offspring, efficiency. They assumed that objectivity improved all outcomes but rarely questioned what "objectivity" meant or whether it was attainable. An important management text, *Personnel Administration,* published first in 1920 and revised repeatedly, echoed the standard refrain, assuming the value of both equal opportunity and impartial selection for training programs, even for executives. It called for a "gauge upon comparative ability" to determine who would gain access to the opportunities such training afforded. Similarly, General Electric expended considerable resources on a mid-1950s guidebook series with the title *Manager Development.* GE assured its employees that only their on-the-job performance determined their chances for future training. As in any "great dynamic enterprise, opportunity should come automatically to the individual who is an outstanding performer on his present assignment."[34]

A 1963 article in the journal *Personnel Administration* echoed that same goal: "performance standards should be selected to measure what the individual does and accomplishes; not general personality characteristics or traits, unless these traits directly affect his work."[35] The escape clause ending this otherwise adamant call for objectivity, however, encouraged the very problem that its author and countless others sought to eliminate. For, in the end, the higher a position lay in the administrative hierarchy, the stronger have been the presumptions that performance of its duties requires "traits" that evade objectivity and therefore must be measured by social gauges.

When Mabel Newcomer summarized several 1950s assessments of executive roles, she found complete agreement: executives' primary functions centered on managing human interrelations. Many earlier analysts had likewise insisted that organizations could best be understood by considering social factors. Chester I. Barnard's *The Functions of the Executive* (reprinted eighteen times between 1938 and 1968) stated authoritatively that organizations operated as systems of "coördinated human efforts." Executives' main task was to guide that coordination. Evaluating individuals for executive roles therefore required assessing their "powers" within their positions and their "determination" to act on them. According to this logic, pertinent questions included "Who is he?" and "What kind of man is he?" as well as "What will he do?" Barnard quite rightly insisted, moreover, that every organization, however formal, functioned within "an informal, indefinite, nebulous, and undirected system"—that is, "society."[36]

U.S. social and legal rules allowed business gatekeepers to maintain their presumptions about what sorts of people were capable of achieving these human relations goals and commanding authority. This allowed only people who resembled or pleased existing leaders to gain opportunities to develop their capacities for authority. The common practice of interviewing job candidates over meals has always privileged the subjective, social nature of judging candidates, satisfying gatekeepers' subjective notions of who merited opportunity to join their networks. As one employer explained in the 1890s, these social occasions gave him a chance to see "just what is in" the candidate. Seventy years later, another authority explained, "When they say 'He's a good man but he wouldn't fit,' that means that he would not fit socially."[37] Table manners mattered.

The mechanisms of social capital, with their tendency to reproduce gatekeepers' traits, perpetuated what *Fortune* described in 1956 as a very stable managerial class. Of executives then under fifty years old, the magazine reported, 51 percent had fathers who had founded or managed companies, or who were professionals. Few came from families that were not "economically comfortable." Some analysts saw this homogeneity as a potential problem. A year earlier, economist Mabel Newcomer asked, "What guarantee is there that the man selected was the best the organization could produce and not just an able but chance favorite of the outgoing executive?" She suggested that increasing professionalization of selection and development could yield executives closer to "ideal."[38] Less social homogeneity could add to the talent pool, but for many years to come diversity was still too high a price for integrating new talent.

First Contacts: Interviews

Even under purposeful attempts to systematize and rationalize personnel operations, interviews provided the venues for selecting managers. As rigidly constructed as interviews might be, some social component had to remain, even after candidates had passed initial screenings for the obvious factors, such as education or experience. Assessment charts abounded in personnel departments, de-

signed to generate consistent and impartial reports on individuals
and thus assist those involved in recruitment, hiring, and promotion. The 1954 General Electric guidebook, for example, proudly
displayed its systematic approach to management training by including a series of appraisal charts. Under the heading "effectiveness in working with others" the key questions seem harmless
enough: "Does he perceive his proper place in the organization, his
own responsibilities and his relationship with others?" "Is he generally respected by his associates?" "Does he gain the confidence of
others?"[39]

Imagine, however, how these questions might be answered for
someone perceived as not socially compatible with peers and superiors or not worthy of respect in the workplace, perhaps because of
class, ethnicity, or sex (that is, a candidate who was not a "he").
How might an interviewer filling out the chart judge such a person's
potential for handling the human relationships at the core of an executive's roles? Under the social and legal conditions that existed
prior to the civil rights and women's movements, any interviewer
who appraised such an outsider as potentially "effective" at managerial levels within a mainstream corporation might well be judged
incompetent, or at least hopelessly unrealistic.

Although interviewing by its very nature must be an idiosyncratic
process, by the 1950s attempts to standardize it aimed for consistent, unbiased appraisals of candidates, including those for lower-
level managerial positions. Some authorities even recommended
team rating processes to help cancel out individual idiosyncrasies in
evaluators. Formatted procedures and rating systems laid out the
necessary conditions under which interviewing might be consistent
and effective. One sample rating form's expressed purpose was to
"obtain information in a systematic manner which will enable us to
evaluate the potentialities" of employees for higher administrative
positions. Detailed questions ranked candidates' judgment on and

interest in technical and people problems, abilities in individual and group "contacts," and "tact and diplomacy." Interview forms for incoming job candidates included questions about "marital status and adjustment"; education financing; "early home life," which included "socio-economic level," "father's occupation" (no mention of mother's occupation), and number of siblings. Other broad categories included "social effectiveness," including self-confidence, maturity, emotional stability, and, of course, "general character and integrity." Favorable ratings went to candidates who demonstrated "conscientiousness" by working their way through college, *and* those whose "social effectiveness" benefited by having been raised in "relatively high socio-economic circumstances."[40] Impartiality and consistency was not easy here, caught between ideals of rags and riches.

Experts warned that poorly conducted interviews risked "unwarranted inferences from limited data obtained in an artificial situation by incompetent observers." However, mainstream critiques prior to the 1960s did not challenge the basic presumption that a well-conducted interview *could* perform valuable selection functions, at least by its evaluating a candidate's "verbal fluency, his sense of humor, [and] his social acceptability." This last point raised quite a barrier for those candidates who were outside the mainstream. Yet, in fairness, executives *must* manage people through socially defined authority and respect. As critic Vance Packard explained, the use of social venues for conducting business called for "sophisticated men who appear at ease in all sorts of social situations," including representing their firms in public arenas.[41] Even now, when it is no longer legal, ethical, or even profitable to presume that one's ethnicity, age, or sex rules out authority and respect, no constraints exist against excluding candidates from executive ladders because of their socioeconomic class or table manners. The problem before the mid-1960s was the total lack of self-consciousness about the profound biases embedded in the phrase "social acceptability." These biases kept most people off key ladders and spared gatekeepers from having to question the process.

Coaching a Business Team

Myles L. Mace's extensive research in 1940s business practices led him to conclude that too few firms developed successors effectively. Two key chapters of his 1950 book *The Growth and Development of Executives* recommended "coaching," which contained components of what we now call networking and mentoring. For Mace, effective coaching included much of what was standard development practice: rotation through departments, challenging tasks, growing responsibilities, support without rigidity, constant proximity to immediate superiors, and broad access to sources of information and authority. The development of managers should not be left to personnel departments or to consultants. To be effective, managerial development had to be intensely personal, building "understandings" as well as skills within "a concrete working situation which is part of the environment in which the subordinate hopes to grow and prosper." In other words, good coaching would generate opportunities for a neophyte's learning, performing, and becoming familiar with, and *to,* a firm's executive community. All this presumed a core of social compatibility and mutual respect.[42]

Mace took "coaching" as a metaphor from sports. He emphasized that preparing future executives required teamwork and that it built effective management teams. A deep knowledge of the players was as fundamental to good coaching and teamwork in business as in sports, he cautioned. Out of historical context, the metaphor seems benign enough, but in 1950, when Mace published his book, professional sports teams and coaches were almost entirely white (Jackie Robinson had just begun major league play for the Brooklyn Dodgers in 1947). Given that cultural context, Mace had no reason to list either "women" or "Negroes" or "race" in his index or to mention such groups anywhere in his book. What could he have said, except that such outsiders had no potential for executive status? Could anyone have applied his counsel on coaching and team building to working with such outsiders? Moreover, in a striking passage that showed just how deeply he assumed the need for homogeneity, Mace quoted an executive's reference to "real coaches" as "the keepers of the secrets of the tribe." He also called for applying the Golden Rule to personal interactions.[43] Yet how could top executives accept reciprocal treatment from people whom they disrespected and whom they could not imagine as their successors or colleagues?

Without anyone to pull strangers in, such outsiders were pushed onto other ladders or kept out of the system altogether. The notion of teamwork had always implied homogeneity. Enoch Burton Gowin's widely used *Developing Executive Ability* (1919) had chapters with such titles as "Team-Work" and "Co-operation," both within a section about executives the author titled "A Man among Men." A few years after Mace, another writer also named coaching as a method of developing a business; he defined it as "the man-to-man relationship which an executive establishes with his subordinates if he is a true developer of men."[44] By assuming that executives had only to learn how to pull people like themselves into their system and assign them to the right ladders, neither Mace nor anyone thinking about mainstream management prior to the 1960s had to think about the fact that his recommended methods involved pushing out everyone other than white men of appropriate classes. When executives pulled "likely" candidates onto and up powerful ladders, their pool of candidates was already relatively uniform. Personnel departments, schools, social venues, and cultural blinders had already screened out any possible alien candidates. Executives could build their teams without having to admit to wholesale biases against large portions of the population. Pulling in is far more gratifying and less troublesome than pushing away.

Contacts and Ladders

Charles Harris's contribution to *Handling Men,* a 1917 manual for managers, argued for letting one's established workers provide new workers. "When Your Men Help You Hire," Harris attested, "capable men" will recruit other capable men, just as "nice" female workers will recruit "nice friends." This system of recruiting can also build a "community of responsibility" among employees based on pride and friendships. Harris quoted a master at this practice as saying that each new recruit benefits because the "older men will sort of 'father' a new man . . .—will help him with infinite patience." They will serve as "several interested and very practical teachers." Even for women hoping to get a foothold on the short secretarial ladder, a 1928 expert asserted that the "most successful methods . . . are through friends, acquaintances, and personal letters of introduction." Only if her networks are of no avail should a young woman formalize her search by approaching an employment agency or writing an application letter. Similar networking prevailed across whole ethnic groups, evinced by the differential employments in 1950 of immigrants to the United States: Italians were barbers at a frequency eight times that for all white men; Irish immigrants were three times more likely to be police or firemen than others; Swedes four times more likely to be carpenters; Greeks twenty-nine times more likely to operate restaurants; and Russians seventeen times more likely to be tailors or furriers. These patterns resulted from the webs of opportunity and information sharing that networks build.[45]

What about those who wish to climb corporate ladders? Not all connections point to the top, so ambitious youths must take care to avoid getting connected with someone whose own ladder may be weak. With luck, judgment, and performance, however, youths can find successful climbers who take them along.

Lido Iacocca was the mid-twentieth century's most prominent case of hitching a wagon to the right star, and then outpacing that star. He became a powerful popular icon as a latter-day self-made man of the corporate style when he, like Carnegie and Morgan, outshone his mentors. Iacocca's success required years. A first-generation Italian American, the son of a smart and hard-driving immigrant entrepreneur, Iacocca began his career in 1948 rather inauspiciously in fleet sales for Ford Motor Company outside Philadelphia. His stellar connection came with his new boss, Charles Rufus Beacham, a college-educated but crude master of salesmanship, who was Ford's regional sales manager for the East Coast. Always "Mr. Beacham" to Iacocca, this man was, to use Iacocca's own emphasis, his mentor and his "*tor*mentor." Obsessed with performance, Beacham drove his underlings fiercely. None of them learned to perform with Lee Iacocca's grim determination, though, and Beacham noticed—though rarely complimented—his apprentice as Iacocca's successes toted up. Beacham did, however, provide promotions, along with stimulating challenges and instruction. After he got the call to join Ford's division headquarters in Dearborn, Michigan, Beacham invited his protégé to join him. There, in 1956, Iacocca met Robert McNamara, then vice president of Ford Motor, who came to share Beacham's enthusiasm for—and mentoring of—this high-powered performer. In 1960, when McNamara became president of Ford, Iacocca had his first substantive conversation with Henry Ford II, who offered him a vice president's office, at McNamara's insistence. Iacocca and his teams developed the Falcon, the Mustang, and the Pinto, and he eventually became president of Ford Motor Company—before Henry Ford II fired him in 1978.[46] Iacocca's performance could not offset conflicts with the one person still higher on the ladder. Chrysler Corporation was worried about its very survival at that point and immediately hired Iacocca to lead the company out of its financial wilderness.

Stereotypes: Social Capital by Any Other Name

Stereotypes fill the social atmosphere that supports the fundamental advantages of class, ethnicity, and sex. Stereotypes are most forceful when they are least recognized. Descriptors such as "good manners," "clean-cut," and "strong handshake" can easily operate as screening codes without any explicit statement of class, ethnic, and sex-based preferences. People with gatekeeping authority in business once saved themselves a good deal of soul searching by holding pictures in their heads, to paraphrase Walter Lippmann's powerful 1922 metaphor for stereotypes, about who did and who did not have potential. With stereotyping, gatekeepers not only could avoid having to admit to ethnic, class, or sex biases or to discrimination based on their personal comfort level; they also smoothed their search for recruits by simply not seeing a majority of the population as eligible for consideration. This is what stereotypes do best: they bring a certain "economy" (again Lippmann's word) to our evaluating and understanding the world. Trying instead "to see all things freshly and in detail, rather than as types and generalities" could be frustrating, adding another burden to one's already "busy affairs." Abbreviated assessments of people (except those with whom we have close personal relationships) not only help order our social universe, but project outward "our own sense of our own value, our own position and our own rights." To continue with Lippmann's elegant phrasing, stereotypes operate therefore as "the fortress of our tradition, and behind its defenses we can continue to feel ourselves safe in the position we occupy."[47]

Just before the U.S. Supreme Court's 1954 decision against school segregation, psychologist Gordon W. Allport published *The Nature of Prejudice*. This monumental work explained stereotypes as cognitive functions that can all too often lead to ethically charged consequences, infusing decision making with blindness to individual characteristics or circumstances. Stereotypes resist contradictory evidence, predict and explain others' behavior without evidence, and impute attributes, also without evidence.[48] Prejudice thereby inclines us to react to categories instead of individuals.

Business gatekeepers, like everyone else, may react more positively to members of some groups and more negatively to members of other groups regardless of the individuals' traits or behaviors. Calling the former "in-groups," Allport showed how they evoke loyalty and comfort, while the "out-groups" evoke discomfort, scorn, and even fear and hostility. Sociologist Robert K. Merton has pointed out that both "insiders" and "outsiders" identify mainstream insiders as superior, especially relative to marginalized outsiders. People who believe that they are insiders enjoy a sense of centrality as well, and rank everyone else according to their social distance from that center. Moreover, disparaging out-groups and their members by applying negative stereotypes strengthens bonds between in-group members.[49] In the realm of making a living, therefore, one's having either insider or outsider status relative to decision makers matters in both practical and subjective ways. Social capital accrues accordingly, and with it the likelihood of gaining entry to desirable authority and peer networks.

Stereotypes perpetuate and justify discriminatory conduct toward people by presuming to predict and explain individuals' behavior according to categories. In other words, stereotypes are vehicles for what Merton called "patterned expectations" about the people identified with a category. For instance, when observers were asked to interpret a simple shoving scene according to who shoved whom, white observers interpreted as violent a black person's shoving a white person more than five times as often as they interpreted as violent a white person's shoving another white person.[50] A jury's verdict based on such assessments obviously puts fairness and objectivity at risk. As in court, so in business. Studies have shown, for example, that what men consider to be acceptable levels of assertiveness by men among men—a good indicator of energy and job potential—they consider to be unacceptable, discomforting levels of aggression by women, anywhere, anytime. The confidently firm handshake that indicates a man's man once branded a woman as too bold and perilously unfeminine, even though a show of timidity would likewise doom any leadership ambitions.

Such expectations become self-fulfilling when they guide gate-

Despite the contributions African Americans made during World War II, often in nontraditional positions, the peacetime boundaries constraining their opportunities quickly snapped back into place. The racially drawn lines between railroad executives and dining car porters shown here around 1950 remained impermeable for decades.

(Courtesy Colorado Historical Society.)

keepers. Challenging and high-profile tasks are assigned to people identified as having potential. Such individuals get invited for a beer after work or for lunch at the club. They find themselves welcomed into authority and peer networks; mentors are delighted to assist their development. They are pulled onto and up the best business ladders. Conversely, people belonging to categories that gatekeepers have stereotyped negatively cannot possess potential. They are invisible when authorities seek recruits. If they have the audacity to approach gatekeepers, they are pushed away. In the mid-twentieth century, African-American men, and women of any ethnicity, still worked at routine tasks and jobs meagerly rewarded by title or income. Decision makers presumed that such workers could not handle the challenges that people with potential could master. This resulted in a frustrating cycle for some, who were hired only for menial work, denied respect and challenge, then judged capable of performing only the work they were doing.

Other sorts of patterned expectations can affect workplace opportunities anywhere. New immigrants, European-American working classes, and African Americans often compete for urban entry-level jobs. Networking and mentoring operate here too as powerful mechanisms that determine what demographic groups dominate what occupational niches. Marginalized groups build networks to share information about employment and to provide references to employers. Employers' stereotypes play into the process: their prejudices reinforce the practical incentive to hire from an ethnic group with whom they are familiar. In return, current employees channel new recruits into their workplace, teach the recruits, assure employers of the recruits' reliability, even punish misbehavior that risks a specific network's control over a given niche.[51]

Stereotyped Potential

Daniel Willard, Walter Carpenter, and Lee Iacocca each possessed remarkable abilities, and each climbed corporate ladders successfully. Someone with authority detected their abilities, identified them as having potential, and decided that they were worth developing and pulling along. Carpenter's mentors had the easiest time of recognizing his abilities, thanks to his close connections to du Pont family leaders and his class, sex, and ethnicity. Still, unlike Jay Hormel and Charles P. McCormick, Carpenter did not have access to a family-based gilded ladder that ensured his success. Instead, his personal and vocational attractiveness induced powerful du Ponts to build personal and professional bonds with him. They bridged the gap between the ladder for which he was initially eligible and what had been a gilded succession tradition. Carpenter's attributes had ample opportunity to gain polish in a privileged environment that welcomed him as a promising novice and allowed him to shine. No social handicaps barred him from access to authority, knowledge, and challenge in his environment.

What it was about Daniel Willard that first captured Frederick Underwood's attention, then James J. Hill's affection? Unlike Carpenter, Willard had no prior nonbusiness connection to either of his mentors. His respectable Vermont upbringing did allow his individual abilities and charm to become visible, thus making him noticed as someone with potential, someone connectable. By contrast, mainstream corporate leaders would not have seen potential in Lee Iacocca at the beginning of the century, when Carpenter and Willard were climbing corporate ladders, because of Iacocca's ethnicity. His talent and drive notwithstanding, Iacocca would not have been connectable in a business world in which his ethnicity precluded the social authority that executive leadership required. His ability could only become visible when cultural and political forces removed blinders from the eyes of corporate gatekeepers after World War II.

Sociologist C. Wright Mills quoted a mid-twentieth-century college president's description of the "ideal graduate in the present employment market of industrial executives." This person was "a fraternity man with a declared disinterest in political or social affairs,

gentile, white, a member of the football team, a student with a record of A in each course, a man popular with everyone and well
known on campus." So unambiguous was this image that he could
be "imagined in twenty years as a subject for a Calvert [whiskey]
advertisement,"[52] a visual cliché for the elite male. Contemporary
business analysts, of course, rarely mentioned all of these qualities
in describing whom authorities and gatekeepers might recognize as
having potential; they simply assumed that person would be male,
white, and gentile. Such positive stereotypes—including the "social
acceptability" deeply embedded in criteria for management—com-
posed the "pull" side of corporate discrimination. Conversely, negative stereotypes made up the push side. Carpenter and Willard fit
comfortably within the positive stereotypes for corporate leadership—both a century ago and today. In contrast, Iacocca could only
fit after corporate gatekeepers' ethnic-based stereotypes had begun
to weaken.

By 1957 the apparent "shortage of executive talent" caused at
least one business analyst to criticize policies favoring the "safety"
of promotion from within firms as risking "decay in all but the largest organizations." Instead of looking for the "mythical 'perfect
executive,'" firms should seek out those with the appropriate abilities, overthrowing "myths and stereotypes" that "stress[ed] age and
appearance." Yet even into the 1970s blinders continued to limit
searches for "fast-track" candidates to "men who are working their
way upward," according to Univac's personnel director in 1972.
This gave only "men who have been around for a while" and who
know the "corridors of power" abundant "opportunity to develop
their abilities."[53] Given this mind-set, marginalized groups remained invisible—or worse.

Stereotyped Failure

If potential for success had a certain "look," failure had many
looks. The *Harvard Business Review* published a survey in the year

of the 1964 Civil Rights Act demonstrating that even though executives objected to any notion of holding a "prevailing image of success," they did admit to a "rather distinct picture of the kind of person who will 'fit in.'" And while their descriptions of characteristics "helpful" to careers almost unanimously featured attributes like "ability to communicate" and "capacity for hard work," only four attributes received at least 75 percent of votes as being "actually" (as opposed to "ideally") "harmful" to careers. In ascending order, from least to most harmful, these were being "Oriental"; from Puerto Rico; female; or "Negro." Executives admitted overwhelmingly that only after screening for these and other social factors, including "pull," "social standing," and religion, did they then consider factors identified as "bearing on job performance."[54]

Popular culture, too, showed little doubt about what business success did *not* look like. African Americans in business management were barely visible prior to the 1970s. Even then, when the pioneer character of George Jefferson emerged to challenge Archie Bunker's white working-class self-esteem in *All in the Family* (1972–1975), then strut and stumble around his own show in *The Jeffersons* (1975–1985), George's financial success had come from building up a small business. Moreover, his blowhard manner compounded his ethnicity in making him an unlikely corporate ladder role model. Neither had the earlier *Sanford and Son* (1972–1977) provided role models for African-American entrepreneurs or corporate managers, given that that series' lead character was a cranky junk dealer. Likewise, a quick review of 1950s, 1960s, and most 1970s television series and magazines leaves no question about which sex had insider status within business, especially management.

Through the nineteenth and most of the twentieth century, mainstream trade journals displayed remarkable insensitivity to people other than their primary audiences. The authors' public portrayals of people without influence make us shudder to think of how businessmen spoke to each other face to face. Flipping through a random issue of *Fortune* magazine—that of January 1950, for instance—makes clear that the dominant business culture of the period could not have considered women as viable leaders. The many images of white males in authority in both advertisements and news items contrast profoundly with the images of women. In news stories, one woman appears as a pin-up style beauty winner; another models a negligee. Others appear as secretaries, consumers, or busi-

The "Follies of the Financial Writers' Association" were aptly named. "Jokes," cartoons, and stunts like this cross-dressing gala reinforced the apparent inappropriateness of women for top management positions. According to *Fortune* magazine's caption, participants in this 1949 event at the Astor Hotel in New York City "jovially lambasted . . . lady aspirants to the directorships of large corporations." Such "follies" encouraged insiders to bond with each other by both distancing themselves from and demeaning outsiders.

(Courtesy Queens Borough Public Library, Long Island Division, the *New York Herald Tribune* Photograph Collection.)

nessmen's wives. An article for Spring Mills textiles features an ad of a startled young woman with a revealing neckline, exposed legs and panties, lifting her skirt to "Beware the Goose!" A photo of the Follies of the Financial Writers' Association went over the top of male-camaraderie-as-business-event, although it is not clear whether manhood or womanhood suffered more. Ten men pranced and danced on a stage dressed in nothing other than underwear, stuffed where necessary. During the course of the festivities, they "jovially lambasted . . . lady aspirants to the directorships of large corporations."[55]

Women, on the rare occasions when they were mentioned in the context of business management, were used as a symbol of the exotic or the irrational—as, for example, when in 1963 an executive intently described the mysteries of office politics to be "as subtle and varied as a woman's moods." Business literature did evaluate women as serious business assets—as wives. The well-regarded 1955 book *Big Business Leaders in America* had two chapters on women: "The Wives of Ambitious Men" and "The Kinds of Women Who Make Successful Wives." This study included no women in its analysis of almost nine thousand "big business leaders," and its index had no entry for "women," only "wives of business leaders." Two cartoons typify many that portrayed wives in management journals. One, in a 1963 issue of *Personnel Administration,* portrayed an attractive wife carping at her newspaper-reading husband. Angry that he had not sacrificed his health for corporate achievements, she blurted out, "Ed Hooper's been with the company only half the time you have, and he's so successful he's had ulcers for years!" Another, illustrating a 1965 *Nation's Business* article, depicted a wide-eyed, adoring wife, happily wiping a dish as she gazed upon her husband, deep in business thoughts, briefcase and papers at his side.[56] Both caricaturized wives' dependency on husbands' labor, making it appear that wives' affection, as well as their own ambition, hinged on their husbands' toil.

A 1958 *Fortune* article did explore the subject of "Women as Bosses" as one article in a series of four on "Women and Business." The other three addressed women's roles as consumers, as non-managerial workers, and as owners. ("To what extent are they merely owners of record . . . ?" this last article asked.) The article evaluated numerical data and anecdotal evidence on women in authority, weighing advantages and disadvantages for women, men, and their companies. One of its informants, an executive from U.S. Steel, declared, "There is no prejudice here against women. They just don't get to the top." Another executive reported, "We never gave women much thought." The *Business Periodical Index* demonstrates this latter remark's accuracy for business literature in general. The January 1958–June 1959 volume listed eighty-nine articles under the category of "executives," two under "women as executives," and six under "working women," one of which was "Are Women Workers Unpredictable?" No separate categories existed for men as executives or for working men, as male was the default category. Two years later the numbers were similar, but three titles merit notice: "Ways of Women (Advice for Supervisors)," "Special Knack of Supervising Women," and "How to Supervise Women: Cartoons with Text."[57] Working with such aliens presented its challenges.

In *The Woman Executive*, Margaret Cussler documented in 1958 what would come to be standard observations in later decades, highlighting men's discomfort around women in business settings. A typical interviewee related that he could not "sit down and confide or talk freely" with a woman in the workplace. Conversely, male business cultures challenged women's comfort levels. A female respondent recommended simply smiling in response to "trivial remarks" about women. Convinced that "the rough days of [feminist] militancy seem to be over," Cussler reported that in the mid-1950s "overt conflict with men over women's rights is as rare as lynchings."[58]

Two decades and a cultural revolution later, women perhaps no longer had to grin and bear "trivial" remarks; but Cussler's explanations for their differential success continued to survive and echo through a large literature. In a chapter titled "The Sponsor and the Protégé," Cussler noted the importance of "prestige by association" and of men's extensive cultivation of informal relationships as central to their business activities. She contrasted women's reliance on "faithful drudgery" against ambitious young males' enjoying coffee, lunch, cards, and golf with "men who would 'count.'" Even where women *could* enter an executive dining room, she noted, "it takes a woman of considerable aplomb to join the gentlemen naturally and uninvited, as a man in her position might. . . . [Therefore] a succession of lonely lunches may drive her to more companionable lunches with secretaries and staff below her on the occupational ladder." Constantly confronted with awkward and conflicting situations, "like the Negro who must be everlastingly neat and industrious to compensate for an unpleasant stereotype, the successful woman quickly learns a kind of chameleon behavior adapted to the needs of the situation."[59]

Rationalized Subjectivity

In the meritocratic world that corporate businesspeople liked to think they inhabited, terms like "potential," "promising," and even "likable" seasoned everyday language. Since the earliest days of recruiting, hiring, and promoting people other than kith and kin, these concepts have labeled candidates worthy of being pulled into networks and companies. Conversely, if candidates discernibly lacked whatever was believed to characterize potential, decision makers found it easier to push them away from opportunities. This pulling and pushing looked fair to gatekeepers because they saw themselves constantly distinguishing between people like themselves based on the hopefuls' ability to perform. They knew, of course, that failure to rank ability objectively occurred too often—regrettable errors attributed to poor personnel functions and office politics. Everyone knew that such errors reduced company productivity and created embittered employees, and efforts to reduce these mistakes consumed countless managerial hours. Yet so powerful were their stereotypes that the "social acceptability" criteria embedded within application and interview processes sounded few alarms about subjective standards. Office politics were mistakenly considered aberrant, not inevitable.

Business procedures have social processes built into them so strongly that social capital was once camouflaged, taken for granted, especially by those whom it benefited. When Edward Bernays worried about how young people lacking connections might gain positions in the mid-1920s, he published a book containing information that luckier job seekers would have been able to get through personal connections. He also wrote letters of introduction for those who had some claim on his own time and reputation. Even earlier, the mechanics of job hunting in the expanded urban and national arenas already involved searching newspaper listings and using employment agencies. How much of a chance did a youth without connections have to latch onto anything but a ladder's lowest rungs? Advice books and articles proliferated about what a reference letter should include and from whom supplicants might best request such letters. But even the most effusive letter could not get a young man on a ladder that stretched to a firm's top layers as well as a quickly scratched note from someone rich in social capital and willing to use it on a youth's behalf.

Despite the formalization of corporate structures and processes throughout a century of incessant efficiency-seeking, uneven personal relationships and social dynamics still defined business relationships in the mid-twentieth century. Bonds of affection and loyalty, plus paternalist succession ambitions, denied bridges to strangers.[60] To be sure, "social acceptability" was, and remains, a reasonable standard for any position that entails social interaction and that requires respect and authority. Offenses against fairness arose when people were considered socially, and therefore professionally, unacceptable because of cultural stereotypes and characteristics over which they have no control, such as sex or race. Myths about self-made success compounded the offense of such biases. They ignored the social factors that determined who could get on what ladder and how people moved on all ladders. They stigmatized the socially handicapped for not climbing ladders that were in fact unavailable to them. As long as businessmen's ambient culture, including the law, allowed businessmen and other gatekeepers to commit these affronts to fairness, the practices would continue, their unfairness unacknowledged. A multilayered system of buffers facilitated recruiting, hiring, and promotion based on social capital criteria even as it protected gatekeepers from facing the ethics and the impact of their refusal to assess individuals as individuals.

CHAPTER 4

Contacts and Buffers

The ambitious J. Pierrepont Finch in *How to Succeed in Business without Really Trying* makes his first big business "contact" by bumping into the Old Man at World Wide Wickets Company, Inc., while seeking a job. J. B. Biggley roars at the bungler to go to the personnel office to apply. Finch happily does just that, telling the "personnel man" that "I was speaking to J. B. Biggley only this morning"; he had "just happened to run into him." With such a powerful contact, how could Finch *not* get his foot in the door of this Park Avenue firm? The rest of Shepherd Mead's tongue-in-cheek guide for the ambitious itemizes steps to obtain and maximize connections: joining the "right country club," avoiding contentious bridge games with "cronies," looking exhausted—surrounded by the signs of work—when the boss comes in on the weekend to pick up his golf clubs, taking up the boss's hobby and/or alma mater, and having a wife who pleases the "influential wives."[1]

Having contacts expedites making connections. At this the audacious Finch excelled. In fact, however, unconnected job applicants other than a fictional hero would not "run into" the big boss exiting an elevator; corporate buildings have long since been designed to constrain promiscuous social interaction. In large firms after 1900, fewer and fewer spaces facilitated cross-rank informal contacts between officers and entry-level employees, apart from such roles as secretaries or clerks. Modern corporate communication systems had no need for male stenographers and office boys of yore, whose role as intermediaries might make their entry-level position the bottom rung of a ladder that went to the top. Yet business analysts and advisors continued to insist that only by "contact with the man himself" could managers know whom to put on development tracks. Within a small firm, a 1972 advisor pointed out, spotting "the men who have the inner drive" was easy. In a large company, however, spotting "high potential" employees without socially based contacts required systematic efforts by both aspirants and employers.[2]

A 1920 counselor to young men "about to graduate in a management course" exemplified how strikingly elites' access to contacts contrasted with others'. Assuming that his audiences would have potent networks available to them, the advisor discouraged college graduates from moving right into a job "through some relationship" such as "Dad." Instead, for at least two years they should develop their "self-reliance," "independence," and "humility" in companies other than their families'. Using their background networks, including schools, to get good positions, they could closely observe "the key man in the enterprise."[3]

So what were other, less connected, ambitious youths to do? How could they get on ladders that were not dead ends? Who might recognize their talents and efforts and help them advance their careers? They needed someone, somewhere, to be their first contact in the world of business. In a small firm, now or in the past, a novice's first contact might be a supervisor, or even the owner of the company. Bureaucratized firms, however, funneled applicants through specialized employment offices that screened candidates. A variety of institutions also played a role, aiding some contacts and buffering against others. Social clubs, colleges, fraternities, and business schools, plus trade and professional associations, took on gatekeeping roles with mixed results. Sometimes they evened out contacts and opportunities, but more often they concentrated contacts and opportunities within already privileged groups.

Do Contacts Matter?

Small businesses still operate with all levels of participants in close proximity, as had most firms when Tom Scott first spotted Andrew Carnegie. With each increment of company growth, however, so grew the distances—physical, social, and procedural—between the expanding layers of operations. The chances of getting noticed and promoted by a firm's top managers decreased with the size of the firm and one's social distance from the top. Analysts who considered success unlikely for unconnected youth in large firms often recommended the small or medium firm for novices, even for young MBAs of the 1960s.[4]

Regardless of the type or size of a firm, the closer a ladder reached to the top of a firm's hierarchy, the more the maneuvers for getting on that ladder and climbing it depended on social capital rather than objective performance. That is, the higher the position, the more connections and socially based impressions counted in a hopeful's interactions with those who would recruit, hire, or promote. An 1890s traditionalist, intending to inspire diligence, declared that "climbing is the only exercise worth while in business."[5] The degree of an advisor's cynicism determined whether he believed that good, hard work might suffice to attract notice, a climber's primary challenge.

If asked for practical advice, rather than inspiration, most twentieth-century business authorities recognized the importance of contacts for top positions. For instance, when asked directly, a "decisive majority" in a 1956 American Management Association survey indicated that "business contacts" were a firm's "most productive source of executive talent." Second in frequency came "knowing somebody" in a social sense, a "time-honored method" for recruiting for the top rungs. Advertisements, consultants, colleges' and professional associations' placement services, and commercial employment agencies, in that order, could also help. Dead last came "unsolicited applications." Only very large firms reported relying on such applications in any significant way because of their need for many managers and these companies' greater use of systematic personnel methods for screening. A detailed analysis of occupational mobility, also in the mid-1950s, concluded that about 80 percent of CEOs had had as their initial contact in the firm either friends or family members.[6] Nonetheless, advisors and pundits have typically ignored these realities in favor of inspiring words of self-made fortune and opportunity for all.

Personnel Departments: Bureaucracy's Buffers

In 1920 the president of a large textile corporation expressed concern that he knew so few of his company's owners and employees. His firm had developed personnel procedures and offices over the previous two decades "to take the place of the lost personal contact," especially the "loss of the old relations between the workers and the management." As top managers became isolated from ownership and other employees, personnel management attempted to balance opposites, formal and informal, personal and impersonal, aiming for what an early text called "humanly scientific standards."[7] Having jurisdiction over screening and training candidates for hiring and promotion made personnel workers into bureaucracies' gatekeepers, buffering top management from often difficult decisions. No wonder J. B. Biggley protested so loudly when corporate novice Finch queried him directly for a job: the personnel system had failed to protect the Big Boss.

Tradition continued to influence personnel professionals' notions of sound hiring techniques, even in large firms. In 1914, an industrialist recommended a formal process by which he intended to replicate the social benefits of community-based hiring and development. His inspiration came from a great merchant who, decades earlier, had always insisted on interviewing each "boy" his firm hired. Developing these boys into "the men to run my business" had resulted in an "aggressive, efficient, and loyal mercantile organization." The industrialist recommended that a vocational school or apprentice supervisor should study each young candidate, reviewing such things as the applicant's school performance, health, parents, and "home surroundings." A neighbor or other person within the youth's background networks would of course know such information. Lacking those connections, a specialized practitioner would have to seek it out. Consequently, firms having strong contacts with employees' neighborhoods and families have been the least inclined to formalize personnel functions, instead maintaining openly social practices.[8]

Despite some lingering desires to hold on to the old ways, as bureaucratic scale and managerial specialization grew over the twentieth century it became impossible for large firms to maintain informal personnel operations for most employees. Schemes to systematize recruiting, hiring, training, and promotion flourished. New and growing departments specialized in such matters, variously called welfare, employment, personnel, benefits, human relations, or, now, human resources. The farther down the corporate hierarchy any particular position was situated, the narrower the job description and therefore the more easily and reliably its occupants could be judged objectively and interchanged, or so the thinking went. Also, the greater the occupational and social distances between personnel specialists and the workers they oversaw, the more appropriate seemed mechanistic policies and attitudes toward workers.[9] Thus, personnel staffs' earliest and most frequent subjects were employees considered "workers" rather than managers. These included blue-collar as well as pink- and lower-level white-

...ALL THE OFFICE MANAGERS *Agreed!*

Yes—they agreed unanimously that the Remington Electric DeLuxe Typewriter lived up to its advance reputation as the finest, all-purpose cost-cutting Electric Typewriter on the market today.

When the Electric DeLuxe arrived, everyone wanted to try typing on it—see the notable difference in finished manuscript—find out if electric typing is *really* faster, easier.

Just a brief trial period at the Remington Electric supplied the answers—*quickly, definitely*. The fast electric action allowed fingers to *fly* over the keys—turn out *more work, better work* with *less effort*. In addition, *all* the correspondence, stencils and carbon copies turned out by the new all-purpose Electric DeLuxe were *uniformly clear* and *distinctive* in appearance

Yes, *all the office managers agreed:* One way to save today is to cut operating costs and increase typing the electric way!

● FREE: For information on how Electric Typing can work for you, write Remington Rand Inc., Business Machines and Supplies Division, Dept. T9, 315 Fourth Avenue, New York 10, for a FREE illustrated booklet, "NEW OFFICE PROFITS THROUGH ELECTRICITY."

Remington Rand THE FIRST NAME IN ELECTRIC TYPEWRITERS

There is no question here about who the managers are in this 1949 Remington Rand advertisement. Managers make decisions about machines, and workers use the machines. In advertisements for office equipment well into the 1990s, that distinction was always gendered, compounding class differences between managers and female workers.

(Courtesy Hagley Museum and Library)

collar employees—that is, manual and office workers on ladders that did not reach outside their box on the organization chart.

As intermediaries between employer and employee, personnel managers have depended on satisfying the former for their management of the latter. To build what a 1917 analyst called "a standard by which to grade the man for the job—a yardstick," personnel professionals developed a series of tools to make their decisions as objective as possible. These tools, all carefully constructed, included job descriptions, training programs, promotion procedures and criteria, as well as quantitative and qualitative measures of aptitude and performance. They applied all these tools to employees starting at the bottom of the corporate hierarchy and as far up as management would allow. Such rationalized policies aimed to "encourage the ambitious and able individuals to come to the front and take advantage of whatever training or understudy positions may be offered for promising individuals."[10]

Rationalized, systematized, formalized personnel operations regulated access to, and progress up, the lower portions of corporate ladders. On balance, the resulting tools for hiring and promotion, as well as for training and development, opened opportunities for many hopefuls who lacked prior connections. They did not, however, eliminate the workings of social capital. Instead, formal personnel procedures restricted opportunities in significant ways, especially before the mid-1960s.[11] Until then, those who managed and developed employees on behalf of their employers could exercise prejudices unchallenged. And the farther up a firm's hierarchy they practiced their art, the more social became the answers to such questions as: Who gets considered but rejected? Who is not considered at all? Who gets notified of opportunities? Who gets tagged for grooming? Despite their intention to rationalize processes, personnel professionals perpetuated mainstream biases through their gatekeeping as they modeled criteria for hires and promotions on people already on the ladders.

Persisting Social Filters

Ironically, formalizing personnel functions in twentieth-century corporations raised, rather than lowered, some socially based barriers for those outside the margins of traditional acceptability. Application forms that appear to be impersonal can actually carry differentiating weights for social factors. A standardized application form for office jobs in a mid-twentieth-century text asked applicants whether they owned their own home and from what source they had learned of the job. It also asked for contact information of "at least two professional persons such as physician, lawyer, teacher, minister, priest, or rabbi, who can vouch for you." Such seemingly reasonable requests actually carried the message that a person without such things was not a good candidate for a white-collar job. The common practice of requiring photographs along with applications and references likewise meant that even structured hiring processes did not rely on objective, ability-related credentials alone.[12] In addition, no matter how structured they may be, interviews—the next step for a candidate beyond application—cannot be free of biases from the interviewers' ambient culture, so they too differentially distribute benefits according to applicants' "social acceptability."

When bosses did their own hiring, which was the case early in the modern business era, contradictions reigned. Common advice to company leaders recommended impartiality and "cool accuracy" in hiring that necessitated "sink[ing] your petty likes and dislikes." In almost the same breath, however, the advice for "high grade positions" often suggested conducting interviews outside of the workplace, at dinner or at "the club," all the better to study a candidate "as a man." A savvy boss was advised to trust his intuition, and he often took pride in his ability to assess people. In any case, bosses had the authority to place anyone they wished upon a ladder that went to the top. A surprise discovery, like that of the starlet at the soda fountain, provided for the occasional spectacular climb. One executive, for instance, recalled giving a chance to "the worst speci-men of long, lean, lank countryman I had ever seen." Tempted to "show him out," this executive instead responded to "some im-pulse which I could not explain at the time" and interviewed the man. Quickly impressed with the candidate's "enthusiasm and in-telligence," the chief put him on a ladder that led to the top in two years.[13] Only a high-level executive could risk making such intuitive decisions.

Bureaucratic personnel workers, in contrast, could have admitted this unlikely candidate to upper management's inspection only at their peril. Screening according to protocol would most likely reject an unpromising candidate off the street. Top executives counted on their personnel department to weed out unconnected and unlikely aspirants. How to separate unpromising from promising appli-cants, however, can be difficult, and failure to screen candidates ef-fectively could carry serious costs, affecting the personnel worker's own career. Stereotypes of all sorts have provided gatekeepers with both shortcuts that simplify judgment and safety nets should that judgment fail. A junior executive worried in 1964 about recom-mending people for promotion solely on merit. As he put it, "I am justifiably afraid that my own judgment will be called into question if I recommend anyone who deviates too markedly from the kind of person I see getting ahead in my company."[14]

Many characteristics lend themselves to the kinds of inferences that people make about others: grooming, clothing style, gait, man-nerisms, and accent. A late twentieth-century advisor warned the ambitious that even such superficial cues could yield evidence of "business or social level" and of whether or not an individual might "match the corporate chemistry." Judgment takes just three sec-onds, and "you've got to get your foot past the door of those tyran-nical three seconds." Class, ethnicity, and sex were at the top of the features by which a personnel officer could, without constraint or qualm, filter candidates prior to the mid-1960s. So, although a top-level manager or owner could elect to run counter to a common stereotype, a personnel worker could not. Only on direct instructions from top management could personnel workers even begin to consider women or ethnically marginalized applicants for positions ordinarily inaccessible to them, even after the 1960s' shifts in legal and cultural norms.[15] As front-line gatekeepers, personnel departments could justify their screening by presumptions about both their bosses' and other employees' prejudices (one would not want to distress present workers, after all). That way, no one had to admit to acting on personal bias.

Above and Beyond the Personnel Department

If personnel specialists functioned to buffer top management from most decisions about employees, they were out of the loop when it came to employment decisions about top managers, and an unconnected applicant for an executive position had little chance. Throughout the twentieth century, personnel specialists and top management disagreed on personnel's proper role. For instance, a personnel professional lamented in 1933 that his field's techniques for evaluating candidates were not respected for their potential to minimize "the part played by personal opinion, company politics, and other undesirable influences" at the top. He either failed to see or refused to accept that executives did not *want* to set personal opinions aside in selecting their own. A widely used, mid-1950s tome criticized the "lack of humility" that too often prevented company officers from seeing the need to go beyond their own judgment in making decisions about "management talent." Personnel specialists insisted that their profession could provide valuable input through "records, rating scales, reports, tests, surveys, and interviews." In contrast, an official of a large company explained in the 1930s that an executive post "involves personal relationships, a knowledge of past company history, and many other features which are thoroughly known and understood only by those with whom they have worked and for whom they would work." For such decisions, "the personnel department is ordinarily not qualified." Two decades later, an authority using circular logic explained that personnel staffs could not hire executives, for whom there were no standardized tests or screens and, furthermore, that there should be no such tests. Those positions required the direct attention of other executives, for only they could understand both the nature of the work and the caliber of people required to do it.[16]

Above a corporation's top executives sits its board of directors. A 1947 Harvard Business School study examined how boards reproduce themselves, select chief executives, and direct corporate management. Because a board's primary responsibility is to ensure the corporation's survival, succession at the top matters, and the decisions relating to that succession bring out all the tensions between formal and informal processes of selection. Contradictions arise between insisting on an "established mechanism" for all such decisions and the social processes by which the decisions actually take place. The authors of the Harvard study favored holding conversations—both casual and purposeful—between directors and their friends in recruiting and selecting candidates. This "usual process of selection" would solicit suggestions from prominent figures in and outside of the firm, then build a "consensus" on the "most desirable" candidate. Because a director's duties entailed "a many-sided problem in human relations," effectiveness required getting along comfortably with the other directors, plus maintaining productive relationships with outside institutions. For these reasons, "the personal factor looms large." Although they rejected a qualification checklist as inappropriate for top executives, the authors did list a CEO's desired qualities, with "compatibility" second only to "honesty and integrity." The "ability to appraise men" ranked farther down the list, but was still prominent. The boards and CEOs that would result from these socially driven selection processes would be "self-perpetuating" bodies, which these authorities saw as a positive outcome.[17]

Candidates who succeeded by social methods could find the process quite gratifying, even when they recognized its pitfalls. Thus, although women in general bore broad and deep disadvantages in business, some women who managed to achieve executive positions took pride in having been chosen as individuals, rather than by an employment department's formal measures. Advocates for women in banking in the 1920s often reflected their class biases more than their sex's interests, noting, for instance, the importance of class to acquiring new accounts as a key to success in banking. Developing new accounts, of course, demanded "a wide and varied circle of friends and connections." One female banker observed that banks never selected managers of women's departments through their employment offices "any more than would a vice-presidency be so filled." Instead, such a sensitive position was "more in the nature of an appointment and is filled by privilege." Thus, social connections were what would first bring appropriate candidates to the attention of senior officers. Only the last step, as she described it, entailed presenting "credentials" beyond those that her reputation and recommendations had already established. While stating her hope that the necessity of this combination of "good luck and friendly gossip" might disappear in the coming years, this female banker noted that men's careers also often required these same chance openings. The major problem for women, she determined, was that women could not climb a bank's ladder to higher positions, as could men. That is, what banks offered as entry-level opportunities for men were either denied to women altogether, or amounted to dead-ends.[18] Achievements in the women's bureau of a bank could not move women to a taller ladder.

Education as Gatekeeping

Nothing has promised—and delivered—the equalizing of opportunity in the post–World War II era more than widely available education. People without prior connections to employers have been able to pass higher levels of formal personnel screening than ever before by virtue of their educational credentials. In this capacity, educational institutions, particularly postsecondary schools such as universities and professional and trade schools, have long since come to serve business as surrogate gatekeepers as well as training sites.[19] As a result, restrictions to school admission have restricted entrance to business and the professions, serving as a first-level screening, all in the name of raising the objective standards for admission to corporate ladders. As educational certification has increasingly determined if and where one enters a vocation, lower and higher education, credible references, and financial resources to acquire degrees and pass licensing examinations have all dramatically raised the barriers to entry.

Yet in business management, unlike law, medicine, engineering, and accounting, growing demands for degrees as job prerequisites often rang hollow. Academically trainable technical skills other than accounting and engineering mattered little for business management until the 1950s. Until then, businessmen tended to criticize rather than praise callow youths who would emerge from academia and expect preferential treatment on preferred ladders. Nonetheless, colleges offering business courses, business schools, and trade associations all grew in number with the rise of corporations because by prescreening candidates these external institutions relieved businesses of gatekeeping burdens.

Social or Human Capital?

Before 1900, most businesspeople presumed that higher education was generally irrelevant to business success. By the turn of the twentieth century, however, a great decades-long debate on the matter had begun. That advocates of specialized business education won the debate had more to do with a changing business environment than it did with any timeless merits in their arguments. In effect, those who built the pre–World War I business culture set the foundations for a bureaucratic system in which they and their own credentials could well have failed, although not for want of intelligence or skills. The demands of this changing business world included specialized training in fields such as accounting and engineering, and, after 1900, management and finance. Schools, in turn, improved their ability to provide competent and useful training.[20] Together these factors of human capital—knowledge and skills—drove much of the rising prestige and attraction of postsecondary formal education.

Another set of variables, this one based on the dynamics of social capital, also contributed to this convergence of interests between business and educational institutions, although this was true more for managerial than for technical positions. The same elite populations that fueled popular nineteenth-century stereotypes of college men as wastrels, undisciplined and overindulged, gave college-educated men the advantage in the competition for top-level business positions. In the era before business-oriented curricula became established in colleges, these institutions functioned largely as depositories for affluent youths not yet ready to leave parental supports. As a result, college experience (if not education) became a strong credential for top management in established industries. William K. Vanderbilt Jr., for example, built a notorious reputation as an all-around cutup as a youth. Yet he moved right into a position high up a gilded ladder on the New York Central Railroad. Anyone who had become his friend at Harvard College joined a peer network that included plenty of well-connected young men. Thus, attending prestigious schools mattered, but not for curricular content, and the "gentleman's C" harmed no one's business career. Graduates of public secondary schools from the 1920s through the 1980s worked much harder on academics in elite colleges than did graduates from private secondary schools. The latter participated more in social organizations and put their efforts into accruing social capital. They were busy building the connections that would determine their future.[21]

For white-collar positions, hierarchies of schools, and hierarchies of fraternities and dining clubs within them, influenced which ladders young men entering business would be offered, and how high they could climb. As a rule, the "objective" credentials—human capital—that applicants earned from school performance had more impact toward the bottom of a hierarchy, as an indication of specific skills or of a "trained mind." In contrast, the connections and connectability developed at school mattered more for positions toward the top of the ladder. The fictional Finch faked having been to college, but not because he needed any academic skills beyond the ability to read *How to Succeed in Business without Really Trying.* He sought a fraudulent claim to social capital by pretending a passionate loyalty to Boss Biggley's Old Ivy. Successful at that ruse, he moved right up the tallest ladder at World Wide Wickets. In this vein, wearing the Harvard Business School "trademark . . . right across the top of your forehead" could be "the single most important thing" in starting a career, as one alumnus put it.[22]

Presumptions about the desirability of a college education for management were so ensconced in the post–World War I business culture that families in the 1920s saw college as the best means of improving their children's lot in life, if only they could afford it. Mabel Newcomer observed in the 1950s that increased access to education had in part compensated for diminishing opportunities since 1900 for the less-than-wealthy to found their own companies. Although they could never have wealthy persons' easy "social contacts with influential businessmen" or their elite education, college experience vastly improved their corporate mobility. A similarly positive impact of education on the mobility of the "lower ranks" in the 1950s was strongest in large corporations, where men with objectively measured abilities could climb onto and up some ladders more freely than they would have been able to do before World

War II.[23] Thus, higher education could grow both social and human capital, improving the career chances of the ambitious youths who had access to it.

Educational Screens

Vance Packard quoted a mid-twentieth-century executive as having avowed that corporate managers "desperately need a means of screening. Education is one quick means of preliminary screening without having to think too much about it." To the extent that businesses' gatekeepers have used educational credentials for prescreening candidates, including those for blue- and pink-collar positions, they increased their firms' hiring efficiency. Screening for high school diplomas avoids companies' having to administer literacy and numeracy tests and tells employment offices whether applicants have at least minimal diligence plus a modicum of family advantages. A college degree holder could have passed higher screening standards, and so on through masters and professional degrees. Such basic preliminary screening served employers, but it greatly raised applicants' costs of entry. Worse, some young people's class, ethnicity, or sex made college attendance impossible, especially at expensive or segregated schools. Because of long-standing traditions, families expended resources on boys' education, often at the expense of, even the labor of, their sisters. Many colleges refused admission to African Americans; the University of Maryland, for instance, only changed its exclusionary policies after the 1954 *Brown v. Board of Education* decision.[24]

Educational rankings generated apparently objective criteria by which personnel professionals could guide their recruiting and hiring, incurring minimal risks of reproach for questionable judgment should a novice fail. Candidates with a college degree who passed through the initial screening could then be ranked by alma mater on seemingly unambiguous scales according to relevant strengths.

Thus, if applicants sought entrance as engineers, economists, or accountants, one ranking of schools applied. If their strengths were managerial—that is, social—then another ranking applied, perhaps by the college's overall prestige or as a social class indicator, such as the Ivy League schools, or by the gatekeeper's own school loyalties, or perhaps even by the reputation of the school's football team. To earn a position on ladders that reached into top management, candidates would be ranked according to their schools, along with their fraternity and alumni clubs, because these indicated the degree of access to valuable networks that the candidates might bring into the firm. Corporations often hired people with little practical preparation for the job, but whose degrees made them connectable.[25]

Campus Recruiting

Constant concern about finding adequate managerial talent moved many corporations by 1900 to send recruiters to college campuses. An important midcentury book on hiring managers included an entire chapter on campus recruitment. It began by pointing out that fewer hourly employees than before were being promoted beyond the position of foreman because they could no longer compete for management positions against increasing numbers of college graduates. Suggestions for firms competing for good candidates on campuses included building relationships with faculty as well as with school placement officers. Corporate recruiters should offer professors technical publications, invitations to pertinent corporate workshops, plant tours for classes, and speakers for classes and student events. The more interaction, the stronger the networks, and the better the chance for leads to top students.[26]

Eager to place their graduates, colleges often encouraged recruiters. Dartmouth College seems to have led the field in institutionalizing liaisons with business. Shortly after 1900 it set up a job placement office. In 1919 it created an associate deanship "to assist the men of the college in making the right contacts at the close of their college course and in beginning their life work advantageously and promptly," according to Richard Husband, who held that position in 1923. Husband included among his responsibilities providing "vocational guidance" and working with the admissions and other college offices to develop students' "intelligence," "forcefulness," "reliability," and "personality." This last factor included "personal acceptability." Dartmouth encouraged companies to send representatives to the campus and used students' records to help match the students to firms' needs. Husband and his subordinates also visited both public and private organizations, attended conferences, and subscribed to trade journals in order to maximize their abilities to facilitate outside contacts for students. In the 1920s, other schools either started or expanded their placement activities, and businesses eagerly received their offerings.[27]

Integrating on-the-job business training within formal education seems to have entered college programs from the periphery of social prestige. Herman Schneider established what was probably the first American cooperative program at the University of Cincinnati in 1905. Modeling his innovation on medicine and law, which by then required or at least encouraged internships prior to licensing, Schneider focused on engineering, a source of many managers in business. By the 1920s, many similar programs prided themselves on making it possible for students to "earn while you learn." In addition to their answering the call for white-collar general and specialized training, these programs benefited their students by providing contacts. Such institutionally mediated contacts could not equal those available to students at elite schools, but they provided entries otherwise impossible to unconnected youths of modest origins. Coordinators acted as liaisons, forging personal contacts for optimizing placements, offering ambitious youths an "escalator" toward their goals. By the mid-1970s, business schools, too, began to build on their growing direct involvement with businesses, providing students with "real-world experience." Their innovations included setting up internships and sending student-run consultant teams out to solve problems for businesses.[28] Internships often turned into jobs when students successfully parlayed their school-based synthetic connections, mastering the jobs and making favorable impressions.

Prerequisites

Many business analysts and practitioners throughout the first half of the twentieth century noted disdainfully that "college boys" expected to be treated differently when they entered employment. Most critics blamed this on college liberties, but the graduates' expectations may simply have resulted from their understanding of their elite status. In 1931, for instance, an article in *Factory and Industrial Management* asked "Do College Men Stick?" A product of new trends in education that taught "industrial facts," these young men flourished best when singled out for "a special job," for rotation, or for assignment to "older men who are executives."[29] In other words, graduates expected to start well up on tall ladders and to receive the benefits of their social standing through challenges and opportunities not available to men without the collegiate badge of class status.

By the 1950s, Mabel Newcomer noted that college had become a "prerequisite" for top management. It is, she wrote, "increasingly the ticket of admission to jobs with big corporations." Her statistics contrasted the "American tradition" of businessmen's scorn for higher education with the roughly 80 percent of executives in 1950 who had been appointed after 1943 and who had college experience. She could not, however, ascertain what "*kind* of education" made for business success. Evaluations about success with either "general" degrees (psychology, management principles, personnel studies) or "specialized" degrees (writing, accounting, law, finance) contradicted each other, as each type had its merits at different rungs on different ladders. Nonetheless, some sort of college degree was increasingly necessary to get on any ladder with good opportunities. In the 1950s, corporate businessmen had attended college almost six times as often as other adult males, and they were eight times more likely to have graduated.[30]

More than half of the Harvard Business School's attendees during its first decade dropped out after a year. The degree itself, and by implication the curriculum, mattered less to either students or their future employers than having studied at that elite institution— for however short a time. Business schools everywhere, and ever since, have wrestled with the content for coursework, certain only that something about business was teachable and somehow their students and business practices could benefit thereby. Amidst vigorous contention about their purpose and direction, the number of programs and the number of students in business schools multiplied, especially after World War I. After the next world war, business schools and businesses sought closer interaction, but still could not agree on curricula. Fittingly, graduates from the Massachusetts Institute of Technology's Masters of Science in Industrial Management in 1955 said that an increase in "personal confidence" was the greatest asset they derived from their education.[31]

Uneven Advantages

Endless discussions in the trade and popular press during the first half of the twentieth century confused cause and effect in assessing the advantages of a college education for those aiming for managerial positions in business. The writers presumed that the characteristics young men took away from college were products of their college experience. Yet many of what observers listed as the advantages of college were in fact advantages of the social status that made college possible in the first place for young people before World War II. A 1920 study of fifty companies reported "potentiality," "mental poise," "perspective," "innate refinement," and "personality" as half of the top ten "qualifications" found more in college men than other businessmen. One of the corporate officers contributing to this survey added "association with men of high mentality" as a benefit of college training. This same executive indicated that his firm "always" hired college men for "a definite position for future advancement." The collegiate screen thus facilitated hiring and placing people, even those who lacked personal contacts. It determined whether a new corporate hire would be assigned to a blue-collar or a white-collar ladder, and Ivy League men started on taller ladders than did most.[32]

Constraints on attending college and graduate school, whether because of class, sex, or ethnicity, exacerbated limitations on corporate opportunity. Lack of access to one could deny access to the other, and each institution could blame the other for the violation of egalitarian principles. For instance, when a woman petitioned the Harvard Business School in 1919 to study life insurance, the faculty voted against her: "since the School aims to prepare for executive positions, it could not at this time logically admit women, as executive positions in business are not ordinarily open to them." Any constraint on equal access to education multiplied obstacles to occupational mobility, and this is one reason why college admissions policies have been hotly contested for decades. Yet, however heated have been the recent debates on affirmative action at colleges, very few have challenged the time-honored practice of legacy admissions. Elite schools' preferential admission standards for alumni's children have been documented since the 1920s, when an increasing number of immigrants' children, especially Jews and Catholics, sought access to education and its benefits. Supposedly meritocratic screening procedures at elite universities still result in ready admission for legacy candidates despite significantly weaker credentials. A U.S. Department of Education investigation in the 1990s, for example, demonstrated that on average legacy candidates at Harvard gained admission despite much lower rankings in SAT scores and every other admissions category except athletics compared to the nonlegacy students.[33] These imbalances carried forward into business opportunities.

When certain groups of people could not gain admission to educational institutions, these groups were not even given the chance to show that they could work harder and better than legacies and others who were more acceptable to admission committees at those institutions. The Wharton School, the University of Pennsylvania's renowned business school, opened in 1881 with a mission to provide business training for "young men." Some business schools did open their gates to women in the 1920s, and women flocked to them—but usually for training in secretarial careers, office management, home economics, and even "household accounts." Women were aliens in separate programs, when they were allowed at all. In the 1940s some business schools began to offer to train the "business men and women of the future," but women's enrollments declined in the 1950s. The Harvard Business School began admitting women in 1961, and Dartmouth's Amos Tuck School did so in 1968. In the 1970s women's business school enrollment growth rates exceeded men's, averaging about 10 percent of enrollments by 1975. African Americans remained largely excluded until the 1960s. Harvard Business School had had only twenty-four African-American students between the end of World War II and 1967, when it admitted twenty-eight.[34] Despite their frustration at gaining access to it, African Americans and women maintained near sacramental expectations for education as a key to mobility.

No Exception to the Rule

What about the late twentieth century's most noted college dropout, Bill Gates? If a college education is universally understood to be a minimal requirement for corporate success, how could he become the richest American, the head of a huge corporation, without a degree? No more than Andrew Carnegie's rise to that same stature a century earlier, Gates's rise is *not* an exception; rather, he too neatly proves the rule of social capital. William Henry Gates III never needed what a college degree offers a young entrant to the business world—a chance at an interview. He had social capital to burn, as well as a million-dollar trust fund from his grandparents, which he never even needed to use in financing Microsoft. A member of a wealthy Seattle family, with connections to governors, senators, and bankers through both parents, Gates was one of those prep school attendees of Ivy League colleges who knew they would never need to send in a cold application to a personnel office. They would never need to get past that first level of objectified prescreening. They could attend to other matters instead, such as playing poker and tinkering with computers.[35]

Gates attended Seattle's most elite prep school. Not just for the rich, but for the rich and talented, Lakeside was the takeoff point for many fortunes. As one of its many advantages, the school introduced its students to computers in the spring of 1968, decades ahead of most high schools (the school provided terminals and bought time on mainframes located elsewhere). Among the students competing with Gates for computer time were Paul Allen, who later became the primary code composer for BASIC and without whom Microsoft would not exist, plus three of the first programmers Microsoft hired. When TRW recruited Gates and Allen, Gates took off time, with permission, from his senior year at Lakeside; Allen, two years older, dropped out of college. The top programmer at TRW recognized Gates's abilities and monitored the boy's work. Once at Harvard, Gates made friends with Steve Ballmer, a sociable and well-connected fellow down the hall from Gates's dorm room, whom Gates later invited to join Microsoft. A major factor in the firm's growth, Ballmer has been CEO since January 2000. An overheard dorm conversation led Monte Davidoff to get involved with solving some of Gates's programming problems, but because he never found his way into Gates's network of friends, he received neither the mention nor the financial rewards of the others.[36]

When Mary Gates tried to dissuade her son from leaving Harvard, she sought advice from a prominent friend, a Seattle philanthropist who had made his fortune in electronics with no college background whatsoever. Gates convinced this man of the merits of his project as the two dined at the venerable Rainier Club, Seattle's prime venue for business and political elites. Mary Gates sat on the boards of some of the Northwest's largest corporations and civic groups; she was the first woman president of Seattle's United Way. Her son had no trouble making connections with leaders at IBM through her networks. In turn those connections provided assurance to IBM during negotiations to license BASIC from Gates's group, as contracting for such an important component with an outside supplier was not its standard procedure. Gates's attorney father helped Gates write up the innovative licensing agreements for BASIC that brought in enough income to make unnecessary either venture capital or family funds, and that contract became a model for software licensing.[37]

Even though Bill Gates combined extraordinary drive, ability, and powerful networks, his success without a college degree still requires some explanation. First, he *did* gain skills and networks from attending elite educational institutions. Both Lakeside and Harvard had facilities and faculty not generally available, and he used them intensively. Second, Gates did not need the credentials a college degree would provide. His success did not require entry into any corporate bureaucracy through its normal channels—through a personnel department to land a job, through a purchasing department to sell his product, or through a credit department to seek a loan. His many networks, including family-based ones, provided whatever institutional access he needed. New, small, and rapidly growing industries typically employ far smaller proportions of degreed people than mature, large, and slowly growing industries do. Moreover, employees are more likely to possess a college degree than are entrepreneurs.[38] Educational institutions have little to teach innovators in rapidly advancing fields beyond the state of the relevant arts, which Gates's privileged schooling did provide. Professionalized standards mean nothing when a field is too new to demand professional stature for its members. Thus, for example, Henry Ford did not need a college education as a pioneer in the automobile industry; but Alfred Sloan did in order to bring that industry into maturity from his post at General Motors. Would Microsoft hire a programmer off the street without college credentials today?

Trade and Professional Associations

Professional and trade associations have flourished over the past century or so, advancing their constituents' and often the public's interests in a variety of ways. Such organizations generate mechanisms that limit access to their fields, facilitating contacts and opportunities between select people while making them more difficult for others. Like education, professional and trade associations can serve the commonwealth by raising standards for vocations. Like schools, they too operate on a principle of exclusion, and as such they have come to serve businesses as remote gatekeepers.

Models of Gatekeeping

Always in the name of improving their fields and services, vocational associations attempt to establish standards based on educational or occupational criteria that appear objective and utilitarian. Historian Harold Perkin called this restriction process "closure," by which skilled workers, whether lawyers or plumbers, aim to "consolidate the financial and psychic rewards accruing from the monopoly of certain kinds of human capital."[39] Effective closure exacerbates differential access to opportunities in business by institutionalizing buffers between business decision makers and strangers. The American Medical Association (AMA) and the American Bar Association have provided the models for vocational groups other than doctors and lawyers. By comparison, professional associations in business have achieved closure unevenly in every way except one: facilitating the application of social capital to benefit some and disadvantage others.

The AMA institutionalized its strongest gatekeeping with educational standards. When it succeeded in imposing its standards on medical schools after 1900, many schools went out of existence, and medical education became more expensive. By ultimately requiring internships and residencies for licensing, the AMA erected barriers for anyone without the resources to sustain such a long, expensive training period. This protracted and expensive education standardized medical care (at least for those who could afford the doctors it produced), but that goal did not require the exclusion of women and racial minorities from internships and residencies. The earlier system of competitive exams had opened licensed medical practice to women, immigrants, and others with limited social capital and financial resources. The AMA's new policies, however, were often administered by establishing quotas or outright prohibitions, which promoted social homogeneity in the profession after 1906. Eventually doctors' access to hospitals required sponsorships that excluded old-time practitioners as well as others who did not fit comfortably within the newly fraternal order of medicine. As a consequence, African-American institutions produced African-American doctors, and the numbers of female doctors declined from their 1910 level, when women comprised 6 percent of doctors. Also in 1910, women made up only 1.1 percent of the number of practicing lawyers, largely because of their exclusion from bar associations.[40]

These were the institutional models to which aspired all other professions, including pharmacists, engineers, morticians, and accountants.

The Walls around Accounting

Accounting rose in importance with the growth of large companies. Andrew Carnegie's accounting skills gave his business ventures a competitive edge. Knowing the cost of each item he produced allowed him to negotiate far more effectively than his competitors. As corporations grew, accounting took on surrogate verification roles as well. When owners were no longer intimately involved with their firms—when they became stockholders and investors rather than owner-managers—they needed reliable sources of information about the firms in which they invested. Following upon the careless securities markets of the 1920s that resulted in the stock market crash of 1929, the New Deal instituted reforms, including the creation of the Securities and Exchange Commission, which required that all publicly traded stocks be audited.[41] Until the deregulations of the 1980s and 1990s, the standards set by the SEC and the accounting profession provided investors with a reasonable basis for their decisions.

As participants in the organizing impulses of the Progressive Era, U.S. accountants affiliated to establish standards for education, training, and admission to the profession. They sought to ensure that practitioners were competent and reliable and had the public's confidence. The American Association of Public Accountants, established in 1887, joined other practitioners in 1916 to form the core of what became the American Institute of Accountants (AIA), which later merged with the American Society of Certified Public Accountants in 1936, eventually becoming the American Institute of Certified Public Accountants (AICPA) in 1957. Following the medical and legal models, accountancy's advocates sought to systematize and restrict entry to the profession. They established as their highest rank the certified public accountant (CPA)—the CPA being a state-licensed auditor sanctioned to certify whether organizations' records meet regulatory standards and accurately reflected managers' actions. Debates raged for years about whether the profession should require apprenticeships or school-based credentials and examinations for the CPA designation. Partisans for each side contended that their preferences would best promote the quality and stature of the accounting profession. Eastern elites tended to argue for apprenticeships, which gave the edge to existing firms, to which they had easy access; Midwesterners and nonelites argued for exams, as they offered a more egalitarian measure of competence. Because a national agreement proved unreachable, states forged their own CPA codes, with New York first to establish its code in 1896. Most states eventually required both a two- or three-year apprenticeship with a CPA firm and qualifying examinations.[42]

The apprenticeship requirement became the flaw in what accounting's gatekeepers could pretend were objective entry criteria. People who passed qualifying exams but failed firms' homogeneity tests for hiring could not fulfill states' apprenticeship requirements for CPA status. State codes that required employment in a CPA firm *before* one took the exams, or that excluded African Americans from taking the exams altogether, raised even greater obstacles to candidates' meeting supposedly objective qualifications. In 1933, the *Journal of Accountancy* published an article entitled "Accounting as a Field for Colored Men." The 1930 census tallied only 163 African Americans working as accountants and auditors, and 7 as CPAs. (A new study lists just 5 African-American CPAs before 1937.) The standards that most states had codified, under the guidance of state chapters of the trade's associations, gave gatekeeping powers to existing firms, which could exclude from apprenticeship anyone they wished. That barrier, plus the broader difficulties that prevailed against the growth of large minority-owned businesses that would need audits, had blocked all but a handful of African-American men from entering the profession. The only African-American CPA to gain the requisite experience in the 1920s within a white firm did so with a Jewish firm in Manhattan.[43]

Each of the pioneering African-American CPAs combined technical achievement and heroic determination to surmount barriers and humiliations. When a young African American named Theodore A. Jones graduated from the University of Illinois in 1933, its placement office refused to assist him in finding a professional position. New Deal programs increased business reporting requirements, and these provided some opportunities for Jones, but only a former professor's supervision and certification for the experience requirement made it possible for Jones to become a CPA in 1940. Two years later, two of his former professors sponsored Jones's admission to the AIA, which claimed to "welcome" every accountant who could meet its "high and rigid standards." Accentuating Jones's alien status, however, the admissions committee refused to take responsibility for deciding on his nomination. Instead, the matter of electing an African-American to the AIA came to a vote on the floor of the annual convention. The vote was positive, but the stigma of strangeness was not. Despite abundant AIA rhetoric about objective criteria for admission, Jones's technical or operational qualifications were not at issue; his race was.[44]

. Where state-sanctioned criteria for professional licensing did not apply, as in hiring accountants below CPA stature, decisions prior to the 1960s were flagrantly subjective. Firms hired people whom they trusted, whom they felt comfortable sending to their clients, and who had claims on their loyalty. Because African-American enterprises and individuals could rarely afford to hire accountants, business conditions failed to provide the patronage that the African-American community did have for medical doctors, teachers, lawyers, and ministers. Meanwhile, mainstream practitioners could claim it was their clients' prejudices that kept them from hiring candidates who were nonstandard in the category of ethnicity, sex, or anything else. It was a potent excuse, because it tied business practices to powerful cultural contexts and seemed to absolve individuals, even in instances when a candidate had passed internal exams or held other credentials but was nevertheless denied a position. One firm asked an African-American candidate to take its exam (which he passed) and then told him bluntly that it had just "wanted to see what a Negro could know about accounting."[45] Business practices changed only after their ambient cultures—including the law—disallowed such excuses.

Within a true profession, cooperation should outweigh competition, and members would share "information and advice," according to the lead article in a 1921 issue of the *Journal of Accountancy*. Participation in meetings would make such things possible, while nurturing "intimate and cordial social and professional relationships," even "beautiful and enduring friendships." Moreover, by attending meetings, both young and mature practitioners could develop "their mental horizons" and become "fitter and better" at their work. As Carl Nau, the author of the article, put it, "I feel that I am a better accountant and a better man" through this "opportunity of contact with others." Two decades after this declaration of camaraderie, Theodore Jones applied for membership in the Illinois State Society of CPAs, and his experiences highlighted the presumption that such productive relationships required homogeneity. Jones gained admission on the merits of his credentials, but only on the condition that he not attend social events. Jones declined the offer of membership. Almost another two decades later, in 1957, Benjamin King attended his first—and last—dinner with the Maryland State Society of CPAs only to watch everyone leave the table at which he took a seat. The AICPA refused even to debate a 1965 motion against racial discrimination that it passed four years later. In reaction to their exclusion, African-American accountants formed a parallel organization in 1969.[46]

Professional and trade associations' exclusionary practices diminished outsiders' chances for achievement in a variety of ways. Insiders have privileged access to the new knowledge and practices that members develop and that association events and publications disseminate. Employers recognize these benefits and often supplement employees' formal training by supporting their participation in trade and professional organizations. Associations also assist in matching employers with specialized candidates. The AIA and some of its state branches, for instance, established "student associates" in the 1920s to foster contacts between students and potential employers. Yet the same 1923 *Journal of Accountancy* editorial that announced these programs chided young people who complained that they could not get jobs because they had no experience, and that they could not get experience without a job. Youths "must be prepared to face a long period of unremunerative struggle." Young men with connections, however, could apparently be exempt from such struggle and not lose their character.[47]

The first sentence in the first article in the *Journal of Accountancy* summarized the field's 1905 priorities at that early stage as "legal recognition and professional education." The second sentence acknowledged medicine and law as the models for professionalization. To reach this standard, each individual practitioner must aim to be "a man of affairs" who can function as "counsellor and adviser" to business leaders, be deserving of a community's full "respect and confidence," and be "trusted with the handling of delicate and important matters."[48] The cultural archetypes that fit those subjective criteria effectively screened out marginalized people, even those who passed state or firms' own qualifying examinations. Only changes in the nation's culture that placed "respect and confidence" in all citizens could take away CPA firms' traditional rationales for refusing to hire women or African-Americans.

Accounting journals published racial "humor" as part of various convention speeches that drew applause and that editors did not choose to omit.[49] Centuries of racial and gendered humor worked against seeing the targets of the jokes as possible colleagues, as reliable, capable, and trustworthy peers. To avoid taking strangers into their midst, accountants, like other professionals, built institutional walls out of social bricks and legal mortar. People without the social capital—connections and connectability—to pull them over those walls were just as effectively pushed away from opportunities that required certification as if the insiders had used rifles instead of humiliation. As with the protection that personnel departments provided for their employers, the CPAs' licensing system made it easy for these professionals—and easier still for their clients—to avoid strangers knocking at the gates. When courageous outsiders challenged them, decision makers fell back on sanctimonious claims to professional standards, as if those standards were objective and equally accessible.

Clubs as Social Screens

Like other types of voluntary associations, social clubs thrive on their ability to provide social contacts for their members, allowing members to distribute opportunities, develop skills, and conduct negotiations. Whether or not clubs function openly as venues for doing business or exist chiefly for service or recreational purposes, some measure of exclusivity characterizes them all. Like children's clubs, adults' clubs provide members with a sense of being special and safe, conditions conducive for business transactions and for building and using social capital. Thus, E. Digby Baltzell's classic sociological analysis of Philadelphia's pre–World War II "gentlemen" showed that business elites, whose occupations required "organizing and personal influence," joined social clubs more than did other professional elites.[50]

Evidence of the relevance of club access to conducting business is everywhere. No less an authority on management than Charles M.

Schwab, who learned networking at the feet of the master, Andrew Carnegie, hosted lunch in an exclusive dining room with his top executives every Saturday. Allowing "not a word of business" until after lunch, Schwab aimed for open discussion and problem solving afterward. A prominent 1920s management text encouraged businessmen to take meals at clubs or executive dining rooms—both restricted environments—because these were "educational" settings wherein new ideas or problems might be discussed during social exchanges. Sharing daily lunches in such venues would build "better acquaintance and personal interchange." In 1954, *Business Week* ran a laudatory article titled "North, South: You Do Business at the Club." Photographs of two elite clubs showed men in suits, working. In one caption, three men proudly reported that they had "just closed a million-dollar deal." Businessmen, the article concluded, were saving the urban club, "an otherwise outmoded institution," because it provided them with "an excellent place to do business." In his 1959 study of American executives, Osborn Elliott called one of his chapters "Club Men All," pointing out that when an employer decided to support a man's membership application and dues, his colleagues figured that he "ought to be watched. He's a comer."[51]

Club memberships were important socializing costs that mid-twentieth-century firms supported for their executives, either through expense accounts or direct payments. A National Industrial Conference Board study found that twenty-five of forty surveyed companies paid for a wide range of club memberships. *Sports Illustrated* featured business activities in its 1962 series on country clubs. An executive explained that the "club is really a kind of grease, like a fraternity. It makes it easier for you to pick up business." Firms reported hiring socially savvy golfers to "soften up prospective clients" and to "bring in the business that's to be picked up around clubs." As a golf aficionado asked, "How often, after all, does one spend four solid hours with somebody these days?"

Satisfactory Results...

Satisfactory results usually emerge when a Chase officer and one of our customers put their heads together to discuss a particular problem. For Chase service has the advantage of *personal* interest and the willingness to take time to understand *all* the conditions involved.

SERVICE TO BUSINESS

Checking accounts
Commercial loans
Credit, trade and investment information
Money transfers
Collection of cash items
Execution of security orders
Safekeeping of securities
Commercial letters of credit
Travelers credits
Foreign exchange
Corporate trust and agency service
Pension trust service

THE CHASE NATIONAL BANK
OF THE CITY OF NEW YORK
HEAD OFFICE: Pine Street corner of Nassau, New York
Member Federal Deposit Insurance Corporation

Doing business at an exclusive club was a good way to ensure that you were dealing with the right sort of people. Plush surroundings and the steady gaze of a dignified master at business helped ensure "satisfactory results" for high-level banking negotiations. Important networking and negotiating also took place in less grand business venues, like union halls. Exclusiveness mattered more than fine upholstery or costly cigars.

(Courtesy JPMorgan Chase Archives; from *Harvard Business Review* 29, July 1951.)

The golf course "provides a nearly Utopian environment in which friendships can flourish," he said, "alternating companionship and solitude while opening us up to each other." Through such shared experiences, "the game offers us more than friendship. It can become a way for two people to learn about each other and form a relationship that becomes a focal point of their lives."[52]

Social settings, in effect, are fruitful places for those who hold job and contract opportunities, for those who might recommend job candidates, and for those wishing to conduct business. As *Business Week* said about men's clubs in 1954, "exclusiveness is the very basis of their character. Without it, they become glorified restaurants—and lose special meaning for their members." Into the 1960s, that often meant separate clubs for Jewish businessmen, and always for African Americans.[53] And of course people could not be interviewed or participate in negotiations over meals at clubs that refused them entry, much less membership. When *Business Week* photographed men and women in two prominent businessmen's clubs, it commented favorably upon their distinct activities. While not all the men pictured were engaged in business-building activities, none of the women were. The latter were clustered in conversational groups with nary a piece of paper to be seen.[54] Women were not people to be taken seriously within any sort of business network. Allowing women on the clubs' premises in limited roles and spaces only reinforced how different they were from the men who did business there.

Exclusivity protects insiders from outsiders, and it fosters behavioral codes that exaggerate and exacerbate outsiders' otherness. In the mid-twentieth-century club world, odd practices that served to remind members of who could not be considered one of themselves still flourished. One such bizarre event was the Womanless Wedding held in 1953 at the Rotary Club in Greenville, North Carolina. This drag event raised a sizable amount of money for the Girl Scouts, but at the cost of belittling both women and marriage.

"One of the greatest benefits from the wedding," one chronicler of the event recalled, "was the tremendous amount of fellowship accrued to the members. They relaxed, they played, they laughed and talked; they got to know each other much better and they came away from the experience with a new feeling of personal appreciation."[55] How better to strengthen insiders' ties than to mock outsiders and emphasize their differences?

Many companies set up internal social and recreational programs to promote company loyalty and improve performance. In 1920, the *American Management Review*'s precursor, the *Bulletin*, included in a list of personnel departments' duties the organizing and operating of clubs. In addition to categorizing company clubs by sex and age (women's, men's, girls', boys'), the *Bulletin* noted separately firms' country clubs for company elites. That same year, another article in the *Bulletin* promoted "the economic value of company clubs" for advancing "understanding" within various levels of employees and managers. Of 137 firms responding to a survey, most had facilities for their executives to meet and dine. Almost every firm that had facilities in addition to those for the top managers differentiated between workers' and executives' clubs, just as they did between women's and men's clubs. Some "circumstances" resulted in company clubs with separate facilities for "American employees," "Negro employees," and "foreigners." The article maintained that executive clubs operated more for utilitarian than for social purposes, facilitating "debate on company policies" and providing a "palatable lunch."[56] Executives, Americans, Negroes, and foreigners were presumably different types of people with different social, business, and dietary needs. All of these in-house mechanisms minimized social contact between people considered too unlike each other to share social and business interactions.

Although clubs and their members emphasize the social activities when defending the clubs' exclusivity and their nonprofit, tax-exempt status, businesspeople have lobbied for and received income tax exemptions for entertainment, including club expenses, since the first pertinent tax codes came into being in 1916. The phrase "ordinary and necessary" as applied to business activities has ever since been the standard terminology used to describe deductible business expenses, and entertainment costs have always fit under that umbrella. According to a tax expert in 1965, food and beverage expenses were deductible "under circumstances conducive to a business discussion . . . , even if business is not actually discussed." The tax code recognized that building social bonds is the foundation for business success. As a result, a businessperson or employer can deduct club dues as long as the ratio of business to personal use is over fifty percent. In the 1960s, when the codes affecting firms and individuals were tightened, the Sun Oil Company responded to those tax code changes with internal decisions regarding reimbursement that evinced the value that management placed on country club activities. It required keeping records regarding the purpose for each occasion of business use, including companions' names and firms. In 1966, company policy declared dues, initiation fees, and locker fees as the only country club costs other than meals that would be reimbursable. That year, the sliding reimbursement scale gave 120 percent of club expenses to employees with salaries below $8,000 but 150 percent for employees with salaries of $24,000 and up.[57] The firm's benefits from social activities paralleled employees' places on the corporate ladder.

Buffers and Excuses

Opportunities get distributed by pulls and pushes. The language and practices of recruiting, hiring, and promoting in business emphasize pulling "the right sort" onto and up company ladders. Despite strenuous attempts to systematize these activities using apparently objective criteria, personal relationships and social criteria—connections and connectability—still determine who gets pulled into networks, who wins a mentor, and, conversely, who gets pushed out. Over the course of the twentieth century powerful institutions evolved to screen candidates on behalf of business, to help decision makers build contacts with some people and avoid them with others. Personnel systems developed as businesses' internal screens for class, ethnicity, and sex as well as for diligence and ability, while schools, associations, and clubs developed ways to prescreen aspirants for firms. In addition to their providing economic benefits to businesses, these screening systems minimized the likelihood of managers' having to experience the unpleasantness of pushing away people who might well have objective qualifications or be capable of obtaining them, but who failed some test of social acceptability. Managers could therefore tell themselves that the candidates they were developing were objectively the strongest, though in fact they made their selection from a relatively small and homogeneous pool.

Protected by these elaborate buffers, corporate managers were rarely forced to admit to their class, sex, and ethnic biases. When institutionalized buffers failed, however, as they often did for smaller firms, managers and even owners could not avoid pushing someone away solely because of stereotypes and negative social capital. The Los Angeles CPA who refused to hire Talmadge Tillman in 1951, saying bluntly, "You are a Negro, I cannot give you the job" was distressed at being forced to make this face-to-face push against a man whose educational credentials had earned him the job. In such cases, a gatekeeper had to admit to bias when no vocational shortcoming disqualified an applicant. But more often a culture of excuses justified homogeneity. One strategy allowed executives and personnel departments to blame lower-level employees for a reluctance to hire strangers.[58] Another rhetorical device allowed gatekeepers to assert confidently, without remorse or guilt, that whole categories of people did not have "potential."

Just as personnel departments could use their superiors' and/or workforces' prejudices and stereotypes as a basis for their gate-keeping, companies that served other businesses used their clients' supposed prejudices and stereotypes in order to deny their own. Through the 1950s, for instance, bankers generally took for granted that women should work with women's and families' accounts, or in small banks. The president of a Boston bank, for example, contended that businessmen coming into the bank for large transactions would be "put out" if they were referred to a woman. Advertisers accepted female account executives to develop campaigns initially for women's products. The brilliant Helen Lans-

Men and women almost always had distinctly different roles in business prior to the 1980s. Men thought, planned, and executed. Women adorned offices and listened attentively to record the fruits of men's decision making.

(Courtesy Corbis.)

downe blazed a path as J. Walter Thompson Company's representative to Procter and Gamble in the 1910s, allowed through the gates
at first to provide the "woman's point of view." One client in the
1950s refused to see a female advertising account executive a second time because he could not "swear at her," apparently for him
an essential part of negotiations. Especially because the advertising
field never established standards for entry, such as education or examinations, admission criteria remained overtly social. Until the
1960s, therefore, Jewish advertising agents worked almost exclusively for Jewish clients. The gatekeepers in accounting, despite that
field's having laid claim to objective educational and performance
standards, still fell back on blaming clients when occupation-based
buffers failed to protect them from strangers. As one accounting
firm executive said in the 1950s, "I could no more send a woman
on that audit job than I could send a negro [sic] although I use both
very effectively within the office."[59]

All these cases of passing the buck presumed a shared culture of
biases and stereotypes. Mainstream practitioners and business theorists alike simply assumed that other businesspeople shared their
attitudes. A 1962 study showed that most accounting firms' recruiters who used the client excuse to deny positions to Asian and African Americans had never actually asked their clients about their
preferences. In 1964 the vast majority of managers believed that integrating management would not affect profits and that it would
improve a firm's public image; but they expected "adverse effects"
in "employee morale." Blanket disqualifications protected gatekeepers from having to make decisions against individuals. They
could instead simply pull in those with whom they felt comfortable
and blame others for pushing out the rest. Using the excuse that
they wished to avoid the risk of offending a potential source of
business had little cost—merely a stranger's prospects for earning
a respectable living. As long as ignoring or pushing aside those
strangers carried no risk and slight moral burden, it made perfect

sense to preserve the status quo. Everything in mainstream businesspeople's social and vocational lives reinforced their stereotypical beliefs about themselves and others and buffered them from the harsh consequences of their behavior. In 1965, psychologist Kenneth Clark pointed out that "privileged individuals may understandably need to shield themselves from the inevitable conflict and pain which would result from acceptance of the fact that they *are* accessories to profound injustice."[60] Insensitivity built cocoons that protected their bearers from worries about what harm they did to others. Today's so-called political correctness breaks up those old, comforting cocoons, reminding us that disrespect has its costs.

Only dramatic changes in the legal and cultural spheres could render excuses for discrimination invalid and make them costly. The 1960s brought just such a change. Millions of previously unheard voices asked why a system that lauded the individual in the abstract refused to evaluate them as individuals. Why did so many layers of screens and buffers keep them away from contact with the people who had the authority to open the gates? People inside and outside of business challenged the institutionalized mechanisms for recruiting, hiring, and promoting that perpetuated homogeneity. Decision makers could no longer deny that they participated in systems that were prejudicial, not meritocratic.

Civil rights activists, later joined by feminists, insisted that the nation recognize and acknowledge the social foundations of business achievement and failure. When the legal and cultural underpinning finally changed, the old excuses no longer held. The buffers that protected decision makers from contact with outsiders and exacerbated the unconnectability of those outsiders slowly began to lose their legitimacy. As one executive put it in 1966: "The luxury of discrimination as I've practiced it is that I don't have to worry about Negroes. But it looks like times are changing. . . . It looks like I'm going to have to hire some Negroes and learn how to manage them."[61] That wasn't all he was going to have to learn.

CHAPTER 5

The Business of Integration

Jerome H. Holland graduated from Cornell University in 1939. He was an elected member of both junior and senior honorary societies and an acclaimed All-American football star. Yet industrial recruiters interviewed every member of his class with a comparable record except him, and only he had not received at least one job offer. A black man, Holland was an alien to recruiters looking for business "potential." Like many other well-educated African Americans, Holland then looked to the nonbusiness professions for his livelihood. He earned a master's degree from Cornell, then a doctorate from the University of Pennsylvania. He became the president of Delaware State College, then of Hampton Institute, a predominantly black college in Virginia. In his book *Black Opportunity,* published in 1969, Holland observed that the previous spring 265 companies had sent recruiters to Hampton Institute, where they interviewed all seniors in the business and technology departments. At least 85 percent of the African-American graduates received job offers at professional, technical, or managerial levels, with salaries equal to those offered to their white counterparts. Such a transformation would have been dramatic enough in comparison to 1939, but the jump from zero interviews to a full schedule at Hampton Institute had come only since 1960! A dozen industrial recruiters had begun the shift by coming to Holland's school in 1961.[1] Holland had witnessed the turning point of business's integration.

Holland considered himself an optimist. He wrote in 1969 that "this new partnership between educated Negroes and corporate industry" was a "mirror of hope." The advances of the 1960s had amounted to a "social revolution that can provide this nation with an image of democracy that may exceed our expectations." Holland credited the remarkable change in part to industry's need for technically competent personnel. But only the decade's civil rights progress had enabled racial minorities to drive through what he called the "breach" in what had been an "unscalable wall that denied all Negroes opportunity to participate on any but the lowest level in the great industrial complex that is the backbone of the American economy." Like everyone working for that progress, Holland redefined "the Negro problem" as an American problem, the failure to "make democracy a *universal* practice, rather than a system that whites will die to defend for themselves and fight to deny to others." He also knew that even if the walls of discrimination came down altogether, and if no one any longer pushed African Americans away from opportunity, black Americans had to be prepared to move into the jobs suddenly available to them. The circularity of the problem was daunting. Disadvantaged people would prepare themselves and their children to the extent that they could be inspired—"'sold' on the idea that there is a place for them." This required "special help," thought Holland—community organizations' and leaders' recruiting and motivating both parents and youths, and industry's offering internships, scholarships, and advice to predominantly African-American colleges and other institutions out of the mainstream. Like many Americans, Holland looked to business as "the sector of the society that *gets things done*."[2] With new laws and a changing cultural climate as incentives, business was a key arena where integration had to start.

Holland's experiences straddled the history of social capital in business from the years before World War II to the late 1960s. During those years, layers of constraints on unconnected individuals peeled away slowly, sometimes painfully, revealing still potent layers as they fell. In the mid-twentieth century, class barriers against white male mobility diminished, spreading connectability more widely than before, especially in bureaucratic workplaces. In particular, the GI Bill helped millions of men move onto corporate ladders by virtue of a college degree, which allowed them to pass through initial personnel screenings. Postwar job growth for skilled tradesmen likewise generated attractive opportunities for many men.

This progress made more visible the still overwhelming discrimination that locked disadvantaged minorities and women out altogether. As a result, civil rights advocates challenged the nation to bring its realities into line with the Cold War's much lauded American creed and business's claims to meritocracy. Reactions to state and federal laws and rulings in the 1960s and 1970s opened up opportunities as employers and unions moved, sometimes reluctantly, toward compliance. Each victory against old barriers reduced exclusion, or "push" discrimination. However, success in business requires pull, too, so reducing push alone did not gain equal mobility for outsiders. The National Urban League worked in the business realm throughout the twentieth century, attempting both to reduce push and to increase pull for African Americans. With the deepening racial crisis of the 1960s, public and private agencies worked with employers to institutionalize pull strategies—often called "affirmative action"—to infuse synthetic social capital into long-disadvantaged groups. At least initially, supporting integration through affirmative action in recruiting and hiring seemed to many in business to advance the American dream of fulfilling each individual's potential.

Different Angles on the American Dream

As much as the Great Depression buffeted the American Dream, the public sector did make some progress toward reducing social and cultural barriers against marginalized people. The New Deal appointed many "firsts"—including working-class activists, women, and African Americans—into cabinet and other top federal positions, with exhortations, if not expectations, that local and regional agencies should follow suit. In the business world, however, precious little changed. Then came World War II. Despite the standard cliché, the war did not end the Depression. Federal deficit spending, distributed broadly through the nation's ranks, did. Just as it took war to propel that spending, the exigencies of war, especially the shortage of preferred white male workers in suddenly bustling industries, opened widespread opportunities for women and African Americans. A few federal directives about distributing the rewards of work helped as well. In particular, responding to pressures from African-American organizations that were stronger than those during World War I, President Franklin D. Roosevelt issued Executive Order 8802 on July 25, 1941, forbidding discrimination by race, color, creed, or national origin in defense industries. In a related effort to ensure national unity under emergency conditions, FDR also required a nondiscrimination clause in all defense contracts. The president's Fair Employment Practices Committee (FEPC) and its successor worked until mid-1946, examining over twelve thousand cases and ameliorating over five thousand cases of discriminatory practices by contractors and unions; these included racially differentiated job advertisements, applications, job placements, and pro-

Railroad executives and locomotive engineers came in all shapes, sizes, and hat styles in the 1940s. But they came in only one sex and one color.

(Courtesy Colorado Historical Society.)

motions. State FEPCs achieved significant progress as well, and continued after the federal FEPC's strangulation by its congressional opponents.[3]

Stories of how women and African Americans contributed their labors and abilities to the war effort are legion. They often managed to earn more than they ever had before, although their pay was lower than that of the white men they replaced and was won often under difficult conditions, including harassment.[4] Even after their welcome into the job corps was rescinded after the war, the expectations of both women and African Americans never quite returned to "normal." The war and the prosperity that followed allowed marginalized people to begin to imagine a world of opportunities in which they could share. Riding a streetcar during the war, a little boy noticed admiringly that its driver was African American, like him; this man was the first African American the boy had seen driving a public conveyance. His mother explained this wonder as a result of the war's requiring that the nation "use all the men we can get—even Negro men!" The boy then asked hopefully, "Will there be a war on when I get big, Mommy?"[5] Nothing fuels ambition better than hope and imagination based on appealing models. In turn, frustration can fuel activism once people begin to imagine worlds beyond their own.

Postwar Opportunities

In the decade after World War II it looked to most Americans as though the American Dream had come true, or was about to. The postwar boom generated vast opportunities for so many people from such diverse backgrounds that opportunity and success for many truly seemed to depend on individual ability and effort—with a dash of luck thrown into the mix. Trying to avoid the problems that soldiers, and therefore the nation, had faced after the First World War, the Servicemen's Readjustment Act of 1944 (the GI Bill of Rights) offered eligible veterans assistance for buying houses, unemployment compensation, and financial aid for education, including tuition and stipends. Half of the 15 million eligible veterans took advantage of some form of training, with 2.2 million of them moving into higher education.

James Conant, longtime president of Harvard University, had led opposition to the higher education part of the bill. He feared "flooding" colleges with the "least capable among the new generation."[6] As it turned out, the veterans raised educational standards all across the country, including at Harvard. Even Conant admitted, years later, that the veterans had contributed to correcting what he had criticized back in 1940 as the "hereditary class" that had dominated higher education. The generous benefits of the first GI Bill remarkably expanded the ranks of people who could attend top schools. Harvard, for example, almost doubled its enrollment in 1946. Five percent of the top fully accredited colleges and universities enrolled 41 percent of the veterans in higher education, dramatically changing those schools' class and ethnic mix. Over 90 percent of the Harvard Business School's class of 1949 entered in 1947 as veterans, 70 percent having been commissioned officers. More than a tenth of this elite-in-training had blue-collar origins, and most came from the middle classes (although about a quarter of the 95 percent in the business school's class of 1949 who already had college degrees had elite college backgrounds). This remarkable new diversity, however, had its limits—the same limits that the postwar boom exhibited in every arena and that defined the new mainstream that was taking shape. Harvard Business School's class of 1949, consisting of more than seven hundred individuals selected from about 2,300 applicants, included no women, only one African American, and a few Asian Americans, plus a few wealthy non-American Asians. Shared wartime and school experiences overcame class differences; military grooming had already eliminated most visual distinctions among them. Many of them later agreed that the content of their courses had less to do with their later business success than did the relationships and ambitions they forged in those intense years in school. As one of their number noted decades later, "Something happened in our lives at the business school that made us very important to each other." Twenty-five years later, they recalled helpful lessons they had learned from each other, in everything from style of dress to job searching.[7] The social capital this peer network built served them all very well as they prepared to take on a future of business challenges.

The GI Bill combined with developments in corporations to make postsecondary education a prerequisite to entering management and advancing therein. Only rarely after the mid-1940s did anyone rise to executive status without some college experience. Postsecondary degrees provided corporate personnel processes with an easy first screen for applicants to white-collar positions, though this screen was originally set up for those belonging to what had been the much smaller prewar middle and upper classes. Thus, veterans' mobility and large, bureaucratized personnel systems coincided with, and helped to fuel, the post–World War II economic boom and its opportunities. Most of the members of the Harvard Business School class of 1949 took a first job that paid less than $75 weekly (about $28,000 annually at turn-of-the-millennium rates).[8] For these and other white males, including those aiming for the skilled trades, these jobs were the entry to what appeared to be a wide-open arena of merit-based opportunities with lowered class barriers. A well-regarded 1955 study of occupational mobility celebrated these dramatic changes in mobility over a single generation for "sons of men from the wrong side of the tracks."[9]

By war's end, nearly a century of efforts to rationalize and systematize corporate personnel practices had convinced many that the system was equitable. With anti-Semitism and prejudices against southern and eastern Europeans somewhat reduced after Americans' experience of World War II, "office politics" seemed to affect individual workers, and not treat entire groups unfairly. When men saw themselves passed up for hiring or promotions by other men who belonged to the same demographic type, they could take those events to be idiosyncratic rather than systemic. Such an interpretation minimized complaints about the system. Likewise, raw nepotism or a boss's whims might foster resentment more than feelings of group-based inadequacy. Other than provoking the eternal cry of modern business—that objectivity should reign—such offenses to meritocracy rarely drew people into challenging the system or its underlying beliefs. With those who were still marginalized, however, constant rejections and limitations dominated their work lives and those of everyone like them. How could they not begin to challenge national declarations about equal opportunity that repeatedly contradicted their own experiences?

Postwar Limitations

Those outside dominant groups still looked at the American Dream through a fog after World War II, its unclear shape raising both expectations and frustrations. Marginalized employees lost both white- and blue-collar gains from wartime service in the workplace; they had gained the most in occupations that had expanded the most during wartime and therefore shrank the most thereafter. Although many state agencies continued to do good work to fight discrimination, political battles had destroyed the FEPC by 1946, with some claiming that the committee's working for economic equality for African Americans indicated communist leanings. In the blue-collar world where women and African Americans had made some wartime gains, they were the last hired and so were the first fired, whether because of unions' seniority rules or outright discrimination in favor of returning white men. Overall, the GI Bill fit the culture more than it changed it, disadvantaging women, African

Americans, and most of the working class relative to middle- and upper-class white men.[10]

Had anyone wondered who owned the opportunities for success in the American mainstream, the decade after World War II made it clear. The blue- and white-collar opportunities that drove social and occupational mobility for white males and their families shined a light everywhere. By reducing class barriers among white males, this wave of mobility illuminated the most basic criterion for workplace success: white manhood. So profound was the effect of this opportunity for white males that, by the end of the century, long-term poverty would be overwhelmingly black or female, or both. Surrounded in every medium of popular culture by representations of others' success, African-American men and women of all races lost vocational stature by comparison, and most lost absolutely. African Americans suffered from a double impact as integration in consumer markets began to reduce entrepreneurial opportunities that had existed behind the wall of segregation. By the late 1950s, African-American insurance companies, retailers, hotels, sports-related businesses, and newspapers had begun to shrink. They lost their hold on their own communities' markets as white firms encroached on them. Although more and more white firms were eager to accept African-American consumers' dollars, they remained unwilling, as a rule, to accept African-American employees for management positions. Too often, if they hired African Americans at all, it was for low-skilled work or as window dressing to attract or reassure consumers in an African-American community.[11]

Thus, as the 1950s boom flourished, African Americans and women saw their workplace opportunities move in reverse relative to the prosperity that the nation's loudest voices proclaimed as proof of the merits of the American economic system. Although white women seem not to have objected routinely to either domesticity or sex-typed job assignments in the 1950s, disadvantaged-minority men and women and their advocates increasingly criticized the systemic discrimination that deprived them of opportunities to share in the abundance they saw around them. Myths do matter, and they can serve opposing masters. Individualist convictions and faith in equal opportunity began to empower those who had neither connections nor advantages in the workplace. After the United States' second war to make the world safe for democracy, African Americans pointed out to the nation the gaps between its principles and its practices. Such gaps between ideals and realities can drive deep reforms if they become sufficiently visible.[12] The gaps for disadvantaged minorities, including Jews, became apparent in the decade leading up to the Civil Rights Act of 1964. In the following decade, the constraints on women—in business and elsewhere—became apparent as well. Meeting the challenges of these two gaps required changing some laws and practices, applying others fairly, and moving toward a new understanding of how success happened.

The National Urban League

Almost a century ago, in 1911, the National Urban League (NUL) began building synthetic networks for people, largely but not exclusively African Americans, with minimal or even negative access to helpful background, authority, and peer networks. Synthetic networks operate through institutions to provide people having little access to social capital with some combination of role models and mentors, practical and social skills, and liaisons with the gatekeepers of opportunity. Like its precursor organizations, the League advanced "racial progress" primarily by developing means for economic advancement in concert with mainstream supporters. Unlike many other twentieth-century organizations promoting African Americans' rights and material conditions, the League did not emphasize political problems and political measures, focusing instead on private activities. With the Great Migration of African Americans into northern cities before, during, and after World War I, the League settled on vocational placement as its major, ongoing focus.[13]

Synthetic Networks and Networking

As the League and its local affiliates began to grapple with the challenge of finding jobs and arranging training for disadvantaged minorities newly confronting urban life, they built patterns that would serve their clients and communities through the century. The League took on the networking roles that more fortunate migrants to cities—like Andrew Carnegie's family, for example—had at their disposal. Recognizing, for instance, that most rural migrants arrived in a city without jobs or employment networks, the NUL began to form liaisons with employers and unions. They introduced their clients to people who controlled jobs. At the same time, local and national branches of the League instructed their clients on urban dangers and cultural expectations, while they provided or arranged for job training. Doing the customary tasks of background, authority, and peer networks, some local affiliates advised their clients in diet, finance, etiquette on and off the job, dress, and hygiene. They held social gatherings and organized sports and recreational events for adults and children alike.[14]

In taking on these customary networking roles as quasi-professional tasks, the NUL and its staffers built and operated networks that were synthetic in the dual senses of being devised and blended. For instance, their mentorlike messages often sounded parental in their admonitions that each migrant held the reputation of the whole race on his or her shoulders. As the Chicago Urban League exhorted African Americans who pioneered in mainstream firms, "Remember that the race, in this new work, is on trial in you."[15] After World War II and the changes that more politically active advocates wrought on the nation's politics, the NUL became a major factor in expanding the opportunities for African Americans, applying the lessons of its earlier decades.

Crashing the Color Line

Ambition cannot exist without hope, and hope must be nurtured. The little African-American boy who innocently hoped for war so that he could have the opportunity to drive a streetcar reminds us that the successful people whom Benjamin Franklin and Andrew Carnegie noticed as youths looked like them. Their role models spoke to them encouragingly, guided them, and often created opportunities for them. As a result, Franklin and Carnegie could imagine futures bright enough to warrant their best efforts. In contrast, the Urban League's clients faced overwhelming disadvantages at obtaining jobs due to low skill levels compounded by discrimination, and they lacked useful role models for corporate and blue-collar achievements. In struggling to prevent abject hopelessness among its communities, the League in the 1930s began a series of annual campaigns, combining publicity and education to augment vocational training. The NUL's Vocational Opportunity Campaign (VOC) tried to counter the often well-meaning but conservative school counselors who endorsed "realistic" goals and thereby discouraged African-American youths from raising their expectations and improving their skills. As a League document put it, "vocational guidance . . . may become another technique by which a minority is encouraged to tolerate and thus perpetuate its restrictive handicaps." The VOC and a wide range of NUL efforts sought to enlighten more pessimistic authority figures and strengthen the optimistic ones in order to inspire youths' ambition and self-discipline while providing them with opportunities to earn credentials. Even when people could not get jobs, the League insisted that they should learn job and life skills so they could contribute to the well-being of the community and strengthen the collective possibilities once prosperity returned. The annual VOC themes therefore were devised with a forward orientation: in 1932, for example, the theme was "After the Depression—What?"; in 1944 and 1945, it was "The Future Is Yours—Plan and Prepare."[16]

The League intensified its work with the war, and the potential of postwar prosperity motivated even greater efforts. Building on earlier successes, the League and its advisors theorized that employers' experiences with minority employees determined their hiring attitudes, and they speculated that positive experiences could ameliorate discriminatory hiring patterns. The problem, of course, was that most employers had only known African-American workers in low-skilled positions. In March 1947, a confidential internal memo proposed a program to break that stereotype. The NUL and its affiliates would "locate exceptionally qualified" young people, then carefully work with employers to place a small number "in jobs where they will have the fullest possible opportunity for advancement and self-improvement." The League would monitor "progress" and its impact on the attitudes of both employers and "white fellow workers." Setting up this Pilot Placement Project (PPP) required the League to collect information on "highly trained people who can be available for the kind of placement we want to make" and to persuade prospective employers to "cooperate." The NUL would canvass its local affiliates and colleges, for whom it already provided placement services, to build the files. It would "use our present industrial and commercial contacts wherever possible," and expand on those contacts. League board member Winthrop Rockefeller applied his family's funds, business sense, and contacts on behalf of the PPP. Knowing full well the power of personal connections and commitment, he recommended in 1946 that the League invite officers of top firms to join a Commerce and Industry Advisory Council. The benefits of this strategy were immediately evident, as by 1950 twenty-five of the nation's largest employers were participating in PPP, and the League had frequent and direct contacts with about two hundred national corporations.[17]

Guidance and placement are core workplace functions of background, authority, and peer networks, whether these networks be synthetic or customary. The first annual report on PPP recognized the novelty of systematically building and using networks of contacts on behalf of people normally excluded from such practices. The successful placements resulted in "no startling revelations." Instead, they reinforced the meritocratic principle that "where people are employed on the basis of ability . . . , and where employers and management people have the decency and courage to recognize this fact [then] employment of all people becomes a matter of personnel policy rather than a so-called 'experiment.'" PPP had already "become a vital force and concept for the integration of qualified Negro workers." It was "a democratic implement" that would improve the whole economy. It could give "real meaning" to "our democratic principles" by defeating traditional barriers to placing qualified people and making "ability alone . . . the sole criterion for the advancement of a worker in an organization, regardless of his race, religion, or national origin."[18]

This expression of urgency and achievement used the contemporary discourses of democratic opportunity and meritocratic personnel management. Yet only NUL's synthetic networks made possible employers' use of objective personnel standards to hire people who had no relevant social capital of their own. So, in a sense, the League reduced the effects of negative social capital, but only by interjecting its own contacts with employers while recruiting and vetting candidates as a sympathetic, surrogate gatekeeper. With luck, the "pilots" so placed could begin to build social capital through more traditional networks for their communities. Such strategic constructions of synthetic networks, with the NUL at the nexus, confirmed its leaders' understanding that they had to create connections deliberately and formally between potential employers and worthy candidates who lacked any other means of entry. In this way some African-American workers managed to "crash the color line," proving their abilities while providing role models and connectability for younger people. But the number of these pilot placements never grew large enough to be self-sustaining. Frustrations with what looked like tokenism to some activists fueled more aggressive civil rights activities as the 1950s wore on.[19]

Throughout the ensuing decades, vocational guidance reform and education remained a focal issue for the League at national and local levels, as it built mechanisms that could mimic the services of customary networks. The Supreme Court's 1954 *Brown v. Board of Education* decision brought new hope to NUL reformers, but they recognized that they had to take that hope into communities where youths' talents had lain fallow for too long. The League and others also understood that organized synthetic networks would have to compensate for deficiencies in background networks from families, neighbors, educational preparation, and so on, relative to the mainstream business world. Tomorrow's Scientists and Technicians (TST) was one such campaign. Begun in 1958, TST embodied League efforts to inspire ambition in a direction pertinent to the post-Sputnik, post-*Brown* era. It addressed children's needs for a positive and inspiring "adult image" and close interactions with "adults from whom boys and girls can get inspiration." NUL president Theodore W. Kheel aimed to provide children "with the additional guidance, and with the incentives that will enable them to get the most out of their schooling, mature their talents, and become equipped to serve the nation's need." TST, like other League activities, tried to overcome the disadvantages children faced because of dispirited parents who could not provide the encouragement, confidence, and coaching that background networks routinely gave to children in the mainstream of American culture. Kheel labeled this program "a challenge to adult community leadership to discover talented youth in their midst." Local Urban Leagues targeted parents by sending volunteers to visit and "enlist their support."[20]

Mobilizing what we now call networks on behalf of disadvantaged people, the League repeatedly urged influential African-American adult fraternities and sororities to engage their members as volunteers. They especially sought volunteer role models and mentors, although not using those terms yet, to supplement unhopeful and unhelpful background networks. In this vein, a chapter of the prominent Delta Sigma Theta Sorority reported on a 1958 project to "motivate a selected group of pupils of good potential toward higher achievement, and to help them establish realistic goals which utilize their abilities." The women intended to visit high school students' homes to talk with parents about future opportunities open to their children, hoping to induce the parents' "encouragement of their children to work toward achievement of their goals." Individual members of the sorority should form one-to-one relationships with students, building "personal contact" with students, their parents, and school authorities.[21]

In a typical appeal, Guichard Parris, director of promotion and publicity for the NUL, lamented to the prestigious Alpha Gamma Lambda Fraternity the "tendency among non-white youth" to "drift into adult employment rather than to train for specific careers in line with their interests and abilities." Citing the 1954 *Brown* decision, Parris looked forward to improved access to both education and jobs for minority children, but they "must have incentive." That had to come from the community, in the way that majority children benefited from their communities. He called for "youth guidance that is based on the use of adult leadership resources" to provide motivation and direction. TST offered one venue, but "adult encouragement and guidance" in any form was essential. He urged "Alpha men" to "develop wholesome friendships" with boys interested in their occupations. Success required "self-assurance, poise, perseverance," and other "personal qualities" that must be taught by example and "assurance" that well-placed efforts could "reap rewards" and not just lead to frustration. The fraternity members should also provide visits to college campuses, tutoring, and discussions about options—part of mainstream family routines unavailable to most disadvantaged youths.[22]

By the mid-1950s, then, national and local branches of the NUL had developed social capital mechanisms based on lessons they had learned from their communities' histories of organization and what they saw routinely at work in the mainstream culture. For instance, when a 1954 proposal from the Akron Urban League affiliate recommended that the NUL work with the Frontiers of America, an African-American men's organization, on a new vocational guidance program, Ann Tanneyhill, a brilliant and dedicated director of NUL programs, wrote in the margins, "Program modeled after Kiwanis and Rotary, etc."[23] While not using the terms, the NUL sought to provide connectability, connections, mentors, and role models to people whose own background, authority, and peer networks failed to provide such things.

Eli Ginzberg, one of the nation's leading researchers on workforce economics and sociology and director of Columbia University's Eisenhower Center for Conservation of Human Resources from 1950 into the 1990s, worked with the NUL. Following his initial contacts with the League, Ginzberg featured racial and, later, gender issues in the center's work. His seminal 1956 book, *The Negro Potential*, predicted that "artificial employment barriers" would gradually fall, but that disadvantaged minorities would have to develop their abilities before they could benefit from expanding opportunities. Conversely, however, until their opportunities for jobs, housing, and education improved, financial and psychological investments in education made little sense. Moreover, "basic preparation for school and for work occurs within the family, the neighborhood, and the community." Ginzberg noted the contrast with white workers, who gained work skills through both informal and formal means, on and off jobs, inside and outside of unions. He proposed that African-American communities take responsibility for preparing children for education and called for increased public resources for all levels of that education. In keeping with the Supreme Court's 1954 call for full integration of education, Ginzberg asserted that "shared experience is a prerequisite for true equality of opportunity."[24]

Although Whitney M. Young Jr. did not have the social capital lexicon at hand, he understood the concepts and kept his focus on building networks and relationships within business to generate opportunities. He became executive director of the League's national office in 1961. Through the following years of intense civil rights activities, he and the NUL stuck to their program of fighting racial disadvantages through interracial cooperation, with integration the highest priority, despite many critics who urged them on to greater militancy. In a 1966 interview subtitled "Powerful Forces for Integration Will Rally against 'Black Power'," Young asked whether he should get off his commuter train in Harlem to "cuss out Whitey to show I'm tough? That will get me a lot of publicity." Or instead, should he "go downtown to the office and call up officials at Ford or General Motors and work on getting 10,000 jobs for unemployed Negroes?" He announced that he was about to tour Europe with nineteen U.S. business leaders, including Henry Ford II and Roger Blough of U.S. Steel. "In the casual give-and-take of a trip like this, . . . I'll be able to say some things to these men."[25]

Title VII

Heroics and doggedness combined to challenge the nation to begin aligning its realities with its ideals. By 1955, African-American unemployment rates had risen from their 1953 low to double that of whites. In 1954, African Americans' median incomes had risen to more than half those of the white population; by 1958 proportional incomes had declined again to below half.[26] Hyperindividualism and anticommunism's constant drone about equal opportunity contrasted starkly with the realities of African-American lives, driving demands for reducing the disparities. Martin Luther King Jr. led campaigns that showed mainstream America the dignity with which African Americans met inequity and brutality. Formal and informal groups pursued civil rights in courts, streets, legislatures, public agencies, schools, and public opinion, sometimes by getting on and sometimes by staying off buses. Moreover, two decades of action by state and national FEPCs had shown time and again that, with few exceptions, strikes and riots did *not* follow from enforced workplace integration, unlike the intense reaction to school and other venues of integration. When bosses firmly called for compliance, workers avoided confrontation that would have violated law and humanity, even in the face of custom and prejudice. Concurrently, popular media began to present racial minorities in less stereotypical modes than they had in past decades. Public figures such as Marian Anderson, Jackie Robinson, and Ralph Bunche helped change attitudes, increasing visibility and respect for African Americans within the white majority culture. Congress had debated equal employment opportunity bills since 1942; finally, in response to activism, public opinion evolved to make the legislation both possible and urgent.[27] The 1964 Civil Rights Act and later revisions in effect made into law beliefs about the priority of individual abilities in distributing access to the workplace.

Title VII of the 1964 law set new national standards for how workers would be recruited, screened, hired, fired, and promoted in the United States. Although enforcement suffered from the reform legislation's underfunding, ambiguity, and built-in impotence, Title VII committed the law of the land to eliminating what had been the most impenetrable and broadly accepted occupational screens: race, sex, color, religion, and national origin. Title VII redirected the history of social capital by disallowing an entire system and its traditions of distributing opportunity according to presumptions about who qualified for what and why. It required that employers and unions and, after 1972, schools and public-sector employers redesign their initial screens to fit skills and characteristics certifiably linked to job performance. Practices formerly taken for granted were finally out of alignment with both the law and mainstream rhetoric about meritocracy.

Blue Ladders and White Screens

Civil rights battles in blue-collar arenas brought powerful social capital mechanisms to the fore. Skilled blue-collar workers, whether unionized or not, rode the post–World War II boom to new levels of affluence and esteem. Like other postwar gains, however, most of these benefits of rising prosperity were distributed unevenly across ethnicity and sex. As gateways to well-paid jobs that did not require college degrees or sedentary work, skilled labor workplaces and unions became high-profile targets for equal employment opportunity efforts as civil rights reforms intensified. The national Equal Employment Opportunity Commission (EEOC) began work July 2, 1965, but state agencies and activist organizations had already built up momentum. The results of civil rights efforts were mixed, however, because unions have never been of one type; some are among African Americans' best allies, while others are their worst antagonists. As unions struggled to gain fair and reasonable conditions and compensation for their members, they sometimes sought solidarity with all workers and sometimes fiercely drew lines to protect their own.[28]

Unions' longtime customs and interest in social capital combined to perpetuate network-based mechanisms. Ancient practices were still in operation in the mid-twentieth century with labels that carried centuries of proud tradition. As in Benjamin Franklin's day, an apprentice held the first rung on the ladder toward manly competence; a journeyman's wages could support a family; and a master could be his own man.[29] In some labor markets, unions have often taken on gatekeeper functions, controlling access to occupations by controlling apprenticeship opportunities. In 1876, a *New York Times* editorial rather hyperbolically attacked trade unions for trying to raise the price of adult labor by driving "boys who might be taught some useful trade into the overcrowded ranks of unskilled labor" or even "into idleness and vagrancy." Constricting competition is a time-honored means of influencing one's livelihood, practiced no more by working-class laborers than by merchants, doctors, and industrialists. It can also protect opportunities for members of one's background networks, just as inheritance laws facilitate the bequeathing of other assets. A union man's 1963 letter to the *New York Times* enjoined civil rights debates by eloquently reinforcing the link between property and livelihood, between financial capital and social capital. Charles Kelly wrote to protect his right "to follow a centuries-old tradition and sponsor my sons for an apprenticeship." He objected to laws that condemned his choosing "a son over all others" as racial discrimination when men who "leave their sons money, . . . large investments, . . . business connections, . . . a profession" have the community's respect. His trade was his "only one worthwhile thing to give."[30] As long as union members could not see themselves as part of the same community with a set of strangers, they objected to sharing their scarce resources—their jobs—and thereby reducing the value of their hard-won social capital.

To the extent that unions sought to gain and maintain control over job and training opportunities, they became targets of civil rights actions.[31] Of all the unions' practices, outright exclusion from entry dominated the integrationists' attention. The President's Committee on Equal Employment Opportunity (PCEEO) sponsored a 1962 conference and published a report titled *The American Dream—Equal Opportunity.* One workshop presentation at

Blue-collar workers lacked the buffers, such as prerequisite college degrees, that often protected white-collar employers and employees from having to make explicit their racial barriers to entry. These union members filled a South Carolina auditorium in 1956 "to hold the color line."

the conference was called "Apprenticeship and Training—An Economic Key"; the speaker "forcibly reminded" everyone about the lack of progress in equalizing "opportunity in apprenticeships," and urged unions "to engage in deep introspection on this issue." Within the next four years, union leaders, the EEOC, courts, and business management did succeed in eliminating discriminatory language from union rules, but this by itself had little effect on actual practices. The EEOC could not even reform common and obvious "push" mechanisms of exclusion, including locals' requiring a membership vote to admit an applicant; oral tests that always failed African Americans who passed written tests; written tests given only to African Americans that asked highly specialized and largely irrelevant questions; and differential rankings on exams. Even less could the EEOC influence the most frequent "pull" mechanism of discrimination: the requirement of sponsorship by one or more members for membership and apprenticeships. Although this mechanism could discriminate against anyone without background networks of family or friends in a local, it disproportionately blocked applicants who could not possibly find or make an ally of men on the inside.[32] Compelling union locals to pull anyone into their ranks violated ancient traditions and often turned union members against civil rights causes.

Urban League chapters worked diligently to integrate their constituents into union locals. At the end of 1964, for instance, a national associate director wrote a background paper for the Community Action Assembly in which he decried the training barriers in apprenticeships as "most unyielding to the Negro's efforts to upgrade his skills. Many persons consider the lack of apprenticeship opportunities the greatest tragedy facing Negro youth who wish employment in some areas." Almost two years later, the draft for an NUL brochure explained for African-American teenagers why so few of their own were employed as skilled craftsmen, citing unions' "father and son tradition." The draft explained what it meant to be an apprentice and a journeyman, what kinds of "words [were] used to talk about apprenticeship," and how the new civil rights laws had already given "minority youths" an opportunity to pass exams to enter apprenticeships.[33]

Why, then, after a decade of trying to enforce the 1964 Civil Rights Act by integrating minority youths into apprentice programs did the National Labor Director for the NAACP write a scathing critique of "apprenticeship outreach" programs? Herbert Hill was angry because African-American and Spanish-speaking teenagers, both male and female, still suffered unemployment rates more than twice that for others. He targeted the "rigid control of training and access to employment by many labor unions committed to perpetuating the racial status quo." These "voluntary associations" had become "a private sovereignty." Title VII had forced unions into giving "the illusion of compliance," but control over apprenticeship programs and job referrals, especially in the building and construction trades, continued to block integration. Hill found such illusions of compliance in a speech by George Meany, in which Meany announced that the AFL-CIO's "Outreach Program" was "reaching out and bringing these people in." Although Hill did not choose to highlight the phrase "these people," it clearly manifests the problem: apparently, Meany felt that African Americans remained strangers to his constituents even as he attempted to put the most positive front on the unions' intentions. Hill cited case after case where men dropped out of apprenticeship programs because they had been assigned to janitorial tasks or low-skilled jobs, or to jobs out of reach to people without automobiles; or they had been graded differentially on tests, or workers had refused to cooperate with trainees, and so on.[34]

Hill stated bluntly that "the basic concept of the Outreach program is a fallacy." This and similar programs created a false sense of hope among African-American trainees because they led these workers to expect to gain respected and well-paid jobs. Construction workers, Hill pointed out, almost always received their training on the job, entering through the "back door" of family and neighborhood sponsorship and rarely having to take a test to get standing. Instead, this Outreach program amounted to a "slow and often futile apprenticeship ladder" that magnified its participants' alienness from their white coworkers. In his extensively documented report, Hill cited acts of violence and humiliation against those who persisted in seeking work in a world that others claimed as their own.[35] Like the synthetic networks that the Urban League constructed, these hard-won apprenticeships were the result of artificial processes that did not facilitate natural job entry into environments where background networks provided access to authority and peer networks.

To resolve "much mutual misunderstanding between the apprenticeship establishment and the civil rights movement," the federal Office of Manpower Policy, Evaluation, and Research sponsored a study that in effect contrasted synthetic with customary networks. The resulting 1967 report summarized the purposes of apprenticeship for union memberships, including the idea of its "maintaining craft identity." The report noted that African-American youths fared less well in apprenticeship programs of all varieties than white youths, attributing this to "poor discipline." Often "some organization [must] see Negro youngsters through the difficult and uncertain process of making proper application to apprenticeship programs, preparing them to take the tests, and seeing to it that they develop proper work habits once they are on the job." But then, immediately following this rather negative portrayal, the study acknowledged that, "Of course, white youngsters also need this kind of attention, but they are more likely to get it from friends or relatives in the trades." In other words, marginalized youths do require synthetic networks to provide the guidance and motivation that labor's mainstream youths get from their background or peer networks. African-American youths did "at least as well" on tests for which they were tutored in some organized way. The investigators concluded that even minor successes in formal apprentice programs could have "great symbolic importance for civil rights groups."[36] That is, role models would help.

Public Sector Opportunities

The history of public-sector job allocation reveals both the power and the malleability of social capital in the workplace. In contrast to trade unions, where laws about allocating opportunity had difficulty penetrating tradition and senses of proprietorship, the public sector has been relatively responsive to the rule of law. As a civil rights era analyst observed, "the public sector is at once the showcase of society, the harbinger of change for the private sector, and a training ground for the induction of change." Moreover, public sector positions, both military and civilian, have for centuries provided class and income mobility for many people locked out of desirable private sector opportunities, especially opportunities that required either financial or social capital. Yet federal progress toward meritocracy has moved in fits and starts. The Jim Crow years saw actual reductions in the number of African Americans in federal jobs despite the growth of civil service. After a major expansion of civil service rules during the latter part of the New Deal, by World War II merit standards covered over 90 percent of civilian federal employees; by 1953, the figure was over 95 percent. Nonetheless, into the 1970s, African Americans consistently possessed higher levels of education than whites who filled the same or similar positions. Even when marginalized people could enter the public bureaucracies, their relative mobility rates therein still suffered from discrimination. Many languished in clerical, dead-end jobs.[37]

The New Deal's expansion of social services opened up many opportunities, especially in areas where clients of the services were nonwhite. This was the context for the National Urban League's first urging its constituency to take public agencies' civil service examinations in 1937. Through the ensuing decades, African Americans did best in newly created positions, where other ethnic groups did not already have a stronghold of preexisting networks by which to pull in their own and push out others. Temporary war agencies experienced the greatest gains during World War II, so the higher an African American's ranking, the more likely it was in a temporary position. When the next surge of federal expansion in social services came during the so-called Great Society of President Lyndon Johnson, Secretary of Labor Willard Wirtz recognized the advantages of shaping new employment patterns in new departments, rather than attempting to integrate old ones and thereby challenging prerogatives within entrenched networks. The resulting growth and the reshaping of federal employment patterns that accompanied it helped to implement the Great Society's commitment to expanding opportunities.[38]

Sociologist Roger Waldinger has examined two centuries of New York City's public-sector employment, showing the survival capacity of "incumbents' networks." Even as civil service coverage expanded through the twentieth century, ethnicity-based patronage flourished. Before World War II, explained Waldinger, "the population of people with ties to municipal workers virtually became the applicant pool." In some cases, "cram schools" prepared the "politically connected" for exams. In most instances, great advantages accrued to those who could learn about openings through friends and family. After passage of the federal Equal Employment Opportunity Act of 1972, which expanded Title VII protection to government agencies and educational institutions, some New York City departments began intensive recruitment outside of employees' networks. The 1972 act allowed outsider groups to challenge civil service exams that were weakly related to jobs and also to challenge unfair and illegal placements. Although New York remained the only major U.S. city lacking a program for public-sector affirmative action in 1989, African Americans' hold on the precious resource of city jobs had begun to exceed their proportion of the city's population. Once again, social capital trumped law. As African Americans moved into positions, including managerial positions, they worked the social capital system just as their predecessors had done. Hispanics, by contrast, remained underrepresented in 1990, laying claim to just one-third as many city jobs as African Americans, although the two groups' residency proportion was about the same.[39]

Civil rights enforcement works best where institutions and laws have the capacity to monitor hiring and recruitment practices, and where bureaucratic personnel procedures can subdue politics. A recent analysis of 1,224 cities and their employment of African Americans points to the functions of social capital in the business world. It concludes that the "most consistently significant determinant" of black municipal job success is the degree to which unions are able to resist integration, which in turn depends on whether or not a city has a "reformed"—that is, professional—management system. Even large minority populations within "unreformed" cities cannot exert enough political influence to counter organized control over opportunities. Removing employment policy from politics promotes equitable employment practices best, the analysis concluded. As a veteran of top posts in New York City explained, "If you consider yourself a professional manager in the 1980s and 1990s, . . . one of the issues you have to deal with is managing diversity." This phrase, "managing diversity," in fact had became code by the 1990s for integrating employee pools across multiple groups. The smaller the employment unit, and the less its visibility to the law, the less likely it is to practice or even claim to practice objective personnel procedures.[40]

Two lessons for success obtain here. First, applying civil service rules in the public sector after 1972 reduced candidates' needs for social capital, making civil service an attractive path to mobility for people without enough social or financial capital for business mobility. As a result, the percentage of employed African-American males in the nation's civilian public sector rose from 5.9 in 1940 and 11.9 in 1960 to 22.5 in 1980. By contrast, the analogous percentages of employed white males rose from 8.6 to 10.5 to 13.5 during those years. Similar ratios continued into the 1990s.[41] Second, in the private sector, the corporations that had developed both the practice and the ethos of formalized, supposedly objective personnel procedures would provide the grandest stages for the civil rights dramas by which aspirants to business achievement would teach themselves—and everyone else—the mechanisms of social capital.

Pride and Prejudice on Corporate Ladders

By the time the civil rights movement came to a head, American corporate culture had built both institutions and doctrines based on what its participants liked to frame as a meritocracy. Only a few outspoken cynics saw systemic flaws rather than idiosyncratic anomalies, such as a particular boss favoring a nephew or a school chum's son. Corporations' successful absorption of white, male veterans in the mid-twentieth century reinforced faith in the fairness of corporate institutions and belief in bureaucratized personnel processes. Moreover, businessmen's belief in impartial and objective personnel practices justified their own status, compensation, self-esteem, and patriotism. Kenneth Miller, the National Association of Manufacturers' (NAM) senior vice president, glorified this ethos in his 1954 speech "The American Negro in Industry." In a stirring tribute to everything from America's technological progress ("against which we are happily powerless") to Americans' "unbounded faith" in their unique mission in the world, Miller emphasized NAM's support for nondiscriminatory policies. The success of America's economy and its classless society relied, he declared, on the "competitive freedom of the individual to advance to any height his energy and ability can take him." He asked his largely African-American audience to be patient, to "play your part in keeping America free," assuring them that "more and more businessmen . . . every day" were lowering their prejudices. "Free competition demands recognition of merit," he affirmed.[42]

The most common corporate responses to the Civil Rights Act a decade after Miller's speech mixed relative confidence about success with huge concerns about compliance. The legislation itself, after all, only required that "push" discrimination be eliminated. That fit well enough with business's creed of equal opportunity, although the accompanying bureaucratic demands did not. Racial tensions, however, continued to increase, and riots from 1964 to 1968 profoundly shook businessmen, as they did everyone else in the nation. The National Advisory Commission on Civil Disorders (the Kerner Commission) analyzed the ghetto riots, and in early 1968 the commission's report provocatively placed the blame on dominant institutions and habits of mind. Title VII had already placed businesses and unions squarely on the front lines of addressing civil rights concerns. Many business leaders were genuinely surprised, even distressed, when forced to notice their firms' operational prejudices. Most sputtered that their firms had espoused nondiscrimination policies, often for decades. After all, they protested, their personnel departments had developed tests to screen applicants fairly. For example, in 1969 Avon Products vice president Norman Haynes insisted that "for many, many years" Avon's personnel policies had provided for equal opportunity. "No, there's no change, it's more a matter of emphasis." Interviewed for an in-house publication, Haynes proudly described Avon's new "additional affirmative steps, such as seeking out people who were denied opportunity elsewhere." Yet all of the firm's managers through the 1960s were white males, most of whom had been with the company for decades.[43]

Making Progress

In the context of social capital, corporate compliance with civil rights ordinances fell roughly into two broad types. One cluster of measures met almost universal acclaim—at least publicly—for advancing the decades-long processes of formalizing personnel processes and removing social capital advantages, furthering efficiency and the meritocracy. The other cluster—affirmative action—consisted of special considerations that did not align so readily with the dominant individualistic ideology, even though the strongest arguments in its favor promised to promote individuals' development, employers' productivity, and the nation's goals. Rather than reducing the influence of social capital, this second cluster attempted to infuse marginalized communities with synthetic social capital. Whitney Young described this in early 1964 as giving an anemic person a blood transfusion before expecting him to compete with someone who was not anemic. He emphasized that "we are not asking for equal time, we are not asking for three hundred years of preferential treatment, but we are asking for unequal inputs for a brief time." At the same gathering of business and community leaders, Charles E. Silberman, a writer for *Fortune,* pointed out that other ethnic groups had moved into the middle class "through political activity." Having been "denied a place in American society because of their group membership, Negroes should inevitably demand admission because of their group membership."[44] In other words, even this business-oriented analyst recommended reversing the direction of social capital's influence for a time.

Equity and compliance through formalized personnel practices could reduce the privileges of social capital by disseminating information about opportunities. One mandated and common remedy for unequal social capital simply called for timely internal postings of job openings, plus widely disseminated ads whenever a company

sought external candidates. New regulations required that all pertinent external communications contain the "equal employment opportunity clause," and none could specify that they wanted "colored" or "white" help. Firms and many unions opened up training
programs, announcing them and making them accessible to all interested parties, with sex and age the only legal limitations, if these
were job requirements that came to be known as BFOQs (bona fide
occupational qualifications). Because civil rights advocates often
criticized tests and educational screens that did not reflect some
jobs' demands, many firms reevaluated job specifications to avoid
screening out capable but undereducated applicants. The Sun Oil
Company, for instance, ceased requiring a high school diploma "as
an arbitrary condition of employment" in 1970, and it had by then
already eliminated employment tests except for secretarial typing.
Upon recommendations from prison boards and probation officers,
Sun even hired people with arrest records who did not present security risks. In keeping with traditions of rotating ambitious employees in order to prepare them for promotion, Sun set a goal in June
1970 to include "two of each" from its groups of minority and female employees among its next fifteen "Rotational Group" members. In order to "reflect the integrated nature of our work force,"
Sun also set a policy of including pictures of ethnic minorities in
publications and advertisements aimed at both internal and external audiences.[45]

In 1966 the journal *Business Management* interviewed five young
African-American men with executive ambitions. Over and over,
they blended the standard business ethos with the themes of Martin
Luther King Jr.'s legendary 1963 speech, "I Have a Dream." All insisted that what they needed most was "to be evaluated on the basis
of what I can do, not on the color of my skin," a "chance to do exactly what my abilities will allow." In keeping with managerial
principles, they asked that any company that wanted the benefit
of their determination to contribute and achieve should address

bigotry head on. It should disseminate antidiscrimination policies broadly, "establish enforcers" who report directly to top management, "make a heroic effort to employ and promote people on their merits, . . . and . . . deal strongly with anyone who is rightly accused of discrimination." The "president has got to lean on the pockets of prejudice," ensuring that company policy was maintained up and down the chain of authority. The "lip service" that filled public and internal statements would not suffice. The five also urged managers to be tough with minority employees, assuming that they enforced rules equally across race. In sum, they called for "respect as a human being, of my capabilities and potential, respect for what I can do for my company." In turn, four of the five rejected use of "the race issue" to advance their careers. The fifth said that he was "not above using my 'handicap' to help me regain ground and catch up." Even so, the consensus was that the "Negro isn't really asking for anything special." Reflecting the dominant tone of the nation, the five expected that eliminating exclusionary discrimination would make them "part of this moving economic and social system. We want what anyone else would want, once we have cleared away this discrimination mess."[46]

These five ambitious, educated, and capable men entering "the white man's business world" asked to be judged according to the American ethos of individualism. A National Association of Manufacturers tract could not have expressed more commitment to that ideal. These five African Americans framed conscientious compliance through formalized personnel procedures as a balance of standardization with appreciation for individual attributes. Explaining this balance in a 1961 *Nation's Business* article titled "Spot and Encourage Initiative" in which he made no reference whatsoever to civil rights, Eli Ginzberg urged owners and managers to cast aside their "rigid hiring criteria" for identifying potential leaders. In the interests of hiring and promoting "men with initiative" and "potential," Ginzberg's first recommendation was that personnel departments avoid relying on their "stereotype of the young man suitable for the executive ladder." Because that in-house stereotype resulted in perpetuation of the kind of people already in top management, such a hiring practice threatened progress in diversity and corporate growth.[47] From this perspective, if the "race question" could be resolved simply by opening doors and no longer automatically pushing marginal people back out of them, the nation's managers could not have objected.

The activism that brought civil rights violations to mainstream America's attention showed African Americans being pushed away from high school and university doors. U.S. marshals and National Guard troops forced those doors open, and that was the last most Americans saw or thought about those new students. Likewise, people within business saw discrimination problems as being of the "push" variety, preventing people from entering the halls where opportunity lay. When workplace doors opened, many African Americans who were willing and able entered the expanding corporate workforce. In New York City between 1960 and 1970, for example, African Americans jumped from 29 percent to 43 percent of the white-collar working population. National proportions also doubled: between 1962 and 1974, African-American clerical workers vaulted from 5.1 percent of the whole to 9.4 nationally. Thus, once "qualified" no longer meant white, an initial surge of often overqualified African Americans found positions. An analyst in the early 1970s likened these individuals who had qualified themselves despite poor prospects to a "pool of Jackie Robinsons" that "quickly drained dry" once mainstream firms began to hire African Americans.[48] The lower ranks of white collar workers began to change their look.

Recruiting Outsiders

As the National Urban League and others had warned, and as one business leader expressed it in his title to a 1970 essay, "Open

Doors Are Not Enough." This vice president of Illinois Bell Telephone Company told his peers that "simply hanging an EQUAL OPPORTUNITY EMPLOYER sign on the door" would not draw enough previously excluded people into their employ. As riots and grossly differential unemployment rates made clear by the late 1960s, color-blind personnel policies that held everyone to the same standards could not solve problems that had evolved over centuries of humiliating discrimination and deprivation. Instead, it would take both "courage, and more important, encouragement to apply today where you were not wanted yesterday—where none of your friends or neighbors ever worked." Like many others, this man called for business leaders to "leave their desks" to recruit among the community leaders who could carry their message. They needed to "re-examine the screens we have used in the past" because perhaps those "tests do a better job of measuring today's ability than tomorrow's potential." Businesses' responsibilities included providing different levels of training to acknowledge that the disadvantaged could not assimilate into the workforce as readily as the advantaged. Affirmative action efforts evolved after the 1964 Civil Rights Act because nothing else seemed adequate to relieve the 1960s' deepening racial crisis.[49]

Of companies' personnel activities, none pertains to opening doors more than recruiting. Therefore none can better illustrate how affirmative action practices imitated social capital and built synthetic social capital where aspirants' identities had zero or negative value in the labor marketplace. Recognizing that, for too many people, opening doors was not enough, recruiters looked outside the ranks of the usual candidates with whom employers and co-workers were familiar. Because distributing information about job availability and encouraging candidates have always succeeded in strengthening networks, the National Urban League and its local chapters worked for decades to create synthetic networks through which to disseminate job information and to encourage and train applicants. Consequently, when businesses across the United States took on integration of their workforces in earnest, they frequently turned to the NUL for help in recruiting. They also called African-American churches, hoping to gain entry into networks that could draw in people who, if not qualified at the start, could be trained. As one businessman, intent on integrating his company, rather indelicately instructed his managers: "You had better call the Urban League or some colored preachers and tell them to send you some colored. We don't want anybody to think we are discriminating."[50]

President Lyndon Johnson understood the importance of engaging businessmen in responding to racial unrest, and he applied powerful political pressure to achieve this end. He inaugurated the National Alliance of Businessmen (since 1979 the National Alliance of Business, or NAB) in 1968 as a liaison between the federal government and private industry. The NAB provided guidance and some compensation for businesses to find jobs, find people, and train the latter for the former—*after* they were hired. As NAB's first annual report explained, "Businessmen were suddenly asked to start hiring persons they wouldn't have let past the plant gate a few years ago." The targets of the NAB were not people ready for white-collar positions, but the "hardcore," people who "had to be persuaded" that the opportunities were real and "not just another 'trick bag'" to raise their hopes. The NAB developed many strategies to recruit and retain workers, and it was justly proud of them, including its innovative blue-collar "'Buddy' system." To assist strangers in adapting to their new environment, the NAB urged firms to assign "experienced workers . . . [to] help the new man with all the problems he encounters—from working problems to personal problems, from transportation problems to financial ones." This recognition of the novice's need for a coworker to turn to describes a synthetic mentoring relationship. Working in fifty cities during its first year, the NAB placed 102,235 "disadvantaged persons" into full-time jobs under the "marching orders" "Hire, Train, Retain."[51]

The NAB's reach into industry was remarkable. Hundreds of companies, including major corporations, participated, "loaned" the labor of 871 staff and executives during the first year, and contributed press and advertising coverage. The degree to which business leaders took on the language of affirmative action, guided by the NAB, was even more remarkable. The NAB and the National Urban Coalition, a private advocacy and information organization formed in 1967, sponsored a series of fourteen volumes in 1969 as a manual "not for the man who has just begun to ask why. This is for the man who asks how." *Training the Hardcore* published model letters from corporate leaders to instruct managers. Top officers at Xerox cited the Kerner Commission report and accepted their firm's responsibility for recent urban riots in Rochester, New York, because their company had failed to employ minority workers. To stop contributing to problems and start contributing to solutions, they pledged to "heavily intensify our recruiting of Negroes and other minorities." They added, "If, as our past experience indicates, they are reluctant to come to us, then we will go to them." They would make all managers accountable for reexamining "their selection standards and training programs," and the firm would also train "unqualified" minorities for entry-level positions. Although Xerox had made progress, "it simply has not gone far enough." The executives concluded that Xerox "will not condone the waste of a great national resource. It will not compromise the conviction on which the success of this enterprise and of the nation depends." Paul Gorman, president of Western Electric, wrote that "the future of the free enterprise system depends on the responsibility of that system to the needs of the society that nurtures it." Henry Ford II added a telling phrase to the common themes and corporate solutions, that Ford Motor Company's programs aimed "not to screen *out* doubtful applicants but to screen *in* if possible."[52] In other words, turn the push to a pull.

A widely distributed 1966 publication, the *Employer's Guide to*

Equal Opportunity, reported on the "affirmative measures" that a broad sampling of companies had taken, with mixed results. Minimal, often token, compliance with state and federal regulations too often resulted in disappointments that confirmed skeptics on all sides. The *Employer's Guide* described habits of discrimination "ingrained in the social fabric" so deeply that no one need make a consciously racist decision in order to practice racism. Managers' simply avoiding "sticky decisions" could perpetuate presumptions that had always diminished the opportunities of disadvantaged groups. Noting that employers could not control broad-based conditions, such as poor communications with minority communities and expectations that applying was hopeless, equalization obliged employers to "compensate for them." By this account, discrimination had come to mean the "*absence of affirmative action.*" A new term, "institutional racism," soon came into common usage because of growing concerns that chronic educational disadvantages, residential segregation, lengthy commutes for people without cars, and long-term exclusion from jobs had generated conditions under which employers and others could justify *continued* exclusion because of what appeared to be the failings of individual applicants. Such conditions allowed decision makers to continue their habits free from self-reproach or legal censure. A 1964 study showed that people who believed that they lacked personal prejudice would discriminate if they believed that fulfilling their "organizational role" as gatekeepers required it. Thus, going about "business as usual" perpetuated existing disadvantages.[53]

Communicating with minority communities remained a core challenge because the relevant networks did not normally intersect. Difficulties in getting employers' messages to the relevant people, including to churches as well as schools and agencies, were compounded by difficulties in making those messages effectively communicate new standards. Showing minority workers on the job was a common publication strategy. Firms that expressed a desire to employ more African Americans often expressed the familiar complaint that not enough who applied were qualified. Companies made the most progress, the *Employer's Guide* reported, by implementing what one firm called "the kind of managerial techniques that have proven so effective in other operations." In a textbooklike approach that worked, one firm analyzed its situation on a unit-by-unit basis, set expectations and targets, offered managers guidance, and made managers responsible for achieving the targets. Another corporation altered its practices for temporary hirings to develop what amounted to an internship program. By actively recruiting "qualifiable" high school students as short-term replacements, the firm built up a cadre of young workers whom the firm knew and who would be able to step into permanent positions that opened up. Another employer who was struggling to find recruits and convince them of his intentions simply quit trying to reach individuals and instead talked to contacts within the African-American community. They in turn took the employer's invitation into the community. The "good people" who came forward and got jobs returned to their communities, "and now the word has got around and people are asking for jobs."[54] What began as a synthetic network took on a life of its own—developing into a traditional, customary network, distributing information about opportunities to its members, as networks do.

As firms of all sizes examined their policies for selecting candidates, they came to realize that they were excluding people simply because they *could,* not because job proficiency required it. As one manager explained, "Screening systems are often devised simply to eliminate a lot of people who don't conform to a set of norms that may or may not be relevant to many of the job requirements." The company figured this out when its president took an interest in employing disabled persons. When standard testing rejected too many people, the president angrily demanded that the personnel department "hire some of them anyway and put them to work where they'll be useful!" After most of the new hires worked out well, the firm's managers realized that their tests might also be screening out minorities and immigrants unnecessarily. Without eliminating the tests, the firm devised a new policy, considering fuller pictures of candidates' abilities, including schooling, work records, and personality. Firms that refined their personnel processes in this or some similar fashion had by 1966 achieved the greatest progress in integrating their workforce, with no measurable harm to their productivity.[55] Moreover, screening people carefully and individually, rather than relying on fast, inexpensive tests, fit more closely with the individualistic ethos of business, while promising a more effective workforce.

Affirmative Action as Synthetic Social Capital

In 1961, the Kennedy administration adapted the phrase "affirmative action" from earlier efforts opposing unfair labor practices. As Eleanor Roosevelt, chair of John F. Kennedy's President's Commission on the Status of Women, explained in a 1962 press release, "a mere statement supporting equality of opportunity must be implemented by affirmative steps to see that the doors are really open for training, selection, advancement, and equal pay."[56] What affirmative action meant in practice for civil rights was not clear then, and the 1964 Civil Rights Act offered no clarification. The phrase instead became a long-standing lightning rod for contention, gathering a conflict-ridden set of meanings along with a corpus of legal decisions, energized by hits from all directions. Norman Haynes, an Avon vice president and the company's representative to the NAB, explained the trade-offs with an example. He had initially worried that redistributing job opportunities could have unfortunate consequences for morale. However, the only adverse effect of "affirmative steps" at Avon that he publicly owned up to in 1969 was "some sacrifice" when the company provided temporary summer jobs for disadvantaged youths. Some employees' children had to find jobs elsewhere, but, he explained, "that's exactly the point. The option was open to them, whereas with the disadvantaged, there was no option—it was Avon or no job at all."[57] In other words, affirmative action devalued the social capital that had traditionally served employees' children for finding summer jobs, in order to infuse synthetic social capital into a community that could not provide its own. From this sort of zero-sum perspective, no wonder affirmative action still elicits intense reactions.

What affirmative action offered, in effect, was an influx of synthetic social capital. People who lacked connections, whose background networks ill prepared them for connecting in the "white man's business world," who had been pushed away from opportunity for centuries with brutality and humiliation needed pull. Even assuming that public laws and private policies in businesses and unions could have eliminated "push" discrimination in short order, pull had to get into the system somehow on the side of the disadvantaged. It has always been there for the advantaged; and disadvantaged groups have done what they could, through political or other means, to strengthen their own pull. Nevertheless, storms over affirmative action still flare up. Most critics have attacked affirmative action for replacing an alleged American individualism with an unfair, even crippling, helping hand.[58] Yet only rarely have critics noted any negative effect on either individuals or the nation from applying social capital to mainstream beneficiaries. For instance, who claims that the GI Bill's veterans' benefits harmed the nation or their recipients by reducing their recipients' self-reliance? And certainly no one ever claimed that Andrew Carnegie's consummate exploitation of his social capital in any way diminished his rise from rags to riches—or injured his psyche.

Nonetheless, few have objected to affirmative action on behalf of African Americans more intensely than African Americans who believe that eliminating "push" discrimination should be all that they need to succeed. The five young men on their way up corporate ladders in 1966 believed that they had *"earned"* every promotion. Thomas Sowell, one of the most well-known such critics of affirmative action, wrote that he pitied people "haunted by the idea that they owed their careers to affirmative action." He considered his life well timed because it placed him "right after the worst of the old discrimination was no longer there to impede me and just before racial quotas made the achievements of blacks look suspect." He could therefore celebrate having "the key inner advantages needed to advance," believing that he had incurred few debts along the way, despite essential advantages he gained from academic mentors. In 1966, Whitney Young praised the Urban League for having placed fifty thousand people in jobs the previous year, but noted that many of the beneficiaries of organized assistance "don't like to admit they got help. They want to feel they did it on their own."[59] Somehow, synthetic social capital—delivered through a formal institution—seems to invalidate individual efforts in a way that "natural," or customary, social capital delivered through personal connections does not. Once the inadequacies of eliminating "push" discrimination became apparent, however, and the racial crisis of the 1960s deepened, institutionalized pull seemed the only solution.

Institutionalizing pull into educational opportunities was an obvious means of moving African Americans toward white-collar positions. Simply opening the gates to graduate business schools raised minority participation, but not enough. In 1967, the U.S. Office of Education created a loan fund for lower-income business students. That year and the next, business schools responded to the ongoing urban and racial crises with recruiting campaigns and fellowships. They got results. For example, from the end of World War II through 1967, the Harvard Business School had had a total of twenty-four African-American students; in 1968 alone, it admitted twenty-eight. The University of Massachusetts featured a program with summer preparatory courses before a year of graduate-level management courses. That same year, the Sloan Foundation funded a five-year "Council for Opportunity in Graduate Management Education" with $1 million for nine of the leading MBA schools to recruit and educate minority students. Through the early 1970s, other schools and foundations continued the process of integrating the means by which minority aspirants could pass through corporate screens.[60] Because admissions are a valuable zero-sum resource, however, crediting minority candidates with synthetic social capital to help them compete continues to raise controversies and Supreme Court cases. In contrast, legacy admission preferences, based on traditional social capital, barely raise eyebrows.

Promoting Strangers: The Next Challenge

Embedded within the practices of corporate personnel departments are both official and unofficial means of nurturing employees for promotion. Who gets the nod for such training measures candidates' social as much as their human capital. Consequently strangers, once hired, climbed corporate ladders slowly, if at all, during the first decades after 1964. African-American accountants, for instance, found themselves working only with minority clients or in the back rooms of large firms. They rarely received the challenging assignments that could develop careers, and they often felt apprehensive about asking even practical and concrete questions of their superiors, much less questions about improving their chances for advancement. Many white-collar novices complained that the hiring of African Americans reflected tokenism rather than integration. Often the newcomers' jobs involved more community work than technical or business work. As one young African-American professional pleaded, "deliver me from presiding over the company table at the annual Urban League benefit dinner."[61]

During the years when civil rights matters were very much in the air, Avon Products issued a series of directives as part of the company's scrupulously detailed appraisal programs that never mentioned race or sex. In the true spirit of managerial professionalism, explained one memo, the "Management Appraisal Program provides formal means of assuring that all designated employees have the opportunity to receive the benefits of personalized guidance," including "day-to-day assistance, counsel and direction." This structured guidance program resulted in "an important contribution to the company and to every employee." When applied to the customary pool of employees, no one objected to practices to ensure that the "right sort" of employees did not fall through the cracks, even though policies to "extend meaningful and personal guidance to each Associate for purposes of his overall career development" amounted to synthetic mentoring.[62] Somehow, however, when similar directives called for applying "personalized guidance" to people outside of the mainstream pools, such treatment looked like reverse discrimination and misplaced favoritism. In some people's eyes, it constituted artificial, government-mandated violations of individualism and meritocracy. These policies seemed tainted when applied to strangers, and they in turn tainted the strangers.

Many people and companies willing to apply affirmative actions to recruit and *hire* marginalized people resisted analogous measures to *advance* employees.[63] Compensatory promotions seemed to violate meritocratic principles more than hiring people who had clearly been victims of exclusionary discrimination. The American business ethos could not approve of "push" discrimination, once it was forced to see it. Systemic "pull" discrimination, however, remained largely invisible for a long time afterward. Once formal—especially government-mandated—policies were put in place to apply pull artificially, even on behalf of previously disadvantaged but capable people, the new practices generated considerable opposition. As debates grew heated, marginalized people and their advocates began to formulate ideas about the role of social capital in everyone's success or failure. After more than a decade of remarkable gains, through legal and moral pressures, against exclusionary discrimination, it became apparent that eliminating such "push" discrimination was not enough. Once in, how could strangers move up? From their new and increasingly cynical perspective as challengers, marginalized people and scholars interested in workplace dynamics began to examine in detail how successful people operated within business and how they differed from the unsuccessful. Realizing that hard work and talent did not suffice, they began to detect visible but previously unseen patterns. Rather than attempting the impossible and trying to eliminate the impact of social capital, they learned to spot it at work, build it, and use it to advantage.

CHAPTER 6

Strangers on the Ladder

At the end of the second summer I spent working in a large Detroit bank during my college years, the vice president of my division asked me to consider continuing there. Although I had fully planned on returning to school, because he and I had a cordial relationship I glibly responded that if he could assure that I would be a vice president in ten years, I would stay. I had meant this as a joke—an impossible request that would relieve me from guilt for saying no. To my surprise, instead of laughing, the vice president was aghast. Well, he stalled, I could be the *secretary* to a vice president.

This was 1966; I had not intended to strike a blow for feminism. Until then, my post-Sputnik education had encouraged me to pursue a profession in science or academics, no less than any of my male schoolmates. But in trying to figure out why this very nice man had recoiled so from my off-the-cuff reply, I realized that his world—the business world—first assigned people to absolute categories and only after that gauged their abilities. As I thought about how men and women and people of various ethnicities were given different jobs throughout the bank, the deep fact of sexual and racial stereotyping in business became apparent. In a sense, the joke was on me. I had assumed that ten years could not prepare *anyone* adequately for a vice president's job. This I thought was the source of my proposal's absurdity. The truth was that this bank vice presi-

How to succeed while you're still young

BUSINESS, today, is too competitive to discriminate against anybody for any reason.

The man who can do the job gets the job . . . whether he's 25 or 55.

But rarely does one give any *serious* thought to his future — beyond the normal concern all of us have — until he begins to stagnate.

Only then does he ask himself: "Where will I be in business two, five, or ten years from now?" "Will I be able to meet the growing expenses of a growing family?" "Can I look forward to retirement at a reasonable age?"

The problem of personal progress is always complex because everybody has characteristics which affect his particular needs.

And that is why the Alexander Hamilton Institute's executive-training plan has been so helpful to more than 618,000 men over a period of 56 consecutive years.

The high regard in which the Institute is held by management men from coast to coast encourages a constant flow of inquiries about the details of the program every year.

A decision only you can make

There's nothing magical about it, other than the "magic" which comes of mastering the fundamentals of business under systematic direction . . . which is essential to scale the heights in business.

Because the final decision must come from you, we have prepared a 32-page booklet factually written to give you the information necessary to reach a conclusion about the program in terms of whatever your individual needs may be.

Free . . . "Forging Ahead in Business"

To men who are looking ahead and want to move ahead, whatever their age, we say this: Time is your most precious commodity. Don't waste it. Send for your complimentary copy of *"Forging*

Ahead in Business" today. It will be mailed to you promptly. Read it carefully, and decide for yourself whether you wish to receive additional information about the program.

Clearly, you have nothing to lose. But nobody can guess how much you may have to gain. The coupon awaits your decision.

ALEXANDER HAMILTON INSTITUTE 235 E. 42nd Street, New York, N. Y. 10017

"Business, today, is too competitive to discriminate against anybody for any reason." Thus begins this 1965 advertisement; yet all of the references in the copy refer to male success. The woman, who seems to be included only as part of the office equipment, is partially obscured by a desktop ornament. The self-help ethos rings throughout this message from a highly respected correspondence school, but it applied only to men.

dent simply could not imagine that any number of years could overcome the limits of my sex. So began my education in the workings of social capital in business. This man could have been a mentor to me, but his vision limited rather than expanded my opportunities.

Although I barely sensed it then, other women were taking up the challenge of expanding women's ambitions and opportunities. Just a few months after my exchange with the bank vice president, the National Organization for Women (NOW) was formed to do battle for women in the cultural, legal, political, and business arenas. Its founders' vision and its members' efforts made it possible for women to achieve in new ways in business and elsewhere. In the previous year the Equal Employment Opportunity Commission (EEOC) had begun to enforce the 1964 Civil Rights Act, but only in 1967 did it reluctantly begin to acknowledge its responsibility to address sex as well as race discrimination. Nonetheless, within a few years the EEOC took on women's workplace rights in earnest. In January 1973, in collaboration with the Departments of Labor and Justice, the EEOC succeeded in turning U.S. business on its head. The nation's largest private employer, American Telephone & Telegraph (AT&T), settled a huge class-action suit by signing a consent decree to eliminate sex and race discrimination.[1] The fight against "push," or exclusionary, discrimination in business was accelerating, and things were looking up for people on the margins. Back in 1954, thinking about the recent *Board of Education* Supreme Court decision, a president of the American Association of University Women had recognized that "*de*-segregation precedes integration—the latter representing a later stage of social re-arrangement."[2] Eliminating the push of segregation was the first step toward integration, and by 1966 "*de*-segregation" had at last begun.

As layers of barriers fell away, people on the margins began to expand their horizons and their strengths. With the support of new legal and cultural pressures, they insisted that gatekeepers apply universally the core principles of individual rights, dignity, and equality with which Americans all want to identify. They called on the business world to adhere to its own rhetoric about following objective standards for hiring and promotion, holding employers up to the equal opportunity rhetoric whose tone was so loud and self-righteous during the Cold War. During the 1960s and 1970s, mainstream businesses, and corporate managers in particular, wrestled with how they could bring so many strangers into their midst, or at least into their employees' midst. Frustrations in every quarter led to valuable insights. Rethinking personnel procedures would bring businesses more into line with their proclaimed ethos of meritocracy. Even so, integration was for them a problem, not a solution.

Strangers as Problems

"The Negro, as a member of a business society that is almost exclusively white, is a stranger." Thus began *Business Management*'s 1966 report on five ambitious young African-American men. This stranger "emerges from another environment to come to work, and at the end of the day, he returns to a world where few white men venture." As a result, the "Negro's ideals and ambitions, his motivations, the many factors that contribute to his social and business personality, are largely unknown"—except to him and his peers, that is. "How is the Negro," this stranger in business's midst, "to be managed?" One of the young men pointed to problems that resulted when managers and peers treated a minority employee "as a *symbol* instead of an *individual*." They and other spokesmen for African Americans wanted opportunities for training and then hoped to be judged on the merits of their performance, in keeping with the modern business ethos. Yet over and over again during the civil rights era, mainstream businessmen expressed their frustration in having to deal with strangers, by race or sex. As one analyst put it to an audience of businessmen, his listeners' unfamiliarity with these new workers revealed a long-term "pattern of unawareness" that was both individual and collective, and it resulted in their feeling "bewildered and frustrated," even when they approached encounters "with nothing but good intentions."[3]

Although well-educated African-American candidates for executive positions benefited from the civil rights activism that had begun to eliminate exclusionary discrimination, they also suffered by having crime, urban unrest, and adjectives like "hardcore" too often linked to their racial identity from the vantage point of the dominant culture. For instance, "Minority Employment and the Hardcore" was the title of a series of managerial meetings at Avon Products in 1968. These meetings were intended to explain Avon's "philosophy and approach to minority group problems," to clarify its "long-standing principles toward Equal Opportunity for all," and to direct "increased action." The agenda identified "hardcore unemployable" as "usually members of minority groups." Although it did not indicate that the latter were necessarily hardcore, the linkage reinforced common stereotypes.[4]

Similarly, at Sun Oil Company in 1969, top-level descriptions of consolidating two cohorts of executives (as the result of a merger) contrasted starkly with discussions about how to bring in and manage people hired through the National Alliance of Businessmen. The former was framed as an opportunity to rationalize corporate policies. Integrating the executives called for moving ahead quickly and optimistically with "sensitivity," keeping in mind "non-financial factors [such as] prestige, ego satisfiers, status symbols," and executive development programs. Integrating disadvantaged hires, by contrast, was seen as a disorienting, externally imposed project with costly inefficiencies. A company document on creating and filling a new managerial position to oversee minority affairs, for example, still exudes obvious discomfort and worry. The writer inquired whether a "relatively temporary position" might suffice to resolve "the problem." He worried that "other groups (including radicals) will take actions (perhaps challenging the basis of the profit system)." The tension between the familiar and the strange emerged full force in the question "Are the factors for having a black incumbent (external company relations) more important than the factors for a white (internal politics, etc.)?"[5] Placing strangers was seen as a difficult problem that had to be weighed carefully. Such strangers could not expect easy promotion through a system to which their meagre social capital barely allowed entry.

The Woman Worker: A Special Problem

Despite their productive experiences in "men's" jobs during World War II, most evidence indicates that the majority of women working outside of female-typed jobs did not expect to retain their wartime positions. Overwhelming cultural and other pressures, including their own beliefs about domesticity, urged white women after the war to return to domestic pursuits, rebuilding the family-based American Dream, complete with male breadwinner.[6] During the postwar boom, having performed managerial tasks from so-called pink-collar positions rarely qualified women for managerial titles and salaries. Conventional wisdom held that it was better to bring in freshly released male veterans, even if they were untrained, given presumptions about women's domestic nature, the nation's interest in encouraging it, and veterans' job needs. Women also lost their places in some colleges, once the schools no longer needed their tuition, thanks in part to the GI Bill's facilitating veterans' schooling. In trying to rebuild the nation, powerful cultural forces bolstered historical sexual divisions of labor at home and in the workplace that wartime liberties had threatened to erode. Even *Independent Woman,* the journal of the National Federation of Business and Professional Women's Clubs (NFBPWC), acknowledged women's worries about losing their wartime positions, but added, "We are all agreed that Johnny should have his old job back if he wants it, or another just as good if he so desires." The accompanying illustration, however, depicted women leaving a workplace in tears.[7] Nonetheless, as for African Americans of both sexes, "normalcy" for many white women after World War II was never quite the same.

Although the percentage of women who worked outside their home increased continuously after a 1947 low (which was still higher than the 1940 figure),[8] women largely remained strangers— outsiders and unknowable—to their bosses. If women tried to develop careers instead of just jobs, they became even more strange, risking their femininity. *Research in Industry,* a 1948 study, featured a section titled "The Woman Worker as a Special Problem." Paternalistically supportive of "the young girl scientists," the publication concluded that women were increasingly accepted into industrial research—as women. It admitted to the "boundaries men themselves place on the fields open to women," but legitimated them by repeating any number of stereotypical notions of sex-based differences. For instance, in both business and science, it alleged, women did not "move forward with the breadth of vision and the will to succeed" found in men of equal ability. Women fared better with mature supervisors than did "a restless young man, impatient for research independence." Moreover, women's strangeness required hiring a female personnel director whenever a firm employed a number of women. Men, after all, could not manage women's "disciplinary or social" problems.[9]

Laws and regulations could, and finally did, require companies and unions to stop pushing female strangers away. Given the social nature of promotion in business, whether corporate or owner-managed, rules could not yet move strangers up the ladders in those organizations. Common notions, held by women as well as men, seemed to preclude women's possessing the kind of "potential" that could get them onto and up executive ladders. Gatekeepers usually

Do clerical bottlenecks leave you thirsting for information?

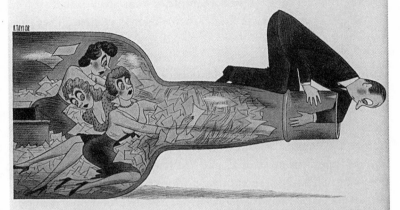

To get the steady stream of facts and figures he needs for sound, timely action, an executive needs a streamlined record-keeping system.

Without it, he'll have to settle for a few sketchy, inaccurate facts that are "pushed through" too late to guide his decision.

But with modern, simple McBee Keysort methods, management can keep up-to-the-minute tabs on every operation, spot developing trends, be in a position to beat competition to the punch.

With your present personnel, *without* costly installations, Keysort cards and machines provide accurate, useful management controls at less cost than any other system. When notched,

the precoded holes along the edges of the Keysort cards make it easy to *collect* a wealth of data ... *classify* it ... *summarize* it ... *file* it ... *find* it ... *use* it ... quickly and accurately.

And because Keysort cards serve as original records, retained from first notation to final report, the delays and errors risked by copying and recopying are completely avoided.

No wonder McBee sales have multiplied *tenfold* in just a few short years, among executives in every kind of business.

The trained McBee representative near you will tell you frankly whether or not McBee can help you. Or write us.

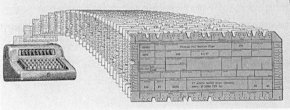

THE McBEE COMPANY

Sole Manufacturer of Keysort—
The Marginally Punched Card
295 Madison Ave., New York 17.
Offices in principal cities.
The McBee Company, Limited,
11 Bermondsey Road, Toronto 13

Secretaries and managers operated on opposite sides of office activities. Both the image and the text of this 1952 ad reinforce then prevailing presumptions about who could be on the managerial side of problem solving.

(Courtesy McBee Systems, Inc.)

did not think of their exclusionary practices as being inappropriate or unfair. Most believed that their judgments were both objective and reasonable; in 1956, for example, a U.S. Steel executive told *Fortune,* "There is no prejudice here against women. They just don't get to the top."[10]

Why would a supervisor invest his time, effort, and reputation in promoting a young woman if he believed that women did not take their careers seriously? A sympathetic presentation of women in the workplace in 1970 appeared in two journals, *Modern Manufacturing* and reprinted in *Management Review,* that referred to women throughout as "they." The article noted that feminists had found "some real problems" in dispelling myths and exposing discrimination based on stereotyped notions of women's supposed impermanence and inability. In doing so, however, they had "aroused a good deal of fury and laughter." The illustration accompanying this seemingly well-intentioned article depicted a young woman reaching for a star with one arm outstretched—and cradling a baby with the other. Could her employer expect only half her effort? And what man could find a potential colleague within this image? A decade later, the *Wall Street Journal* reported a survey according to which 75 percent of 280 male executives, mostly bank officers, believed that working women quickly lost interest in their job, got pregnant, fell in love, and abandoned business for domesticity. Well into the 1980s, managers still feared that women were more interested in their appearances than career goals and that training them would be wasted.[11] They neglected to take into account whether their refusal to consider women for promotions served to discourage women's ambition.

Selling Opportunities

Like Martha Harper, Annie Turnbo Malone, and Madame C. J. Walker at the turn of the twentieth century, and Brownie Wise in the mid-twentieth century at Tupperware, enterprising women aroused an almost devotional loyalty among the sales teams that they generated by the tens of thousands—made up largely of women. The leadership of these women derived in no small part from their being charismatic role models at the center of effective authority networks. Their networks institutionalized mentoring that met many of their followers' needs. Brownie Wise and her earlier cohorts communicated genuine affection for their agents, and inspired and guided them. As one Tupperware dealer wrote to Wise during a sales session, "I wonder if you can ever realize . . . the really deep and abiding gratitude that most of us (me in particular) feel for this wonderful opportunity in business we now enjoy. Thank you Brownie for being a constant shining example."[12]

Another mid-twentieth-century dynamo, Mary Kay Ash, held an indomitable belief in business as the means for women's attaining the personal independence that was every American's due. She combined both an intense conviction about women's rights and a pink-colored hyperfemininity. For her, cosmetics and knowledge of how to use them could help a woman feel "pretty on the outside" and thereby "prettier on the inside, too"—better able to serve her family and community and to prosper as a strong individual. In the 1940s, Ash was a dealer for Stanley Home Products. At the first sales convention she attended, she strode right up to the company's founder and announced that she intended to win the sales award and be crowned "queen" the next year. According to her frequent retelling of the story, the executive took her seriously and said, "You know, somehow I think you will." His acceptance of her ambition spurred her on, she declared, and Ash convinced that year's queen to hold a model sales party for a group of other salespeople, at which Ash took nineteen pages of notes. With grim determination, buttressed by what she had learned, Ash did become queen of sales the following year.[13]

Despite her successes at Stanley and other companies, Ash grew frustrated as she noticed that even the most exceptional women achieved only limited authority and recognition. Too often she found herself training men who then moved above her on the corporate ladder. As a divorced mother, she had a family to support, so she loathed that standard argument for favoring men over women. Peremptory dismissals of women's suggestions also infuriated her. After being passed by for promotion yet again in the early 1960s, she determined to stop working for others and, in 1963, began her own "dream company." Like her predecessors in direct selling, Ash fostered networks among dealers and clients; her first nine dealers were her friends. Ash deliberately altered the normal corporate balance of social capital and individualism in her company, Mary Kay, Inc. She took Cold War rhetoric about individualism to heart and devised merit-based reward systems that featured precise and objective criteria for movement up and down Mary Kay's "Ladder of Success." She prided herself in shaping an operation that offered truly "equal advancement opportunities to all" and that "*guarantees* that the best people will be promoted to top levels of management." While dealers could and should use their personal connections for recruiting and selling, Ash insisted that they did not need connections to learn the means of advancement. She complained that in her former employment "nobody let you know what you had to do in order to advance in your job." What she failed to recognize, of course, was that people in the know *did* share rules and expectations, but nobody told *her*—or other people with inadequate social capital—how to advance. In contrast, if any one of Ash's dealers needed individualized guidance, she could call and ask for it. Every woman was connectable. Ash believed that her company gave women "the maximum opportunity to earn." It served as "a vehicle to help women all over the world," with no "door marked For Men Only."[14]

Mary Kay Ash and the notable beauty sellers before her sought the independence that the American dream promised. They constantly spoke of the links between economic independence and personal independence, and therefore of the necessity for women's business opportunities. In contrast, Elizabeth Arden and Helena Rubenstein were beauty entrepreneurs whose early lives had seen more privilege than Harper, Malone, Walker, Wise, and Ash. They achieved fortune and influence by selling products in high volume through extensive advertising campaigns and mainstream outlets, focusing on product sales, not training and directing armies of women to become self-sufficient.[15] Ash's methods and principles were more in keeping with those of Harper, Malone, Walker, and Wise than with those of Arden and Rubenstein; she was determined to make her own fortune by pulling other women up the economic ladder with her, rather than merely selling to them. All these women, however, regardless of sales organization, found that their best means to economic independence lay in owning their own firms. In this, they were predecessors of a great many women in the late twentieth century, whose frustrations on corporate ladders propelled them into self-employment.

Imagining Equality

Women came to imagine equality from as many directions as there were niches in their social and economic worlds. To make any generalization at all about modern women's history risks neglecting the diversity that both divided and united women in the mid-twentieth century. The roots of the women's movement spread through organized labor; middle-class, college-educated suburbia; professions and businesses; the New Left; African-American communities; and other sources as well.[16] Many forms of activism have sprung from workplace-related issues, as power, esteem, and standard of living directly and indirectly ride upon these issues. Female union activists of the 1940s and 1950s sought less to challenge sex-typing in job allocations than to gain fair working conditions and compensation sufficient to support their families. Betty Friedan's 1963 wake-up call to middle-class women, *The Feminine Mystique,* urged women to seek professional development through a paid job, saying that "society" pays for work it values.[17] Like the women who built businesses in the beauty industry, feminists of the 1960s often looked to economic power as the foundation of individual strength and self-determination. Cold War rhetoricians had not aimed to teach women to value their own individualism through economic activity, but how could women avoid picking up such a lesson? A telling confrontation of capitalist and communist ideologues, after all, took place in 1959 in a model American kitchen set up in Moscow, when Richard Nixon and Nikita Khrushchev debated the purported material benefits of self-determination in the United States against conditions in the Soviet Union, where women had careers but not beautiful kitchens.

Most interpreters of the post–World War II version of the American Dream, mainstream and otherwise, male and female, assigned women to stay-at-home roles whenever possible, in order to nurture their families and communities. For many women, the standard dream coincided perfectly with their own hopes and ambitions. For others, however, living the so-called dream left too many bills unpaid—bills for the homes, cars, appliances, and school supplies that the consumerist modernity of the 1950s and 1960s required. And more than a few other women found this standardized dream stifling. By the mid-1960s, the growing corps calling for female equity in the nation's workplaces included blue- and pink-collar women, housewives who were suffering from Betty Friedan's "problem that has no name," civil rights or New Left activists who were angered by their male colleagues' insensitivity, and businesswomen who saw male coworkers with less skill and experience pass them on corporate ladders. Whether or not these and other women took on the label of "feminist," they had rising expectations and sought to understand and ameliorate the conditions of their frustration—in themselves, in others, and in institutions.

White middle- and upper-class women faced more mixed conditions and options than other women, but American women overall shared diminishing postwar options. These were in part a result of their own choices, though these were made within contexts that discouraged other choices. Although college attendance remained high among middle- and upper-class women, less than half at the end of the 1950s completed their degrees, as young women married and either started families or worked to support their husbands' education. A woman's prestige hinged on her marrying young, and a family's prestige and material well-being argued for maximizing the male breadwinner's income, at a time when women's careers still met formidable barriers. From living rooms to television stages, self-appointed humorists referred to women's "MRS" and "Ph.T." (putting husband through) degrees, mocking women's renunciation of their education in one breath, but in the next chiding "old maids" who chose other paths. These deeply ingrained cultural presumptions limited what even the most fair-minded people, male or female, could imagine for women's economic independence, for women's careers.[18]

Nonetheless, by the mid-1950s, the percentages of women working full- and part-time outside the home were up, for women both married and single, with and without children at home. Three times as many married women worked outside the home in 1970 as in 1940, and the proportion of married women among the workforce doubled between 1940 and 1960. The material abundance paraded in the consumerist popular culture prompted women to seek gainful employment; often, just buying groceries necessitated it. Many working-class women and their allies brought their 1940s organizing spirit and techniques, such as women's caucuses, into the 1950s. They helped to build the feminist movement of the 1960s and 1970s, even though their own career goals often kept them from seeing discrimination in sex-typed job postings. Female union activists served on John F. Kennedy's President's Commission on the Status of Women, which reflected union women's views more than those of their middle-class sisters. Gerda Lerner, a pioneer women's historian, brought her leftist, pro-labor insights into that era's feminist activism. After reading *The Feminine Mystique,* she suggested that Friedan consider the hardships that "economic discrimination" added for working-class and African-American women. In an important insight for the battles to come, Lerner pronounced working-class women as "most important in reaching *institutional* solutions to the problems of women."[19]

Feminist activists outside of the white working class aimed their postwar workplace-related efforts in two general directions: first, they aimed to eliminate "push" discrimination; and second, they hoped to raise ambitions among their constituencies. What had always appeared to mainstream businesspeople to be simply pulling in people with potential and pushing away those without it appeared to women and members of disadvantaged minorities to be blanket rejection that ignored their credentials and job readiness. Centuries of such rejection had impaired these groups' ambition, and progress required both reducing "push" discrimination and fueling ambition. Betty Friedan's appeal to both fronts combined her own Ivy League education with years of labor activism on behalf of women. She addressed women whose mothers had been financially able to be stay-at-home housewives, who had given up "careers" (not just jobs), and who could afford to be bored. Although Friedan described only a fraction of American womanhood, even of suburban womanhood, in *The Feminine Mystique,* she and a growing legion of activists sought to rally all women to surmount a combination of barriers, humiliations, and misdirected desires that diminished all of their ambitions save for domesticity.[20]

The intense activism that had made the 1964 Civil Rights Act possible highlighted for all Americans the power of "push" discrimination in distributing opportunity. The national discussions on racism legitimated, energized, and instructed the budding new wave of feminism that arose out of the frustrations women experienced in jobs, in the New Left, in the suburbs, and in the civil rights and black power movements.[21] Through their own experiences and their observation of other groups who were striving for their civil rights, women began to find other ways to relieve their frustration beyond the domestic diversions that popular culture advised. Thus, the civil rights movement taught women of all ethnicities to think about public discrimination as a source of their economic dependence and to consider legislative, judicial, and political amelioration. As women learned to expect equity, they learned that social capital mattered, that they could build it, and that they could use it in business politics just as much as in legislative politics.

Small Groups and Big Ideas

From as many directions as came incentives for women to change their circumstances came the understandings and the means for them to do so. Everywhere, small groups of women talked together, formally and informally, discussing their needs, concerns, hopes, and frustrations, all the while building relationships with each other. Some groups formed for workplace-related purposes, but even groups with more intimate agendas more often than not explored business-related issues as well. Economics pervaded too many facets of women's lives for it not to infiltrate almost any subject—relationships, identity, and just getting through the day. Precedents for such group-based problem solving could easily be found. Working-class women had long engaged in collective bargaining to redress wage, promotion, and other grievances, and often they used local caucuses to determine their priorities and to plan. The Negro American Labor Congress urged African-American women to form local workshops to address issues particular to them. By the 1970s, caucuses gained wide use as a collective-action tool for raising women's consciousnesses (to use the era's phrase) about the nature and consequences of deeply gendered expectations and sex-based discrimination.[22]

Working women at the opposite end of the political spectrum

from unions also moved toward group-based solutions for sex-based discrimination. The NFBPWC resolutely subscribed to conventional notions of individualism. Yet from its start in 1919 the membership sought collective means to their various ends, including business achievement and legislative reform. After a half century of activism on behalf of women in business, including supporting the Equal Rights Amendment since 1937, the NFBPWC took on a more aggressive stance in the 1950s. It changed its magazine's title from *Independent Woman* to *National Business Woman* in November 1956. Women's goal of being independent in earning their own living required "a cooperative spirit in every phase of citizenship responsibilities," so the word "independent" was inappropriate. The *National Business Woman* eliminated fashion and food preparation from its features soon thereafter; the last cluster of four fashion articles in the January 1957 issue contrasted noticeably with the July issue later that year, which highlighted arguments for women's equal rights.[23]

In 1956, the organization's executive director, Helen G. Hurd, emphasized the importance of local clubs' assisting women, who were otherwise "free-floating" in male-dominated business environments. Hurd rejected "mere organization," preferring that the group take an active role in helping "individual women to solve some of the concrete problems with regard to their relations in the social structure," as the social structure, more than anything else, she believed, held women back. Continuing to promote the synthesis of social capital through local assistance, a 1963 article encouraged members to engage in "sharemanship" in their local clubs, recruiting new members as a means of gaining "full partnership in our socio-economic society."[24]

Feminists developed insights and mechanisms for business achievement through sometimes unlikely activities. Perceiving themselves as operating on the margins of the dominant culture, women everywhere constructed small groups of varying degrees of formality through which they defined and advanced their objectives, including goals attainable only through paid work. Betty Friedan considered women's informal gatherings within their suburban neighborhoods as possible keys to what she called self-realization and faith in nondomestic ambitions. Friedan argued that postwar glorification of a "feminine mystique" had valued women solely for fulfilling domestic duties and had thereby created a disabling "problem that has no name." This malaise paralyzed women by limiting their own sense of options. Only by sharing with each other, within secure groups, their dissatisfaction with domestic, unpaid work could women expand their horizons. Friedan claimed to have first heard women refer to "the problem" in 1959 when a mother voiced her frustration to four other mothers over coffee. The others understood her immediately, and they all knew at last that they were not alone.[25]

Friedan published *The Feminine Mystique* in 1963, and three years later she was among those who created NOW. The group's founders sought to build an action organization for women's civil rights, with specific legislative and workplace goals. To their dismay, as NOW's membership grew, many of the newer members were less sure of what NOW's goals should be. (By 1974, NOW had seven hundred chapters and forty thousand members.) Many of these new members wanted to explore what feminism could mean for them on a personal level. Adapting the notion of a caucus from earlier stages of women's activism—when aggrieved women congregated in ghettos, community centers, schools, or workplaces—NOW chapters sponsored local "rap groups." Organization leaders recognized the value of these groups for fostering political and social understanding of what most women and men had perceived as personal problems. Consequently, many chapters formalized workshops for educating and shaping feminists—"consciousness raising," as Kathie Sarachild, a peace and civil rights activist, called it in 1968. Participant Jo Freeman's 1975 history of "women's liberation" described the rap group as "an artificial institution which provides some degree of structured interaction" akin to the women's clubs of feminism's first wave a century earlier. Once the members of any given group felt that their needs for consciousness raising had been met, the group usually disbanded. Its members would move into their communities, carrying their new perspectives to friends and coworkers.[26] These synthetic networks thus increased women's abilities to function in every aspect of American life.

The small, informal consciousness-raising group was the defining mechanism of this "second wave" of feminism. After decades of rhetoric about opportunity, and the experience of having joined in or observed civil rights and New Left activities, participants in women's groups began to build what was traditionally characterized among men as "potential," including such features as self-confidence and nondomestic ambitions. Discussions often turned to work-related concerns, even when a group's agenda and lead-off questions did not mention jobs. Women taught each other about on-the-job strategies, such as the inappropriateness of responding to workplace situations with nervous or flirtatious smiles. (As one woman said in a New York City session, "To be masculine is to take action; to be feminine is to smile.") They also taught each other the merits of competing for workplace rewards instead of competing for other women's men. They taught each other that "we're not dumb because we can't get good jobs, we're discriminated against in hiring." They learned that they shared the encumbrance of economic dependence because of the difficulties of earning a solid wage. In these peer networks, women learned to trust each other and to call upon each other for worldly assistance and advice. By the early 1970s, women's caucuses were flourishing in more than one hundred corporations, crossing status and sometimes race lines. In these groups women sought the means for achieving equal pay for equal work, respect, grievance procedures, and opportunities, and they gained understanding and self-confidence.[27]

Examining 1970s' consciousness-raising topics in different contexts reveals the growing awareness of social processes for men's and women's workplace development. Women's sessions often addressed job-related humiliation, discouragement, and alienation, as they described experiences ranging from having to smile at sexist jokes, resisting advances of the sort now labeled harassment, and enduring limited assignments that more often included making coffee than making deals. Inequitable compensation, rigid limits to development opportunities, and presumed obligations to further husbands' careers would come up in the sessions, even those initiated for more intimate topics. June Arnold, for example, recalled that her group in 1970 linked gender roles with success and failure on corporate ladders. Because of what she learned from her group, Arnold came to denounce the sexism "sustaining the Horatio Alger myth of America which benefits only the ruling males." Tying the notion of the corporate ladder into her polemic, and (mistakenly) imputing the eponymous myth to Alger himself, Arnold described women as "rungs" supporting "Horatio's" climb. Promoting the rising tide of these group-nurtured epiphanies, the Los Angeles chapter of NOW formalized the process of consciousness raising and produced a handbook in 1974. The following year, a revised edition rapidly sold out worldwide. A third edition was published in 1976, in which the section on women and economics began with the equation "MONEY = POWER." The book emphasized the idea that women needed to learn to compete confidently within the workplace and to question the differences in respect and compensation between "women's work" and "men's work." It urged women to seek access to business and financial resources and to support other women in business.[28]

In contrast, a section on men's consciousness raising in the NOW *Guidelines* did not ask men to consider how they might improve their business opportunities and effectiveness. Instead it asked them to consider the roles their wives played as business assets. Reversing a standard question put to women, it asked men what jobs they might have chosen had they faced women's constraints. A series of questions focused on the domestic maintenance chores that fell to women at home and to minority men and women in public. The text associated freedom from these tasks with business success, because having to perform those tasks drained women's productivity. Professional and executive men were advised to consider whether they could have achieved their "'self-made' status" without help from women.[29]

The so-called men's liberation movement of the early 1970s did not deplore occupational limitations, although it was inspired by women's insights, motivation, and techniques for liberation from gendered constraints. Whether based on small-group consciousness raising or individual therapy, the activities of the men's movement gave middle- and upper-class men the opportunity to focus on self-reflection, on enriching their relationships with both men and women, and on becoming emotionally healthier and more fulfilled. To reach these goals, advisors encouraged men to *reduce* their occupational efforts in order to upgrade personal and familial involvements. In 1976, Herb Goldberg, then a California State University professor of psychology, wrote a book titled *The Hazards of Being Male: Surviving the Myth of Masculine Privilege*. He feared for those victims of gendered expectations whom he characterized as "successful male zombies." Men, he asserted, were just as much casualties of cultural pressures as women, but they suffered from a paradoxical burden, apparently running the show by oppressing others but failing to gratify themselves. Learning competitiveness in order to achieve in the workplace, men too often knew nothing else. Goldberg analyzed men's job-related tensions and fears, not in order to urge them on to climb to greater heights on corporate ladders, but to have them recognize the cost and the "impossible binds" of ambition. Goldberg, like most advocates of men's liberation, counseled men on what he called the "lost art of buddyship." By this he meant noncompetitive relationships with other men that were supportive but not instrumental. Such buddy relationships should grow without focusing on common targets, as in the pursuit of war (international or gang), business dealings, or women. By contrast, Goldberg called most male relationships "manipulative": they operated only as long as they served "a mutually beneficial feed-off, such as occurs in the business world," often between powerful men and their subordinates.[30] Ironically, by the time Goldberg published his book, women were discovering the merits of the patterns of behavior he decried.

These explorations of how individuals related to their social environment through cultural expectations illuminated connections between the private and the public spheres that had long been invisible. With the political intensity of the Cold War, the civil rights movement, and the Vietnam War as background, in 1968 former civil rights worker Carol Hanisch coined the phrase "The personal is political." Politics in this sense reigned wherever power differentials ranked individuals, such as in business. Women's status in business and elsewhere should therefore not be blamed on women's individual failings. The problems were systemic, and they required systemic solutions.[31] Legal changes, most notably civil rights enactments and enforcements, provided one type of solution; they would make exclusion from schools, public places, and jobs illegal and culturally unacceptable. Accordingly, much of women's and disadvantaged minorities' first decade of efforts after 1964 focused on gaining entry to previously inaccessible arenas where opportunities existed.

Advocates for marginalized groups also recognized the importance of fostering hope and ambition in people too long prevented from exercising ambition. Consciousness raising, inspired and supported in one form or another by a growing women's press and through women's groups small and large, became women's most visible early tool to promote these feelings. Individual women who responded to this cultural revolution by moving into business with newfound ambition thought that eliminating barriers would be all that was needed for them to fulfill their ambition. Yet the lessons women and others had learned in the early 1970s about working together and building peer networks contributed to a mind-set that would soon create a new awareness of an old set of tools for success.

Sex on the Ladder

Corporate America has always distributed women through its ranks in complete accordance with gauges of social capital. Although women have always owned or managed small and medium-sized businesses, the larger the firm—and therefore the more power it took to acquire status within it—the less likely women were to rise beyond a company's lower rungs. Mid-twentieth-century analysts occasionally noted that a few women did hold top management positions, disproving the rule that women could not manage but proving the rule that social capital mattered above all else in distributing opportunity. The two primary ways for a woman to control a firm were for her to have founded it or to have inherited it through a male relative. Prior to the 1980s, no woman made it to a top position of a major corporation any other way. In 1973, *Fortune* reported on finding 11 women among approximately 6,500 officers and directors of the largest 1,220 American corporations. Of those women, one had only a titular position, three had founded their companies with their husbands, one had founded her company "virtually singlehandedly," and four had gained their influence through family ownership. Among the ten active managers, seven of the nine women who were married worked in the same companies as their husbands. Two of the eleven did rise through the ranks "the way most men do . . . without family sponsorship," although social capital mattered in those cases too: the father of one had been president of a different firm in a related industry; and the other woman had been promoted to the position of vice president from that of the CEO's executive secretary; when the CEO retired, she reduced her activity with the firm. *Fortune* concluded that founders or inheritors benefited by not having either to begin in dead-end sex-typed positions or to climb through a discriminatory "corporate hierarchy."[32] Social capital had a hand in all of these women's careers, not just "family sponsorship" in the sense of glaring nepotism.

Most of the ten high-level women *Fortune* interviewed for its 1973 report, including Katharine Graham, had little sympathy for vocal feminists. Four years earlier, Caroline Bird's popular book *Born Female: The High Cost of Keeping Women Down* had named Graham among the "loophole women," very successful women whose privileges had enabled them to bypass typical obstacles. In 1963 Graham had inherited a fortune that included controlling interests in the *Washington Post* and *Newsweek*. When Bird interviewed her, Graham asserted that her "situation is so unusual that it has very little relevance for other people." Over time, however, Graham did come to admit that gender mattered. Like most white American women of the time, she had started off believing that her anxieties and feelings of inadequacy in meetings full of men were personal, not cultural. She blamed her own feelings of alienness—not speakers' thoughtlessness—for her discomfort when speakers addressed their audience as "Gentlemen and Mrs. Graham." As the women's movement grew, colleagues and friends of Graham, including Gloria Steinem, challenged Graham's lack of perspective, suggesting books and acting as private consciousness-raising tutors. Why, they asked, did she accept her frequent invisibility among men no more influential than she, or accept being denied admission to the Economic Club of New York? When Graham said in a 1969 interview that a man could perform her job better than she, a female reporter and editor threatened to quit the *Post*. Once Graham's eyes opened, however, she began to notice countless slights, rebuffs, and insults—usually phrased as jokes to which she felt obliged to smile; and she finally objected to the custom of ladies being "dismissed" from after-dinner business and political conversations. By the time Steinem began laying the foundation for *Ms.* magazine, Graham was ready to give seed money and support.[33]

Katharine Graham came to realize that her privileged class position could put her at the head of a major corporation but that it could not override the constraints of gender altogether, including her own self-imposed constraints and limited vision. By the mid-1960s, however, restless women of all classes had begun to see past gendered constraints in themselves, the law, and the workplace. They would have to fight exclusion and generate the will to do so. In 1964 an analyst observed that feminists could have a difficult time making a revolution, as they still lacked a driving ideology.[34] Yet, out of their consciousness raising in the next decade, women did generate an ideology, one that linked the personal and the political.

Applying the New Left's conception that politics encompasses all relationships governed by power, women linked their personal lives and attitudes with the politics of the workplace. They began to see the flaws in traditional advice literature that pinned responsibility for success solely on individuals' talents and efforts. Like African-American men, women came to know better. They concluded that no amount of effort could build opportunities for people without social capital. Ordinary women and African Americans should be able to rise as high as ordinary white men, they often said. They learned that there were no individual solutions, and they exchanged their limited, self-blaming imagination for what sociologist C. Wright Mills called the sociological imagination. These newfound insights brought relief to countless women: they realized that they were not alone in their frustration and their inability to move into rewarding employment. As laws and cultural conditions changed, exclusion grew less acceptable, vindicating activist Carol Hanisch's 1970 assessment that "there are no personal solutions."[35]

A Corporate Feminist at AT&T

Lois Kathryn Herr began her twenty-six year career at American Telephone & Telegraph (AT&T) and NYNEX expecting that such a large and prestigious corporation would operate rationally. Eager and alert, her ambition grew in the mid-1960s when she saw other women move into nontraditional positions, filling technical needs in a fast-growing, high-tech industry. Impressed by the technological progressiveness of AT&T's Bell Laboratories, Herr became perplexed, and then angered, by rules both formal and informal that seemed to her to have no logical connection to the work. For instance, women were not to wear pantsuits; somehow miniskirts were deemed more professional. She and others asked why Bell Labs insisted upon using "Miss" and "Mrs." to indicate women's marital status. Why did they hire men and women with the same qualifications at different salaries and with different benefits? Why did her supervisors praise Herr's work but refuse her requests for more challenging positions? As Herr began to think in terms of a career rather than just a job, her frustration grew. Too many rules exaggerated the differences between men and women within the firm. By August 1970, Lois Herr had become a feminist—a "corporate feminist," to use her term. She began to organize other women at Bell Labs and became increasingly active in NOW. As Herr read the growing feminist literature, she, like so many others, expanded her concerns and possible solutions beyond her own career and life. The rules had to change everywhere, she decided; and AT&T was a good place to start. NOW and the EEOC also identified AT&T as a prime target to use as an example for change. The leviathan AT&T was then the nation's largest private-sector employer and employed one of every fifty-six working women.[36]

The restraints on Lois Herr's ambition at AT&T followed from the overriding logic of sexual stereotyping. Her library still contains well-worn copies of books that helped her understand that those restraints, and their ultimate remedies, were social and political: Caroline Bird's *Born Female,* Saul Alinsky's *Rules for Radicals,* Pamela Allen's *Free Space: A Perspective on the Small Group in Women's Liberation,* and Robin Morgan's *Sisterhood Is Powerful.* Herr read widely in the mainstream business press as well, including from leading newspapers and the *Harvard Business Review,* as well as from the Business and Professional Women's publications list.[37] She also attended meetings and lectures, such as one in 1971 whose speakers included Bird and Cynthia Fuchs Epstein, an academic sociologist whose work had a major impact on feminist thinking. Herr was a dedicated corporate feminist, but she was not unusual in her efforts to learn what she needed in order to participate fully in the workplace. She and others saw Epstein and Bird speak, read their works and the many others in circulation, and helped disseminate them to other women. Herr published a newsletter within AT&T; *The Private Line* disseminated questions, reading lists, and news. NOW also encouraged its members to read, listen, and participate. Films, sometimes produced by progressive companies such as IBM, made the rounds. Betty Friedan's leadership in NOW formed another prominent link between feminist authors and activists.[38] All the theorists and all the activists may not necessarily have agreed with one another, but they did inform one another.

Lois Herr never wavered in her loyalty to what the corporate world claimed as its ethos: work hard and well, and expect even-handed, objectively distributed opportunities to work even harder and better. Yet corporate America had not lived up to its own principles with respect to women. That explains why Herr—and many other—corporate feminists turned to Saul Alinsky's *Rules for Radicals*. In 1972, as Herr worked out her ideas about corporate feminism, the points she itemized as "Alinsky Tactics" included urging feminists to insist that their targets "live up to [their] own book of rules." That same year Herr prepared a report for AT&T Corporate Planning that she later revised under the title "External Realities: Feminists and the Corporation." Laying out external and internal sources of feminist pressure on corporations, Herr assured "the corporation" that corporate feminists did not threaten it; "they are out to make it better."[39]

Herr and other corporate feminists included corporate documents and literature about managerial principles in their cases, as did NOW and the EEOC. Although this business literature suggested how pull operated in mainstream men's favor and therefore contained the clues to corrective strategies, neither Herr nor others who objected to corporate inequities in the early 1970s saw past the pressing need to eliminate exclusionary discrimination. Push was too overwhelming for the outsiders to see what pull offered. Consequently, in the early phases of this era's feminism, male managers often recommended "special efforts" to move women into managerial positions. They well understood the need to apply "pull" mechanisms for entering and climbing corporate ladders. Women, in contrast, were more likely to insist that all they required was "just . . . an equal chance," just an elimination of push. For instance, Ann London Scott, an academic who helped frame NOW's affirmative action policy and testified for the EEOC during the AT&T hearings, explicitly described affirmative action's synthetic pull into jobs as "self-destruct" programs—short-term remedies. Once the system worked properly, these programs would become unnecessary. Scott emphasized that women must be allowed access to training programs and other sources of opportunity under "good management" practices, thus framing the solution in terms of getting in, of ending exclusionary discrimination.[40]

A 1970 Bell System report on women in management sounded all the right notes about inserting women into existing standard managerial practices. In exploring why men were promoted "sometimes at the expense of more competent women," the authors noted that "fact-finding" had found that "many traditional beliefs concerning women [were] quite unreasonable." They also found attitudes and presumptions about managerial qualifications that gave men advantages but were unrelated to the actual positions. In order to live up to corporate ideals, "the System [had] to provide the best female talent with the opportunities to be selected, developed and utilized in the best possible way." Reading like a management textbook, the report identified three components of success in management: "*ability, motivation* and *opportunity.*" Only in opportunity did men and women differ "significantly." Typical of the "organizational factors" that resulted in "different *opportunity* factors for our women managers" was the fact that personnel departments excluded women in the "manpower planning program" for middle and upper management. Although women received promotions "*into* management at about the same rate as men, the likelihood of promotion *within* management for women is negligible." Management decision makers saw women as impermanent, "filling a position rather than as moving through it." Women's positions were dead-ends rather than opportunities because management neither considered nor evaluated women for further promotion. Other inequities included differential recruiting practices for college graduates, the exclusion of women from special training programs and rotational assignments for development, and a complete bar on women in the upper ranks of management. Every corporate practice that enhanced men's progress inhibited progress for women. All this led the reporting group to attach "a definite urgency" to the problem, in part because the "typical management person in the Bell System did not perceive a problem concerning women in management."[41] Women were aliens within the managers' world, and most top managers saw no contradiction between their corporate ethos of objective opportunity and women's lack of access to it.

Because managerial practices at AT&T did not reflect its progressive corporate pronouncements, women's and African Americans' complaints to the EEOC mounted. By 1970, the EEOC had received more discrimination complaints against AT&T, then the nation's largest private employer, than against any other firm. Teaming up with the Federal Communications Commission (FCC), which required equal employment opportunity of the industries under its purview, the EEOC had a powerful ally with which to challenge the giant Bell System. In December 1970, the EEOC charged AT&T with a host of violations against codes that extended beyond the FCC rules to the Equal Pay Act of 1963, the Civil Rights Act of 1964, various executive orders, plus state laws and city ordinances, even the U.S. Constitution. AT&T's size and stature gave this case enormous significance, and organizations ranging from NOW to the National Association for the Advancement of Colored People to the American Civil Liberties Union filed statements in support of the charges. For two years, the EEOC and the FCC negotiated with AT&T and argued their cases in hearings before the three parties finally came to terms. The January 1973 settlement on race and sex discrimination put every U.S. corporation on notice. As Lois Herr described the results, the affirmative action principles embedded in this settlement aimed to "structure the personnel practices of business to help corporations achieve a goal of equity." They sought to make "equal opportunity . . . a part of the routine."[42]

General Electric, in contrast to AT&T, built a positive image for itself by the early 1970s in combating race and sex discrimination. Its widely distributed 1972 report, *Women and Business: Agenda for the Seventies,* laid out a progressive course of affirmative action. It called for women to gain positions by the company's eliminating exclusion, opening occupations, and eradicating "all institutional barriers." The investigators concluded that "the main thrusts of the women's movement is to get 'in'"—to gain the multiple benefits of responsible and challenging jobs. Written from the perspective of improving management, the GE report also suggested strategies beyond mere entry. After the typical, and lengthy, description of "myths and issues" about women in the workplace, a brief section titled "Equality of Opportunity" concluded that U.S. corporations had failed to meet the modern corporate mission "to ensure the full utilization of all our human resources." In something of an understatement (and with revealingly infelicitous phrasing), the report stated that "our manpower systems have simply neglected, on the whole, to factor women into their planning." Other company failings included "well-intentioned protection" that held women back, "male chauvinism," and "women's own attitudes and aspirations." Proposed corrections through the establishment of affirmative action included considering *all* qualified people for promotion, seeking out qualified women, and requiring that women be included in all appraisal, training, and development programs. The report, in effect, proposed using what for men were simply standard personnel practices, recognizing that innovation entailed merely applying existing rules and practices to everyone. GE's words did not reflect its practice, however, and in 1973 the EEOC filed a complaint. The resulting 1978 settlement called for GE essentially to practice the management it preached. As Eleanor Roosevelt had insisted in 1962, "a mere statement supporting equality of opportunity must be implemented by affirmative steps to see that the doors are really open for training, selection, advancement, and equal pay."[43]

Corporate Ladders at Avon

Avon Products, Inc., wholeheartedly endorsed the standard U.S. corporate ethic. Objective criteria and fair procedures for entry and promotion inspired many heartfelt words. The gap between beliefs and actions at Avon, however, was also typical, as at GE, whose public advocacy of affirmative action did not forestall the EEOC's case against its actual practice. The white men who ran Avon and most corporations in the 1960s and 1970s struggled with their suspicion that following meritocratic ideals and the law meant violating deep convictions about who did and did not have potential for management.

Avon's annual reports, like all corporate annual reports, were filled with platitudes that expressed the image the firm wanted to project to its various publics, especially investors. In keeping with prevailing values, Avon's annual reports of the 1950s always differentiated "management" from its roughly ten thousand employees and over one hundred thousand "representatives"—the female "independent contractors" who presented Avon's face to the public, on whose "loyalty and ability" management depended. Avon had always developed its managers from within. (In 1964, the average age of Avon's corporate officers was fifty, each having an average of twenty-four years with the company.) This policy continued into the mid-1960s with no sense that the company's "program to assure the development of a continuing supply of executives" should produce anything but more of the white men in suits who populated all of the executive and board pictures in the reports until 1967, when a lone woman appeared in the top ranks. Internal documents show that Avon's development programs fit snugly into the standard corporate managerial ethos and practices. Personnel department bulletins emphasized that "the development of people is a fundamental responsibility of management. Effective personnel development must be an everyday function." Properly conducted, personnel procedures would ensure a "spirit of harmony and cooperation," which in turn would contribute "to an efficient and productive organization."[44] No management textbook could ask for more.

By the late 1960s, "fair and equitable treatment" had joined harmony and efficiency as managerial goals at Avon. A 1968 bulletin noted a policy shift by which all exempt employees (salaried, not hourly or on commission) became eligible for the "Appraisal Program," not just those already in management. Although the announcement still used only masculine pronouns when referring to eligible employees, this shift in policy did extend career development to women outside of male-dominated management enclaves. Avon's personnel departments also received notice in 1969 that "all eligible non-exempt associates are considered for advancement." Still, when the 1969 "Guidelines for Conducting the Performance Appraisal Interview" outlined all the usual recommended features of a proper corporate evaluation ("comfortable," "individualized," using "equitable comparisons . . . based on similar standards of performance," and with "development plans" such as company-supported training), it referred only to men. The change to inclusive or gender-neutral presumptions took decades.[45]

In 1971, all twenty-eight top positions at Avon still belonged to white males. The following year saw accelerated efforts to remedy that imbalance, as the men at the top struggled to integrate strangers—women and ethnic minorities—into their midst. Their efforts evinced both good intentions and uncomfortable squirming. Without admitting to previous sex- or race-based exclusion, Avon's executives began to apply basic management principles to the task of replacing pushes with pulls.[46] Though not as effective as conventional, social capital–based pull, institutionalized pull—in the form of affirmative action—did make the entry of formerly excluded groups possible. This was a necessary first step.

A telling 1972 Avon document brought together the standard

corporate ethos and the problems of applying it to strangers. The awkwardness of this transitional phase is evident. On the one hand, "Managing a Woman Effectively"—the title of the document—unequivocally labeled women as strangers. The integration of these aliens required "climate control"; for one thing, managers' informal discussions with each other, as well as their official statements, should include pronouns and other phrases that referred to women as well as men. Managers could use their lunch and other conversations with each other to expose "their own biases, and make them aware of other male points of view." Managers should advise women about problems of "acceptance by peers and subordinates," and they should not preemptively exclude women from opportunities, such as travel and conferences. The rest of the recommendations followed standard personnel practices, now to be applied to everyone. Most important, the document started and ended with reminders of the corporate ethos. "When discussing the effective management of women," it began, "we are actually talking about management techniques which should be applied with all Avon employees." The conclusion conveys the prevailing tension:

> As you surely noticed, all the above are simply good management techniques. Our concern should be that we are doing all we can to promote the development and success of all individuals in Avon, including women. Because we might tend to regard women as fitting a narrow stereotype and not consider them for non-traditional opportunities (training programs, assignments or positions), we should be especially attentive to her individual needs and interests. . . . By being open-minded, and willing to experiment, we can add much to the breadth of opportunities available to women in Avon. With the support of all management, we can continue to add a valuable resource to Avon's management team.[47]

Even the most standard of "good management techniques" were experimental when applied to strangers.

That same year, 1972, Avon formed a Corporate Social Responsibility Committee, responding to what its report called "society's growing complexity." Of course, society had always been complex, but corporate managers had been able to shield themselves from much of it until then. The "new challenges [that had] emerged" included "the women's movement, [and] the need to draw minorities more fully into the mainstream of American life." In Avon's files for that year lies an extensively annotated article from the National Association of Manufacturers titled "Women in Management—Past, Present, Future," which recommended, among other things, "an open promotion policy" and active recruitment of women for "professional level jobs." One sentence expressed both the ongoing transition and the continuing dichotomy in perception that was its target: "Actually, it is the moment of decision for both women and for management." In keeping with this spirit, in its most dramatic and public action that decade, the Avon board of directors appointed its first woman member, Cecily Cannan Selby, in 1972. The following year, Ernesta G. Procope, an African-American businesswoman, became the second female board member.[48]

Avon's "Corporate Responsibility Plan 1973" included marketing strategies such as making products for all skin tones and types so minority women could sell Avon products to their peers. It also urged seeking out minority suppliers. This confidential report laid out plans for integration because they were "economically and morally proper [and therefore] within the letter as well as the spirit of the Avon tradition." A revised "Procedure Bulletin" laid out the rationale and the means for both preventing discrimination and enacting affirmative action to recruit African Americans aggressively, including through the use of community outreach and organizations such as the National Urban League and the National Alliance of Businessmen. Counter to Avon's tradition of promoting from within, this plan emphasized recruiting women for upper management from the outside as well as from internal development programs. Throughout, the tone of the text communicates a sense that managers felt they were assimilating and training aliens, emphasizing the importance of inculcating Avon's "philosophy" and policies. Workshops of various sorts for employees and top managers attended to "cultural differences" and included "racial awareness seminars" and "women in management awareness training programs." In the end, promotions should depend upon the corporate ethos—that is, "solely upon merit, ability, initiative, and dependability, and when other factors are equal, the employee having the longest period of service with the company receives the preference."[49] That last clause, of course, left little room for women and other new arrivals. Without some infusion of synthetic social capital, not even substantially greater talent and effort could overcome the strangers' historic lack of access.

Avon's programs and policies hint at the depth and breadth of how it and every major corporation wrestled to begin integrating strangers of various stripes into their midst. As the Avon records make clear, if upper-level managers made the connection between the need to integrate previously excluded groups and the values to which the company laid claim—universal access to the American dream through objectively and fairly distributed opportunities—they would apply considerable resources to the project. Lest these efforts seem extravagant, as critics asserted, Francine E. Gordon made an analogy between integrating people and integrating what were in the mid-1970s technological strangers—computers—into a company's practices. Speaking to a 1974 conference for corporate executives on women in management at the Stanford Graduate School of Business, Gordon described how corporations facilitated the changes that their first computers required. She contrasted the top priorities, performance incentives, and high-level authorities assigned to introducing computers against the low-level, low-budget, peripheral personnel staff to whom nobody reported typically assigned to the equal employment "problem." Moreover, she pointed out, top executives' involvement in equal employment too often ended after they simply proclaimed an inspiring statement crafted by public relations—unless the EEOC, another outside authority, or public protests intervened to ensure their interest.[50]

Gordon's analogy was brilliant. We can no longer imagine any business operating without computers; we all know the costs that institutions unhesitatingly incur to integrate even questionable new computer applications into their operations. Yet some institutions and individuals still consider the effort required to integrate some human beings into their organizations to be an unreasonable burden. Battles have continued over the use of affirmative action as a synthetic mechanism to pull people onto and up corporate ladders. While those battles took place, however, advocates for the marginalized uncovered the social capital mechanisms by which these individuals might succeed once the doors had been pushed open.

Uncovering Social Capital

Years before the exclusionary discrimination that pushed women away from opportunities in business became illegal, the NFBPWC had begun to recognize the importance of socially based pull to business success. In 1956, the organization's executive director, Helen G. Hurd, wrote an article titled "Leadership Problems for the White Collar Woman Worker" for the organization's magazine, *Independent Woman*. In just two pages Hurd laid out issues that would not capture feminists' full attention for decades—not until corporate feminists began to wonder why reducing the push against them had not assured their success. Hurd recognized that leadership was a social phenomenon and that social factors were what most seriously constrained women's ambitions, often including women's own training and presumptions. Hurd observed that women were "free-floating" within the male-dominated and male-defined business culture because they lacked men's "sponsorship which assists in the development of attitudes and loyalties." That sponsorship protected men and advanced the contacts that facilitated their career mobility. Women's absence from professional societies and service clubs, including Rotary and Kiwanis, kept women from "the easy camaraderie and gossip of the local business world." Nor did women typically develop the required confidence and skills for public competition, as did young men; this further limited their occupational choices and effectiveness. Moreover, a powerful double bind branded women as overly aggressive if they were assertive, and "just a woman" if they were not.[51]

At around this same time, NFBPWC sponsored a study by Margaret Cussler, which was published in 1958 as *The Woman Executive*. Cussler interviewed fifty-five female executives and concluded that, except for women who had founded their own firms, in each case, "something—or someone—gave her a push up the ladder while others halted on a lower rung." Working harder and longer than others did *not* open doors for women, whom Cussler identified as a minority, like African Americans, because of their "inferior place in society." In her second chapter, "The Sponsor and the Protégé," Cussler insisted that that relationship was the key—a "magic formula"—that explained why so few women had risen in firms they did not own. Sponsors protected protégés, trained them, and recommended them for openings. Cussler found that too few women "recognize[d] the importance of the informal relationships so readily cultivated by men."[52]

Cussler contrasted women, who by "faithful drudgery" could rise only to the top of the secretarial ranks, against ambitious young men, who filled their calendars with coffee breaks, lunches, golf dates, and card games with men who "count." She advised ambitious women to expand their limited notions of what their jobs entailed to include social events where "clinching the deal" occurred.

Although Cussler did not indicate *how* women could break down barred doors, she argued that they must make more use of their social interactions, either joining men in the executive dining room or eating there alone if necessary, rather than with secretaries. Status and prestige accrued by association, and Cussler insisted that women should overcome feeling awkward about cultivating contacts. She cited a *Fortune* study as evidence that ambitious men connected everything they did to their careers, urging that women do deliberately what successful men were doing as a matter of course. *Fortune* did not highlight men's merging of leisure and labor as a mercenary tool for advancement but as an admirable characteristic of men who were so passionate about their work that they could only enjoy what pertained to it.[53]

Cussler's observations about office politics contrasted sharply with those of most contemporary business analysts on the topic. Although a few cynics scoffed at any denial of the impact of politics, most decried its effects as blemishes on an otherwise objective meritocracy. As outsiders looking in, however, Hurd and Cussler could see how the dynamics of office politics—social capital—kept women out of power. As Hurd put it, "Men move in a prefabricated recognized pattern; women move on their own." Although Hurd and Cussler overlooked it, white middle- and upper-class women did, however, possess a great advantage over ethnic minorities. Whether as members of executive men's families or as private secretaries and assistants, they were in a position to see those social patterns at work. Relatives and acquaintances also gave them access to information and what economist Eli Ginzberg called "informal communications networks [that can] serve as important informational and hiring channels." Almost two decades after Hurd and Cussler, Ginzberg noted that women still felt awkward about using personal contacts, though "men have always made use of such contacts."[54]

Women too often trained young men only to watch them march

past them up corporate ladders. This indignity spurred on some women, like Mary Kay Ash, either to build their own ladder or to figure out how to use the rules of social capital to advance their own career. As invited guests who participated only as ornaments, facilitators, and cheerleaders, women at least could see how business success happened.

Beyond Push

In the 1960s, excluding women from corporate opportunities not only became illegal, but it also came under growing criticism from advocates of the corporate ethos who sought to employ fully the nation's talents. The business press increasingly repeated arguments that had appeared earlier in *Independent Woman* and other women's publications, debunking the standard myths by which gatekeepers had justified excluding women from executive positions. In a 1960 issue of *Office Executive,* the journal of the National Office Management Association, the president of the Los Angeles Metropolitan College of Business objected to the scarcity of women in top positions. He itemized a typical list of "reasons" for discriminating against women, then refuted each of them, concluding that either the reasons were "sheer fiction" or they resulted from correctable educational or social habits.[55]

Responding to the new legal climate, the *Harvard Business Review* joined this current in 1965 with an article asking "Are Women Executives People?" The article concluded that although few men admitted to operating according to stereotypical beliefs about women, they overwhelmingly agreed that "*only the exceptional,* indeed the overqualified, *woman can hope to succeed in management.*" In other words, women were not people in the same way men were. They could not therefore rely on purportedly objective personnel procedures to advance their careers, despite respondents' repeated references to the "American creed of freedom of choice" and the "principle of selection on individual merit."[56] But if push was now illegal, and fewer business leaders would openly admit to the stereotypical excuses for excluding women, what remained?

Gatekeepers' comfort was what remained, and by the mid-1960s it had become a target of analysis. Because people feel comfortable around and cooperate best with others whom they can predict, trust, and communicate with readily, gatekeepers' comfort levels have given social capital much of its power. Yet the issue of gatekeepers' comfort rarely entered into analyses of business success until the mid-1960s, when variations on words like "comfort" and "uncomfortable" began to appear to explain both "push" and "pull" mechanisms in business. In 1964, for instance, the *Harvard Business Review* reported on the relative weights of objective and subjective variables in executive advancement. From surveys of thousands of executives and many interviews, Garda W. Bowman demonstrated that a candidate's degree of difference from decision makers overwhelmingly determined promotability. Despite the depth of her analysis, however, Bowman focused on "push" discrimination against ethnicity and sex.[57] So close to the passage of the Civil Rights Act of 1964, it was difficult to see much beyond this vantage point.

Although the 1964 legislation did not include any sort of call for affirmative action, various efforts in that direction soon began. Some advocates, such as Eleanor Roosevelt and the National Urban League, had earlier recognized the need for building in pull to make up for centuries of "push" discrimination. By 1967, people who were concerned with ethnicity-based discrimination against African Americans and other groups, including Jews, developed the concept of institutional racism to explain the residual impact of past discrimination, such as unevenly distributed education and presumptions about who fit into good jobs. Going about business as usual, they realized, could not redistribute opportunities. Insight about institutionalized discrimination helped to legitimate affirmative action as a means of pulling people into opportunities, but analysts continued to emphasize how existing systems built barriers and pushed people away. For instance, Caroline Bird wrote in 1968 that women could do almost any job, however rigorous or high-pressured, if they could only get it.[58]

To move ahead—to identify the pull that marginalized people still lacked and that kept them from competing on and ascending corporate ladders—required a new language of business relationships. As advocates learned to identify the problems that prevented strangers from succeeding in business, they invented new terms and revised others as ways of labeling and explaining their observations and then naming the solutions. In 1970, for example, such terms as "role models," "mentors," and "networks" were not in Americans' general vocabulary. By 1980, however, the language of social capital had largely taken shape, and by the mid-1990s those expressions had become embedded in our everyday language. How could that happen so quickly?

CHAPTER 7

Uncovering the Power of Pull

How could a woman attend a meeting at the New York Stock Exchange in 1967? By sneaking up to the conference room floor in a service elevator, escorted by janitors. Attending this meeting was part of Joan Lappin's job as an analyst at Equity Research Corporation. Her exclusion from the NYSE's lunchroom—and any number of other social venues where only white males could conduct business—was part of a problem that took decades to resolve. By the mid-1980s, revamped personnel policies and procedures had resulted in formerly excluded people being hired for *some* corporate jobs. But getting a job did not assure a career's progress. Barriers to the social venues where business was conducted still limited access to opportunity, hampered performance, and highlighted the alien status of the newcomers relative to the "insiders." Hostile behavior often frustrated ambition. As an indication of their growing frustration, 10 percent more female managers in 1990 believed that the "male-dominated corporate culture" hindered their success than had been the case two years earlier. Like many women during the 1980s who believed that they could climb no higher on corporate ladders, Joan Lappin founded her own firm in 1986, and succeeded brilliantly. In 1992, *Business Week* featured her among its list of the top fifty businesswomen in the United States. Lappin's firm handled investment accounts of a half million dollars or more, and she received rave reviews for her investment skills.[1] She never returned to a large corporation, even though she can now take the front elevator to the Big Board's lunchroom any time she likes.

As they discovered how to succeed, women, African Americans, and their advocates exposed the "pull" mechanisms of social capital that had lain hidden under heavy smoke screens of exclusionary discrimination and rhetoric of self-made, individualist success. As the haze of the worst of "push" discrimination began to clear, the "pull" mechanisms by which the fortunate succeeded in both small and bureaucratized businesses came into focus, challenging the self-made rhetoric. As age-old practices received names—"networking" and "mentoring" in particular—previously marginalized people could begin to identify these essential mechanisms, first as factors that limited their success, then as tools for advancement. Nonetheless, two decades after "push" discrimination was outlawed from most workplaces, frustrations continued, finding expression in 1986 with a new term, the "glass ceiling." Fresh attention to this old but newly named barrier further uncovered the mechanisms of social capital.

Sun Oil Company and the Sun Women's Organization

"I'm just like you" is a refrain in a verse found in the files of the Sun Women's Organization (SWO). This 1977 "Open Letter to an Employer" asserts that employees share a common humanity with their employers; they need not be strangers. Women and their supervisors at Sun Oil Company (Sunoco) spent the 1970s struggling to figure out their new world, but upper management continued to see women and ethnic minorities as strangers. Still wrestling with racial issues, Sun managers, like those of other firms, wondered whether "females (regardless of race) [should] be considered a minority group" despite their large numbers. Both women and African-American men remained unknown and alien aspirants, requiring special treatment. Often this "special" treatment simply meant equalizing access to information and opportunity following standard personnel practices, but expanding their reach. For instance, Sun readily adopted policies for the public posting of all openings and for establishing a "formalized career planning process." However, policy statements about managerial promotion still referred to male candidates, and only to those identified by their superiors as having "high potential," with the phrase encased in quotation marks in a 1970 document as if to point out its contested nature.[2]

Responding to Equal Employment Opportunity Commission (EEOC) and Labor Department guidelines, in 1970 Sun managers determined that all company policies regarding women had to be revised. The revisions, however, had little impact on women's position in the firm. Then the EEOC's 1973 settlement against AT&T put all U.S. corporate leaders on notice. Finally, in 1975, Sun accelerated and deepened what had been perfunctory efforts to remedy the inequities; the gentlemen present at a January 1975 Sun Executive Committee meeting were asked to ponder the matter of "promotable / high-potential females." One participant recommended encouraging and counseling "females to raise their career goals." Another proposed restructuring jobs to fit women's "capabilities." Yet another suggested a program for "infusing women into higher positions." In response, Sun president and COO Ted Burtis designated a Human Resources Task Force to address "the problem" of women's "upward mobility." In keeping with standard managerial procedures, the resulting recommendations featured formalizing for women and ethnic minorities the very types of activities that had long been standard for pulling mainstream men up corporate ladders, such as job rotation and training seminars, augmented with "possible short term 'catch-up' benefits" to accelerate progress.[3]

In essence, Sun's Female Upward Mobility Task Force had to determine how to synthesize and institutionalize pull for the newcomers to management-level positions. Modeling their proposals on existing programs at General Electric and IBM, the Sun task force prepared a document titled "Developmental Process for Individual Career Planning," which was intended to balance individual and corporate responsibilities, in keeping with orthodox management principles. A section titled "Special Emphasis" admitted that earlier efforts in the 1960s to eliminate "push" discrimination had brought new people into entry-level positions but had not made available the means of advancement. "Phase Two of our Affirmative Action Program" recommended expanding basic personnel advancement practices to *all* employees and maximizing the flow of information about opportunities throughout the firm. Following standard practices for men identified as having potential, the task force recommended institutionalizing promotional pull for women by listing middle- and upper-management positions likely to open up over five years, then identifying and training "qualifiable" women employees.[4]

In the course of Sun's forays into EEOC compliance, its human resources department received assignments to survey and coach managers in career counseling, performance appraisal, and "awareness." One survey exposed an array of widely held myths and stereotypes hindering women's advancement. A sampling of comments suggests the strain of incorporating strangers into what had been a relatively homogeneous elite.

- "Our customers aren't ready for a woman sales rep. Besides, working with the dealers is not a woman's job."
- "I'd hate to get beaten out of a job by a woman—so why develop them?"
- "I usually don't tell a woman exactly what's on my mind— they're not used to taking it straight."
- "I'd rather take a guy under my wing and develop him; he's a better risk. A woman would weaken the department."

- "We managers have an 'expectation' problem. We don't expect the same quality or quantity of work from the women as we do from the men."
- "Men understand the male viewpoint. How do we understand the female viewpoint?"
- "Affirmative Action means unqualified people get the jobs."
- "There are very few women who are emotionally and psychologically equipped to be anything but a secretary."
- "I interviewed men and women for an opening, but only the men had *potential*."

When asked to describe "potential," this last respondent said, "It's hard to describe. I guess it's a gut feel."[5]

With this evidence in hand, Sun's task force for EEOC compliance recommended a variety of actions and incentives, including that the company run a series of workshops for managers and women. Attendance at the workshops would be mandatory for all supervisors; all nonsupervisory women would be invited. Lending his authority to the project, President Burtis volunteered to deliver the introductory speech at the first session. The script prepared for him emphasized the benefits that would accrue to the firm from developing "woman-power," and asserted that discrimination violated the firm's "belief in the respect for the individual." The speech asked managers to consider whether they had genuinely tried to evaluate and counsel each woman to maximize her potential contribution.[6] Addressing both push and pull issues related to gender, Burtis asserted that not pulling women in ignored the spirit of equal opportunity, as well as the new legal climate.

Thirteen years after the Civil Rights Act, eleven years after the founding of the National Organization for Women (NOW), four years after the AT&T/EEOC settlement, and two years after Sun Oil Company had apparently recommitted itself to advance women into management, continuing frustrations of the women at Sun prompted the founding of the Sun Women's Organization (SWO) in 1977. Lest anyone question their resolve, the first adjective the founders used to describe their intentions was "serious." Their initial goals included building compensatory social mechanisms for women at the company, such as a support system for women moving into nontraditional positions. The eight founders were inspired to activism after having attended one of the company's awareness sessions; they sought a "forum in which women may serve as a resource to each other by sharing experiences and insight." They also believed that women at Sun nationwide needed an organization through which to gain top management's attention and respect in ways they could not as individuals.[7]

SWO's founders began gingerly, first seeking approval from President Burtis and then informing other top mangers of their intentions. Initial reactions from their managers ranged from dismay to cautious support. By this time, however, court decisions and the managerial and popular press had warned business leadership that superficial efforts did not fulfill a company's obligation to improve opportunities for women and ethnic minorities. The American Management Association, for example, had published a guide to EEO compliance in 1975 that informed its readers that "initiating . . . remedial activities . . . involves primarily the proper application of well-known personnel policies and practices"— "proper" meaning universal. Annotated excerpts from key court decisions showed managers and gatekeepers that firms were legally obligated to remove all barriers unrelated to job performance and that results, not efforts, measured compliance. Thus managers, as well as union leaders, had to overcome the "systemic discrimination" and "poor personnel practice" that allowed seemingly neutral decisions to have unequal consequences on different populations. An effective Affirmative Action Plan would "break the chain of discrimination" and its "chilling effect" on past victims.[8]

Despite the court rulings, however, some Sun managers were worried about the formation of the SWO, thinking that "an organized alliance could evolve into a militant organization." One naysayer softened his opposition in light of two pending class action suits and other EEOC action, but still expressed his concerns about "these women." In a confidential memo to Burtis, he wondered, for instance, why the women's proposal went directly to Burtis rather than through the women's immediate supervisors and "normal business channels." He also warned that some would view a female alliance as "a sexist group," and that could be detrimental to the women's cause. Burtis, however, decided that the benefits to the company and its female employees outweighed the risks. He repeatedly announced his "keen personal interest" in SWO, and at least one other executive praised him for an innovation that could "unblock a number of the traditional organization constraints."[9]

In October 1977, SWO's founders invited female Sun employees around the nation to join them, and they received a strong response. Despite official support, however, the women encountered obstacles from the mundane to the intensely political. Deciding when to meet presented problems because few women could commit to attending sessions after working hours. Participants also wanted to avoid the appearance of forming "a clique" or engaging in a "bitch session" or "grievance forum." SWO, especially outside the Northeast, aroused male colleagues' misgivings for its gendered exclusivity, though some of these men thought nothing of attending exclusive golfing parties or all-male clubs or using executive dining rooms. Some of SWO's regional groups even alluded to "setbacks of a . . . more pernicious nature." Still, enough women were seeking mutual career supports, organized information sharing, heightened communications between women, and links between women and management to initiate the groups. As an SWO newsletter put it, "We work in the same place five days a week and hardly know one another."[10]

An organizational meeting in November 1977 discussed agenda suggestions, which included distributing job and resource information, organizing problem-solving sessions, circulating bibliographies, and holding book and article discussions. Founders wanted "an arena in which women would feel free to share experiences and understandings as they relate to employment at Sun Co." In language derivative of consciousness-raising literature, leaders advised recruits not to expect the necessary "atmosphere of mutual trust and support" to exist immediately. By mid-1978, the SWO newsletter referred to the importance of forming a "support network," and soon thereafter the Philadelphia section offered monthly "RAP Sessions" on building careers, exploring sexual politics, setting up "informal communication networks," and figuring out "how to be part of the 'in' group." A local newsletter summarized points from its members' readings, including a recommendation that ambitious women "open up communications with your superiors and persons who are involved in or who can influence your career planning and development."[11]

Corporate feminists around the nation in the late 1970s were exploring workplace dynamics as they found their way in from the periphery of business. In keeping with this trend, respondents to an SWO survey stated that they preferred meetings about office politics over legislative politics. Women now inside the workplace knew that the law supported their growing ambitions, but they did not know how to get onto their company's career ladders, much less how to climb them. Two documents point to the importance of this period as a transition for Sun women in thinking about social capital. A memo of December 1977 listed possible speaker topics that ranged from skills like interview techniques and career planning to problems like peer pressure and supervising men. Although the memo included the item "job resource network" without explanation, the listing for mentoring not only placed quotation marks around "mentor" but explained the term as "how to get help from supervisor." But just five months later, in mid-1978, an SWO newsletter featured a speaker on mentoring, and this time the term was printed without quotation marks. After the presentation, the newsletter reported, the audience discussed "how realistic is it to approach someone to be your mentor," who could be a good mentor, and the "need for a company sponsored career counselor/mentor available to all women."[12]

This five-month shift indicates that women within this cohort of explorers eagerly adopted not-yet-fixed concepts as tools and guides, sharing their sources and expanding their insights as they went. Just as Lois Herr and her colleagues at AT&T distributed reading lists to each other, SWO recommended books, films, and articles. In fact, the first *Sun Women's Organization Newsletter* in January 1978 devoted one of its four pages to a bibliography of books featured as "useful and enlightening." Of the seven titles listed, three had come out just the year before, and none predated 1971, an indication of how rapidly this literature was growing. Moreover, SWO presented copies of one of the books, Rosabeth Moss Kanter's *Men and Women of the Corporation,* to ten senior Sun executives. This scholarly book, written by a professor of sociology, found its way onto lists throughout the ranks of corporate feminism, along with many other academic studies. Other popular and often-discussed titles were more colloquial in nature, such as *The Woman's Dress for Success Book* and others of the how-to-succeed genre. Betty Harragan's *Games Mother Never Taught You: Corporate Gamesmanship for Women* frequently found its way into lists and discussions, including those of the SWO. Some women found Harragan's cynical exposition of the necessity for playing office politics distressing. However bitter corporate feminists might have been about their lack of progress, for some, attacking beliefs about meritocracy seemed too threatening. They hoped to succeed without playing office games.[13] Ambitious women, especially those without a New Left or civil rights background, were often reluctant to accept that social capital trumped merit throughout the business world.

Naming and Reframing Strategies for Success

By the end of 1972, women had won 178 of 208 discrimination cases in lower courts, and the EEOC was working through a battery of complaints on both racial and sexual discrimination, often with significant success. Some individuals' lawsuits made quite a splash in the press as well, such as Elizabeth McDonald's suit against thirty-two companies because they interviewed only men for executive trainee positions. (She got an interview when she applied with her brother's name.) Like the women at Sun Oil Company, many still-marginalized people were looking up the ladders. "Tokenism" received growing notice, and public opinion often reproved firms that placed women and African Americans in positions with more show than authority. Legal settlements, like EEOC's with General Electric, filed in 1973 and settled in 1978, required universal implementation of standard personnel practices, such as an "open-promotion system." Yet progress of women and African Americans toward the top of corporate ladders remained painfully slow.[14] As in any transitional environment, analysis and advice thrived; insights flowed from every angle, through every medium. The lists and recommendations that corporate feminists shared with each other, plus highly visible popular publications, track these activists' evolving understanding of social capital. Through the growing literature, the mechanisms of social capital gained names and popular profiles.

Many core insights in this literature came from scholars, and one of the first sociologists to turn up in corporate feminists' reading lists was Cynthia Fuchs Epstein. By the time Lois Herr at AT&T heard Epstein speak in 1971, she had already testified before the EEOC and published in both the scholarly and the popular press. Her 1970 book *Woman's Place: Options and Limits in Professional Careers* explained what women faced in their "struggle for the right to a chance to succeed." She helped introduce terms such as "gatekeeper" to the business world. Gatekeepers, she observed, viewed women attempting to enter business and professional spheres with "suspicion, hostility, and amusement" and therefore refused to assign them to roles with authority. In another widely read publication, Epstein argued that "gatekeepers can structure success for those whom they judge will become competent." Most gatekeepers in high-prestige vocations were men who held stereotyped presumptions that women and minority men must fail, so they would not sponsor anyone who did not "fit the *image* of competence."[15] Epstein was describing precisely how the universal language of "potential" was used to pull select people onto and up career ladders.

For newcomers in a vocational arena, Epstein noted, "success is difficult because they have not shared the same worlds as their colleagues and cannot count on them for the same assistance that people from the same backgrounds informally offer to one another." That, in a nutshell, is the essence of how social capital works: it tends to favor homogeneity and exclude strangers. Discriminatory workplace practices included what Epstein called "the protégé system," in which sponsors teach their favorites "crucial trade secrets" through a mix of formal and informal relationships that "assure continuity of leadership." So undeveloped was the language of social capital when Epstein was writing, however, that even a section on "the club context" and its impact on bestowing favors did not include the word "network" or even the concept of a closed communication system. The index to Epstein's book included no entries for "sponsor," "role model," and "mentor," although Epstein did use the words "sponsor" and "role" in the text.[16] The lexicon of social capital had not yet taken shape.

Mentoring

A groundswell of interest in social capital as a positive tool rather than solely as an exclusionary weapon began to emerge in the mid-1970s. Analysts advised that the mechanisms that moved gatekeepers' favorites up business ladders had to be taken up by newcomers. A 1971 *Harvard Business Review* article titled "Women in Management" recognized that all successful businessmen needed mentors and concluded that women needed them even more. Presuming that women should mentor women, these analysts found the dearth of senior female managers to be an almost insuperable problem. Popular writer Gail Sheehy brought mentoring into popular discourse when her book *Passages: Predictable Crises of Adult Life* made the best-seller lists for 1975–1978. Writing about vocational experiences within the context of adult development, she used the concept of mentoring freely as a major social factor affecting adult lives. Sheehy's interviews indicated that most women in the early 1970s did not recognize the word or even the concept of mentoring. The paucity of women in positions of strength and authority, plus possible erotic complications with male guides, Sheehy argued, had prevented most women from developing a sense of what mentorship could offer. Noting that "career women" who did well were "at some point nurtured by a mentor," Sheehy concluded that those who lacked information that was available only through "the grapevine or the mentor system" missed "a mentor relationship, even if they don't know what to call it."[17]

In *The Seasons of a Man's Life,* published in 1978, Daniel Levinson and his coauthors added academic complexity and legitimacy to the mentoring concept. Together, Levinson's and Sheehy's books, plus myriad journalistic offshoots in the popular press, publicized the concept, forging it into an umbrella term. Like Sheehy, Levinson had found that "no word currently in use is adequate to convey the nature of the relationship we have in mind here." His concept covered "teacher," "sponsor," "host and guide," "exemplar," "counsel," "moral support," plus inspiration, "to support and facilitate the *realization of the Dream.*" Clustering all these functions under a single term promoted its rapid dissemination into popular language. Not optimistic about women's careers because of "the current reality," Levinson gave little attention to women as either mentors or protégés. He believed that powerful male mentors too often took advantage of women, and he did not consider other options.[18] This dismissal, however, did not discourage women from taking the ideas that held promise for their ambition.

The 1977 best-seller *The Managerial Woman,* by Margaret Hennig and Anne Jardim, each with a Ph.D. from the Harvard Business School, received widespread, positive reviews. The book showed up in the SWO lists, where it was "particularly recommended." *The Managerial Woman*'s index included no entry for "mentoring" because Hennig and Jardim described the men who assisted women's professional development in terms of their various roles as "supporter," "teacher," "buffer," "protector," and "sales agent." They concluded that "without exception" the successful corporate women they studied began as secretaries or administrative assistants and moved up with their bosses. The most successful of the women they studied had benefited from both fathers and supervisors who had downplayed their strangeness as females in male domains, thereby encouraging and enabling them to develop their intellect and skills.[19]

Harragan's 1977 *Games Mother Never Taught You* mentioned "mentor" once, at the end. She concluded, simply enough, that finding "one of them" improved a woman's "chance of winning the game of corporate politics . . . one-hundredfold." Also in 1977,

Rosabeth Moss Kanter published *Men and Women of the Corporation,* the book that the SWO gave to top executives shortly after its publication. It quickly became the standard work on social systems in business. Instead of "mentor," Kanter preferred the more traditional word "sponsor," under which she subsumed two functions: coaching and fighting for "a favorite." Sponsors could also help subordinates to "bypass the hierarchy" and could confer "reflected power" on them. Kanter also emphasized that if "sponsors are important for the success of men in organizations, they were absolutely essential for women, [who] need even more the signs of such influence and the access to real power provided by sponsors." Precisely because of their personalized nature, however, sponsors for women were "harder to come by," because "leaders choose to promote the careers of socially similar subordinates." As one executive told her, powerful people take on a protégé when they can see what they would like to imagine as a "younger version" of themselves. "Who," this man asked, "can look at a woman and see themselves?"[20]

Mentoring had long been an acknowledged means of pulling up novices in the arts and literature, as well as education, athletics, and politics, but explicit mentions of it challenged the individualist rhetoric that prevailed in twentieth-century business.[21] This did not, however, deter ambitious women from taking it up. Thus, by mid-1978, SWO newsletters no longer confined the term within quotation marks or felt the need to define it. One of the books recommended by the SWO illustrated how the word had moved into common usage. The 1975 edition of the American Management Association's *Ambitious Woman's Guide to a Successful Career* mentioned mentoring in passing in a chapter titled "Developing Your Boss as a Resource to You." The 1980 edition, by contrast, included five pages on mentoring in a new chapter, "Special Concerns of the Career Woman." The 1980 edition distinguished between sponsors and mentors, noting that mentoring was a more personal relationship. Gaining either a sponsor or a mentor, the authors wrote, requires "exceptional performance" that attracts the attention of influential people and makes them want to identify with this "young potential."[22]

By 1978, mentoring had reached the mainstream business press. *Business Week* proclaimed "Women Finally Get Mentors of Their Own" in an article that contained several interviews with women in upper management who advocated providing deliberate and focused assistance to other women. One noted that women are "good at their tasks but not good at politicking" and that mentors should focus on teaching those skills. Another observed that women lagged behind men in knowing "how to look around for their best opportunities"; she saw that as her particular gift to protégés. Another female executive answered one of social capital's ancient riddles: what do mentors gain by mentoring? She believed that successful mentoring offered "proof of the executive woman's power and a means of impressing it upon others." Also in 1978, the *Harvard Business Review* chronicled the careers of four chief executives at a single major corporation, applying notions of mentorship to explain how one generation of leaders produced the next. Predictably, the oldest of the four acknowledged mentoring as nothing more than his predecessor's recognizing his ability and letting him do "things my way." When it came time for this man to groom a successor, he simply went with "a feeling" that his pick "had it." Even as he described examples of mentoring, he assured the interviewer that each of his protégés had "earned everything he got." In contrast, the fourth in this line of chiefs discussed how his career had benefited from the third's special interest in him, noting that neither had used the word "mentor" back in the 1950s. He did, however, recognize that such "close human relationships" were essential to success, "whatever it might have been called." He concluded, "Everyone who succeeds has had a mentor or mentors."[23]

Six months later, another *Harvard Business Review* article announced its subject as "Much Ado about Mentors." This report noted that mentoring in "the business world [had been] largely unheralded," despite long traditions of acknowledged mentoring in the arts, sports, philosophy, and the military. A survey of 1,250 top executives revealed nonetheless that a high proportion of them had been mentored or sponsored. These reported higher earnings, a better education, earlier achievements, and higher job satisfaction than those who reported no such personal aid. Evincing the ongoing changes in perception and attitude, acknowledgement of having been mentored was highly correlated with male respondents' ages. However, *all* of the tiny number of women surveyed (less than 1 percent of the whole) acknowledged having been mentored.[24]

These articles heralded an explosion of interest in mentoring. Hundreds of articles, including business-related items, appeared in a wide range of media. By the mid-1980s, some analysts were complaining of "mentormania," but the topic continued to find ready audiences, especially among feminists and disadvantaged minorities.[25]

Rarely did an analysis of mentoring, under whatever name, fail to discuss the personal nature of such relationships, which could take on parental or erotic overtones. Kanter borrowed the term "office uncles" from British usage, and she documented the use of "rabbi" and "godfather" among her corporate informants. She even quoted a protégé who was concerned that these relationships often developed into "a father/son issue as well as business." The often-quoted 1978 article "Everyone Who Makes It Has a Mentor" mixed the individualist tones of a nineteenth-century saga of success with profoundly familial notes. As one of the men in that article asked rhetorically, "Who knows where close human relationships start?" All of these men readily admitted to the respect and affection, even a "father and son" type of love, that their intense, mutually supportive relationships entailed. Such comments suggested the difficulties women and other strangers faced in gaining that kind of support.[26]

Networking

African-American men at Xerox formed the most well known of the early corporate caucuses put together by newcomers. Thanks to the participants' diligence and an unusually supportive upper management, this system of peer networks yielded a dozen African-American vice presidents at Xerox by 1987. Top managers at Xerox had responded to the 1960s race riots in Rochester with resolute participation in programs sponsored by the National Alliance of Businessmen, developing their own projects as well. Aggressive hiring brought so many African Americans into the firm that some critics referred to it as "the ghetto." Effective programs gave credibility to rhetorical promises. Many of the new recruits moved into sales because their efforts in that arena would produce the most objective evidence of results. Even there, however, the newcomers soon realized that individual effort would not suffice; they were routinely assigned the least profitable territories and suffered other inequities.[27]

African-American sales representatives for Xerox in the San Francisco area organized an intensive mutual self-help caucus beginning in 1969. In the Washington, D.C., area, another group began meeting in 1971. Members of these groups met regularly to coach each other, sharing what they learned about company culture and policies, effective strategies, and hidden dangers. A. Barry Rand, who began his three decades with Xerox in 1968, called their intensive interaction "revolution by telephone," building new "communication channels, because we were not part of the old-boy network." Although these caucuses raised some concerns among white employees, top management recognized both the value of these groups and their members' concerns; management's discussion with the caucuses often led to policy changes, such as open job postings. In 1971, in response to a pending legal action by members of the San Francisco caucus, the company president and another top executive flew out to investigate. Among other remedial actions, they immediately restructured regional operations to resolve unfair opportunity distribution.[28]

As Rand moved up Xerox's ladder and into national headlines, he always credited the combination of individual effort and intensive networking and learning from role models for his success. "We couldn't risk having low performers," Rand declared. Nor could individual newcomers succeed alone. Xerox top management accepted the caucuses and continued to work with them after their initial 1971 confrontation in San Francisco. By 1974, six caucuses had formed, and they voiced two constant themes: committing to excellent performance and counterbalancing exclusion from the informal, customary networks of management. A participant explained, "Our goal is self-help and helping the company be better and helping us be better, but," he added, "you'd better deal with us." These ambitious men were not looking for a favor; they insisted on the need to excel. The caucuses sought opportunities to perform, to improve individual performance, and to protest when superior performance led to a dead-end.[29]

Marginalized people had long traditions of organizing to pool their information and strengths and to synthesize social capital. Local communication networks among community organizers, including civil rights activists, for example, had contributed to the resurgence of feminism in the 1960s. What Jo Freeman called "friendship networks" operated both locally and nationally. Freeman's own work experiences lay in academia, and she described in detail women's exclusion from the informal networks through which male faculty shared information, advice, and camaraderie with male students. She had observed women forming their own caucuses on campuses across the country in order for them to piece together the benefits of networking, maintain self-esteem, and lobby for women's practical concerns. These techniques could serve women everywhere, she declared in 1975.[30]

Although the concept of social networks was generally known, especially in the social sciences, the terms "networks" and "networking" emerged in the popular and business press in the mid-1970s. Even Kanter's pioneering 1977 book did not include an entry for networks in the index, despite its detailed analyses of networks in action. The transition of networking to center stage came around that time, however, as the SWO newsletter showed. Just as the American Management Association's two editions of *The Ambitious Woman's Guide to a Successful Career* bracketed the dissemination of "mentoring" within corporate feminism, it identified the spread of "networking" as well. The 1975 edition had no mention of networks in the index, whereas the 1980 index does carry an entry for the term, with ten pages referenced, although the difference in the number of pages devoted to networks in the two editions was less than these numbers might suggest. Both editions contained five pages on networks in a chapter titled "Building Effective Relationships with Peers." There, each edition had an identical discussion of informal internal organizations and how people can be "in" or not, plus information on building "an extensive communication network." The later edition, however, contained five additional pages, in the same new chapter that featured mentoring, "Special Concerns of the Career Woman."[31] The main difference was the spotlight that was finally shining on the concept.

One of the high-profile books on the SWO lists, Hennig and Jardim's *Managerial Woman* (1977), contributed to the dissemination of the idea of networks, if not the word itself. Repeating a civil rights admonition that legislation can prohibit segregation but cannot force integration, they cautioned women to be alert to informal systems, which by their very nature react to threats by closing their doors to outsiders. Because informal business structures were then populated, built, and operated by men, women had access only to the formal structures. Hennig and Jardim worried that women did not "even recognize" the existence of informal systems. Even so, almost all of the successful businesswomen whom they studied had obtained their positions because of fathers' or family friends' connections. Moreover, in many instances, these women, who mostly entered business in the 1930s, had initially moved into jobs "specially created as a favor to the father or friend."[32]

Without using the term "social capital" or even "network," Hennig and Jardim laid out a course for career-seeking women that would build social capital through authority and peer networking. They advised such a woman to try to identify "someone in a more senior management position who can teach her, support her, advise her, critique her." This required presenting "herself as someone worth investing in," someone with whom the mentor (they also used such terms as "coach," "godfather," "godmother," and "advocate") would want to identify. Likewise, women must not hesitate to "use" friendships they had formed through volunteer work or other social means. Some of those contacts were likely to be business gatekeepers, who could help identify positions or become mentors. Because such authorities were rarely available to women, however, Hennig and Jardim urged women to build peer networks as well. A women's "support group" offered the best way to learn about opportunities and share assessments about which authority figures were helpful and which were risky. Such a group could also provide its members with invaluable guidance and feedback, as well as enhance their esteem, all based on trust and shared understanding—just what men gained in their groups.[33]

During this period, women were learning to appreciate networking from many different perspectives. Some converted to feminism's social capital approach to business from the individualist dead-ends that were the final resting places of most women's careers. In 1977, Marcille Gray Williams, in *The New Executive Woman,* described the unexpected consciousness raising that grew out of her attempts to understand why she could not find a role model. She concluded that women needed to construct peer and authority networks, and her advice found its way to the SWO reading lists. Similarly, Letty Cottin Pogrebin confessed to once having "cast [her] lot with the ruling class" as a "queen bee" who refused to see a common interest with other women. She eventually rejected individual solutions, which are "pointless, selfish and often counterproductive."[34]

Also in 1977, an article in *Redbook: The Magazine for Young Women* asserted that women's organizing—formal and informal, inside and outside of firms—was the key to their "getting better jobs." Organizing could "make the law against sex discrimination work" and help women move up career ladders. Internal caucuses within corporations would help women make progress by pursuing lawsuits, conducting negotiations, and providing mutual support and information sharing. As a founder of the Woman's Committee for Equal Employment Opportunity at NBC told that firm's top executives, "What we want from you is what you have given each other, and what we would give you: a *chance*—a *choice*—and *respect.*" A feminist at Polaroid commented that the "Women's Movement was very much in the air in Boston" in 1971. "It was becoming okay to think as I did," she said. "I was getting support from everything I read." A group called Women Organized for Employment built both "inside networks" and "outside networks" to help the efforts within one another's companies. The article ended with advice on "how to make working together work," the final item of which was "*Keep in touch, no matter what.*"[35]

By 1979, networking was in everyone's sights—and in all the books on how women might succeed in business. Some tried out other words, such as "huddling," in a book by that name from the

American Management Association; but they did not catch on. "Networking," with meanings from social science, feminism, and even the fading counterculture, was broadly used to refer to social connections within and between organizations. The generally conservative group Business and Professional Women/Inc. defined itself as a "'women helping women' organization." Its president-elect in 1978 urged its members to build "New Girl Networks" in order to provide women with contacts and connections and to compensate for their lack of access to the "hidden job market" and other business benefits of men's social connections. For a time, in fact, it seemed that networks received credit for almost every tie that binds humans together. The 1982 book *Networking: The First Report and Directory* promoted networks to facilitate sharing "work, aspirations, and ideals." The 1986 edition noted that the term "networking" still lacked a dictionary definition in its new post-1960s sense of "people connecting with people, linking ideas and resources." A popular title by Marilyn Ferguson, *The Aquarian Conspiracy: Personal and Social Transformation in the 1980s,* promoted networks as tools of "transformation" on both a personal and a global scale, their "mutual aid and support" benefiting everyone.[36]

The semantic roots of the term "network" were many and varied, from fishnets and old school chums to railroads and telegraph lines to broadcast systems and computers. In the 1970s, it was used in mathematics, sociology, and anthropology. Dictionaries of popular usage identify "networking" in a business sense as dating from the mid-1970s. They identify the origins of the term in business as being linked to women's efforts to counter or parallel men's social connections for business success; not until the 1990s did a dictionary give a social capital definition of networking that was not associated with feminism. A 1993 dictionary observed that "networking" in the business sense "first appeared in the 1970s but achieved greater popularity in the 1980s."[37] The *Business Periodi-*

cals Index, which has catalogued business articles since 1958, confirms the feminist origins of "networking" in the business–social capital sense. The first entries for "Networks" in the social capital sense appeared in the 1981–1982 edition of the index and referred only to three citations under "Women's networks." The next year, the index added "Business Network Clubs" as a second entry in the social sense of networking, but "Women's networks" continued as an entry into the twenty-first century.[38]

The Glass Ceiling

In 1980, the Sun Women's Organization put together a document titled "Proposal for a New Cooperation on the Advancement of Women at Sun." They reported progress on some fronts, noting that, a decade earlier, women at Sun had held only 2.3 percent of exempt, managerial jobs, whereas in 1979 they held 12.5 percent of such jobs. Taking a line from a then ubiquitous advertising campaign, however, they rejected the temptation "to think we've come a long way." Instead, "a lot of us have come part-way." For most women at Sun, "there are tremendous strides to be made before those senior management positions become close enough to see." For good reasons, the language they used to describe their situation was the language of obstacles and barriers. Although these and other women, as well as male African Americans, could almost see the top, they could not reach it. They had realized by then that moving into lower-level management did not assure further promotions, and they used a variety of metaphors to describe the barriers that still confronted them now that they were finally on the lower rungs of previously inaccessible ladders.[39]

Of course, barrier metaphors in the context of the workplace were not new. The famous Hawthorne Works study from the 1920s and 1930s reported that young men expressed satisfaction with the lower ranks only if those were not "viewed as a ceiling." In the

1930s, the National Urban League distributed a set of pamphlets based on a common phrase for racial barriers: *He Crashed the Color Line!* and *They Crashed the Color Line!* Metaphors for barriers and their destruction—or forced passage through them—multiplied with the rising expectations of the 1960s and 1970s. Caroline Bird's 1968 book *Born Female* described an "invisible bar" into which even the most capable and well-trained women crashed. The following year, an important analysis of institutional racism repeated a 1945 reference to the "job ceiling" long blocking African Americans. Twenty years after the 1964 Civil Rights Act, a *Fortune* cover story explored a range of factors that built an "invisible ceiling" that one female executive estimated women "hit" about eight or ten years into their careers.[40]

The 1984 *Fortune* article expressed considerable uncertainty about what discrimination involved in these cases, since the worst of the coarse, old-fashioned sexism had faded. The trade journal *Industrial Week* also examined conditions limiting women's success in "reaching for the top." Focusing on an elite group of women who were already top executives, the article cited with little comment a few claims that sex and race no longer disqualified aspirants. It emphasized instead the "wide range of non-business-related traps crimping their climb." In particular, the "clones" populating management's "inner circle" rarely recruited outsiders as candidates for fear of their peers' reproach. Powerful men did not spot capable female candidates and guide them through the "sometimes-treacherous corporate jungle," one female senior executive explained, because "it's a cultural, rather than a prejudicial thing."[41] Equating "prejudicial" attitudes with deliberate and crude "push" discrimination, this executive, and many others, male and female, failed to see that the cultural attitudes that kept men from considering women as CEOs were also prejudicial, in that they resulted in an uneven distribution of pull.

Finally, a special report titled "The Corporate Woman" in a 1986 issue of the *Wall Street Journal* coined—or at least made famous—the "glass ceiling" metaphor to explain the paucity of women in top positions. The glass ceiling, an "invisible barrier that blocks [women] from the top jobs," pushed strangers down and out of competitive pools and kept them from getting pulled in or up. This "caste system" for women resulted from many things: their difficulties in finding sponsors; men's discomfort in working with them; women's assignment to support, human resources, and public relations (staff) positions rather than sales or production (line) positions; their (usually) nontechnical education; and their "subtle, even unconscious" exclusion from meetings and social occasions. "Up to a certain point," one respondent asserted, "brains and competence work. . . . But then fitting in becomes very important. It's at that point that barriers against women set in." Uninvited or unable to participate in many social activities, women missed a "lot of male bonding and informal mentoring." Women simply did not make the lists of candidates who seemed appropriate—that is, who had potential—for top leadership. Sometimes, as lone or rare examples of strangers near the top, women felt as if they were "on display under glass," noticed mostly for their apparent abnormality.[42]

The "glass ceiling" term quickly spread. Several months after the *Wall Street Journal* piece appeared, *New York Times* columnist Maureen Dowd quoted Betty Friedan as applying the term to political as well as corporate limitations on women's progress, contrasting it to "overt discrimination." A 1988 article on African Americans' progress urged applying force from below—"cracking" the ceiling, now that they could see it. Between the introduction of the term in 1986 and the end of 1990, twenty-four articles in the *New York Times* featured it, with hundreds more during the early years of the 1990s. The *Business Periodicals Index* caught onto the trend with its 1990–1991 volume, when it listed three business journal articles under the heading. Both that year and the following, when it listed twenty-four, it appended to the term the parenthetical explanation "(Employment)" and added bracketed definitions to clarify the meaning of this metaphorical innovation.[43]

The first book featuring the glass ceiling—Ann M. Morrison's 1987 *Breaking the Glass Ceiling: Can Women Reach the Top of America's Largest Corporations?*—described the "wall of tradition and stereotype that . . . keeps women out of the inner sanctum of senior management, the core of business leaders who wield the greatest power." Morrison and her colleagues interviewed a group of successful women and collated the twenty-two factors these women credited for their successes. Of the six most frequently mentioned factors, five were personal characteristics related to ability and drive. The top factor, however, was "help from above." Morrison emphasized that this was the "*only* point in the entire study on which all of our savvy insiders agreed!" However, "wide-ranging support from one person over an extended period of time" was uncommon for women. When women did have an "unusually strong advocacy of at least one influential person higher in the company," that "extra" helped them to "break through."[44]

Business Week observed in 1991 that the federal government had yet to tackle "the touchiest area" of employee relations, "the dominance of white men in top management jobs." It announced the end of that neglect because federal promotion of equal employment opportunity was about to focus on the top of the ladder. In 1989 the Department of Labor, under Secretary Elizabeth Dole, undertook a Glass Ceiling Initiative. The result of its several-year investigation identified the "artificial barriers based on attitudinal organizational bias that prevent qualified individuals from advancing upward in their organization into management level positions." Following the initiative's 1991 report, Senator Robert Dole of Kansas introduced the Glass Ceiling Act, which became Title II of the Civil Rights Act of 1991. Senator Dole praised the report for confirming "what many of us have suspected all along—the existence of invisible, artificial barriers blocking women and minorities from advancing up the corporate ladder to management and executive level positions." "For this senator," he concluded, "the issue boils down to ensuring equal access and equal opportunity." The resulting Glass Ceiling Commission continued the initiative until 1996.[45]

The Department of Labor's investigation and hearings documented possible causes of a "plateau" in managerial progress among women and minority men. They also showed that, despite a few high-profile exceptions, the "glass ceiling existed at a much lower level than first thought." Stereotypical attitudes placed non-mainstream applicants into staff positions, rather than line positions from which top executives typically rose. Ongoing corporate practices still favored promotion largely from within and according to time-honored and restrictive "pipelines." Moreover, the higher a position, the more likely it would be filled "outside the formal recruitment process," without consulting firms' Equal Employment Opportunity directors and without full posting. Networking, defined by the Glass Ceiling Initiative as "word of mouth" and "employee referrals," received much of the blame. The first (1991) report noted that standard managerial practices of spotting and developing "high potentials" through rotation and extra training, both internal and external, failed to include nonmainstream personnel. Highlighting key mechanisms of social capital, the report determined that mentoring, grooming, and sponsoring reinforced the glass ceiling, perpetuating a system of self-reproduction that had no place for strangers.[46]

The Glass Ceiling reports called for enforcement of its recommendations among all but small employers by extending upward personnel procedures that had long been standard at lower levels, and to improve the monitoring of these procedures. Corporations' formalized personnel practices for managers had never taken women and minority men into account until excluding them lost its legal and cultural license. Even after that, inclusion was often perfunctory, stopping at low-level management. The Glass Ceiling Initiative clarified the links between corporate personnel practices as problems *and* as possible solutions. It noted that effective top managers took years to groom. These executives also had to be able to assert authority, and—more important—others had to recognize that authority. Reforms aimed at the glass ceiling therefore had to take a longer view than did earlier reforms whose aim had been immediately to improve the numbers of entry-level women and minority men. Compliance required that firms ensure the diversity of the pools from which they selected candidates with top-level potential. And they had to put into place—at all employment levels—an environment in which previously excluded people could do their best and be recognized for it.[47]

A population for which these considerations have only recently received attention is the disabled. Like disadvantaged minorities and women, people with physical limitations performed many production and other jobs during World War II, gaining them, as a group, workplace credibility, if not permanent positions. The Rehabilitation Act of 1973 forbade discrimination against qualified persons with disabilities, who were defined as those who can perform a job with "reasonable accommodation." This legislation used similar strategies against discrimination as had earlier executive orders against other forms of discrimination—that is, prohibiting discrimination by agencies, contractors, and institutions receiving federal funds. The 1990 Americans with Disabilities Act applied the principles to all private-sector employers with fifteen or more employees. A 1994 report, funded in part by the Glass Ceiling Commission, documented parallels between discrimination against persons with disabilities and other marginalized people. Here, too, stereotypes profoundly affected employers' decisions, including assumptions that functional impairment leads to impaired personhood; that the disabled engender pity, or, conversely, are heroic; that their presence causes discomfort in others; and that they and their impairments are best treated as though they are invisible. The report also noted that supervisors and employers expect too little and are reluctant to correct persons with disabilities on the job, replacing proper training with misguided kindness, a problem that women often experienced, as well. This "kindness" slows or even prevents performance improvement, and accompanies a reluctance to give challenging tasks to marginalized individuals. The report concluded that technological and environmental accommodations, along with awareness training, could reduce the impact of this particular glass ceiling.[48]

Solutions to the Glass Ceiling Problem

Once previously excluded people could get on ladders that some people climbed to the top, what had been a concrete ceiling turned into glass. The barrier remained impenetrable, but critics' being able to see through it made possible a reformulation of what business achievement required, and allowed outsiders to imagine climbing higher. As in prior stages of the revelation of social capital, diminishing the potency of some constraints on equal opportunity made other constraints more visible. The metaphor of the glass ceiling was a powerful one, which inspired those frustrated by it to talk of dismantling, cracking, chipping away, throwing stones, breaking through, and shattering it. Yet assaults from below, however forceful, could not succeed alone. What was needed was what social capital could provide: a hand reaching down from above to pull someone up through that glass ceiling. If those in power continued to ignore people they considered to be strangers, if gatekeepers pulled up only those with whom they felt comfortable and whom they saw as having "potential," the glass ceiling would remain in place.

The Glass Ceiling Commission recognized these problems and explained that a combination of "push" and "pull" discrimination was responsible for strangers' being kept from top management. Its

1995 report, *Good for Business*, marshaled analysis of societal, governmental, and "internal business" barriers to advancement. Stereotypes and lack of access to education fueled prejudice. Governmental failings allowed violations of the law to continue. A key factor, according to the commission, was the feeling of discomfort, a "perception of loss" and "white male anxiety" on the part of those in power in response to newcomers' incursion into competitive pools and the consequent changes in workplace culture. These sorts of emotional reaction against integration that was finally and inescapably enforced by law and that was changing national values had only served to harden the glass ceiling. Although top officers (like the CEOs at AT&T, Avon, Sun, and Xerox) rarely felt threatened and often manifested considerable grace during equal opportunity crises in their organizations, accepting responsibility for integrating their firms, their middle managers often resisted.[49]

The Glass Ceiling Commission thought of full integration as the next step in a century's efforts at rationalizing business procedures, adding that personnel tools already established through those efforts could be effective in meeting that new goal. The remaining barriers all pertained to social capital. The commission identified problems in three areas: outreach and recruitment, with firms not knowing where or how to recruit nonmainstream candidates; "corporate climate," as characterized by differing communication and behavioral styles and values; and eleven "pipeline" policies, both formal and informal, by which companies groom their leaders, too often assigning strangers to dead-end positions, excluding them from opportunities to prove themselves, and failing to rotate them through departments. By the time that the concept of the glass ceiling was formulated, mentors, networks, and role models were well accepted as mechanisms for success, and the commission assumed that all were important factors unavailable to nonmainstream candidates.[50]

Elliot W. Springs assumed leadership of what is now Springs Industries almost seventy years before his granddaughter, Crandall C. Bowles, became CEO in 1997. When Colonel Springs crowned the winner of an employees' beauty contest in 1949, women's contributions to the business

environment were generally gauged by their manual skills and social acquiescence. In contrast to those limitations, Bowles holds an MBA from Columbia University and heads the firm.

(Courtesy Springs Industries.)

Escaping the Glass Ceiling

Flight often makes sense when a fight seems inevitable and winning seems impossible. When newcomers' accelerating ambition rushed past corporations' willingness to absorb them into top management, many enterprising men and women forswore salaries for opportunity. By the late 1980s many ambitious women and African-American men were jumping off corporate ladders. Although the number of African Americans who ranked as corporate managers and officials grew by 83 percent from 1972 to 1982, many felt relegated to what they called "ghetto" positions, such as overseeing staff or public relations. They felt underused on the job and were almost never invited to social events outside of the workplace. As a result, the *Wall Street Journal* recorded a "resurgence of black rage" in 1984, the result of African Americans' frustration over hitting endless white-collar barriers. Rapid ascents partway up corporate ladders halted "abruptly," time and again. Entrepreneurship, with the chance to share ownership and authority, looked far more attractive to these well-educated, ambitious people in the 1980s than it had a decade earlier, when corporations first welcomed racial minorities.[51]

The original 1986 glass ceiling article in the *Wall Street Journal* indicated that many women were resolving their frustrations within corporations by becoming entrepreneurs. Executives remained largely unaware of this "brain drain" for the very reasons it was occurring: marginal people were invisible or unwelcome, regardless of their performance. The number of self-employed women increased 43 percent in the preceding decade, while that of self-employed men rose less than 10 percent. Countless examples of this "new breed of female entrepreneur" said that they had determined to "make things happen" for themselves outside of unwelcoming and unnurturing corporate environments. Between 1977 and 1980 women began new businesses at three times the national rate of start-ups, and during the 1980s at twice the national rate. As a result, whereas in 1980 less than 5 percent of U.S. small businesses were owned by women, in 1988 that percentage had rocketed to about 28 percent. Although women may have taken this avenue out of frustration, they did very well at it. Women-owned small business revenues from 1980 to 1985 increased by 78 percent, compared to overall small business revenue growth of 31 percent. As one analyst concluded in 1984, "The problem of the 1970s was bringing women into the corporation. The problem of the 1980s is keeping them there." The trend continued into the 1990s, as women continued to seek greater flexibility, challenge, and recognition off corporate ladders than they could find on them.[52]

Adding Insult

Frustration from stalled ambition was not all that drove new arrivals out of corporations. The perennial problems of workplace racial and sexual harassment acquired names and legal standing only in the 1970s, as these problems became newly visible. Social capital is part of the larger story of how and why this came to pass: harassment was long tolerated as a way for workplace insiders to exercise and enhance their power at the expense of others' vulnerability. According to analyst John P. Fernandez in 1981, retreat into "a self-imposed ghetto" was sometimes "the only psychological defense against the unbearable pain" of "discrimination, humiliation, insult, and denial of opportunities." He emphasized the "stress under which minorities and women are placed as they become isolated in middle- and upper-management levels." Institutionalized discrimination and harassment expressed mainstream males' sense of diminished control over "their" environment once law and custom no longer prevented strangers from invading it.[53]

A century ago, some men resented women's entering the business world as secretaries and typists. Although almost all women remained in subservient service positions during that initial invasion, their presence vexed many men anyway.[54] That first invasion coincided with the woman suffrage movement, further threatening men's dominance. The second invasion of women into business likewise accompanied a wave of feminism plus a civil-rights-inspired influx of members of ethnic minorities, two populations that had never before challenged mainstream bastions of workplace authority. Sexist and racist harassment humiliated, demoralized, and intimidated its targets, driving them out of the workplace or into submission; it was a significant and well-documented cause of absenteeism and quitting. Gossip, disparaging comments, epithets, and deprecating jokes also serve to tighten bonds between in-group members. Because people who behave this way may not indulge in more severe degrees of prejudice, such as physical attack, they may well deny their prejudice, masking it as humor. People who laugh at others' prejudice-driven humor or, worse, physical affronts, such as groping at female interlopers in their workplace, strengthen their bonds with the worst of the offenders while condemning the victims to alien, outsider status. Rosabeth Moss Kanter pointed out that small numbers of strangers invading corporate management serve as "instruments for under*lining* rather than under*mining* majority culture." Men lauded their exploits, sexual and otherwise, shared off-color jokes, and drank more when just a few female workers were present than when either zero or many females were present. Above all, men let it be known that whether they acted in a chivalrous or an obscene manner, they could not be "natural" in the presence of women. Their constant marking and remarking of boundaries precluded newcomers' assimilation.[55]

Like other dynamics of social capital, harassment gained visibility as other constraints dropped away—in this case, as insiders were finding it harder to keep strangers out. Once again, the two editions of the American Management Association's *Ambitious Woman's Guide to a Successful Career* suggested just when harassment began to become visible. The 1975 edition devoted just three pages to "dealing with sexism." The text of these pages addressed the overall manifestations of prejudice, including those that would soon fall under the category of harassment, such as sexist jokes and labels, as well as anatomical references. The index for that edition listed nothing under the entry "harassment," although a few passages in the text alluded to dealing with sexual advances and avoiding office affairs. The 1980 second edition carried a new section entitled "Sex with the Boss" and included an index reference to a five-page section with the title "Combating Sexual Harassment," which included advice regarding legal recourse, should matters come to that.[56] Over these same years, the *Business Periodicals Index* also reflected changing conceptions. In the second half of the 1970s it carried listings under the category "Sex in business"; the listings referred mainly to articles about office affairs. In the 1978–1979 edition and into the 1980s, the new entry "Sexual harassment" simply referred readers back to the older category, "Sex in business," as if harassment were basically business as usual. By 1979–1980, the listings in this category juxtaposed the older, trivializing style of article carrying such titles as "Love in the Office" and "How to Tame the Office Wolf—Without Getting Bitten" with articles carrying more serious titles, such as "EEOC Says: Sexual Harassment of Workers Is No Joking Matter" and "Sexual Harassment Lands Companies in Court."[57]

Sexual and racial harassment both reflects and exacerbates outsiders' presumed ineligibility as peers. Most feminist advice against office affairs in the 1970s and 1980s went beyond pointing out the practical and emotional risks. It also addressed the danger of perpetuating stereotypes of women as sexual objects that, in turn, would keep women from being perceived as colleagues and worthy competitors. Likewise, laughing at sexist jokes, not objecting to anatomical references, tolerating inappropriate touching, even acquiescing in making coffee reduced women's professional credibility.

The *National Business Woman* directly engaged the issue in 1984, asking readers how many times they had heard "I was only joking. Can't you take a joke?" Remarks about full coffee pots and physical appearance—or any nonprofessional subject, for that matter—were distractions for everyone and harmed the victim. Rather than suggesting that they emulate insiders, this conservative publication advised women to be willing to appear humorless, to confront "jokers," and even to raise their coworkers' consciousness about the effect of humor that camouflaged "hostility or harassment."[58] Otherwise, women would always be outsiders, under glass in one sense or another.

Racial harassment in the workplace was successfully prosecuted in 1971, and later in the decade courts began to draw parallels with sexual harassment. After many courtroom failures, the EEOC adopted new guidelines in 1980 that defined sexual harassment as a form of discrimination under Title VII of the 1964 Civil Rights Act. Both "quid pro quo," by which victims' reactions to sexual advances influence the terms of their employment, and "conduct [that] has the purpose or effect of unreasonably interfering with an individual's work performance or creating an intimidating, hostile, or offensive work environment" became actionable. Peers and subordinates could be held guilty of interference and disturbing the work environment, using harassment to rob women of dignity and of even enough self-respect for them to function and remain healthy. Superiors, of course, could be found guilty of both types of offenses.[59]

In 1991, an editorial in *Business Week* used the glass ceiling metaphor to link harassment and women's lack of job progress. "Pull Down the Pinups, Raze the Glass Ceiling" applauded court decisions that enforced reform at companies that had "winked at intimidation as the normal behavior of 'boys' at play." The editorial condemned "sexual bullying" and urged managers to "educate workers on proper etiquette between the sexes."[60] The glass ceiling began to lose its power to deflect ambition, although high-profile cases in the 1990s indicated that insiders still subjected newcomers to racial and sexual harassment. The Glass Ceiling Commission's *Good for Business* list of barriers ended with the entry "counterproductive behavior and harassment by colleagues."[61] In 1980, this phrase might have seemed overly ambiguous. By 1995, its meaning was quite clear.

Quarantine

Private clubs exacerbated perceptions of the ineligible as aliens by drawing sharp barriers between members, nonmembers, and staff that recapitulate class and other differences. For instance, although Rotary International had multiracial membership by the 1960s, its Club Number One in Chicago sat for a portrait of a "typical luncheon meeting" in 1965 that displayed rigid segregation. A sea of white men in suits filled a hotel banquet hall and were served by uniformed, adult, male African-American waiters. How could this weekly experience not incline Rotary members to consider any not-white-male-in-a-suit as incapable of being a peer?[62]

Almost thirty years later, the Greenwich Country Club, the most elite of the eight then white-only country clubs in that wealthy Connecticut town, refused even to hire an African-American man as a waiter. Lawrence Otis Graham, graduate of Princeton and Harvard Law School, went undercover to assess how his career suffered by exclusion from the clubs where his white colleagues networked. He had noticed, for instance, that African-American executives and lawyers felt obliged to ask their white peers and even subordinates for invitations to racially exclusive clubs in order to conduct business. Graham's telephone queries gained him offers to apply to several of Greenwich's clubs, only to be rejected on sight. He could, however, be a busboy at the century-old Greenwich Country Club, and he took the position. Among the indignities Graham experienced there was learning that the Greenwich Country Club had a staff dormitory originally built for African-American workers and still called the Monkey House in the 1990s. Like many elite clubs, this one also restricted women's access to some dining areas.[63] Restrictions like these impeded pull for racially alien men, and women of any ethnicity.

Enforced absence from social venues for business, or presence in very different roles from the power brokers, sets people apart as aliens and slows the dissolution of stereotypes. If certain individuals

Fishing and camping trips often provided men the freedom to build personal bonds and discuss business in relaxed settings and comfortable clothes. They could leave behind people and conditions that might constrain their camaraderie and confidential discussions. These railroad executives in 1945 brought along staff whose dining car uniforms, poses, and race made clear that they were present to serve, not participate. It did not matter if these outsiders overheard off-the-record conversations.
(Courtesy Colorado Historical Society.)

are present only as waitstaff, begowned wives at holiday parties, objects of curiosity or charity, or renegades having to arrive via the service elevator, they cannot be seen as equals or dislodge insiders' wariness. Insiders' lack of awareness of their own prejudices led to some peculiar observations. Harvey Scott, president of the ultra-elite Bohemian Club, for example, declared in 1987, "We don't discriminate against anybody. We are a men's club, however." Another club's defender said that he did not consider excluding women to be "discrimination." The title of Gwendolyn Parker's autobiography, *Trespassing,* communicates her unending sense of alienation in what she called the "halls of privilege," despite her successes there. This brilliant African-American lawyer joined a top Wall Street law firm in 1976, one of two African-American professionals there at the time. She never felt so alienated, however, as when she left the premises on business. Once, when she was to have lunch with a senior partner at his club, her party was escorted around the male-only areas of the club after her host announced to the club staff, repeatedly and in her presence, "Three for lunch, and one of us is a woman." As she moved through the club and then sat down, well-heeled men stared, Parker observed, with "no need to hide the look, no need to be polite."[64]

Parker might well have appreciated one of Rosabeth Kanter's corporate metaphors. Kanter called a "quarantine" the process by which gatekeepers, both authorities and peers, kept the small number of women managers, like other unassimilated people, from participating in informal occasions. This word was apt for the 1970s, when Kanter was writing, because it conveyed the sense of preventing the spread of contagion. The occasions that quarantines were enlisted to protect ranged from "pre-meeting meetings" to social events—occasions that nurtured business alliances and planning. At the upper levels of management, where male-only social institutions and events were both widespread and important, quarantines abounded. To make matters worse, top executives in the corporation Kanter studied were aware that quarantines constrained women's access to important conversations. Yet, following a deadening circular logic, instead of worrying about how to do away with the quarantines, they worried about how the women's lack of access limited their "business effectiveness" and promotability.[65] As women, African Americans, and their advocates became aware of the existence of quarantines, they developed and publicized their understanding of the importance of social capital to succeeding in business.

Poking Holes in Social Screens

Until the importance of social activities to business success became widely evident, negative publicity based on civil rights principles remained the primary weapon against discrimination by private clubs. Even the 1964 Civil Rights Act excluded private clubs from its equal protection requirements. Ethical principles alone were not enough to override traditional constitutional interpretations that have subsumed freedom of association under freedom of speech and the right to assemble. In the 1970s, new laws made some inroads, denying tax-exempt status and other state-based benefits to associations with written discriminatory policies. As late as the mid-1980s, however, all private clubs retained unquestioned legal privileges to discriminate as they wished, and many still do, with or without discriminatory written policies. Most of the progress in eliminating such policies has relied on arguments about doing business in social venues. Protests against exclusion have typically combined both ethical and business arguments, such as General Motors' top officers' withdrawal from the Bloomfield (Michigan) Country Club in 1994 when it refused membership to an African-American GM vice president.[66]

As women's frustration grew with their slow progress toward the top of business ladders, they objected to their exclusion from the social venues where business was conducted. Suburban country clubs had become more accessible to women in the 1950s and 1960s, although women were usually admitted only as members' spouses or daughters. Well into the 1990s, country clubs often denied access to women without men—even those who had been members prior to their divorce. A Long Island club, for instance, revoked a woman's membership after her divorce, even though her parents had been founding members and she had spent much of her free time there her entire life; her ex-husband retained his membership. As owner of an insurance agency, this woman tried to join more than two dozen clubs because doing so was a good "business move," but clubs told her that they had no memberships for "single women." The Nassau County, New York, chapter of NOW discovered that in 1993 only two of the county's thirty-seven country clubs allowed unmarried women to join. A decade later, the Augusta National Golf Club still denied membership to women.[67] Because of the growing appreciation for the importance of personal contacts and other forms of social capital in business, their concerns gained support.

In the mid-1980s, women's advocates quoted Ruth Bader Ginsburg on the importance of equal access to private clubs as "a traditional avenue for self-development, economic and political opportunity, and advancement." That members deducted dues as business expenses and companies subsidized dues and related expenses affirmed the business importance of clubs. Even so, advocates for the status quo insisted that private clubs should be exempt from antidiscrimination regulations because they were social institutions, where comfort and relaxation—not business—supposedly reigned. Nonetheless, the president of the Citadel Club in Austin, Texas, reportedly grumbled that women would distract from the business discussed at lunch, like a "gaggle of magpies." A former officer of New York City's University Club feared that allowing women would destroy the club's sedate atmosphere: "the chatter and noise will be like Macy's basement at a post-Christmas sale." Ginsburg credited all this resistance to a "tree-house mentality," according to which children "want to keep something that's strange to them out." With no sense of irony, men complained that no one criticized women's institutions for not allowing men. Of course, when women's organizations have opened to men, few apply;[68] insufficiently powerful connections reside there.

Federal Supreme Court decisions in 1984, 1987, and 1988 established the rights of states and cities to insist on equal access to clubs that have large memberships and so are similar to public accommodations like restaurants and hotels. This overturned decisions from the 1960s that had equated all clubs with homes in arguments for the protection of privacy and freedom of association. Although these more recent decisions allowed so-called intimate clubs to continue discriminating, the rulings had a huge impact, most immediately for the Jaycees (Junior Chamber of Commerce) and Rotary International, which were parties to the first two suits. These and other large clubs were thereafter required to abide by state and local antidiscrimination laws. The third decision supported New York City in prohibiting discrimination by large clubs where business transactions occur and valuable personal contacts develop. After these legal decisions, many elite clubs restructured themselves in an attempt to qualify as strictly private and therefore exempt from legal constraints, ridding themselves of "commerce" by eliminating corporate memberships, company reimbursements, and tax deductions. That clubs then complained bitterly about having to raise dues to offset these measures belied their original claims to have been commerce free and confirmed the importance of business to their traditional, basic functions.[69] Today's "no papers on the table" rules for club dining rooms do not diminish the business benefits of being able to hold exclusive discussions and interviews, cement transactions, and build profitable social relationships in a club setting.

Access to business lunch venues and golf courses came to be seen for what it was: a necessary tool for doing business and therefore a protectable right within a nation that wished to see itself as enabling equal opportunity for business success. NOW argued that groups like Rotary and the Jaycees serve first and foremost as business arenas and that discriminatory policies placed excluded populations at a significant disadvantage. The California attorney general who made that case against Rotary International before the U.S. Supreme Court asserted that "the state has a compelling interest in ensuring that women have equal access in the business world." The antidiscrimination law in question, she said, targeted "business establishments of every kind whatsoever." Attitudes and laws were in fact changing. In 1978, delegates to the Rotary International annual convention had voted overwhelmingly against reinstating a renegade California local chapter that had admitted women; the vote was 1,060 to 34. By the time of the Supreme Court decision in 1987, however, Rotary chapters throughout the United States readily and often comfortably complied with the new norms. By then, many major cities had enacted laws to bring business-oriented private clubs under the same antidiscrimination principles that applied to all public institutions.[70]

The growing understanding of mentoring and networking as tools for the ambitious gave new urgency and justification to integrating social arenas for fulfilling business ambitions in the 1980s. By the time of the Glass Ceiling Initiative, the "old boys' network" was more than a bad joke; it had become a model. The mechanisms of pull had acquired high-profile names. Businesspeople and business analysts explored and lauded the power of networks, mentors, and role models. Courts and laws lent their authority to ambitious but marginalized people who were fighting exclusion from overtly social venues, such as country and city clubs, where business transactions shared space with golf balls and martinis. In the 1990s, both those in the mainstream and the invaders would act on what they had learned about social capital, especially their new appreciation of the power of pull.

CHAPTER 8

Social Tools for Self-Help

Nowadays, strategies for individuals' success in business highlight networks, mentors, and role models—the key mechanisms of pull. Advocates for workplace equity were the first to identify these mechanisms and name them as barriers to newcomers on the road to opportunity. They soon realized, however, that the same dynamics of social capital that blocked progress could also help. Naming and analyzing these mechanisms, reformers also attempted to create them as a means of enabling outsiders to fulfill the nation's promise of equal opportunity. Business analysts and mainstream businesspeople quickly adopted the newly recast names for the old office politics. In the 1980s and 1990s enthusiasm spread for both using traditional social capital and building synthetic social capital as tools for success. The mysteries of the "secret handshake," as one enthusiast put it, were laid open. Books on networking in business hit a high in 1993; mentoring in business peaked in 1999. By the turn of the millennium, *Achieve Success through Social Capital* seemed a perfectly reasonable title for yet another book on how to succeed in business.[1]

Despite this newfound awareness of the power of pull, America's historic moralizing about the merits of individual effort as the ticket to business success continues almost as fiercely as ever. Attacks on synthetic social capital persist, while the power of already

311

privileged groups faces few challenges. If some commentators had their way, even nepotism would regain its pre-Enlightenment glory. Using one's connections and connectability has not enjoyed such high public esteem since the American Revolution challenged the principles of patronage. In this latest twist in the history of pull, social capital can be as openly managed as stock holdings. Ambitious people grow their social assets when they can and convert them into opportunities; but the nation has yet to accord synthetic social capital the same stature as the customary form.[2] Americans seem to have forgotten that "networks," "mentors," and "role models" received both their names and their current legitimacy from the efforts of people who were trying to move in from the margins of business.

Synthesizing Pull: Women

The growing appreciation for the role of social capital in business achievement has added social interaction to the traditional self-help repertoire of hard work, diligence, and training. This twist on self-help has come to include organized means to individual ends, with varying degrees of structure and formality to make social capital more accessible. At the informal end of the spectrum, some women have taken it upon themselves to assist others. As Gail Sheehy wrote in *Passages* (1974), "The fervent sisterhood abroad in the land today has committed many already successful women to being mentors for their eager juniors." Others have promoted themselves as they shared their insights, like the authors of *Women's Networks: The Complete Guide to Getting a Better Job, Advancing Your Career, and Feeling Great as a Woman through Networking* (1980); *Networking: The Great New Way for Women to Get Ahead* (1980); *Is Networking for You? A Working Woman's Alternative to the Old Boy System* (1981); and *Members of the Club: The Coming of Age of Executive Women* (1993).[3]

In 1979 the *Wall Street Journal* noted the phenomenon of what it called "Sisterhood Inc.," the "ever rising flood of 'how to succeed' courses" and workshops that offered to teach ambitious women the "art of 'networking'." Sociologist and consultant Rosabeth Moss Kanter, author of 1977's acclaimed *Men and Women of the Corporation,* told women to work hard, of course, but also advised them to learn workplace rules and reward systems, which often required personal advising. Courses could be useful, but "women need contacts, not training." She recommended forming a "network of connections" on the job. Other experts noted that public courses were better than nothing at getting women started, since few firms in 1979 offered internal aids to initiate women into the social mysteries of management. Courses that offered interaction and exercises that simulated real offices could best guide women trying to break into the "mainstream of the working world."[4]

Networking can proceed on any scale and with almost any degree of formalization. Many advocates for women's progress lauded the merits of creating informal "old girls' networks" that mimicked men's undeclared, customary practices with declared, synthetic ones.[5] Some women, however, worried that one-on-one, informal counseling would not suffice. They sought out or created organizational venues and tools for devising and disseminating advice and other assistance, creating a multitude of organizations of all sizes and shapes. Not long after business schools began accepting women, networking groups appeared there. Local and specialized organizations, plus chapters of national organizations, multiplied. As a promotion for the Business and Professional Women/ USA (BPW/USA) organization put it in 1986, "Issues . . . networks . . . skill development. These are the strengths of a locally-based working women's organization." By the end of the 1990s, *Women's Enterprise* had grown into a national newspaper and active Internet Web site, featuring advice to women that encouraged and facilitated their networking and mentoring, highlighting a "Mentor of the Month." The elite "Committee of 200" formed in 1982 to raise money for the National Association for Women Business Owners, then continued to promote women's top-level business activities. Formal learning about informal mechanisms of social capital appeared in 1991 in yet another venue, the Ladies Professional Golf Association (LPGA). Women, the LPGA asserted, could advance their business careers by using golf as a "relationship-building sport" that can serve as "an integral part of the game of business" and an "effective networking and business tool." The title of the book *Feminist Organizations: Harvest of the New Women's Movement* (1995) succinctly summarized the abundance of resources.[6]

Internal networks flourished in firms everywhere through the 1990s, as they had in the 1980s. As women improved their lot in corporations, enough felt a responsibility to assist those coming behind them to develop and often formalize mentoring efforts. *Mentoring at Work* came out in 1988 as a scholarly book, and although it did not mention gender in its title, it targeted women, and business writers often cited it. Lois Herr, corporate feminist at AT&T during the 1970s, continued her activism through the 1990s, focusing on mentoring. Like many other women, after the momentous EEOC settlement in 1973 Herr had optimistically returned to a focus on her own career. After AT&T's 1984 divestiture, she moved to NYNEX, one of the Baby Bells, where she learned that women still could not prosper on their own. The push had diminished, but women still lacked pull. As a result, she and a colleague designed "Mentoring Circles" in 1990 for synthesizing networks across managerial levels at NYNEX, hoping that the formal contacts would encourage informal, "true," mentoring to evolve. Faithful to her feminist roots, Herr based the processes and structure of these groups on consciousness-raising models, first building confidence and rapport, and then greater comprehension about succeeding, even leading, in business.[7]

The New York–based organization Catalyst began its work in

1962, an innovative and aptly named group for sponsoring, gathering, and disseminating research on women and their working conditions. It generated a mountain of compelling publications through which it interpreted mentoring, networking, and role models as both traditional impediments to women's business successes and as potential tools for progress. In 1999 Catalyst published a three-year survey, *Women of Color in Corporate Management: Opportunities and Barriers,* in which its respondents listed "not having an influential mentor" as their most serious barrier and "lack of informal networking" as the second most serious. Three years later, a follow-up study found that women of color were gaining ground through increased levels of mentoring and informal networking. Catalyst's recommendations called for even and ability-based distribution of well-understood, opportunity-generating development activities, such as rotation and high-visibility assignments, once reserved for candidates with traditional, socially defined potential for achievement. The Labor Department's Glass Ceiling Commission sponsored several of Catalyst's research projects in the 1990s, all of which insisted that businesses will prosper when women can prosper within them.[8]

The American Association of University Women (AAUW), founded in 1881, had been working for almost a century prior to feminism's second wave to eliminate exclusionary discrimination against women. Like other formalized organizations advocating for marginalized populations, AAUW developed insights into the mechanisms of pull all along, encouraging networking and mentoring while publicizing success stories to provide role models decades before any of those terms became commonplace. Building on its long experience, the AAUW instituted the concept of Advocacy Networks in the 1980s, through which it and other groups could target reform efforts. Its leaders praised the proliferation of feminist networks, urging existing groups to reach out beyond their immediate cohorts to form bridges to other communities. An AAUW policy report in 1983 explained that a "collective voice" could succeed when "personal access to resources or influence is insufficient to produce the desired outcome."[9]

Beginning in 1983, AAUW linked together its fellowship recipients with a newsletter, *Fellows Network*. It also promoted career networking at the local level as a means of keeping working women involved with the organization despite their often harried lives. Local meetings assisted members in developing leadership and technical skills through a variety of programs for projecting "the image of AAUW as a network." Annual conferences facilitated "Networking for Personal and Professional Growth," an activity offered first in 1983. The 1985 conference, titled "Milestones to Success," included a session called "Developing Mentoring Skills," along with other business-oriented sessions. "Leaders for a New Century," the 1991 conference, included in its agenda "Eat and Network" and "Open Caucuses," promoted as opportunities to meet others with common interests. AAUW conferences continue to feature sessions on mentoring and networking, plus informal opportunities for making connections.[10]

Synthesizing Pull: Ethnic Minorities

During the 1980s and 1990s, members of disadvantaged minorities and their advocates continued to develop social capital through informal and formal efforts. Many successful African Americans felt what Frank Savage, senior vice president at The Equitable Companies in the 1990s, described as "a tremendous sense of obligation to serve as a mentor." Business and popular literature urged successful members of minorities to cultivate networks with authorities, peers, and novices. In 1990 *Black Enterprise* magazine sponsored a Corporate Roundtable where Ralph Thomas, vice president of a Citicorp subsidiary, advocated both authority and peer networking. He and his colleagues at the roundtable lamented African

Americans' overspecialization, imposed by their limited options, and their resulting narrow connections, which left them vulnerable to downsizing and limited advancement. In particular, Thomas urged senior managers to recruit and take risks for "our own folks . . . because that's what happens on the majority side."[11]

Earl Graves, founder, owner, and publisher of the influential magazine *Black Enterprise,* often lauded the merits of networking. The ambitious, he asserted, "never forget that business is personal" and that the person who "builds the strongest relationships wins." Graves used a "storming the castle" metaphor to encourage his readers to use skillful and thoughtful networking to get inside the gates, instead of fighting discrimination with bludgeons and winding up in the moat. When he found himself unable to meet a CEO directly, for example, he figured out how to reach him through people who might know the CEO socially or professionally. Graves cautioned, however, that networking was "a social-first, business-second activity" and should not be approached cavalierly. Concerned that the term was already overused by 1997, he was reluctant to use "networking" in the book he published that year, *How to Succeed in Business without Being White.* Too many people, he worried, engaged in the "networking nonsense" of mechanically foisting business cards and unreasonable requests on acquaintances they barely knew. Nonetheless, Graves was proud to have disseminated the idea of networking among African Americans. "Twenty years ago," a 1990 article in his magazine pointed out, "the terms 'networking,' 'mentoring,' and *Black Enterprise* were not part of the vocabulary of most black professionals," but all three had now become "important ingredients" for success.[12]

The semiformal caucuses that flourished at Xerox in the 1970s continued to bear fruit after their initial successes. The Xerox groups were among the best known and most effective internal African-American corporate peer networks in the nation prior to the late 1980s, joined to a lesser degree by groups at Corning, AT&T,

and DEC. At the top of the Xerox success stories was A. Barry Rand, who by 1992 was executive vice president at Xerox. One of the founders of Xerox's original support networks, Rand credited participation in those networks for his and others' successes—along with hard work and Xerox's progressive personnel practices. Rand recognized that his pioneering made him a role model, whom one analyst called "the Jackie Robinson of the corporate world."[13]

Internal self-help groups burgeoned at U.S. corporations during the 1990s. These synthetic networks helped otherwise marginalized employees to function more effectively within their companies and to maximize both opportunity and recognition, enabling these employees to compensate for a lack of connections within the corporate hierarchy. In addition to being a forum for sharing information, contacts, and strategies, such caucuses also provided occasions for members to test and improve their skills, plus bolster their confidence. They also served as conduits to management for the concerns and suggestions of those who lacked informal access to authorities. Companies' attempts to recruit for diversity and pursue community outreach were aided by the existence of such groups. Nonetheless, management and employees from nonminority groups often remained anxious about such groups, whether they met during or off company time. Formal gatherings sometimes prompted concern about participants' intentions or possible divisiveness, or even that a caucus might become a union. However, because these caucuses brought together employees with managerial ambitions, its members were usually able to reassure employers that their intentions were compensatory self-help, not threats to corporate goals.[14]

By the civil rights era, African Americans' social organizations had long and venerable traditions of building social capital. As part of the changes that took place during the civil rights period, ambitions rose for the elite members of minorities, along with expectations about putting some of their social capital to use on behalf of the less advantaged. Lawrence Otis Graham, a member of what he calls "America's black upper class," noted the growing visibility of that accomplished elite and its establishments, many with deep roots in activism. With the civil rights era, some took on responsibilities as role models and mentors. A member of Links Incorporated, a prominent African-American women's social, service, and philanthropic organization, declared, "We are smart women with money and clout, and we should use it to help blacks who need our connections and our mentoring." For this woman, "need" did not mean impoverishment; it was an invitation to any capable and ambitious African American who could benefit from a network of well-positioned, experienced individuals.[15]

The organization One Hundred Black Men brings together top business and professional men for both individual and community assistance. Unlike the elite social clubs, it was founded in 1963 primarily for professional networking and service. In the 1990s, it allocated 34 percent of its budget to educational and mentoring programs. In addition to informal networking between members, the organization sponsored mentoring for children, about which one of its presidents wrote an inspirational book in 2000, *The Miracles of Mentoring: How to Encourage and Lead Future Generations.*[16]

Professional organizations flourished as African Americans raised their expectations. They established professional organizations parallel to those that already existed, organizing, for example, such groups as the National Association of Black Accountants and the National Association of Minority Contractors, both in 1969. The National Minority Supplier Development Council, begun in 1972, was formed to facilitate contacts between its constituents and contractors, thriving in part by raising the latter's confidence in the former. The National Black MBA Association was instituted in 1970 and had thirty-nine chapters by 2003. Its goals included executive skills development and helping constituents to form corporate connections and other networks. In 1996, a four-hundred-page directory, *The African American Network,* was published, containing lists of more than five thousand people and organizations with contact information, plus a chapter on how to write letters of inquiry.[17]

In 1992, South Asian immigrants to Silicon Valley, California, formed The Indus Entrepreneurs (TiE), bringing together successful and novice high-tech businesspeople. The group's explicit networking goals included instruction in American business methods and cultural expectations, as well as on how to build contacts through social interaction. With thirty-eight chapters worldwide by 2004, TiE honored its slogan "One Mission: Fostering Entrepreneurship Through Mentoring, Networking, Education." [18]

Experimentation continued and came to include the Internet as a connector medium. *GlobalMecca.com* was an organization that initiated an ambitious, Internet-based plan in 1999 to attract professional and business mentors to assist in raising the number of African Americans in top management. Its founder hoped that people with valuable experience would find mentoring to be "one of the most rewarding experiences of your professional career."[19]

The National Urban League (NUL) continued to develop formal networking and mentoring programs out of its national office and in local chapters. Ann E. Tanneyhill, longtime NUL program director, lobbied in the 1970s to recruit club women and men—and their clubs—to contribute financial assets and connections to NUL efforts.[20] Some local offices provided formalized networking. For example, the Akron, Ohio, Urban League Training and Employment Center demonstrated in a 1972 brochure what structured networking could achieve for people repeatedly rejected from job opportunities because of prejudice or lack of training. Over two years, this center placed 320 people, most of whom still held the same or better jobs at the end of the program. The program's success came from careful placement and training, based on personal contacts between individuals and employers. Leah Greer, a white League worker in Akron since 1966, described herself as "a believer in all that stuff about liberty and justice for all in the United States until I went to graduate school, first met blacks and began to see the rebuffs they had to face every day." One of Greer's young African-American female placements expressed the sentiment with which the brochure concluded, placing the nation's self-help ethos into the context of institutionalized, synthetic pull: "Black people seem to give up easily, but that is only when they think they have no future. It can be our time now. All we need is a helping hand. We can do this for ourselves."[21]

Formalizing Personnel Tools for Ambitious Strangers

That hopeful young woman in Akron blended self-help with a "helping hand" to explain what success for the disadvantaged required. Since then, decades of political and cultural battles have swirled around the merits and means of facilitating this mix. It has also become clear that this mix applies to the advantaged as well. They differ from the disadvantaged, of course, in their ready access to social capital and helping hands. *Everyone* needs *something* on the social side of the scale, if only to deter "push" discrimination. If someone's background networks provide no social capital of value in venues where opportunities exist, what can be done to gain access to empowered authority and peer networks?

Historical examples abound of companies' attempts to institutionalize social means for helping employees fit in and grow. In 1925, for instance, the book *Personal Leadership in Industry* suggested that leaders take a "personal interest in the men" under them. Establishing a "ritual of shaking hands" could help newcomers to "overcome hostility." Newcomers should be introduced "particularly to one man of longer service" to answer questions and provide guidance. A "sponsor" of the same age was likely to have the best chance at making the newcomer "feel at home most quickly" and forming a "friendship." General Electric's training programs in the 1950s stated, "Effective education may be described as a man and a boy, walking along a road, talking together in a friendly atmosphere." The best way to develop leadership, given this "personal nature of successful education," results from the neophyte's "good fortune" to "work under the guidance of seasoned, successful managers of men."[22]

These pre-1960s suggestions for integrating new people as potential peers all assumed a basic compatibility between newcomers and veterans. Integrating people who were true strangers, however, generated tension and alienation. Thus, women in corporate managerial positions during the 1980s and even into the 1990s often described "feeling like a complete outsider," as if their "company is a foreign country" or even feeling like a "Martian." "We know," one woman explained, "that men have worked, fought, played, and even showered together for years, and that, as women, we are intruders in their midst." Addressing this, a 1995 Glass Ceiling Commission report highlighted "corporate climates that alienate and isolate minorities and women" among the "structural barriers" that companies could and *should* improve.[23]

Whether the newcomers experienced harassment or just felt that they did not belong, enlightened personnel professionals had a ready solution, and that was formalizing—and thereby, it was hoped, equalizing—the processes by which management welcomed everyone. They believed that formalizing, rationalizing, and universally enforcing standards of managerial behavior could start breaking down barriers. Although no one argued that formalization offered a panacea, most saw it as a beginning. The idea was to manage and redistribute what was already "going on under their noses," as one woman put it. In this vein, a 1971 *Harvard Business Review* article laid out an early case for institutionalizing remedial mechanisms of pull. It urged top executives "to bring more women into responsible positions," in order both to avoid legal difficulties and to improve their firms' performance. Analysts asserted that equal employment opportunity required formally implementing for women all of the opportunities standard for men of equal ability and ambition. Business as usual would not suffice. Executives would have to "plan the new policies and practices essential if women are to assume responsible positions."[24]

Advocates for people excluded from the mainstream understood the importance of bringing those individuals into that mainstream. To do this, businesses must forbid overt harassment and segregation, and require at least the appearance of fair treatment—as a start. In 1977, Rosabeth Kanter recommended "opportunity-enhancing efforts" and "empowering strategies." She called for assessments of the different job ladders to which "tokens" and "dominants" were assigned. Performance reviews and career counseling must take *everyone* seriously, and she insisted that the word "everyone" be taken literally. Institutionalizing information flows and formalizing development programs could spread knowledge and managers' assistance deliberately and evenly instead of informally and therefore unevenly. Sharing training programs could also cause "peer alliances" to spring up among all sorts of people. Kanter suggested that "artificial sponsorship" and "foster sponsors" could help advance those who had been denied the benefits of informal sponsorship. To prepare women for jobs previously held by men, managers could rotate assignments in order to broaden both experience and contacts—these, after all, were the same reasons firms had always given in using job rotation to develop people with potential.[25]

Through the 1980s and 1990s, calls for formalized procedures to redistribute opportunities for advancement continued to multiply. Both employees and executives agreed, sometimes grudgingly, that companies could improve progress in providing equal opportunity by clarifying criteria for advancement and making minority and female advancement an explicit goal in company business plans. Analysts and activists urged the development of systematic mentoring programs, structured career planning, monitoring, individualized attention, and proactive human resources departments that worked to maximize opportunities for *all* capable employees. A free and universal flow of information about everything from business procedures and goals to social practices, such as whether to wear a jacket into the executive dining room, could very well be institutionalized, avoiding both inefficiency and awkwardness.[26]

Lawrence Otis Graham highlighted firms with compensatory social capital programs in his 1993 book, *The Best Companies for Minorities*. His criteria for inclusion were such things as whether or not the company supported minority caucuses; the existence of diversity and sensitivity training, as well as mentoring, internship, and management training programs for minority individuals; and to what ranks minority executives had risen. Graham ranked Xerox at the top, a model firm. Open, straightforward, and universally applied personnel practices at Xerox and other progressive firms benefited minority employees, argued Graham. Such even-handed practices also minimized resentment against incoming strangers.[27]

The Glass Ceiling Commission's 1995 report, *Good for Business*, itemized "what works to overcome the business barriers" to strangers' success: having formal programs with strong and visible CEO support for *all* employees; tracking improvements; and making managers and other gatekeepers accountable for progress. Effective programs recruited from broader population bases than were traditional; once the newcomers were hired, synthesized social capital helped move capable people up. Pointing out that informal mentors and networks have always aided successful businesspeople, the report found that structured programs succeeded when business goals, such as productivity, ranked high in statements supporting them. A participant in a formally established network praised the sharing it promoted: "Those who are close to or through the glass ceiling tell others where the cracks are and what size hammer to bring." Effective programs at Xerox, Procter & Gamble, and IBM validated formalized programs for women as well as for minority men and people with disabilities. IBM's sophisticated Mentoring Program, for example, engaged *all* new employees, with specific aids geared to each job level. Overall, "comprehensive, systemic approaches" succeeded, whereas "one-shot or ad hoc approaches" failed.[28]

The development of diversity management raises the value of nonmainstream workers to the organization. Business school courses and corporate vice presidents have taken on the tasks of institutionalizing mechanisms of social capital within routine human resource practices. Increasing diversity as a business strategy, they argue, benefits employers by increasing the talent pool, widening the range of creative solutions, and improving the performance of all employees. In the 1980s, for instance, Alcoa sought racial and gender diversity for both its managers and its workers as a way to improve productivity and remain competitive despite its reputation for being "tradition-bound." In this spirit, sixty-eight corporations filed amicus briefs in support of affirmative action in a 2003 U.S. Supreme Court case, commending the overall benefits of a mixed workforce.[29]

The Limits of Synthetic Pull

Despite all of the fanfare about mentoring, many critics warned against unrealistic expectations. One authority on mentoring, Kathy Kram, wrote in 1988 that the "popular press" was overselling mentoring as a simple key to success. The popular media could not resist stories of the successful pairing of a wise chief and a dedicated disciple. Earl Graves, Kathy Kram, and others pointed out that these types of human relationships at work were fragile under the best of conditions. Without storybook luck or ready-made connections, they asked, how could junior people actually find mentors willing and able to help them? Could formal programs find places for people as well as background networks do? Could "facilitated mentoring" foster comfortable relations between strangers, especially when those involved were strangers in many ways—gender, race, national origin, religion?[30]

Everyone who admitted to the problem agreed that relationships formed spontaneously have the best chance at fulfilling mentoring's promise. As the magazine *Essence* explained in 1980, "You don't just ask someone to be your mentor. Mentorships tend to develop gradually as two parties come to recognize and admire each other's talent." Even relationships with optimal beginnings, however, could become frayed. Sexual tension, a change in relative professional status, coworkers' resentment, disappointed expectations, and myriad job pressures could complicate, alter, or even destroy affiliations. Complete meltdowns could harm a business and even impair an affected person's health.[31]

For the same reasons that customary networks can foster comfortable and productive interactions, social distance can generate awkwardness and uncertainty between the most well meaning of people. Businessmen who volunteered as consultants to minority businessmen in the many outreach programs begun in the 1960s often found themselves at odds with their clients. Some consultants tried to impose their recommendations, while others were reluctant to challenge; clients often resented the volunteers, or devalued or misunderstood their advice. What made perfect sense in one culture too often jarred with another. In some cases, clients were unable for one reason or another to follow sound counsel.[32] Studies in the 1980s and 1990s showed repeatedly that simply having someone tagged as one's mentor or sponsor was not enough to provide equal opportunity. Cross-race and cross-sex developmental relationships seldom provided the same level of social and psychological support as same-race and same-sex relationships. Since majority-group male protégés almost never needed to cross race or sex lines to build authority networks, differential advantages continued. In some firms, women likened diversity programs to "pushing rocks up hills" because of stereotype-driven corporate cultures. Despite these problems, however, formal programs in firms with strong top-level commitment produced positive results.[33]

Finding a mentor could be like blind dating, with similar chances for either serendipity or calamity. "Forced matching," as one analyst put it in 1983, "ignores a characteristic crucial to the more intense mentor relationships—that the two people involved are attracted to each other and wish to work together." When that mutual attraction did not occur spontaneously—socially—care in selecting and training those who would become involved in mentoring was essential. Poorly put together programs usually did more harm than good: those being mentored were in danger of being further stigmatized by enforced attention and unwanted publicity. Too often, companies that neglected personnel development generally would institute formal mentoring programs as a panacea, not as a real solution to a serious problem, and the supposed beneficiaries would gain nothing but ill will from their coworkers. Labeling marginal people as needful of "fixing" exaggerated their strangeness.[34]

Some experts suggested that the components of mentoring be separated into more objective, less personal activities. Although "mentoring" became the umbrella term for person-to-person assistance, simpler, though still formal, programs could avoid some of the perils of mentoring, such as unfavorable matches, unrealistic expectations, and emotional closeness. For instance, providing straightforward practical advice carried little emotional freight, but still offered a novice many benefits.[35] As always, programs worked best when they were designed for all employees—minimizing differences between strangers and mainstream employees.

In creating environments that fostered social capital, effective training programs never imposed relationships on anyone. They provided occasions for people to mingle in business settings for business-related purposes, and from the resulting encounters supportive relationships evolved on their own. The Mentoring Circles that Lois Herr helped initiate at NYNEX in 1990 reflected her understanding of both the importance of mutual cooperation and the impossibility of forcing people into genuine mentoring relationships. "Classical mentoring, like the wind," she observed, "is usually noticed more by its effect than its existence." Nonetheless, she advised women to create synthetic networks in the hope that "real mentoring" would develop out of them. Herr's guidelines called for juniors to arrive at workshops with no expectations beyond the likelihood of learning from seniors. Personal relationships might blossom after the structured contacts, but no one should expect or assume that they would.[36] In short, formal contacts might lead to personal connections.

Still Strangers

A 1960s advertising executive once wondered aloud how television commercials could include more African Americans, given the limited roles for waiters and shoeshine boys. Another enthusiastically offered to help an African-American applicant, not by offering employment but by offering an introduction to someone who aided the handicapped. In the 1970s, a young African-American woman who had graduated with honors from the University of Maryland devised a well-regarded marketing plan for her firm. Before she left to present the plan to the client, her manager made her rehearse it over and over for fear she would forget her own plan. He took her to lunch and explained to her how to make her way in the airport, how to check and retrieve luggage, and how to rent a car. She finally put a halt to the lesson by asking her boss if she should pin a note to herself with the company's name so that Traveler's Aid could send her home if she got lost. The manager had the good grace to be embarrassed, and he realized that he had never worried about whether his white subordinates knew how to take a plane trip. Thus, even as overt racism was declining in corporate America, its traces lingered on.[37]

A 1998 Catalyst study showed that women of color, bearing the burdens of a double stereotype, ranked social capital factors as more important than white women did. While high percentages of all the surveyed female groups felt that they had to exceed the average performance standards to receive promotions, women of color ranked higher the barriers from not having network assistance from peers and superiors. An African-American manager noted, "Access to opportunities is easier for white women because they share informal experiences with the power structure." She continued, "Networking is a game that not everyone plays; somebody has to ask you to play. But you have to recognize that there's a game being played in the first place." Another observed that she had never "learned about exposure in informal ways. African-Americans are twenty years off in learning their way through the organizational culture—that it's more than performance and education that leads to advancement."[38]

Like beauty, potential resides in the eye of the beholder. At every level of opportunity, it mattered whether or not those in a position to recruit, hire, or promote saw an aspirant as someone with "potential." Gatekeepers would not willingly advance someone with whom they were uncomfortable, whose behavior they feared they could neither predict nor trust, or whose stereotype was all they could see. Who could deny the importance of what a 1997 author highlighted as the critical first "three seconds"? The statement "Enter a room, and it's already happened" would not have surprised a businessman eighty years earlier who could hire a man in "three minutes" because "there are labels all over a man's appearance and actions."[39] Neither of these commentators, at nearly opposite ends of the twentieth century, mentioned class, race, or sex as being relevant; yet no one needs even three seconds to detect these differences.

Thus, although formalized pull can offer a boost, the disadvantaged remain at a disadvantage. Moreover, individuals worry over whether their job performance will confirm negative stereotypes. Perversely, opinion may also turn against people whose behavior runs counter to stereotype. Although women have been held back for supposedly feminine weakness, others have been condemned because of "aggressive" behavior that in a man would have been considered aptly decisive. Residual prejudice comes through even when well-intentioned people attempt to override their predispositions, but inadvertently exhibit them by evaluating members of different groups against stereotyped standards. An African American who scores well on a technical skills test is more likely to be considered exceptional than someone from a different ethnic group. Even something as straightforward as height is subject to bias: men assume that women are short and so estimate women to be shorter than do women.[40] Strangers remain strangers.

A New Politics of Success

The Harvard School of Public Health Center for Health Communication initiated the Harvard Mentoring Project in 1998 as a public service campaign, using coverage from television networks, radio stations, major newspapers, and magazines to urge adults to mentor children and to thank their own mentors, using the slogan "Who mentored you?" The U.S. Postal Service even issued a stamp to mark the occasion, with a man pointing the way for a boy and copy that read "MENTORING A CHILD: VALUES • GOALS • SKILLS." The campaign promoted the work that Big Brothers / Big Sisters of America and other child-oriented organizations had been doing for a century, and expanded further the now ubiquitous term "mentoring." To cap the campaign, President George W. Bush declared with much fanfare that each January, beginning in 2002, would be National Mentoring Month.[41] Certainly, mentoring had become a hot topic, both in and out of business.

Networking spread its magic everywhere, as well. A 1999 college campus job fair, for instance, was dubbed a "Networking Job Fair." A brightly colored flyer announced that the National Coalition of Employers "extends a personal invitation to you and your friends" to participate. Applying the latest buzz words, promoters urged students, "Start networking now for the best jobs . . . !"[42] Under the expanding connotations for "networking," even the most alienating, intimidating, and hurried information exchange could masquerade as the offerings of supportive connections.

Fields that, like business, have strong individualist traditions have faced recent exposés of their social dynamics. Science, for instance, has come under scrutiny over the past two decades. In 2000, the book *Athena Unbound: The Advancement of Women in Science and Technology* explored the impact of gender on success in those fields. The authors showed that women's low social capital undermined their careers, despite excellent knowledge and skills. As a result, women were able to move ahead only if they could overcome isolation and discouragement. Despite popular culture's notion of a scientist working alone in an ivory tower, modern science is a social enterprise based on trust within and between networks.[43]

African-American scientists were therefore at a disadvantage because of their outsider status, and some have countered with network building akin to internal business caucuses. African-American molecular and cellular biologist Roland Owens, for instance, recognizes the importance of networking and mentoring to his own education and career. As one of the few African-American senior investigators at the National Institutes of Health (NIH), he helped found the NIH Black Scientists Association in late 1994 and has chaired its Career Enhancement Committee. The organization developed a mentoring program and a self-help network to compensate for the social distance that leaves minority scientists at a disadvantage. Owens and his colleagues in science built social capital for themselves for all the same reasons as did their counterparts in business: they wanted access to guidance, feedback, and challenging assignments. In 2002 Owens was honored as one of two Meyerhoff Mentors of the Year for his work with young minority scientists in a scholarship program. Summarizing his rationale for developing social capital, Owens reflected, "I have always felt that my own future in science is inextricably linked to the success of other minority scientists."[44]

By the last years of the twentieth century, the importance of the mechanisms of pull had become conventional wisdom. Many fields initiated mentoring awards to encourage the practice.[45] The popular excitement about the not-really-new tools of mentoring and networking caused them to be applied to every endeavor, from business to raising children to science. But the antidiscrimination activism that brought these practices to the fore has begun to fade from memory. Severing today's popular acceptance of growing and using the mechanisms of social capital from the history that named and legitimated them has serious consequences. It makes possible a backlash against attempts to synthesize pull for outliers while promoting pull for people who are already connectable is perceived as acceptable, even laudable. Two recent trends are pushing reformist links out of memory: companies are encouraging, even exploiting, the development of social capital among their employees in order to boost productivity; at the same time, advice on how to use social capital has abandoned reformist and community-oriented messages, retaining only lessons for the ambitious.

Employers Put Social Capital to Work

Recently, companies have attempted to reframe old problems by promising to raise productivity through synthetic social capital. This new management approach expects to facilitate recruiting, hiring, training, and promotion by generous doses of techniques based on the concepts of role models, mentors, and networks. Of course, advocates for integrating nonmainstream employees always promoted these practices as being beneficial to firms, mentioning in particular productivity, long-term morale, and a general furthering of the nation's progress toward its becoming an equal opportunity meritocracy. The issue here is balance. The perceived potential of social capital for boosting companies' productivity has fueled business analysts' ongoing excitement about networking and mentoring. The Academy of Management, for example, chose a familiar buzzword for its 2002 conference theme: "Building Effective Networks." Publicity for the conference declared that "network" had become "one of the most widely used words in our everyday vocabulary" and that participating in networks was "a source of competitive advantage for both people and organizations alike." Firms benefit if their employees are "well connected" and "excel in collaborative teamwork."[46]

Advocates of synthetic mentoring in business have increasingly focused on its purported usefulness in solving management problems. For instance, the human resources journal *HR Focus* urged managers to mentor their recruits so they "can spend more time being productive and less time *learning* to be productive." A 1999 American Management Association book laid out this set of assumptions in its title: *Coaching, Counseling, and Mentoring: How to Choose and Use the Right Technique to Boost Employee Performance.* According to this book, firms should set up three-tiered programs to encourage or arrange "mentoring" for "exceptional employees," "coaching" for all employees, and "counseling" for "poor performers." Responses from almost four hundred managers to a 2002 survey asking about their firms' mentoring practices made clear that they used mentoring for meeting "work-related needs of the company" and for "building the skills of individual employees." Just under 98 percent of the respondents said that they expected their firm to be the primary beneficiary of these mentoring programs. Just one respondent named "society" as a potential beneficiary, and only seven named employees. Some firms have tracked employees' e-mail correspondence, not to learn how to develop these employees, but to learn what personal connections the firms might exploit.[47]

A Social Spin on Self-Help

Mentors, networks, and role models now populate the index of every management book and every how-to-succeed treatise. No longer thought of as aberrations in the meritocracy of the business world, manipulating social capital now reigns as a legitimate tool for achievement, wielded best by the best. In the tradition of self-help literature, recent how-to books are filled with happy stories. It seems that anyone with enough ambition can succeed by following the rules for building social capital. Personality types matter, of course: "schmoozers" do better than people less adept at pleasing others and building bridges across organizational distances.[48] But even personality disadvantages can be overcome by adhering to the right advice—and being cheery about it. Women's special differences may still get mentioned, but no insurmountable problems break through the optimism. Affirmative action, if mentioned at all, appears as an obstacle to the true heroes of ambition. Individuals can conquer all, even if they know now that getting allies is part of the challenge of climbing the ladder. Thus, the new instructors on success show us how to pick and use mentors, how to create and operate within networks, how to manage the impression one makes, how to appear dedicated to one's company, how to get others to divulge information without becoming obligated to them, how to gain autonomy, loyalty, impact, visibility—and how to appear sincere all the while. They turn the mutual assistance component of social capital on its head in service of individual ambition.

Even luck, one pundit contends, is a by-product of one's forming a multitude of social contacts. Pluck makes luck—again. And one never outgrows the need for help from connections. Guidance from mentors and support groups benefits even CEOs and senior officers, along with pull and advice gleaned through connections of all sorts.[49] Mentors gain, as well, by spreading their influence as their protégés move through mazes of networks. The umbrella of pull has grown so large that it sometimes seems to encompass almost every sort of helpful relationship in business. All part of a day's work.

Just as the Horatio Alger cliché does not reflect Alger's original message, today's advice on using social capital slights the goals for which it was originally uncovered. The new conventional wisdom implies that class, ethnicity, and gender problems are over, and that all contenders can now fend equally for themselves. Most writers ignore the fact that the workings of social capital were uncovered only through civil rights and feminist activism; some actually disparage those roots. In doing so, they contribute to the backlash against community and institution-based aid, all the while promoting the exploitation of pull with tools newly highlighted and honed precisely because of earlier, progressive concerns.[50]

Promoting social skills on behalf of personal ambition is not new. Dale Carnegie was only the most famous of many old-time promoters of building connections, but he did not scorn the political origins of the tools he sold. According to current business gurus, success comes to whoever is ambitious and clever enough to combine social savvy with objective, on-the-job ability. Thus, even in the heyday of social capital, the individual remains the hero, and the assumption once again is that there is equal access for all. Individual "merit" has come to include how much pull one has.

Uncovering the social tools for advancement and self-remaking at least means that they are no longer unacknowledged, uncontested prerogatives. Pull no longer operates unchallenged. A century of business analysts and activists have made clear its power and application.[51] The legacy of ambitious strangers guides and inspires all striving souls who apply social tools to their own individual quest. The tools disadvantaged people and their advocates uncovered, named, and made legitimate now serve everyone, including those in the mainstream, more effectively than ever. With our present awareness, every career story now should prompt us to ask: What was the social capital behind that success or failure? How did social capital determine the pushes or pulls?

Pull remains indispensable for business achievement. Neither wealth, nor talent, nor skill can predict achievement. Luck alone is not enough; lottery winners rarely make a mark in business. Neither a gregarious personality, like Andrew Carnegie's, nor a secretive one, like Jay Gould's, is a standard feature of successful people. Neither a nurturing upbringing, like Henry Ford's, nor a dysfunctional one, like John D. Rockefeller's, determines success. Neither Benjamin Franklin's social skills nor Bill Gates's social ineptness guarantees anything. But take away access to the circles that control and distribute opportunity and information, and no combination of other characteristics can fully compensate. Even the most extraordinary people cannot achieve ordinary success alone.

The language and ethos of pull have made their ways into our common understanding of how people succeed in business. Yet not all ambitious people exploit every bit of social capital to which they can lay claim, nor do they work at synthesizing more. Many people are content to earn their livelihood and climb a short way up the ladder by using only their on-the-job labor. They do not wish to sacrifice their private lives to build the social capital that purposeful networking requires. Because of the reduction of "push" discrimination, career paths now often seem deceptively uncomplicated by social capital constraints, especially where objective personnel procedures minimize the need for pull for modest success. Overt networking, including seeking out mentors, may be perceived negatively in some workplaces as awkward aggressiveness—office politics—with those engaging in it judged to be insufficiently focused on their job responsibilities. This diminution of the influence of social capital in more meritocratic workplaces is the effect of four decades of restructuring American business and the larger culture in which it resides. We think differently now about who can have potential. Capable and ambitious people, including individuals who were previously marginalized, can increasingly take for granted access to many of the authority and peer networks from which previous generations were excluded. Thanks to this access and to their own network building, they can get reasonable jobs, and they can build challenging careers.

We can expect that ethnicity and gender will continue to decline as overriding variables in determining who has "potential." The influence of social capital will not be eliminated, but its distribution will be evened out; "push" discrimination will be minimized. Class will continue to matter for the foreseeable future, and office politics will certainly continue. Whether or not individuals try to advance their career by exploiting pull, they will at least be aware of the existence of social capital and its effects. Connections and connectability will always affect where they begin, to what they aspire, to what education, information, and opportunities they have access.[52]

Gatekeepers use different criteria for "potential" than they did a half century ago, but they still exercise the same authority. Social factors, especially class, continue to determine connectability; pull still determines who makes connections. The grand career successes of the 1990s, as well as the corporate scandals after that decade, proved again the power of social capital, the indispensability of pull. Background, peer, and authority networks still retain the power to instill hope and inspire ambition. Diminished exclusionary discrimination cannot compensate for a lack of role models and mentors. Minimizing "push" discrimination does not generate pull.

Knowing the real stories of how Americans have succeeded in business should help us balance individual and social factors for achievement. Successful businesspeople have used assets besides talent and effort, whether in colonial shops or modern corporations. Ignoring the evidence of social dynamics, as traditional stories of self-made business heroes have done, fosters the neglect, even disparagement, of people who simply lack connections and cannot get them. Revealing the existence of social capital and how it works embeds individuals' stories into their social and cultural context. These newly enriched narratives highlight the consequences of differential access to social capital and the benefits of synthesizing it on behalf of the meritocracy of our ideals. These fuller stories can foster hope and nurture ambition through helping people understand what they can do for themselves and what networks make possible. It may be that reaching the perfect balance of individual and social factors for success in business—making America truly the land of equal opportunity—is a dream. But it remains the American Dream.

NOTES

INDEX

Notes

Abbreviations

AAUW	American Association of University Women Library, Washington, D.C.
Avon/HM&L	Avon Products, Inc., Avon Archives, Accession no. 2155, Hagley Museum and Library, Wilmington, Delaware
Chandler/HM&L	Elva M. Chandler Papers, Accession no. 2057, Hagley Museum and Library, Wilmington, Delaware
HM&L	Hagley Museum and Library, Wilmington, Delaware
LKH	Lois Kathryn Herr Personal Document Collection
LofCMD	Library of Congress Manuscript Division, Washington, D.C.
NAM/HM&L	National Association of Manufacturers Archives, Accession no. 1411, Hagley Museum and Library, Wilmington, Delaware
NUL	National Urban League Archives, Library of Congress Manuscript Division, Washington, D.C.
Sun/HM&L	Sun Oil Company, Archives, Accession no. 1317, Hagley Museum and Library, Wilmington, Delaware

341

Introduction

1. Walter R[aleigh] Houghton, *Kings of Fortune, or the Triumphs and Achievements of Noble, Self-Made Men* (Chicago: Loomis National Library Association, 1888), p. 5. The vast literature on the self-made myth includes John G. Cawelti, *Apostles of the Self-Made Man* (Chicago: University of Chicago Press, 1965); Richard M. Huber, *The American Idea of Success* (New York: McGraw-Hill Book Co., 1971); Edward Chase Kirkland, *Dream and Thought in the Business Community, 1860–1900* (Ithaca, N.Y.: Cornell University Press, 1956); Richard Weiss, *The American Myth of Success: From Horatio Alger to Norman Vincent Peale* (New York: Basic Books, 1969); Irvin G. Wyllie, *The Self-Made Man in America: The Myth of Rags to Riches* (New Brunswick, N.J.: Rutgers University Press, 1954).

2. Educator and reformer L. Judson Hanifan seems to have used the phrase "social capital" first in 1916. Sociologists Pierre Bourdieu in the 1970s and James S. Coleman in the 1980s also used the term "social capital," which had arisen in various venues during the twentieth century. Economist Glenn C. Loury used it in the 1980s to refer to the economic development needs of African Americans; see his "New Dividends Through 'Social Capital,'" *Black Enterprise* 15 (July 1985): 36–37. Robert Putnam's 1990s work culminated in his best-seller *Bowling Alone: The Collapse and Revival of American Community* (New York: Simon and Schuster, 2000), pp. 19, 350, 358. See also Putnam, *Making Democracy Work: Civic Traditions in Modern Italy* (Princeton: Princeton University Press, 1993); "Bowling Alone: America's Declining Social Capital," *Journal of Democracy* 6 (1995): 65–78; and Putnam, ed., *Democracies in Flux: The Evolution of Social Capital in Contemporary Society* (New York: Oxford University Press, 2002), esp. pp. 4–14. For examples and overviews of the literature and its growing concern with the exclusionary effects of social capital, see Mark Granovetter and Richard Swedberg, eds., *The Sociology of Economic Life,* 2nd ed. (Boulder, Colo.: Westview Press/Perseus Books, 2001); and James Farr, "Social Capital: A Conceptual History," *Political Theory* 32 (2004): 6–33. For examples of historians who use the term, see Dario Gaggio, "Do Social Historians Need Social Capital?" *Social History* 29 (2004): 499–513; and Sheilagh Ogilvie, "How Does Social Capital Affect Women? Guilds and Communities in Early Modern Germany," *Ameri-*

can Historical Review 109 (2004): 325–359. Economists and other specialists have begun to explore these possibilities as well. See Kenneth J. Arrow and Ron Borzekowski, "Limited Network Connections and the Distribution of Wages" for a review of economists' appraoches to social capital questions and correlations between social capital "disparities" that "engender further inequality" (quotation on p. 13), FEDS Working Paper no. 2004-41, August 2004, http://ssrn.com/abstract= 632321 (accessed 7 May 2005). See also Michael J. Mazarr, "Culture and International Relations: A Review Essay," *Washington Quarterly* 19 (Spring 1996): 177.

3. I will be using the term "ethnicity" and its variants to denote groupings of people by ascribed and cultural characteristics, including characteristics often considered racial. Also, "minority" will not necessarily refer solely to African Americans. Further, not all minorities are marginalized or disadvantaged (consider, for example, elite white males), and not all those who are disadvantaged or marginalized are minorities (such as women and, one could argue, the working classes, who include lower-level white-collar workers).

4. Gary S. Becker, *The Economics of Discrimination,* 2nd ed. (Chicago: University of Chicago Press, 1971; 1st ed., 1957), pp. 10–11, 160. In 1992, Becker received the Nobel Memorial Prize in Economic Sciences for linking econometrics and social processes.

5. For cases of race-based "push" discrimination, see Theresa A. Hammond, *A White-Collar Profession: African American Certified Public Accountants since 1921* (Chapel Hill: University of North Carolina Press, 2002), quotation p. 60; and Thomas J. Sugrue, *The Origins of the Urban Crisis: Race and Inequality in Postwar Detroit* (Princeton, N.J.: Princeton University Press, 1996), esp. chap. 4.

6. See Naomi Lamoreaux, *Insider Lending: Banks, Personal Connections, and Economic Development in Industrial New England* (Cambridge: Cambridge University Press, 1996); Richard White, "Information, Markets, and Corruption: Transcontinental Railroads in the Gilded Age," *Journal of American History* 90 (2003): 19–43; and Mark R. Wilson, "Gentlemanly Price-Fixing and Its Limits: Collusion and Competition in the U.S. Explosives Industry during the Civil War Era," *Business History Review* 77 (2003): 207–234.

7. Seymour Martin Lipset, *The First New Nation: The United States in Historical and Comparative Perspective* (New York: Basic Books,

1963), quotation p. 321. Thanks to Daniel Pope for suggesting this source. For other sociologists on this issue, see Reinhard Bendix, *Work and Authority in Industry* (New York: John Wiley and Sons, 1956); and Gunnar Myrdal, *An American Dilemma: The Negro Problem and Modern Democracy* (New York: Harper and Brothers Publishers, 1944). C. Wright Mills addressed the systemic consequences of social advantages and how they limited equal opportunity. He traced the webs of influence between American elites, most notably within what he called the "power elite" and also within labor unions and the "white collar" middle classes. Mills found nonmeritocratic institutions operating within every sector, unevenly distributing authority, wealth, and other benefits of power. Mills, *The Power Elite* (London: Oxford University Press, 1956), pp. 11, 329–330, 342; Mills, *White Collar: The American Middle Classes* (New York: Oxford University Press, 1951). For Mills on labor union elites, see "The Trade Union Leader: A Collective Portrait," in *Power, Politics, and People: The Collected Essays of C. Wright Mills,* ed. Irving Louis Horowitz (New York: Oxford University Press, 1963), pp. 77–96.

8. Shepherd Mead, *How to Succeed in Business without Really Trying: The Dastard's Guide to Fame and Fortune* (New York: Simon and Schuster, 1952); *How to Succeed in Business without Really Trying,* script by Abe Burrows, Jack Weinstock, and Willie Gilbert, music and lyrics by Frank Loesser (play opened at the 46th Street Theatre, New York, 14 October 1961; film released in 1967).

1. Social Capital and the Mechanisms of Success

1. Benjamin Franklin, *Benjamin Franklin: The Autobiography and Other Writings,* ed. L. Jesse Lemisch (New York: Penguin Putnam, 1961), pp. 82–88. Additional references, unless otherwise noted, are to this edition. Gordon S. Wood calls Franklin "the architect of his own fortune" and the "archetype of the self-made man," though he also notes that patronage was "the basic means of social mobility in the eighteenth century, and Franklin's rise was due to it." *The Americanization of Benjamin Franklin* (New York: Penguin, 2004), pp. 2, 16, 25–28, 246. Other recent biographies that detail social factors but credit personal factors for success include Ron Chernow's *Titan: The Life of John D. Rockefeller* (New York: Vintage, 1998), and his *Alexander*

Hamilton (New York: Penguin, 2004). A rare exception that balances both types of factors is Charles W. Cheape's exemplary *Strictly Business: Walter Carpenter at Du Pont and General Motors* (Baltimore: Johns Hopkins University Press, 1995).

2. Franklin, *Autobiography,* pp. 35–41. Henry Steele Commager called Franklin's "origins" "middle class" in his introduction to the *Autobiography* (New York: Random House, 1944), p. xi.

3. Thomas L. Purvis, *Colonial America to 1763,* Almanacs of American Life (New York: Facts on File, 1999), pp. 136, 222, 227–229. This calculation set sixteen years as the dividing age for adulthood.

4. Franklin, *Autobiography,* pp. 24, 27.

5. Another ship's captain mentioned the young Franklin's erudition to the governor of New York, who also invited him to call. This, wrote Franklin, "for a poor boy like me was very pleasing." (Franklin spelled Homes as "Holmes" here.) Ibid., pp. 35–43, 46–48, 50–55, 69.

6. Ibid., pp. 69–73.

7. Judith A. McGaw, *Most Wonderful Machine: Mechanization and Social Change in Berkshire Paper Making, 1801–1885* (Princeton, N.J.: Princeton University Press, 1987), pp. 127, 130–131, 137–146. For an analytical overview of the most important statistical mobility studies, see Walter A. Friedman and Richard S. Tedlow, "Statistical Portraits of American Business Elites: A Review Essay," *Business History* 45 (October 2003): 89–113. See also Alan B. Krueger, "The Apple Falls Close to the Tree, Even in the Land of Opportunity," *New York Times,* 14 November 2002, p. C2; Edward Pessen, ed., *Three Centuries of Social Mobility in America* (Lexington, Mass.: Heath, 1974); and Kevin Phillips, *Wealth and Democracy: A Political History of the American Rich* (New York: Broadway Books/Random House, 2002), esp. chap. 1.

Indications are that even to this day there is less mobility onto the top rungs of business than promised by two centuries of rhetorical politics. Peter Temin recently concluded that while the American political elite has become more representative of the general population over the past century, the business elite has not done so. "The American Business Elite in Historical Perspective," in Elise S. Brezis and Peter Temin, eds., *Elites, Minorities, and Economic Growth* (Amsterdam: Elsevier Science B. V., 1999), pp. 19–39.

8. Andrew Carnegie, *Autobiography of Andrew Carnegie* (Boston: Northeastern University Press, 1986; first published 1920), p. 1;

Thomas Mellon, *Thomas Mellon and His Times,* 2nd ed., ed. Mary Louis Briscoe (Pittsburgh: University of Pittsburgh Press, 1994), p. 5. William M. Thayer, *Onward to Fame and Fortune; or, Climbing Life's Ladder* (New York: Christian Herald, 1893), p. 3; Wood, *Americanization,* pp. 1–8, 238–243; Daniel J. Boorstin, "The Secret of Success: Benjamin Franklin Created a New Type of Book, the ABCs of Getting Ahead." *U.S. News and World Report* 113, no. 9 (31 August 1992): 82–83.

9. Mellon, *Thomas Mellon,* pp. 33, 62; William Larimer Mellon and Boyden Sparkes, *Judge Mellon's Sons* (privately printed, 1948), p. 22. Franklin's *Autobiography* was one of only eleven books, other than the Bible, that sold at least 40,000 copies in the United States from 1790 to 1799. Frank Luther Mott, *Golden Multitudes: The Story of Best Sellers in the United States* (New York: R. R. Bowker Co., 1947), p. 305. Franklin's 1758 "Way to Wealth" also became immensely popular, reprinted well beyond the colonies in time and space. Franklin, *Autobiography,* pp. 187–196.

10. Mansel G. Blackford and K. Austin Kerr, *B. F. Goodrich: Tradition and Transformation, 1870–1995* (Columbus: Ohio State University Press, 1996), p. 10; Ralph W. Hidy, Frank Ernest Hill, and Allen Nevins, *Timber and Men: The Weyerhaeuser Story* (New York: Macmillan, 1963), pp. 4–7. The inscribed copy of Franklin's *Poor Richard's Almanac* (Aldus; no place or date of publication) was a gift to Sarah Maud Weyerhaeuser; courtesy Walter S. Rosenberry III.

11. Carnegie, *Autobiography,* chaps. 3–6; Harold C. Livesay, *Andrew Carnegie and the Rise of Big Business* (Boston: Little, Brown and Co., 1975), chap. 2; Joseph Frazier Wall, *Andrew Carnegie* (New York: Oxford University Press, 1970), chaps. 5–6.

12. Carnegie, *Autobiography,* chaps. 3–6; Livesay, *Andrew Carnegie,* chaps. 3–4; Wall, *Andrew Carnegie,* chaps. 5–6.

13. Wall, *Andrew Carnegie,* pp. 87–89.

14. Carnegie, *Autobiography,* pp. 67, 69; Wall, *Andrew Carnegie,* p. 115; C. W. Gale to Roy G. Munroe, 31 August 1931, quoted in Mark H. Rose, *Cities of Heat and Light: Domesticating Gas and Electricity in Urban America* (University Park: Pennsylvania State University Press, 1995), p. 128n26. For an analysis of the "affective relations between men . . . concealed within the image of bureaucracy as a machine," see Michael Roper, *Masculinity and the British Organization Man since 1945* (Oxford: Oxford University Press, 1994), pp. 78–81, 98–100. See

also Toby L. Ditz, "Shipwrecked; or, Masculinity Imperiled: Mercantile Representations of Failure and the Gendered Self in Eighteenth-Century Philadelphia," *Journal of American History* 81 (1994): 51–80.

15. Ditz, "Shipwrecked"; Tamara K. Hareven, ed., *Family and Kin in Urban Communities, 1700–1930* (New York: New Viewpoints, 1977); Naomi Lamoreaux, *Insider Lending: Banks, Personal Connections, and Economic Development in Industrial New England* (Cambridge: Cambridge University Press, 1996).

16. Albert Ellery Berg, ed., *The Universal Self-Instructor* (New York: Phillips and Burrows, 1882), pp. 501–502; James D. McCabe, *The National Encyclopedia of Business and Social Forms* (Boston: E. W. Sawyer and Co., 1884), pp. 256–259. Henry Clews, *Fifty Years in Wall Street* (New York: Arno Press, 1973; originally published New York: Irving Publishing Co., 1908), pp. 1061–62. See also S. Roland Hall, "Applying for a Position as Office Clerk," in Clarence M. Woolley et al., *Employer and Employee* (Chicago: System Co., 1907), pp. 132–149.

17. Robert D. Putnam, *Bowling Alone: The Collapse and Revival of American Community* (New York: Simon and Schuster, 2000), pp. 19–21. See also Robert K. Merton, "Insiders and Outsiders: A Chapter in the Sociology of Knowledge," *American Journal of Sociology* 78 (July 1972): 9–47; Monica Biernat and Melvin Manis, "Shifting Standards and Stereotype-Based Judgments," *Journal of Personality and Social Psychology* 66 (1994): 5–20; Mark Granovetter and Richard Swedberg, *The Sociology of Economic Life,* 2nd ed. (Boulder, Colo.: Westview Press/Perseus Books, 2001); Clyde Griffen and Sally Griffen, eds., *Natives and Newcomers: The Ordering of Opportunity in Mid-Nineteenth-Century Poughkeepsie* (Cambridge, Mass.: Harvard University Press, 1978); Roger Waldinger, *Still the Promised City? African-Americans and New Immigrants in Postindustrial New York* (Cambridge, Mass.: Harvard University Press, 1996).

18. Mary Ryan, *Cradle of the Middle Class: The Family in Oneida County, New York, 1790–1865* (Cambridge: Cambridge University Press, 1981), pp. 183–185. Carnegie, *Autobiography,* pp. 31–32, 37, 45–47, 82; Wall, *Andrew Carnegie,* pp. 85–86.

19. Wall, *Andrew Carnegie,* pp. 65–68, 72–74, 79, 81, 87–89; Carnegie, *Autobiography,* pp. 28–35; Peter Krass, *Carnegie* (New York: John Wiley and Sons, 2002), p. 14.

20. Carnegie, *Autobiography,* pp. 35–38; Wall, *Andrew Carnegie,* pp. 89–

91; Krass, *Carnegie,* pp. 31–32. For analysis of Pittsburgh's ethnic groups, see John N. Ingham, *The Iron Barons: A Social Analysis of an American Urban Elite, 1874–1965* (Westport, Conn.: Greenwood Press, 1978), pp. 6–7, 21.

21. Carnegie, *Autobiography,* pp. 38–42; Wall, *Andrew Carnegie,* pp. 102–104. In addition to Pittsburgh's central position in iron, steel, and railroads, it was also the home of the industries founded by George Westinghouse and H. J. Heinz, plus that of Joseph Newton Pew during the formative decades in natural gas and what became the Sun Oil Company; see Mark David Samber, "Networks of Capital: Creating and Maintaining a Regional Industrial Economy in Pittsburgh, 1865–1919" (Ph.D. diss., Carnegie Mellon University, 1995). John D. Rockefeller's Cleveland base was nearby. Jocelyn Maynard Ghent and Frederic Cople Jaher show a similar growth pattern for Chicago, namely that the "leading Chicago businessmen became less Algeristic in origins with each successive birth cohort." "The Chicago Business Elite, 1830–1930: A Collective Biography," *Business History Review* 50 (Autumn 1976): 288–328.

22. Carnegie, *Autobiography,* pp. 42, 52–57, 61, 69–70; Wall, *Andrew Carnegie,* pp. 102–104.

23. Carnegie, *Autobiography,* pp. 37, 40–41; Wall, *Andrew Carnegie,* pp. 89, 91. Samber, "Networks of Capital," pp. 76–79. "Carnegie Has Made Forty-Three Millionaires," *New York Times,* 11 February 1911, 3. The newspaper counted forty-seven to Carnegie's forty-three.

24. Carnegie, *Autobiography,* p. 167; Wall, *Andrew Carnegie,* pp. 297–360. For a case of Carnegie's acting as a mentor, see Robert Hessen, *Steel Titan: The Life of Charles M. Schwab* (New York: Oxford University Press, 1975).

25. Michael Klepper and Robert Gunther, *The Wealthy 100: From Benjamin Franklin to Bill Gates—a Ranking of the Richest Americans, Past and Present* (Secaucus, N.J.: Citadel Press, 1996); and Klepper and Gunther, "The *American Heritage* Forty: A Ranking of the Wealthiest Americans of All Time," *American Heritage,* October 1998, pp. 56–74. Klepper and Gunther calculated their rankings by dividing the U.S. GNP by each individual's wealth, either at death or in 1995 (if the person was still alive); the results differed between the two rankings in part because of the movement of Bill Gates from 31 to 5.

Maury Klein found more to praise about Gould than have most, including Gould's "magnificent performance" in perpetuating his "longest and noblest deception": hiding his tuberculosis for four years from everyone except his doctor. According to Klein, this refutes the frequent assessment of Gould as "unmanly, cowardly, physically afraid." *The Life and Legends of Jay Gould* (Baltimore: Johns Hopkins University Press, 1986), pp. 404–405.

For analyses that contrast character with personality, see Judy Hilkey, *Character Is Capital: Success Manuals and Manhood in Gilded Age America* (Chapel Hill: University of North Carolina Press, 1997); David Riesman, with Reuel Denney and Nathan Glazer, *The Lonely Crowd* (New Haven: Yale University Press, 1961); Warren I. Susman, "'Personality' and the Making of Twentieth-Century Culture," in *Culture as History: The Transformation of American Society in the Twentieth Century* (New York: Pantheon, 1984), pp. 271–285; Irvin G. Wyllie, *The Self-Made Man in America: The Myth of Rags to Riches* (New Brunswick, N.J.: Rutgers University Press, 1954), pp. 34–35. On the masculine sociability of business, see Michael Grossberg, "Institutionalizing Masculinity: The Law as a Masculine Profession," in *Meanings for Manhood: Constructions of Masculinity in Victorian America,* ed. Mark C. Carnes and Clyde Griffen (Chicago: University of Chicago Press, 1990), pp. 133–151; Anthony Rotundo, *American Manhood: Transformations in Masculinity from the Revolution to the Modern Era* (New York: Basic Books, 1993), chaps. 1, 8, and 9.

26. The gunfire occurred in 1860, when Gould and his allies stormed a tannery in Gouldsboro, Pennsylvania, to take possession of it in a dispute with a former partner. Klein, *Jay Gould,* pp. 42–51, 53–61, 71–74, 112–114.

27. Ibid., pp. 76–81.

28. Ibid., pp. 76–81, 102–14; Gould quoted p. 109.

29. Ibid., pp. 128, 134, 140–141, 212, 317–318, 493; Klepper and Gunther, "The *American Heritage* Forty," pp. 56–74; Paul Sarnoff, *Russell Sage: The Money King* (New York: Ivan Obolensky, 1965), pp. 149–156.

30. Sarnoff, *Russell Sage,* p. 210; quotation from *New York World* in Klein, *Jay Gould,* pp. 481–482.

31. Wall, *Andrew Carnegie,* p. 144.

32. Horatio Alger, Jr., *Helping Himself* (New York: New York Book Co., 1912; first published 1886); quotations from pp. 45, 51–52; *Ragged*

Dick, or Street Life in New York with the Boot-Blacks (Philadelphia: Henry T. Coates and Co., 1895; first published 1868). See also Carol Nackenoff, *The Fictional Republic: Horatio Alger and American Political Discourse* (New York: Oxford University Press, 1994).

33. Alger, *Ragged Dick,* pp. 69–70, 127–128. See also Nackenoff, *The Fictional Republic,* pp. 134–141.

34. Surveys of the entire runs of the *Wall Street Journal* and *New York Times* demonstrate this evolution. The U.S. population began at one-seventh and ended at one-fourth of its present size when Alger's readership achieved such high numbers. For scholarly analyses of the changing meanings attached to Alger's name and message, see Gary Scharnhorst, *Horatio Alger, Jr.* (Boston: Twayne Publishers, 1980), pp. 42, 65, 121–127; Scharnhorst and Jack Bales, *Horatio Alger, Jr.: An Annotated Bibliography of Comment and Criticism* (Metuchen, N.J.: Scarecrow Press, 1981), p. x; and Scharnhorst with Bales, *The Lost Life of Horatio Alger, Jr.* (Bloomington: Indiana University Press, 1985), pp. xix, 149–156. See also R. Richard Wohl, "The 'Rags to Riches Story': An Episode of Secular Idealism," in *Class, Status and Power: A Reader in Social Stratification,* ed. Richard Bendix and Seymour Martin Lipset (Glencoe, Ill.: Free Press, 1953), pp. 388–395, 693–694; and Mott, *Golden Multitudes,* p. 159.

35. In addition to Benjamin Franklin and Andrew Carnegie, all of the well-known dramatic American business successes required entry into influential social networks. Examples include John Jacob Astor, Jay Cooke, Henry Ford, Jay Gould, Thomas Mellon, and John D. Rockefeller. In fact, I have found no biography of a business success that does not reveal the benefits of social capital, most obviously mentoring.

36. Sarah K. Bolton, *Poor Boys Who Became Famous* (New York: Thomas Y. Crowell and Co., 1885), pp. v–vi. Bolton published *Girls Who Became Famous* the following year. Her famous female subjects, however, need not have been raised in poverty, nor did any earn their way into the book through business. (New York: Thomas Y. Crowell and Co., 1886). See also Daniel Walker Howe, *Making the American Self: Jonathan Edwards to Abraham Lincoln* (Cambridge, Mass.: Harvard University Press, 1997), p. 108. Judy Hilkey estimates that by 1900, several million copies of advice books were in circulation: Hilkey, *Character Is Capital,* pp. 21–22.

37. P[hineas] T[aylor] Barnum, *Dollars and Sense: or, How to Get On*

(New York: Henry S. Allen, 1890), pp. 77–79. Russell H. Conwell, *Acres of Diamonds* (New York: Harper and Row, 1915), p. 21.

38. John T. Faris, *Men Who Made Good* (New York: Fleming H. Revell Co., 1912), p. 6. Sigmund Diamond, *The Reputation of the American Businessman* (Cambridge, Mass.: Harvard University Press, 1955), chap. 4, quotation p. 82.

39. Karen Halttunen, *Confidence Men and Painted Women* (New Haven: Yale University Press, 1986), pp. 25–28, 36–43; Rotundo, *American Manhood.*

40. "Sons of Millionaires Who Have Made Successes," *New York Times,* 10 April 1910, sect. 5, p. 6; "The Rich Man's Son—How He Is Being Trained to Succeed His Father," *New York Times,* 14 January 1906, sect. 3, p. 6; Hill quoted on his own sons by Charles H. Ingersoll, "The Good Fortune of Being Born Poor and Having a High Ideal," in *Touchstones of Success* [no editor] (Philadelphia: Vir Publishing Co., 1920), p. 68.

41. C. Wright Mills created the classic study on the "sociological anchor of the community of interest, the unification of outlook and policy, that prevails among the propertied class": *The Power Elite* (London: Oxford University Press, 1956), p. 123. Sven Beckert's *The Monied Metropolis: New York City and the Consolidation of the American Bourgeoisie, 1850–1896* (Cambridge: Cambridge University Press, 2001) provides an analysis of class-preserving processes. Arguing that monied people formed a cohesive and restrictive class, Beckert shows that they built up a structure through which they could exert their power throughout the nation's political and economic systems. John Ingham provides an especially close analysis of these self-perpetuating dynamics, including both biographical and statistical data, in his book *The Iron Barons.*

For a classic study of background networks operating within an elite business community, see Robert F. Dalzell Jr., *Enterprising Elite: The Boston Associates and the World They Made* (Cambridge, Mass.: Harvard University Press, 1987). For studies of family at other levels of business activity, see Alan Dawley, *Class and Community: The Industrial Revolution in Lynn* (Cambridge, Mass.: Harvard University Press, 1976); Richard Grassby, *Kinship and Capitalism: Marriage, Family, and Business in the English-Speaking World, 1580–1740* (Cambridge: Cambridge University Press, 2001); and Hareven, *Family and Kin.*

42. Jean Strouse, *Morgan: American Financier* (New York: Random House, 1999), pp. 30–34, 54; Junius Morgan quotations on p. 32.

43. Ibid., pp. 67–72, 77, 137, 142; Junius Morgan quotations on pp. 67, 72, 77.

44. For evidence of women's nonstereotypical business activities, see Angel Kwolek-Folland's encyclopedic *Incorporating Women: A History of Women in Business in the United States* (New York: Twayne Publishers, 1998), esp. chap. 3; and Susan Ingalls Lewis, "Women in the Marketplace: Female Entrepreneurs, Business Patterns, and Working Families in Mid-Nineteenth-Century Albany, New York" (Ph.D. diss., State University of New York, Binghamton, 2002).

45. Ralph M. Hower, *History of Macy's of New York, 1858–1919* (Cambridge, Mass.: Harvard University Press, 1946), pp. 65–66, 115; Curtiss S. Johnson, *America's First Lady Boss* (Norwalk, Conn.: Silvermine Publishers, 1965), pp. 14–26, 29, 32, 34–35, 50–56.

46. Hower, *History of Macy's,* pp. 123–128, 157–160; Johnson, *America's First Lady Boss,* pp. 40–63, 69–75, 84, 97, 102, 162.

47. Hower, *History of Macy's,* pp. 123, 157–160, 226.

48. Andrew Dawson, *Lives of the Philadelphia Engineers: Capital, Class, and Revolution, 1830–1890* (Aldershot, Eng.: Ashcroft, 2004), esp. pp. 4–9, 79–109; Donna J. Rilling, *Making Houses, Crafting Capitalism: Builders in Philadelphia, 1790–1850* (Philadelphia: University of Pennsylvania Press, 2001), pp. vii–vii, xi, 36–37.

49. Rilling, *Making Houses,* pp. 15, 17–25, 38.

50. Ibid.

2. Organizing and Synthesizing Social Capital

1. The AAUW took on its present name in 1921, following two key mergers. Marion Talbot and Lois Kimball Mathews Rosenberry, *The History of the American Association of University Women, 1881–1931* (Boston: Houghton Mifflin Co., 1931), pp. 4–9, 36. Barbara J. Balliet borrowed Mary Livermore's post–Civil War era question for her dissertation, "'What Shall We Do With Our Daughters': Middle-Class Women's Ideas about Work, 1840–1920," in which she demonstrates the breadth of women's concerns on the topic (Ph.D. diss., New York University, 1988, p. 3).

2. Talbot and Rosenberry, *History,* pp. 7–11, 17, 35–37, 93, 104, 228–

233, 313–314; Susan Levine, *Degrees of Equality: The American Association of University Women and the Challenge of Twentieth-Century Feminism* (Philadelphia: Temple University Press, 1995), p. 24; Karen J. Blair, *The Clubwoman as Feminist: True Womanhood Redefined, 1868–1914* (New York: Holmes and Meier Publishers, 1980), pp. 84–85.

3. Alexis de Toqueville, *Democracy in America*, ed. J. P. Mayer, trans. George Lawrence (Garden City, N.Y.: Anchor Books/Doubleday, 1969), p. 513. On the early organizing impulse, see Robert A. Gross, *The Minutemen and Their World* (New York: Hill and Wang, 1976), pp. 172–175; Paul E. Johnson, *A Shopkeeper's Millennium: Society and Revivalism Rochester, New York, 1815–1837* (New York: Hill and Wang, 1978), esp. chaps. 2, 3; Stuart M. Blumin, *The Emergence of the Middle Class: Social Experience in the American City, 1760–1900* (Cambridge: Cambridge University Press, 1989), chap. 6. On the importance of organizing in the Progressive Era, see Blair, *The Clubwoman as Feminist*; Mark C. Carnes, *Secret Ritual and Manhood in Victorian America* (New Haven: Yale University Press, 1989); Jeffrey A. Charles, *Service Clubs in American Society* (Urbana: University of Illinois Press, 1993); Mary Ann Clawson, *Constructing Brotherhood: Class, Gender, and Fraternalism* (Princeton, N.J.: Princeton University Press, 1989); Robert D. Putnam, *Bowling Alone: The Collapse and Revival of American Community* (New York: Simon and Schuster, 2000); David P. Thelen, "Social Tensions and the Origins of Progressivism," *Journal of American History* 56 (1969): 323–341.

4. The clasic work on American reactions against what seemed to be floods of "strangers" is John Higham, *Strangers in the Land: Patterns of American Nativism, 1860–1925* (New York: Atheneum, 1970; first published 1955). For studies of other reactions, especially gendered ones, see Gail Bederman, *Manliness and Civilization: A Cultural History of Gender and Race in the United States, 1880–1917* (Chicago: University of Chicago Press, 1995); Carnes, *Secret Ritual and Manhood*; Mark C. Carnes and Clyde Griffen, eds., *Meanings for Manhood: Constructions of Masculinity in Victorian America* (Chicago: University of Chicago Press, 1990); Karen Halttunen, *Confidence Men and Painted Women: A Study of Middle-Class Culture in America, 1830–1870* (New Haven: Yale University Press, 1982); John F. Kasson, "Civility and Rudeness: Urban Etiquette and the Bourgeois Social Or-

der in Nineteenth-Century America," *Prospects* 9 (1985): 143–167; Kasson, *Rudeness and Civility: Manners in Nineteenth-Century Urban America* (New York: Hill and Wang, 1990); Kasson, *Houdini, Tarzan, and the Perfect Man: The White Male Body and the Challenge of Modernity in America* (New York: Hill and Wang 2001); E. Anthony Rotundo, *American Manhood: Transformations in Masculinity from the Revolution to the Modern Era* (New York: Basic Books, 1993); and Peter N. Stearns, *Be a Man! Males in Modern Society,* 2nd ed. (New York: Holmes and Meier, 1990).

5. Frederic H. Curtiss and John Heard, *The Country Club, 1882–1932* (Brookline, Mass.: The Country Club, 1932), pp. 139–140, 144–145. See also James M. Mayo, *The American Country Club: Its Origins and Development* (New Brunswick, N.J.: Rutgers University Press, 1998).

6. George L. Beiswinger, *One to One: The Story of the Big Brothers/Big Sisters Movement in America* (Philadelphia: Big Brothers/Big Sisters of America, 1985), pp. 3–34; Marc Freedman, *The Kindness of Strangers: Adult Mentors, Urban Youth, and the New Voluntarism* (San Francisco: Jossey-Bass Publishers, 1993), pp. 25–30.

7. Burton J. Bledstein, *The Culture of Professionalism: The Middle Class and the Development of Higher Education in America* (New York: W. W. Norton and Co., 1976), p. 86. Louis Galambos, *Competition and Cooperation: The Emergence of a National Trade Association* (Baltimore: Johns Hopkins University Press, 1966); Galambos, "Technology, Political Economy, and Professionalization: Central Themes of the Organizational Synthesis," *Business History Review* 57 (Winter 1983): 471–493; Thomas L. Haskell, *The Emergence of Professional Social Science* (Urbana: University of Illinois Press, 1977); Bruce A. Kimball, *The "True Professional Ideal" in America* (Cambridge, Mass.: Blackwell Publishers, 1992); Harold Perkin, *The Rise of Professional Society: England since 1880* (London: Routledge, 1989); Robert H. Wiebe, *Businessmen and Reform: A Study of the Progressive Movement* (Cambridge, Mass.: Harvard University Press, 1962); Wiebe, *The Search for Order, 1877–1920* (New York: Hill and Wang, 1967).

8. Paul Starr, *The Social Transformation of American Medicine* (New York: Basic Books, 1982), pp. 40, 91–92, 117–124; Darlene Clark Hine, "Black Professionals and Race Consciousness: Origins of the Civil Rights Movement, 1890–1950," *Journal of American History* 89 (2003): 1279–1294.

9. J. E. Sterrett, "Education and Training of a Certified Public Accountant," *Journal of Accountancy* 1 (November 1905): 15; W. L. Harrison, "A Message from the American Society," *Accounting Review* 1 (March 1926): 70–73.

10. See Benedict Anderson, *Imagined Communities: Reflections on the Origin and Spread of Nationalism,* rev. ed. (London: Verso, 1991; originally published 1983); Karl W. Deutsch, *Nationalism and Social Communication: An Inquiry into the Foundations of Nationality* (Cambridge, Mass.: M.I.T. Press, 1953), esp. chap. 4; Francis Fukuyama, *Trust: The Social Virtues and the Creation of Prosperity* (New York: Free Press, 1995), esp. pp. 26–28; Halttunen, *Confidence Men;* Kasson, *Rudeness and Civility;* Naomi Lamoreaux, *Insider Lending: Banks, Personal Connections, and Economic Development in Industrial New England* (Cambridge: Cambridge University Press, 1996); Robert K. Merton, "Insiders and Outsiders: A Chapter in the Sociology of Knowledge," *American Journal of Sociology* 78 (July 1972): 9–47; Putnam, *Bowling Alone;* Steven Shapin, *A Social History of Truth: Civility and Science in Seventeenth-Century England* (Chicago: University of Chicago Press, 1994), esp. chaps. 1 and 2.

11. Stephen Fox, *The Mirror Makers: A History of American Advertising and Its Creators* (New York: William Morrow and Co., 1984), pp. 286–287; Reginald Horsman, *Race and Manifest Destiny: The Origins of American Racial Anglo-Saxonism* (Cambridge, Mass.: Harvard University Press, 1981), esp. pp. 139–145, 288–303; Stephen Jay Gould, *The Mismeasure of Man* (New York: W. W. Norton, 1981); Cynthia Eagle Russett, *Sexual Science: The Victorian Construction of Womanhood* (Cambridge, Mass.: Harvard University Press, 1989), esp. pp. 182–206; Starr, *The Social Transformation of American Medicine,* pp. 49–50. For a discussion of how observable differences can become the basis for explanations of discrimination, see Stanley Lieberson, *A Piece of the Pie: Blacks and White Immigrants since 1880* (Berkeley: University of California Press, 1980), pp. 382–383. Some of these reasons included attitudes about gendered differences in alcohol use, home responsibilities, and divergent recreation and rituals. For an introduction to the literature on nineteenth-century masculinity and femininity, see note 4.

12. Blair, *Clubwoman as Feminist;* Patricia M. Hummer, *The Decade of Elusive Promise: Professional Women in the United States, 1920–1930*

(Ann Arbor: UMI Research Press, 1979), p. 124. See also Anne M. Boylan, *The Origins of Women's Activism: New York and Boston, 1797–1840* (Chapel Hill: University of North Carolina Press, 2002); Nancy F. Cott, *The Grounding of Modern Feminism* (New Haven: Yale University Press, 1987), pp. 22–23, 224, 230–231, 243; Sarah Deutsch, "Learning to Talk More Like a Man: Boston Women's Class-Bridging Organizations, 1870–1940," *American Historical Review* 97 (1992): 379–404; Anne Firor Scott, *Natural Allies: Women's Associations in American History* (Urbana: University of Illinois Press, 1991).

13. Blair, *Clubwoman as Feminist*, pp. 12, 15–21; Glenna Matthews, *Just a Housewife: The Rise and Fall of Domesticity in America* (New York: Oxford University Press, 1987), chap. 6.

14. In 1873, Sorosis and the New England Woman's Club joined to form the Association for the Advancement of Women, which they continued as an explicitly elite women's institution. Blair, *Clubwoman as Feminist*, pp. 21–25, 29–30, 39, 44–56, 108–111.

15. Ibid., pp. 73–85.

16. Elizabeth Kemper Adams, *Women Professional Workers* (Chautauqua, N.Y.: Chautauqua Press, 1921), pp. 8–9, 28–31.

17. Fox, *The Mirror Makers*, pp. 286–287; Matthews, *Just a Housewife*, pp. 168–170. Quotation from "Founder's Section," p. 2, 1947 typescript for a history of the Advertising Women of New York by Dorothy Dignam, Box 1, Folder 3, Advertising Women of New York Records, Schlesinger Library, Radcliffe Institute for Advanced Study, Harvard University, Cambridge, Mass.

18. Quotation from "Preamble" in "Founder's Section," pp. 10–11, typescript.

19. Ellen S. More, "The American Medical Women's Association and the Role of the Woman Physician, 1915–1990," *Journal of the American Medical Women's Association* 45, no. 5 (1990): 165–180, quotation on p. 166; Association of Bank Women, *Yearbook* (New York: Association of Bank Women, 1928), pp. 7, 13–14, 17. See also Anne Seward, *The Women's Department* (New York: Bankers Publishing Co., 1924), p. 112; and Hummer, *Decade of Elusive Promise*, pp. 122–125.

20. Adams, *Women Professional Workers*, pp. 30–31; Geline MacDonald Bowman and Earlene White, *A History of the National Federation of Business and Professional Women's Clubs, Inc., 1919–1944 Inclusive* (New York: National Federation of Business and Professional Wom-

en's Clubs, 1944), pp. 12–29, quotations on p. 14. See also Cott, *Grounding of Modern Feminism,* pp. 89–90.

21. Ida Clyde Clark[e], "Intellectual Wine," *Can Happen* 1 (16 July 1919): 1; Clarke, "Handicaps Are Out of Date," *Can Happen* 1 (17 July 1919): 1; Gail Laughlin, "Illimitable Opportunities," *Can Happen* 1 (1 October 1919): 1.

22. Mary E. Bulkley, "Every Woman for Herself or Federation," *Can Happen* 1 (1 October 1919): 5. See also "President Laughlin's Trip East," *Independent Woman* 1 (February 1920): 11; Bowman and White, *History,* p. 17.

23. "What Shall We Name the Bulletin?" *Bulletin* 1 (1 December 1919): 5; *Independent Woman* 2 (January 1920): 3. Bowman and White, *History,* p. 23. See also "We Need a Slogan," *Independent Woman* 1 (January 1920): 5; Marjorie Shuler, "An Organization of Business Women," *American Review of Reviews* 66 (19 September 1922): 309–310.

24. "Vocational Luncheon," *Can Happen* 1 (17 July 1919): 2; Beatrice E. Carr, "The High Cost of Inefficiency," *Independent Woman* 1 (February 1920): 10; "President Laughlin's Trip East," *Independent Woman* 1 (February 1920): 11–12; Mae B. Wilkin, "Leader of Business Women," *Independent Woman* 2 (May 1921): 26. See also "Don't Be a Human Scarecrow," *Independent Woman* 1 (January 1920): 5; Seward, *Women's Department,* pp. 101–103.

25. Shuler, "An Organization of Business Women."

26. Jane R. Plitt, *Martha Matilda Harper and the American Dream* (Syracuse, N.Y.: Syracuse University Press, 2000), pp. 5, 14, 16, 34, 39–41, 72, quotation on p. 5; Kathy Peiss, *Hope in a Jar: The Making of America's Beauty Culture* (New York: Metropolitan Books, 1998), p. 75.

27. Plitt, *Martha Matilda Harper,* pp. 52, 60–61, 63, 65, 67–72, 87, 107–108.

28. Ibid., pp. 51, 56, 64, 70; Charles Van Doren and Robert McHenry, eds., *Webster's American Biographies* (Springfield, Mass.: Merriam-Webster, 1984), pp. 793–794.

29. Peiss, *Hope in a Jar,* pp. 67–77, 80–81, 89–94, 209, quotations on pp. 81, 91. Tiffany Gill, "Civic Beauty: Beauty Culturists and the Politics of African American Entrepreneurship, 1900–1965" (Ph.D. diss., Rutgers University, 2003), pp. 16, 18, 28, 53–74; Darlene Clark Hine, "Booker T. Washington and Madam C. J. Walker," in *Speak Truth to*

Power: Black Professional Class in United Sates History (Brooklyn, N.Y.: Carlson Publishing, 1996), pp, 95–104; Juliet E. K. Walker, *The History of Black Business in America: Capitalism, Race, Entrepreneurship* (New York: Twayne Publishers, 1998), pp. 208–211; Julie A. Willett, *Permanent Waves: The Making of the American Beauty Shop* (New York: New York University Press, 2000), pp. 19, 22–26. On the history of selling, see Walter A. Friedman, *Birth of a Salesman: The Transformation of Selling in America* (Cambridge, Mass.: Harvard University Press, 2004), esp. pp. 190–208, 242–245.

30. Transcript quoted in Jean Strouse, *Morgan: American Financier* (New York: Random House, 1999), p. 13.

31. Lamoreaux, *Insider Lending,* especially pp. 4–7, 22–27, 159. Tyler Anbinder, "From Famine to Five Points: Lord Lansdowne's Irish Tenants Encounter North America's Most Notorious Slum," *American Historical Review* 107 (2002): 351–387; David L. Mason, *From Buildings and Loans to Bail-Outs: A History of the American Savings and Loan Industry, 1831–1995* (Cambridge: Cambridge University Press, 2004), pp. 54–56. For an intriguing interpretation of character, corruption, and personal connections among high-flying speculators, see Richard White, "Information, Markets, and Corruption: Transcontinental Railroads in the Gilded Age," *Journal of American History* 90 (June 2003): 19–43.

32. A polished builder of social capital on many fronts, Giannini married into a fortune and thereby gained himself a bank director's position. Marquis James, *Biography of a Bank: The Story of Bank of America* (New York: Harper and Bros., 1954), pp. 3, 7–13, 17, 20, 36, 211–212, 216–218.

33. Mary Vail Andress, "Banking," in *An Outline of Careers for Women,* ed. Doris E. Fleischman (Garden City, N.Y.: Doubleday, Doran and Co., 1928), pp. 69–75; Beatrice E. Carr, Orra E. Carroll, and Florence Spencer, "The Woman in the Bank—Has She a Future?" *Independent Woman* 1 (June 1920): 8–9; Seward, *Women's Department,* pp. 9–10, 24–25, 43–44, 47–48, 50, 89; Shuler, "An Organization of Business Women." Nancy Marie Robertson, "A Room of Their Own: Banking and Women's Departments in the United States," paper delivered to Business History Conference, 10–12 March 2000, Palo Alto, California, copy in author's possession; cited with permission. See also Angel Kwolek-Folland, *Engendering Business: Men and Women in the Cor-*

porate Office, 1870–1930 (Baltimore: Johns Hopkins University Press, 1994), pp. 5–6, 105–106; Kwolek-Folland, *Incorporating Women: A History of Women and Business in the United States* (New York: Twayne Publishers, 1998), pp. 109–110.

34. Walker, *The History of Black Business in America*. See also Robert Higgs, *Competition and Coercion: Blacks in the American Economy, 1865–1914* (Cambridge: Cambridge University Press, 1977); and Stephanie J. Shaw, "Black Club Women and the Creation of the National Association of Colored Women," *Journal of Women's History* 3 (Fall 1991): 10–25.

35. Monroe N. Work, "Secret Societies as Factors in the Social and Economical Life of the Negro," in *Democracy in Earnest,* ed. James E. McCulloch (New York: Negro Universities Press, 1969; originally published by the Southern Sociological Congress, 1918), pp. 342–350; J. H. Harmon, Jr., Arnett G. Lindsay, and Carter G. Woodson, *The Negro as a Business Man* (College Park, Md.: McGrath Publishing Co., 1969; originally published 1929), pp. 57–58; Shaw, "Black Club Women," pp. 11–14; Walker, *Black Business in America*, pp. 85–86, 183–187. See also Allison Dorsey, *To Build Our Lives Together: Community Formation in Black Atalnta, 1875–1906* (Athens: University of Georgia Press, 2004), esp. pp. 76–77, 111–116, 120; Willard B. Gatewood, *Aristocrats of Color: The Black Elite, 1880–1920* (Bloomington: Indiana University Press, 1990), p. 14; Steven Hahn, *A Nation under Our Feet: Black Political Struggles in the Rural South from Slavery to the Great Migration* (Cambridge, Mass.: Harvard University Press, 2003), esp. chap. 7; Theda Skocpol and Jennifer Lynn Oser, "Organization Despite Adversity: The Origins and Development of African American Fraternal Organizations," *Social Science History* 28 (2004): 367–437, esp. pp. 372, 418–422.

36. Walker, *Black Business in America,* pp. 164–166, 168–169; Dorsey, *To Build Our Lives Together,* pp. 46–47; Harmon, Lindsay, and Woodson, *Negro as a Business Man,* p. 88. On African-American elites' social organizations and networks, see Gatewood, *Aristocrats of Color,* chap. 18; and Lawrence Otis Graham, *Our Kind of People: Inside America's Black Upper Class* (New York: HarperCollins Publishers, 1999).

37. Walker, *Black Business in America,* pp. xix, 85–86, 164–172, 183–193, 219–223; Abram L. Harris, *The Negro as Capitalist: A Study of Banking and Business among American Negroes* (College Park, Md.:

McGrath Publishing Co., 1968; originally published 1936), pp. ix–xi, 47–55; Harmon, Lindsay, Woodson, *Negro as a Business Man,* pp. 57–58, 87, 110–111; M. S. Stuart, *An Economic Detour: A History of Insurance in the Lives of American Negroes* (New York: Wendell Malliet and Co., 1940), pp. xvii–xxiii, 35–36. See also Martha L. Olney, "When Your Word Is Not Enough: Race, Collateral, and Household Credit," *Journal of Economic History* 58 (1998): 408–431; Robert E. Weems Jr., *Black Business in the Black Metropolis: The Chicago Metropolitan Assurance Company, 1925–1985* (Bloomington: Indiana University Press, 1996), esp. chap. 4.

Other groups, especially immigrants, the poor, or the working classes, also formed mutual aid societies for similar reasons. See David Beito, *From Mutual Aid to the Welfare State: Fraternal Societies and Social Services, 1890–1967* (Chapel Hill: University of North Carolina Press, 2000), esp. chap. 1; and John Charles Herbert Emery and George Neil Emery, *A Young Man's Benefit: The Independent Order of Odd Fellows and Sickness Insurance in the United States and Canada, 1860–1929* (Montreal: McGill–Queens University Press, 1999).

38. Harmon, Lindsay, and Woodson, *The Negro as a Business Man,* pp. iv, 8, 13, 24, 32–35, 88. See also John Sibley Butler, *Entrepreneurship and Self-Help among Black Americans: A Reconsideration of Race and Economics* (Albany: State University of New York Press, 1991); Harris, *Negro as Capitalist,* pp. ix–xi.

39. Harmon, Lindsay, and Woodson, *Negro as a Business Man,* pp. 7–8, 19, 24, 27, 35–37, 39. Higgs, *Competition and Coercion,* p. 90. Robert E. Weems Jr. identifies the "Don't Buy" slogan with the 1930s, but the idea can be found as early as the 1890s. *Desegregating the Dollar: African American Consumerism in the Twentieth Century* (New York: New York University Press), pp. 27, 57–58; Harris, *Negro as Capitalist,* pp. 50–51.

40. The Consolidated Bank and Trust Company, the result of 1929–1930 mergers between the St. Luke Bank and two others, continued to operate into the 1990s. Harmon, Lindsay, and Woodson, *Negro as a Business Man,* p. 88; Harris, *Negro as Capitalist,* pp. 46–49; Stuart, *An Economic Detour,* pp. 1–3, 11, 33. On Walker, see Charles Willis Simmons, "Maggie Lena Walker and the Consolidated Bank and Trust Company," *Negro History Bulletin* 38 (1975): 345–349; Walker, *Black Business in America,* pp. 188, 315.

41. Louise Day Putnam Lee, "A Business Woman's Club," *Independent Woman* 1 (September 1920): 6–7; Martha Tracy, "Are Women Good Mixers?" *Independent Woman* 3 (August 1921): 20. See also "How to Acquire, Finance, and Operate a Club House," *Independent Woman* 1 (September 1920): 14; "The Club Tea Room," *Independent Woman* 3 (November 1921): 10.

42. Seward, *Women's Department,* p. 26. Sociologists and other scholars have frequently assessed the business significance of club memberships, noting the high correlation between business ranking and club membership. For classic works on this subject, see E. Digby Baltzell, *Philadelphia Gentlemen: The Making of a National Upper Class* (Glencoe, Ill.: Free Press, 1958), chap. 13; Robert S. Lynd and Helen Merrell Lynd, *Middletown: A Study in American Culture* (New York: Harcourt Brace Jovanovich, 1929), pp. 76–77 and chap. 19; W. Lloyd Warner and Paul S. Lunt, *The Social Life of a Modern Community* (New Haven: Yale University Press, 1941), pp. 87–88, 143–148; C. Wright Mills, *The Power Elite* (London: Oxford University Press, 1956).

43. Henry W. Bellows, *Historical Sketch of the Union League Club of New York, Its Origin, Organization, and Work, 1863–1879* (New York: Club House, 1879), pp. 13–14. See also Sven Beckert, *The Monied Metropolis: New York City and the Consolidation of the American Bourgeoisie, 1850–1896* (Cambridge: Cambridge University Press, 2001), esp. chap. 8.

44. George D. Bushnell, "Chicago's Leading Men's Clubs," *Chicago History* 11, no. 2 (1982): 78–88; John N. Ingham, *The Iron Barons: A Social Analysis of an American Urban Elite, 1874–1965* (Westport, Conn.: Greenwood Press, 1978), esp. pp. 96–98, 117–127, 222–228; Osborn Elliott, *Men at the Top* (New York: Harper and Bros., 1959), pp. 161–167, 170–171.

45. Herbert L. Satterlee, *J. Pierpont Morgan: An Intimate Portrait* (New York: Macmillan Co., 1940), pp. 126, 235, 430, 456, 534; Strouse, *Morgan,* pp. 10, 113, 217, 276. See also Beckert, *Monied Metropolis,* p. 246; Ingham, *Iron Barons,* p. 227. Mills, *The Power Elite,* pp. 61–62, 123; see pp. 383–384 for details of 1938 and 1950 interlocking directorates.

46. Vernon F. Snow, *A Child of Toil: The Life of Charles Snow, 1831–1889* (Syracuse, N.Y.: Syracuse University Press, 1999), pp. 184–185, 221–223. See also Jon M. Kingsdale, "The 'Poor Man's Club': Social Func-

tions of the Urban Working-Class Saloon," *American Quarterly* 25 (1973): 472–489.

47. *American Federation of Labor: History, Encyclopedia, Reference Book* (Washington, D.C.: American Federation of Labor, 1919), pp. 26, 300–301. For labor solidarity issues and cases, see David Montgomery, *The Fall of the House of Labor* (Cambridge: Cambridge University Press, 1987), pp. 2, 82–85, 100, 111; Carl I. Meyerhuber Jr., *Less Than Forever: The Rise and Decline of Union Solidarity in Western Pennsylvania, 1914–1948* (Selinsgrove Pa.: Susquehanna University Press, 1987); Thomas Dublin, *Women at Work: The Transformation of Work and Community in Lowell, Massachusetts, 1826–1860* (New York: Columbia University Press, 1979), pp. 103–105, 198–207; and Richard Jules Oestreicher, *Solidarity and Fragmentation: Working People and Class Consciousness in Detroit, 1875–1900* (Urbana: University of Illinois Press, 1986), esp. pp. vx–xix, 109–110, 168, 191–197, 244–253, and chaps. 2, 4. On race and labor solidarity, see Roger Horowitz, *"Negro and White, Unite and Fight!" A Social History of Industrial Unionism in Meatpacking, 1930–1990* (Urbana: University of Illinois Press, 1997); A. T. Lane, *Solidarity or Survival? American Labor and European Immigrants, 1830–1924* (New York: Greenwood Press, 1987); Melton Alonza McLaurin, *The Knights of Labor in the South* (Westport, Conn.: Greenwood Press, 1978), pp. 139, 144, 153–156, 159, 168; and Kim Voss, *The Making of American Exceptionalism: The Knights of Labor and Class Formation in the Nineteenth Century* (Ithaca: Cornell University Press, 1993), esp. pp. 223–224, 232–237. For a focus on gender rather than race, see Mary H. Blewett, *Men, Women, and Work: Class, Gender, and Protest in the New England Shoe Industry, 1780–1910* (Urbana: University of Illinois Press, 1988).

48. Oren Arnold, *The Golden Strand: An Informal History of the Rotary Club of Chicago* (Chicago: Quadrangle Books, 1966), pp. 10–11, 13–16; Charles, *Service Clubs,* pp. 9–10, 44.

49. Arnold, *Golden Strand,* pp. 11–13, 21–25, 28; Charles, *Service Clubs,* pp. 9–10, 39–40, 49, 1910 recruiting letter quotation on p. 39; C[harles] Sylvester Green, *Fifty-Eight Years of Rotary in Greenville, North Carolina* (Greenville, N.C.: Rotary Club, 1977), pp. 11–13; Paul P. Harris, *This Rotarian Age* (Chicago: Rotary International, 1935), pp. 54–56; Lynd and Lynd, *Middletown,* pp. 301–306; University of Chicago, Social Science Survey Committe, *Rotary? A University*

Group Looks at the Rotary Club of Chicago (Chicago: University of Chicago Press, 1934), pp. 6–7, 10–11.

50. Arnold, *Golden Strand,* pp. 7, 25–26, 41–42; Charles, *Service Clubs,* pp. 24–25, 29–30, 37, 40–44; Harris, *This Rotarian Age,* pp. 72, 75–77, 107, 129, 194; F. Melvin Lawson, *A Saga of Service, 1913–1985* (Sacramento, Calif.: Rotary Club of Sacramento, 1986), pp. 8–9; Frank H. Lamb, *Rotary: A Business Man's Interpretation* (Hoquiam, Wash.: Rotary Club of Hoquiam, 1927), pp. 6–7; Carl A. Zapffe, *Rotary!* (Baltimore, Md.: Rotary Club of Baltimore, 1963), pp. 115–116. See also Laura Tuennerman-Kaplan, *Helping Others, Helping Ourselves: Power, Giving, and Community Identity in Cleveland, Ohio, 1880–1930* (Kent, Ohio: Kent State University Press, 2001), pp. 63–65.

3. Social Rungs on Corporate Ladders

1. Edward L. Bernays, ed., *An Outline of Careers: A Practical Guide to Achievement by Thirty-Eight Eminent Americans* (New York: George H. Doran Co., 1927), pp. v–vi.
2. Ibid.
3. Alfred D. Chandler Jr., *The Visible Hand: The Managerial Revolution in American Business* (Cambridge, Mass.: Belknap Press of Harvard University Press, 1977), pp. 99–107, chaps. 12, 13; JoAnne Yates, *Control through Communication: The Rise of System in American Management* (Baltimore: Johns Hopkins University Press, 1989), pp. xvii, 1–20. Biblical references abound to heavenly ladders; the multitude of nineteenth-century secular ladders to material success include the golden ladder pictured on the cover of A. Craig, ed., *Room at the Top: or, How to Reach Success, Happiness, Fame and Fortune* (Chicago: Henry A. Sumner and Co., 1883), as well as the subtitle of *Onward to Fame and Fortune; or, Climbing Life's Ladder* by William M. Thayer, shown in the introduction. On corporate ladders see Clark Davis, *Company Men: White-Collar Life and Corporate Cultures in Los Angeles, 1892–1941* (Baltimore: Johns Hopkins University Press, 2000), esp. pp. 9–11, 159–164; Angel Kwolek-Folland, *Engendering Business: Men and Women in the Corporate Office, 1870–1930* (Baltimore: Johns Hopkins University Press, 1994), chap. 1; and Olivier Zunz, *Making America Corporate, 1870–1920* (Chicago: University of Chi-

cago Press, 1990), esp. chap. 2. On the decline of self-employment, see Spurgeon Bell, *Productivity, Wages, and National Income* (Washington, D.C.: Brookings Institute, 1940), p. 10; and Gail Bederman, *Manliness and Civilization: A Cultural History of Gender and Race in the United States, 1880–1917* (Chicago: University of Chicago Press, 1995), p. 11. C. Wright Mills estimated that in 1870 about 85 percent of the middle classes, including farmers, owned the property from which they made their living, whereas by 1940 the number had fallen to 44 percent. Mills, *White Collar: The American Middle Class* (New York: Oxford University Press, 1951), pp. 5, 13, 63–65. Daniel Starch, *How to Develop Your Executive Ability* (New York: Harper and Bros., 1943), p. 10.

4. Shepherd Mead, *How to Succeed in Business without Really Trying: The Dastard's Guide to Fame and Fortune* (New York: Simon and Schuster, 1952); *How to Succeed in Business without Really Trying*, script by Abe Burrows, Jack Weinstock, and Willie Gilbert, music and lyrics by Frank Loesser (play opened at the 46th Street Theatre, New York, October 14, 1961; film released 1967); Edward J. Hegarty, *How to Succeed in Company Politics* (New York: McGraw-Hill Book Co., 1964), p. iii; "How to Clamp Down on Office Politics," *Business Management* 24 (August 1963): 26–30, 50–52.

5. Quotation by Walter H. Cottingham, President, Sherwin-Williams Co., in Enoch Burton Gowin, *Developing Executive Ability* (New York: Ronald Press Co., 1919), p. 12. Literature on systemizing labor is vast. For particularly useful sources, see Kwolek-Folland, *Engendering Business*, pp. 72–76; Daniel Nelson, "Scientific Management and the Workplace, 1920–1935," in *Masters to Managers*, ed. Sanford M. Jacoby (New York: Columbia University Press, 1991), pp. 74–89; Nelson, *Managers and Workers: Origins of the Twentieth-Century Factory System in the United States, 1880–1920*, 2nd ed. (Madison: University of Wisconsin Press, 1995). Nelson demonstrates that preoccupation with productivity and efficiency influenced industrialists' rhetoric more than it did their practices on the shop floor.

6. F. J. Roethlisberger and William J. Dickson, *Management and the Worker* (Cambridge, Mass.: Harvard University Press, 1939), reported the Hawthorne experiments; see esp. pp. viii, 336, 338, 351–352, 559. These Hawthorne experiments reports were reprinted fifteen times over

thirty years and are still cited prominently. See also Nora K. Moran, "'The Importance of Being Excellent': Human Relations and 'Corporate Culture,' 1930–1995," *Economic and Business History* 14 (1996): 229–248; Nelson, *Managers and Workers,* p. 120.

7. H. A. Worman, "How to Secure Factory Workers," in Clarence M. Woolley et al., *Employer and Employee* (Chicago: System Co., 1907), pp. 51–58.

8. Herbert J. Hapgood, "How to Select and Develop Office Boys" and "How to Select and Train Office Clerks"; John V. Farwell Jr., "Building a Business Machine"; Clarence M. Woolley, "Selecting and Training Executives"; all in Woolley et al., *Employer and Employee,* pp. 13–17, 23–28, 65–70, 71–75.

9. "Office Boy to Director," *New York Times,* 12 July 1927, p. 36.

10. Margery W. Davies explains how lower-level office positions came to be defined as women's work in *Woman's Place Is at the Typewriter: Office Work and Office Workers, 1870–1930* (Philadelphia: Temple University Press, 1982). Jean Hortense Norris, "Law," in *An Outline of Careers for Women,* comp. and ed. Doris E. Fleischman (Garden City, N.Y.: Doubleday, Doran and Co., 1928), pp. 271–281; the "business advisor" quotation in Reeve Schley, "Banking," in Bernays, *An Outline of Careers,* pp. 87–88. For an overview of gendered expectations in early corporations, see Kwolek-Folland, *Engendering Business,* chaps. 1, 2.

11. Even the literature on this literature is vast. Key sources include John G. Cawelti, *Apostles of the Self-Made Man* (Chicago: University of Chicago Press, 1965); Arthur Gordon, *One Man's Way: The Story and Message of Norman Vincent Peale* (Englewood Cliffs, N.J.: Prentice-Hall, 1972); Judy Hilkey, *Character Is Capital: Success Manuals and Manhood in Gilded Age America* (Chapel Hill: University of North Carolina Press, 1997); Richard M. Huber, *The American Idea of Success* (New York: McGraw-Hill Book Co., 1971); and Richard Weiss, *The American Myth of Success: From Horatio Alger to Norman Vincent Peale* (New York: Basic Books, 1969).

12. "Success and How to Achieve It," *New York Times,* 17 February 1919, p. 12; "Gives Nine Rules to Succeed," *New York Times,* 31 July 1938, sect. 3, p. 9; "J. P. Day Radios Rules for Success," *New York Times,* 13 January 1925, p. 10; Murray Teigh Bloom, "This Way to Success,"

Coronet 23 (February 1948): 99–104; Harold Mayfield, "How Champions Reach the Top," *Supervisory Management* 12 (September 1967): 14–15.

13. George J. Kienzle and Edward H. Dare, *Climbing the Executive Ladder: A Self-Training Course for People Who Want to Succeed* (New York: McGraw-Hill Book Co., 1950), pp. vii, 4–8, 19–20, 233–234.

14. Charles P. McCormick, *Multiple Management* (New York: Harper and Bros., 1938), pp. 1–6.

15. Chandler, *Visible Hand,* pp. 387, 390, 415–418. George Presbrey Rowell, *Forty Years an Advertising Agent, 1865–1905* (New York: Printer's Ink Publishing, 1906), pp. 145, 468. See also Pamela Walker Laird, *Advertising Progress* (Baltimore: Johns Hopkins University Press, 1998), pp. 168, 238–240.

16. Gowin, *Developing Executive Ability,* pp. 417–418; "These Are the Basics of Good Management," *Business Management* 22 (June 1962): 39–43.

17. Andrew Carnegie et al., *Personality in Business* (Chicago: System Co., 1910), pp. 66, 71; n.a., *Handling Men* (Chicago: A. W. Shaw Co., 1917), p. 7. Morgan quoted in George F. Redmond, *Financial Giants of America,* vol. 1 (Boston: Stratford Co., 1922), p. 61.

18. David M. Vrooman, *Daniel Willard and Progressive Management on the Baltimore and Ohio Railroad* (Columbus: Ohio State University Press, 1991), pp. 7–11; Edward Hungerford, *Daniel Willard Rides the Line: The Story of a Great Railroad Man* (New York: G. P. Putnam's Sons, 1938), pp. 88–89, 101–103.

19. Vrooman, *Daniel Willard,* pp. 11–13; Hungerford, *Daniel Willard Rides the Line,* pp. 107–110, 121–123, 131–134, 292.

20. For recent studies of the relationship between manhood and livelihood see Ava Baron, "An 'Other Side' of Gender Antagonism at Work: Men, Boys, and the Remasculinization of Printers' Work, 1830–1920," in *Work Engendered: Toward a New History of American Labor,* ed. Ava Baron (Ithaca, N.Y.: Cornell University Press, 1991), pp. 47–69; Baron, "Acquiring Manly Competence . . . The Demise of Apprenticeship and the Remasculinization of Printers' Work," in *Meanings for Manhood: Constructions of Masculinity in Victorian America,* ed. Mark C. Carnes and Clyde Griffen (Chicago: University of Chicago Press, 1990), pp. 152–163; Lawrence B. Glickman, *A Living Wage: American*

Workers and the Making of Consumer Society (Ithaca, N.Y.: Cornell University Press, 1997); Anthony Rotundo, *American Manhood: Transformation in Masculinity from the Revolution to the Modern Era* (New York: Basic Books, 1992), esp. pp. 167–185; and Peter N. Stearns, *Be a Man! Males in Modern Society,* 2nd ed. (New York: Holmes and Meier, 1990), chaps. 3, 5.

21. Joseph Frazier Wall, *Andrew Carnegie* (New York: Oxford University Press, 1970), p. 144. Baron, "An 'Other Side' of Gender Antagonism at Work"; Baron, "Acquiring Manly Competence"; Glickman, *A Living Wage;* Rotundo, *American Manhood,* pp. 53–55; Stearns, *Be a Man!,* pp. 49–50, 134–135, 152–153. Quotation from Hungerford, *Daniel Willard,* pp. 101–103.

22. Anonymous, "Definition of a Boy," *Coronet* 23 (February 1948): 104.

23. Michael Roper, *Masculinity and the British Organization Man since 1945* (Oxford: Oxford University Press, 1994). For a compelling analysis of many of these factors among nonelites, see Roger Waldinger, *Still the Promised City? African-Americans and New Immigrants in Postindustrial New York* (Cambridge, Mass.: Harvard University Press, 1996). Theresa A. Hammond, *A White-Collar Profession: African American Certified Public Accountants since 1921* (Chapel Hill: University of North Carolina, 2002), pp. 59–61.

24. Hungerford, *Daniel Willard,* p. 110.

25. Ibid., p. 293.

26. M. Joseph Dooher and Elizabeth Marting, eds., *Selection of Management Personnel,* vol. 1 (New York: American Management Association, 1957), pp. 194–195.

27. Louis F. Swift and Arthur Van Vlissingen Jr., *The Yankee of the Yards: The Biography of Gustavus Franklin Swift* (Chicago: A. W. Shaw Co., 1927), pp. 22, 140–152; the Sears quotations in Carnegie et al., *Personality in Business,* pp. 66–69; Myles L. Mace, *The Growth and Development of Executives* (Boston: Division of Research, Graduate School of Business Administration, Harvard University, 1950), pp. 114–121, 160–161. On managers' developing their own successors, see Woolley, "Selecting and Training Executives," pp. 65–70; and Mace, *Growth and Development of Executives,* p. 159. For a more recent statement of this policy, see Mary Kay Ash, *Mary Kay on People Management* (New York: Warner Books, 1984), p. 173.

28. Richard Dougherty, *In Quest of Quality: Hormel's First Seventy-Five Years* (Austin, Minn.: Geo. A. Hormel and Co., 1966), pp. 128–133; John T. Landry, "Corporate Incentives for Managers in American Industry, 1900–1940" (Ph.D. diss., Brown University, 1995), pp. 214, 237; W. A. Viall, "Training the Owner's Son," *Commerce and Finance* 16 (8 June 1927): 1145–1146.

29. Mabel Newcomer, "Professionalization of Leadership in the Big Business Corporation," in *The History of American Management: Selections from the Business History Review,* ed. James P. Baughman (Englewood Cliffs, N.J.: Prentice-Hall, 1969), pp. 244–252, esp. 248–249. Charles W. Cheape, *Strictly Business: Walter Carpenter at Du Pont and General Motors* (Baltimore: Johns Hopkins University Press, 1995), esp. chap. 1; Landry, "Corporate Incentives," pp. 214–215, 237–238.

30. Mabel Newcomer, *The Big Business Executive: The Factors that Made Him* (New York: Columbia University Press, 1955), pp. 132–133, 149–151. For a sampling of arguments on behalf of promotion from within, see T. F. Bradshaw, *Developing Men for Controllership* (Boston: Graduate School of Business Administration, Harvard University, 1950); M. Joseph Dooher and Vivienne Marquis, eds., *The Development of Executive Talent: A Handbook of Management Development Techniques and Case Studies* (New York: American Management Association, 1952); Woolley, *Employer and Employee;* and, for a later example, Paul J. Cathey, "Future Managers: Spot Them Fast, Challenge Them Often," *Iron Age* 209 (15 June 1972): 23.

31. Landry, "Corporate Incentives," p. 238; Dooher and Marquis, *Development of Executive Talent,* p. 377; Mace, *Growth and Development of Executives,* pp. 3–16; Ordway Tead and Henry C. Metcalf, *Personnel Administration: Its Principles and Practice,* 2nd ed. (New York: McGraw-Hill Book Co., 1926 [first published 1920]; reprinted New York: Arno Press, 1979), pp. 158, 227, 231. Bradshaw, *Developing Men,* pp. 55, 214, 218.

32. Editors of *Fortune, The Executive Life* (Garden City, N.Y.: Doubleday, 1956), p. 213. See also Robert D. Hulme, "Fifteen Ways to Develop Managers," *Management Methods* 16 (August 1959): 61–64; "Survey Shows How to Succeed," *Nation's Business* 50 (June 1962): 38–39, 44–46; Thomas J. Murray, "The Rise of the Fast-Track Executive," *Dun's Review* 91 (January 1968): 34–35, 72–74.

33. Hulme, "Fifteen Ways to Develop Managers," p. 62; McCormick, *Multiple Management,* pp. viii, x, 1–12, 33–43; Dooher and Marquis, *Development of Executive Talent,* pp. 115–120.

34. Joseph A. Litterer, "Systematic Management: The Search for Order and Integration," *Business History Review* 35 (1961): 461–476; Dooher and Marting, *Selection of Management Personnel,* vol. 1, p. 95. Tead and Metcalf, *Personnel Administration,* pp. 156, 158; General Electric, *Manager Development,* Guidebook 2 (New York: General Electric, 1954), p. 3 and unpaginated "Self-Development Planning Workbook."

35. Robert J. House, "Prerequisites for Successful Management Development," *Personnel Administration* 26 (May–June 1963): 51–56, quotation on p. 53.

36. Newcomer, *Big Business Executive,* pp. 133–134; Chester I. Barnard, *The Functions of the Executive* (Cambridge, Mass.: Harvard University Press, 1968; first published 1938), pp. vii, 39, 67, 78–79, 94–95. See also Editors of *Fortune, The Executive Life,* p. 64; Melvin T. Copeland and Andrew R. Towl, *The Board of Directors and Business Management* (Boston: Graduate School of Business Administration, Harvard University, 1947), p. 7.

37. Herbert J. Hapgood, "Engaging and Keeping an Employee," in Woolley et al., *Employer and Employee,* pp. 3–12; quotation on p. 5. Thomas O'Donovan quoted in Vance Packard, *The Pyramid Climbers* (New York: McGraw-Hill Book Co., 1962), pp. 108–109.

38. Editors of *Fortune, The Executive Life,* pp. 42–43; Newcomer, *Big Business Executive,* pp. 149–154. For measures of managerial immobility see also W. Lloyd Warner and James C. Abegglen, *Occupational Mobility in American Business and Industry* (Minneapolis: University of Minnesota Press, 1955).

39. General Electric, *Manager Development,* "Self-Development Planning Workbook," p. 15. On testing, see Lewis B. Ward, "Putting Executives to the Test," *Harvard Business Review* 38 (July–August 1960): 6–7, 10–12, 165–180.

40. Dooher and Marting, *Selection of Management Personnel,* vol. 1, pp. 295–302, 355–357, 486–489, 496–517, 531; Dooher and Marquis, *Development of Executive Talent,* pp. 329, 337–344, 368–377, 477–479. See the latter, pp. 408–414, for other attempts at objectivity in appraising employees for promotion. Recent studies have shown

continuing hiring biases when interviews prescreen candidates. Philip Moss and Chris Tilly, *Stories Employers Tell: Race, Skill, and Hiring in America* (New York: Russell Sage Foundation, 2001), pp. 229–232.

41. Dooher and Marting, *Selection of Management Personnel,* vol. 1, pp. 279–281; Packard, *The Pyramid Climbers,* p. 108. See also Harry L. Wylie and James Q. Harty, *Office Management Handbook* (New York: Ronald Press, 1958), p. 3.5 [*sic*].

42. Mace, *Growth and Development of Executives,* chaps. 6, 7; quotations on pp. 12–13, 109n2, 157–158, 185–186, 193. First published in 1950, the book was in its tenth printing by 1967.

43. Ibid., pp. 108, 142–146.

44. Gowin, *Developing Executive Ability,* Part 8, chaps. 24, 25; Dooher and Marquis, *Development of Executive Talent,* p. 343.

45. Charles Harris, "When Your Men Help You Hire," in [n.a.] *Handling Men* (Chicago: A. W. Shaw Co., 1917), pp. 24–30. Ruth M. Crawford, "Secretarial Work," in *Outline of Careers for Women,* ed. Fleischman, p. 470; Stanley Lieberson, *A Piece of the Pie: Blacks and White Immigrants since 1880* (Berkeley: University of California Press, 1980), p. 379. See also Waldinger, *Still the Promised City?* and Scott Cummings, ed., *Self-Help in Urban America: Patterns of Minority Economic Development* (Port Washington, N.Y.: Kennikat Press, 1980).

46. Iacocca began with Ford as a student engineer in 1946; he used his connections there to move into sales, where his career really began. David Abodaher, *Iacocca* (New York: Macmillan, 1982), chaps. 2, 5; Lee Iacocca and William Kovak, *Iacocca: An Autobiography* (New York: Bantam Books, 1984), pp. 29–38; Peter Wyden, *The Unknown Iacocca* (New York: William Morrow and Co., 1987), pp. 25–29, chaps. 4, 5. Regarding Iacocca's stature as a nationally known charismatic CEO, see Rakesh Khurana, "Good Charisma, Bad Business," *New York Times,* 13 September 2002, www.nytimes.com/2002/09/13/opinion/13KHUR.html.

47. Walter Lippmann, *Public Opinion* (New York: Free Press, 1965; originally published 1922), pp. 59, 63–64.

48. Gordon W. Allport, *The Nature of Prejudice* (Garden City, N.Y.: Doubleday Anchor Books, 1958; first ed. 1954). See also Arthur G. Miller, ed., *In the Eye of the Beholder: Contemporary Issues in Stereotyping* (New York: Praeger Publishers, 1982), pp. 77, 84–85, 119.

49. Allport, *The Nature of Prejudice,* pp. v–vii, 10, 26–27, 45, 49, 349.

Allport's foreword to the 1958 edition focused on implications of his work for the ongoing national civil rights crisis. He insisted both that "legal prods are necessary" to overcome prejudice and that "folkways" would eventually change, taking their negative stereotypes with them. Robert K. Merton, "Insiders and Outsiders: A Chapter in the Sociology of Knowledge," *American Journal of Sociology* 78 (1972): 9–47. For more recent analyses on stereotypes in action, see Miller, *In the Eye of the Beholder,* esp. chaps. 1–5. For a discussion of "social distance" within a corporation, see Roethlisberger and Dickson, *Management and the Worker,* pp. 359, 556.

50. Allport, *Nature of Prejudice,* p. 187; Merton, "Insiders and Outsiders," pp. 12–13; Miller, *In the Eye of the Beholder,* chap. 3; for experiments, see ibid., pp. 116–117.

51. Waldinger, *Still the Promised City?,* pp. 3–4, 21–26.

52. Mills, *White Collar,* p. 267.

53. Mace, *Growth and Development of Executives,* pp. 18–23, 145–146, 190. Dooher and Marting, *Selection of Management Personnel,* vol. 1, pp. 195–197, 403. Paul J. Cathey, "Future Managers: Spot Them Fast, Challenge Them Often," *Iron Age* 209 (15 June 1972): 23.

54. Garda W. Bowman, "What Helps or Harms Promotability?" *Harvard Business Review* 42 (January–February 1964): 6–26, 184–192, quotations on pp. 10, 14–15.

55. *Fortune* 41 (January 1950): 11–22, 66–68.

56. "How to Clamp Down on Office Politics," p. 30. W. Lloyd Warner and James C. Abegglen, *Big Business Leaders in America* (New York: Harper and Bros., 1955). "Negro men of ambition," by contrast, could anticipate moving into leadership in another generation; ibid., p. 227. Cathy Joachim, cartoon, *Personnel Administration* 26 (May–June 1963): 53; cartoon, *Nation's Business* 53 (August 1965): 78.

57. Katharine Hamill, "Women as Bosses," *Fortune* 53 (June 1956): 105–108, 213–220; *Business Periodical Index.* See also Nancy F. Cott, *The Grounding of Modern Feminism* (New Haven: Yale University Press, 1987) for extensive documentation of men's sense of women's strangeness within business and professional settings prior to 1930.

58. Margaret Cussler, *The Woman Executive* (New York: Harcourt, Brace and Co., 1958), pp. 62, 66, 71.

59. Ibid., pp. 17, 20–25.

60. Roper, *Masculinity,* pp. 2, 12. See also David W. Ewing, *The Manage-*

rial Mind (New York: Free Press of Glencoe, 1964), pp. 76–77; Sexton Adams and Don Fyffe, *The Corporate Promotables* (Houston: Gulf Publishing Co., 1969), pp. 61–65.

4. Contacts and Buffers

1. Shepherd Mead, *How to Succeed in Business without Really Trying: The Dastard's Guide to Fame and Fortune* (New York: Simon and Schuster, 1952), pp. 3–4, 8–9, 107–108; *How to Succeed in Business without Really Trying,* script by Abe Burrows, Jack Weinstock, and Willie Gilbert, music and lyrics by Frank Loesser (play opened at the 46th Street Theatre, New York, 14 October 1961; film released in 1967).

2. Angel Kwolek-Folland, *Engendering Business: Men and Women in the Corporate Office, 1870–1930* (Baltimore: Johns Hopkins University Press, 1994), chaps. 1, 4, pp. 25–27; JoAnne Yates, *Control through Communication: The Rise of System in American Management* (Baltimore: Johns Hopkins University Press, 1989), chaps. 1, 2; Olivier Zunz, *Making America Corporate, 1870–1920* (Chicago: University of Chicago Press, 1990), chap. 4. Paul J. Cathey, "Future Managers: Spot Them Fast, Challenge Them Often," *Iron Age* 209 (15 June 1972): 23.

3. Mark M. Jones, "If I Were About to Graduate in a Management Course," *Personnel* 2 (June 1920): 1–5.

4. For example, see Ronald E. Herington, David C. Dionne, et al., *The Young Businessman: Small Company or Large?* (New York: Hobbs, Dorman and Co., 1967).

5. H. A. Worman, "How to Work up Through the Ranks," in Clarence M. Woolley et al., *Employer and Employee* (Chicago: System Co., 1907), pp. 169–177.

6. M. Joseph Dooher and Elizabeth Marting, eds., *Selection of Management Personnel,* vol. 1 (New York: American Management Association, 1957), pp. 404–410; W. Lloyd Warner and James C. Abegglen, *Occupational Mobility in American Business and Industry, 1928–1952* (Minneapolis: University of Minnesota Press, 1955), p. 163.

7. William M. Wood quoted in editorial, "The Functions of Management of a Modern Business Organization," *National Association of Corporation Schools (NACS) Bulletin* 7 (July 1920): 289–293. Ordway Tead and Henry C. Metcalf, *Personnel Administration: Its Principles and*

Practice (New York: McGraw-Hill Book Co., 1926, first published 1920; reprinted New York: Arno Press, 1979), pp. xi, 243, chap. 1.

8. Thomas E. Donnelley, "Some Problems of Apprenticeship Schools," *NACS Bulletin* 1 (April 1914): 43–48. This was the second issue of the *Bulletin* of the National Association of Corporation Schools, ancestor of the *American Management Review* and the American Management Association. The industrialist gave this speech at the association's first annual meeting. Walter Licht, "Studying Work: Personnel Policies in Philadelphia Firms, 1850–1950," in *Masters to Managers,* ed. Sanford M. Jacoby (New York: Columbia University Press, 1991), pp. 55, 64.

9. Licht, "Studying Work," pp. 43–73; Cyrus Curtis Ling, *The Management of Personnel Relations: History and Origins* (Homewood, Ill.: Richard D. Irwin, 1965), chaps. 1, 15. F. J. Roethlisberger and William J. Dickson, *Management and the Worker* (Cambridge, Mass.: Harvard University Press, 1939), chaps. 16, 24, esp. p. 556.

10. Ling, *Management of Personnel Relations,* p. 495; Tead and Metcalf, *Personnel Administration,* pp. 227–231. Quotations from Carroll D. Murphy, in [n.a.], *Handling Men* (Chicago: A. W. Shaw Co., 1917), p. 45.

11. Philip Moss and Chris Tilly, *Stories Employers Tell: Race, Skill, and Hiring in America* (New York: Russell Sage Foundation, 2001), chap. 6.

12. Harry L. Wylie and James Q. Harty, *Office Management Handbook* (New York: Ronald Press, 1958), pp. 3.6–9 [*sic*]. Terry Mitchell, "Do College Men Stick?" *Factory and Industrial Management* 81 (May 1931): 788–790.

13. Clarence M. Hapgood, "Engaging and Keeping an Employee," in Woolley et al., *Employer and Employee,* pp. 3–12.

14. Garda W. Bowman, "What Helps or Harms Promotability?" *Harvard Business Review* 42 (January–February 1964): 6–26, 184–192, quotation on p. 7. See also Eli Ginzberg, "Spot and Encourage Initiative," *Nation's Business* 49 (April 1961): 74–78.

15. Camille Lavington with Stephanie Losee, *You've Only Got Three Seconds: How to Make the Right Impression in Your Business and Social Life* (New York: Main Street Books, Doubleday, 1997), pp. xiii, xv, 1–3; Ziva Kunda, *Social Cognition: Making Sense of People* (Cambridge, Mass.: MIT Press, 1999), pp. 351, 392–393; Charles Stangor, ed., *Stereotypes and Prejudice: Essential Readings* (Philadelphia: Psychology

Press, 2000), pp. 251–252. Frances M. Fuller and Mary B. Batchelder, "Opportunities for Women at the Administrative Level," *Harvard Business Review* 31 (January–February 1953): 112–113.

16. Pearce C. Kelley, "Selecting Executives," *Personnel* 10 (August 1933): 8–27. Dooher and Marting, *Selection of Management Personnel,* vol. 1, pp. 18–19, 194, 203, 327, chap. 13. Myles L. Mace, *The Growth and Development of Executives* (Boston: Division of Research, Graduate School of Business Administration, Harvard University, 1950), pp. 86, 109–112.

17. Melvin T. Copeland and Andrew R. Towl, *The Board of Directors and Business Management* (Boston: Graduate School of Business Administration, Harvard University, 1947), pp. 1, 35, 45, 179–181, 186–187.

18. Mary Vail Andress, "Banking," in *An Outline of Careers for Women,* comp. and ed. Doris E. Fleischman (Garden City, N.Y.: Doubleday, Doran and Co., 1928), pp. 69–75; Anne Seward, *The Women's Department* (New York: Bankers Publishing Co., 1924), pp. 102–104, 109–110.

19. Currently, many schools seek to enhance their service to business by developing curricula for "competency-based learning." See, for instance, Alice Bedard Voorhees, "Creating and Implementing Competency-Based Learning Models," *New Directions for Institutional Research* no. 110 (Summer 2001): 83–95; Karen Paulson, "Using Competencies to Connect the Workplace and Postsecondary Education," *New Directions for Institutional Research* no. 110 (Summer 2001): 41–54.

20. Carter A. Daniel analyses these processes in his book *MBA: The First Century* (Lewisburg, Pa.: Bucknell University Press, 1998). See also Tead and Metcalf, *Personnel Administration,* pp. 164–165; Alfred D. Chandler Jr., *The Visible Hand: The Managerial Revolution in American Business* (Cambridge, Mass.: Belknap Press of Harvard University Press, 1977), pp. 465–468.

21. "Sons of Millionaires Who Have Made Successes," *New York Times,* 10 April 1910, sect. 5, p. 6. Richard L. Zweigenhaft, "Prep School and Public School Graduates of Harvard," *Journal of Higher Education* 64 (1993): 211–225.

22. Marilyn Wellemeyer, "The Class the Dollars Fell On," *Fortune* 89 (May 1974): 228.

23. Daniel, *MBA,* esp. chaps. 1–2; Robert S. Lynd and Helen Merrell Lynd, *Middletown: A Study in American Culture* (New York: Harcourt Brace

Jovanovich, 1929), pp. 49, 185–187. Mabel Newcomer, *The Big Business Executive: The Factors That Made Him* (New York: Columbia University Press, 1955), pp. 145–148; Warner and Abegglen, *Occupational Mobility,* p. 31.

24. Statement made during a study by the McKinsey Foundation for Management Research, quoted in Vance Packard, *The Pyramid Climbers* (New York: McGraw-Hill Book Co., 1962), p. 33. Theresa A. Hammond, *A White-Collar Profession: African American Certified Public Accountants since 1921* (Chapel Hill: University of North Carolina Press, 2002), p. 58. Mary Ryan, *Cradle of the Middle Class: The Family in Oneida County, New York, 1790–1865* (Cambridge: Cambridge University Press, 1981), pp. 162, 169–172.

25. See, for instance, Zunz, *Making America Corporate,* pp. 48–49; and E. Digby Baltzell, *Philadelphia Gentlemen: The Making of a National Upper Class* (Glencoe, Ill.: Free Press, 1958), pp. 340–341. Susan Ariel Aaronson argues that top business schools prepared students poorly for nonsocial executive functions even after World War II. "Serving America's Business? Graduate Business Schools and American Business, 1945–1960," *Business History* 34 (January 1992): 160–183.

26. Daniel, *MBA,* p. 102; Dooher and Marting, *Selection of Management Personnel,* vol. 1, pp. 391–403, 410. For other observations on the growing distinction between a professional management class and employees who should not expect to rise above supervisory positions, see ibid., pp. 20–21, 327–329.

27. Richard Wellington Husband, "Training Students for Their Life Careers," *Personnel Administration* 11 (January 1923): 7–11; Daniel, *MBA,* pp. 36–37, 102.

28. Joseph E. Barbeau, *Second to None: Seventy-Five Years of Leadership in the Cooperative Education Movement* (Boston: Custom Book Program of Northeastern University, 1985), pp. 9, 14, 19, 74–78; Northeastern University Libraries, Archives and Special Collections Department, online finding aid on Division of Cooperative Education A-16, www.lib.neu.edu/archives/collect/findaids/a16find.htm (accessed 18 October 2001). Daniel, *MBA,* pp. 177, 202–211.

29. John T. Landry, "Corporate Incentives for Managers in American Industry, 1900–1940," (Ph.D. diss., Brown University, 1995), pp. 124–126; Zunz, *Making America Corporate,* p. 65; Mitchell, "Do College Men Stick?"; Tead and Metcalf, *Personnel Administration,* p. 165.

30. Newcomer, *Big Business Executive,* pp. 75, 147–148; Newcomer, "Professionalization of Leadership in the Big Business Corporation," in *The History of American Management: Selections from the Business History Review,* ed. James P. Baughman (Englewood Cliffs, N.J.: Prentice-Hall, 1969), pp. 244–252, quotation on p. 245. See also "The Commercial Value of College Training," *NACS Bulletin* 7 (September 1920): cover, 395–414; Christopher Newfield, *Ivy and Industry: Business and the Making of the American University, 1880–1980* (Durham, N.C.: Duke University Press, 2003); Packard, *Pyramid Climbers,* pp. 33–35; Tead and Metcalf, *Personnel Administration,* p. 165; Warner and Abegglen, *Occupational Mobility,* p. 28, chap. 4, esp. p. 108. See also Anthony Rotundo, *American Manhood: Transformation in Masculinity from the Revolution to the Modern Era* (New York: Basic Books, 1992), pp. 248–249, 260.

31. Daniel, *MBA,* chaps. 2–4, 7–8, quotation on p. 155.

32. "The Commercial Value of College Training," p. 396; Landry, "Corporate Incentives," pp. 130–131. For mid-1950s' warnings against relying on a degree, see Editors of *Fortune, The Executive Life* (Garden City, N.Y.: Doubleday, 1956), pp. 216, 218, 220.

33. Jeffrey L. Cruikshank, *A Delicate Experiment: The Harvard Business School, 1908–1945* (Boston: Harvard Business School Press, 1987), p. 72. Mark Megalli, "So Your Dad Went to Harvard: Now What About the Lower Board Scores of White Legacies?" *Journal of Blacks in Higher Education,* no. 7 (Spring 1995): 71–73; John D. Lamb, "The Real Affirmative Action Babies: Legacy Preferences at Harvard and Yale," *Columbia Journal of Law and Social Problems* 26 (1993): 491–521; Judith Lichtenberg, "How the Academically Rich Get Richer," *Philosophy and Public Policy Quarterly* 24 (Fall 2004): 19–27. Megalli demonstrates the flaws in the argument that admitting legacies results in higher college donations.

34. C. Wright Mills, *White Collar: The American Middle Class* (New York: Oxford University Press, 1951), pp. 137, 265–272. Daniel, *MBA,* pp. 31, 93–94, 143–144, 185–186, 198.

35. James Wallace and Jim Erickson, *Hard Drive: Bill Gates and the Making of the Microsoft Empire* (New York: John Wiley and Sons, 1992), pp. 13–15, 61, 66.

36. Ibid., pp. 18–21, 24–25, 49–50, 62–63, 77–78, 99.

37. Ibid., pp. 14, 89–94, 136, 188–189; Daniel Ichbiah and Susan L.

Knepper, *The Making of Microsoft* (Rocklin, Calif.: Prima Publishing, 1993), pp. 2–3; www.microsoft.com/presspass/exec/steve/default.asp (accessed 13 October 2003).

38. Warner and Abegglen, *Occupational Mobility,* pp. 31, 143, 153; Mills, *White Collar,* pp. 266–269.

39. Harold Perkin, *The Rise of Professional Society: England since 1880* (London: Routledge, 1989), pp. 288, 439. See also Burton J. Bledstein, *The Culture of Professionalism: The Middle Class and the Development of Higher Education in America* (New York: W. W. Norton and Co., 1976); Louis Galambos, "Technology, Political Economy, and Professionalization: Central Themes of the Organizational Synthesis," *Business History Review* 57 (Winter 1983): 471–493; Bruce A. Kimball, *The "True Professional Ideal" in America* (Cambridge, Mass.: Blackwell, 1992); Robert H. Wiebe, *Businessmen and Reform: A Study of the Progressive Movement* (Cambridge, Mass.: Harvard University Press, 1962); Wiebe, *The Search for Order, 1877–1920* (New York: Hill and Wang, 1967). Roger Waldinger analyzes an informal closure dynamic at low-level occupations in *Still the Promised City? African-Americans and New Immigrants in Postindustrial New York* (Cambridge, Mass.: Harvard University Press, 1996), p. 21.

40. Paul Starr, *The Social Transformation of American Medicine* (New York: Basic Books, 1982), pp. 102–105, 110, 117–119, 123–125, 168; Martha Tracy, "Medicine," in *An Outline of Careers for Women,* comp. and ed. Fleischman, pp. 344–345; Michael Grossberg, "Institutionalizing Masculinity: The Law as a Masculine Profession," in *Meanings for Manhood: Constructions of Masculinity in Victorian America,* ed. Mark C. Carnes and Clyde Griffen (Chicago: University of Chicago Press, 1990), pp. 133–151; Patricia M. Hummer, *The Decade of Elusive Promise: Professional Women in the United States, 1920–1930* (Ann Arbor: UMI Research Press, 1979), pp. 47–48, 134–136. See also Corinne Lathrop Gilb, *Hidden Hierarchies: The Professions and Government* (New York: Harper and Row, 1966), pp. 46, 49, 119, 128–129, 159, 231. For earlier roots of professional organizations as gatekeepers, see Rosemary O'Day, *The Professions in Early Modern England, 1450–1800* (Essex: Longman, 2000).

41. Margaret Levenstein, *Accounting for Growth: Information Systems and the Creation of the Large Corporation* (Stanford, Calif.: Stanford University Press, 1998); Paul J. Miranti Jr., *Accountancy Comes of*

Age: The Development of an American Profession, 1886–1940 (Chapel Hill: University of North Carolina Press, 1990); Chandler, *Visible Hand,* p. 464.

42. Hammond, *White-Collar Profession,* pp. 3–4; Miranti, *Accountancy Comes of Age,* chaps. 1, 3, p. 62; J. E. Sterrett, "Education and Training of a Certified Public Accountant," *Journal of Accountancy* 1 (November 1905): 15; W. L. Harrison, "A Message from the American Society," *Accounting Review* 1 (March 1926): 70–73.

43. I. Maximilian Martin, "Accounting as a Field for Colored Men," *Journal of Accountancy* 55 (February 1933): 112–116; Hammond, *White-Collar Profession,* pp. 1–2, 5–7, 16–21.

44. Hammond, *White-Collar Profession,* pp. 33–35; Carl H. Nau, "The Aims of the Institute," *Journal of Accountancy* 31 (1921): 321–328, quotations on p. 324.

45. Quoted in Hammond, *White-Collar Profession,* p. 61.

46. Nau, "The Aims of the Institute," pp. 322, 326–327; Hammond, *White-Collar Profession,* pp. 37–38, 58, 76–78, 82, 87.

47. Tead and Metcalf, *Personnel Administration,* pp. 163–164; Dooher and Marting, *Selection of Management Personnel,* vol. 1, p. 410; Hummer, *Decade of Elusive Promise,* pp. 133–135; A. P. Richardson, "Editorial," *Journal of Accountancy* 36 (1923): 27–30.

48. Sterrett, "Education and Training," quotations on pp. 1, 2, 4, 8.

49. Hammond, *White-Collar Profession,* pp. 35–36. Endless racist and sexist "jokes" and cartoons have filled trade journals in many fields, from hardware store operation to printing. For a survey of common images of a range of minority groups, see William M. O'Barr, *Culture and the Ad: Exploring Otherness in the World of Advertising* (Boulder, Colo.: Westview Press, 1994).

50. Crane Brinton, "Clubs," in *Encyclopedia of the Social Sciences,* ed. Edwin R. A. Seligman and Alvin Johnson (New York: Macmillan, 1949), pp. 573–577. See also Henry W. Bellows, *Historical Sketch of the Union League Club of New York* (New York: Club House, 1879), p. 159; George D. Bushnell, "Chicago's Leading Men's Clubs," *Chicago History* 11, no. 2 (1982): 78–88; and Frederic H. Curtiss and John Heard, *The Country Club, 1882–1932* (Brookline, Mass.: The Country Club, 1932), p. 145. E. Digby Baltzell, *Philadelphia Gentlemen: The Making of a National Upper Class* (Glencoe, Ill.: Free Press, 1958), chap. 13, quotation on p. 335.

51. Enoch Burton Gowin, *Developing Executive Ability* (New York: Ronald Press Co., 1919), pp. 440–441, chap. 11; Tead and Metcalf, *Personnel Administration,* p. 164. See also Lynd and Lynd, *Middletown,* p. 287. "North, South: You Do Business at the Club," *Business Week,* 5 June 1954, pp. 90–98; Osborn Elliott, *Men at the Top* (New York: Harper and Bros., 1959), p. 164.

52. Newcomer, *Big Business Executive,* p. 123; Packard, *Pyramid Climbers,* pp. 251–252; Robert H. Boyle, "The Ways of Life at the Country Club," *Sports Illustrated* 16, 26 February 1962: 50–56, and 5 March 1962: 68–74; Lorne Rubenstein, *Links: An Exploration into the Mind, Heart, and Soul of Golf* (Rocklin, Calif.: Prima Publishing, 1991), pp. 158–159, 162. See also Lavington, *You've Only Got Three Seconds,* pp. 82, 190.

53. On clubs' exclusiveness, see "North, South," quotation on p. 94; Willard B. Gatewood, *Aristocrats of Color: The Black Elite, 1880–1920* (Bloomington: Indiana University Press, 1990), p. 47, chap. 8; Lawrence Otis Graham, *Our Kind of People: Inside America's Black Upper Class* (New York: HarperCollins Publishers, 1999), chaps. 1, 2, 6, 7.

54. Fuller and Batchelder, "Opportunities for Women," p. 120; "North, South."

55. C[harles] Sylvester Green, *Fifty-Eight Years of Rotary in Greenville, North Carolina* (Greenville, N.C.: Rotary Club, 1977), pp. 58–60.

56. "Activities of the Personnel Department," *NACS Bulletin* 7 (June 1920): cover, 250–252; "The Economic Value of Company Clubs," *NACS Bulletin* 7 (March 1920): cover, 123–134. See also "A Survey of Personnel Activities of Member Companies," *NACS Bulletin* 7 (August 1920): 346–350. For an analysis of firms' support of social functions, see Clark Davis, *Company Men: White-Collar Life and Corporate Culture in Los Angeles, 1892–1941* (Baltimore: Johns Hopkins University Press, 2000), chap. 4.

57. Norman J. Ginstling, "Social Clubs Coming under Closer IRS Scrutiny," *Journal of Taxation* 23 (September 1965): 162–167; and Heather Anne Keith, "A History of Taxation: Club Dues Deductability," *Club Director* 11, no. 1 (1993): 18–23. The following are all from Sun Oil Company Records: Thomas S. Horrocks, memo, 27 June 1963; F. N. Kaye, memo, 19 July 1963; Donald P. Jones, memo, 25 January 1966; C[harles] A. Pfahler, memo, 27 January 1966; Accession 1317, Box 469, folder "A to C," HM&L. See also "Travel, Entertain-

ment, Gift, and Car Expenses," Internal Revenue Service Publication 463 (Washington, D.C.: U.S. Government Printing Office, 2003), pp. 9–13.

58. Hammond, *White-Collar Profession,* p. 60. For one of many examples of blaming workers for discrimination by personnel departments, see Nancy J. Weiss, *The National Urban League, 1910–1940* (New York: Oxford University Press, 1974), p. 186.

59. Andress, "Banking," in *An Outline of Careers for Women,* comp. and ed. Fleischman, pp. 71–74; Fuller and Batchelder, "Opportunities for Women," pp. 116–117; Daniel Pope and William Toll, "We Tried Harder: Jews in American Advertising," *American Jewish History* 72 (1982): 26–51; Pamela Walker Laird, *Advertising Progress: American Business and the Rise of Consumer Marketing* (Baltimore: Johns Hopkins University Press, 1998), pp. 286–287, 311–322.

60. Hammond, *White-Collar Profession,* p. 69; Bowman, "What Helps or Harms Promotability?" p. 10. Gordon W. Allport, *The Nature of Prejudice* (Garden City, N.Y.: Doubleday Anchor Books, 1958; first ed., 1954), p. 11; Kenneth Clark, *Dark Ghetto* (New York: Harper and Row, 1965), p. 75.

61. "What It's Like to Be a Negro in Management," *Business Management* 29 (April 1966): 60–64, 69–77, quotation on p. 60.

5. The Business of Integration

1. Jerome H. Holland, *Black Opportunity* (New York: Weybright and Talley, 1969), pp. vii–viii. Holland was later ambassador to Sweden (1970–1973), and he chaired the American Red Cross and Planned Parenthood. He also served on nine corporate boards, including AT&T and General Motors, and was the first African American to sit on the New York Stock Exchange board, serving from 1972 to 1980. http://www.aaregistry.com/african_american_history/649/Educator_and_Diplomat_Jerome_Holland (accessed 23 March 2003).

2. Holland, *Black Opportunity,* pp. viii–xiv, 260–269.

3. Paul D. Moreno, *From Direct Action to Affirmative Action: Fair Employment Law and Policy in America, 1933–1972* (Baton Rouge: Louisiana State University Press, 1997), pp. 66–74, 107–108; Andrew Edmund Kersten, *Race, Jobs, and the War: The FEPC in the Midwest, 1941–46* (Urbana: University of Illinois Press, 2000), pp. 2–6; Steven

M. Gelber, *Black Men and Businessmen: The Growing Awareness of a Social Responsibility* (Port Washington, N.Y.: National University Publications, 1974), pp. 24–29, 35, 217; Thomas J. Sugrue, "Affirmative Action from Below: Civil Rights, the Building Trades, and the Politics of Racial Equality in the Urban North, 1956–1969," *Journal of American History* 91 (2004): 145–173. See also Darlene Clark Hine, "Black Professionals and Race Consciousness: Origins of the Civil Rights Movement, 1890–1950," *Journal of American History* 89 (2003): 1279–1294.

4. See Alice Kessler-Harris, *Out to Work: A History of Wage-Earning Women in the United States* (New York: Oxford University Press, 1982), pp. 274–279, 286; Angel Kwolek-Folland, *Incorporating Women: A History of Women and Business in the United States* (New York: Twayne Publishers, 1998), pp. 133, 149–154; Elaine Tyler May, "Pushing the Limits: 1940–1961," in *No Small Courage: A History of Women in the United States,* ed. Nancy F. Cott (New York: Oxford University Press, 2000), pp. 476–484; Juliet E. K. Walker, *The History of Black Business in America: Capitalism, Race, Entrepreneurship* (New York: Twayne Publishers, 1998), pp. 238–248.

5. Samuel F. Yette, typescript of address to National Council of Jewish Women, Toledo, Ohio, 17 February 1965, p. 8; Part II, Series I, Box 7, NUL.

6. Joseph C. Goulden, *The Best Years, 1945–1950* (New York: Atheneum, 1976), pp. 56–60, 67–68; Michael J. Bennett, *When Dreams Came True: The GI Bill and the Making of Modern America* (Washington, D.C.: Brassey's, 1996), pp. 3, 11, 21, 155, 161. Keith W. Olson, *The G.I. Bill, the Veterans, and the Colleges* (Lexington: University Press of Kentucky), pp. 23–24, 101–102.

7. Bennett, *When Dreams Came True,* pp. 18–21, 235, 238–240, 243–245; Conant quoted on pp. 133, 241. David Callahan, *Kindred Spirits: Harvard Business School's Extraordinary Class of 1949 and How They Transformed American Business* (New York: John Wiley and Sons, 2002), pp. 16, 18–19, 26–27, quotation on 40; Marilyn Wellemeyer, "The Class the Dollars Fell On," *Fortune* 89 (May 1974): 224–229, 340–352. For criticisms of the GI Bill's limitations, see Lizabeth Cohen, *A Consumer's Republic: The Politics of Mass Consumption in Postwar America* (New York: Alfred A. Knopf, 2003), pp. 137–143, 155–160, 166–173.

8. Callahan, *Kindred Spirits,* p. 12.

9. Bennett, *When Dreams Came True,* pp. 156, 235; W. Lloyd Warner and James C. Abegglen, *Occupational Mobility in American Business and Industry, 1928–1952* (Minneapolis: University of Minnesota Press, 1955), quotation on p. 36; Cohen, *A Consumer's Republic,* pp. 155–160.

10. After World War II, notions of "whiteness" crystallized into those that prevail in the United States to this day. Matthew Pratt Guterl, *The Color of Race in America, 1900–1940* (Cambridge, Mass.: Harvard University Press, 2001), pp. 13, 187–189. Kersten, *Race, Jobs, and the War,* pp. 126–134; Moreno, *From Direct Action to Affirmative Action,* chap. 5. Bennett, *When Dreams Came True,* pp. 268–273; Michael K. Brown et al., *Whitewashing Race: The Myth of a Color-Blind Society* (Berkeley: University of California Press, 2003), pp. 76–77; Cohen, *A Consumer's Republic,* pp. 137–143, 166–173.

11. Brown et al., *Whitewashing Race,* pp. 68–70; Thomas J. Sugrue, *The Origins of the Urban Crisis: Race and Inequality in Postwar Detroit* (Princeton, N.J.: Princeton University Press, 1996), esp. chap. 4; Robert E. Weems Jr., *Desegregating the Dollar: African American Consumerism in the Twentieth Century* (New York: New York University Press, 1998); Walker, *History of Black Business in America,* pp. 254–258, 263.

12. Samuel P. Huntington, *American Politics: The Promise of Disharmony* (Cambridge, Mass.: Belknap Press of Harvard University Press, 1981) p. 3. See also Eli Ginzberg, ed., *The Negro Challenge to the Business Community* (New York: McGraw-Hill Book Co., 1964), p. 41.

13. Nancy J. Weiss, *The National Urban League, 1910–1940* (New York: Oxford University Press, 1974), pp. 6–7, 88–92, quotation on p. 88.

14. Ibid., pp. 108–111, 114–125.

15. Ibid., pp. 124–125, 127, 181–187, 205, 251; Guichard Parris and Lester Brooks, *Blacks in the City: A History of the National Urban League* (Boston: Little, Brown and Co., 1971), pp. 260–266, 275; Weiss, *National Urban League,* pp. 250–255.

16. Quotation from *Toward Job Adjustment* in Ann Tanneyhill, "Discussion on Vocational Counseling," 1 July 1948, Part I, Series VII, Box 2, NUL. References to improving guidance run throughout NUL files. See, for instance, items in Career Guidance Project (1951), Part I, Series VII, Box 2, NUL. Parris and Brooks, *Blacks in the City,* pp. 210–213,

312–313; Weiss, *National Urban League,* pp. 255–260. Vocational guidance was not invented for disadvantaged youth; colleges began such programs in the 1920s to prepare their students for careers. See, for example, Richard Wellington Husband, "Training Students for Their Life Careers," *Personnel Administration* 11 (January 1923): 7–11.

17. Parris and Brooks, *Blacks in the City,* pp. 312–313, 333–339, 348, 359. Lester Granger to Ann Tanneyhill, memo, 12 March 1947; and Julius A. Thomas to LeRoy W. Jeffries, memo, 11 December 1947, Part I, Series VII, Box 5, NUL.

18. LeRoy W. Jeffries, memo to Executive and Industrial Secretaries, "Pilot Placement Project," 7 January 1948; and Jeffries, "Annual Report: Pilot Placement Project," 31 December 1948, p. 12; both Part I, Series VII, Box 5, NUL.

19. Other NUL operations included forming a Trade Union Advisory Council in 1949 to further cooperation with unions. That same year, the league introduced corporate employers to traditionally African-American colleges for recruiting. Not relying on the outcome of recruiters' simply showing up on campuses, the NUL set up innovative "career conferences," which included speakers from industry; luncheons; and seminars. All were geared to encourage useful exchanges and learning—by all parties and in both directions. Parris and Brooks, *Blacks in the City,* pp. 334–337. Thomas Sugrue makes a compelling argument that the failure of what Philadelphians called "breakthrough" placements in construction jobs was a major factor in polarizing and energizing racial activism in the 1940s and 1950s. "Affirmative Action from Below," pp. 149–150.

20. Ann Tanneyhill, "Report on the Invitational Conference on Encouraging Personal Incentive for Higher Education among Talented but Disadvantaged Youth" (1959), Part I, Series VII, Box 1, NUL; Lisli Carter Jr., opening remarks for Planning Conference (1958), Part I, Series VII, Box 19, NUL; Press Release, written 23 May 1958 for release 15 June 1958, Part I, Series VII, Box 20, NUL; "League Volunteers Spark TST Program in Columbus [Ohio]," *TST Bulletin* 2 (January–February 1959): 1, Part III, Box 474, folder 1, NUL. Parris and Brooks, *Blacks in the City,* p. 357. Kheel was president of the NUL 1956–1960.

21. "Pilot Project of the Gamma Nu Sigma Chapter of the Delta Sigma Theta Sorority" [ca. January 1958], Part I, Series VII, Box 2, NUL.

22. Guichard Parris, "Youth Incentives—A Challenge to the Community," typescript of speech [1958 or 1959], Part I, Series VII, Box 20, NUL. See also "Proposal for the Fifth Annual Vocational Opportunity Campaign 1937" typescript carbon (1937), Part I, Series IV, Box 8, NUL; "Proposal for a Pilot Project in Youth Guidance" (1957), Part I, Series IV, Box 11, NUL.

23. Thomas Augustine to Lester B. Granger, 14 October 1954, Part I, Series VII, Box 3, NUL.

24. Eli Ginzberg's *The Negro Potential* was published in 1956 and had had six printings by 1968. (New York: Columbia University Press, 1956), pp. ix, 7, 12–13, 92–93, 97–98, 104–106, 111–115, 119; quotation on p. 111.

25. "Coming: Wide-Open Split among Negro Leaders," *National Observer,* 10 October 1966, pp. 1–2; reprinted by National Urban League, Part III, Box 385, folder 8, NUL. In 1968, the league added new strategies aimed at improving ghetto conditions, including very successful "street academies"; Parris and Brooks, *Blacks in the City,* pp. 457–471.

26. Michael Bennett argues for strong links between the GI Bill and civil rights activism in *When Dreams Came True,* pp. 27, 268–275; see also Moreno, *From Direct Action to Affirmative Action,* pp. 135, 138–139.

27. Gordon Allport, *The Nature of Prejudice* (Garden City, N.Y.: Doubleday, 1958; first ed. 1954), pp. 47–56, 195, 314, 471, 477; Holland, *Black Opportunity,* pp. 123–125; Paul H. Norgren and Samuel E. Hill, *Toward Fair Employment* (New York: Columbia University Press, 1964), pp. 30–33; Paul Burstein, *Discrimination, Jobs, and Politics: The Struggle for Equal Employment Opportunity in the United States since the New Deal* (Chicago: University of Chicago Press, 1985), pp. 5–9, 37–38, 125, 180–182, 186. See also Henry Allen Bullock, "Racial Attitudes and the Employment of Negroes," *American Journal of Sociology* 56 (March 1951): 448–457.

28. John H. Bracey Jr., August Meier, and Elliott Rudwick, eds., *Black Workers and Organized Labor* (Belmont, Calif.: Wadsworth Publishing Co., 1971), pp. 1–4. For a union's solidarity across race, see Roger Horowitz, *"Negro and White, Unite and Fight!" A Social History of Industrial Unionism in Meatpacking, 1930–1990* (Urbana: University of Illinois Press, 1997). Timothy J. Minchin shows the importance of civil rights law and enforcement in the blue-collar workplace in *The Color of Work: The Struggle for Civil Rights in the Southern Pa-*

per Industry, 1945–1980 (Chapel Hill: University of North Carolina Press, 2001).

29. Arthur B. Mays, *The Problem of Industrial Education* (New York: Century Co., 1927), pp. 16–18. For a contrast between pre- and post-unionized practices, see Horowitz, *"Negro and White, Unite and Fight!"* pp. 89–90.

30. "The Apprentice System," *New York Times,* 30 January 1876, p. 6; Charles Kelly, "Apprenticeship as Heritage," letter to *New York Times,* 8 August 1963, p. 26, col. 5.

31. Lawrence Plotkin, "Negro Job Quota Upheld," letter to *New York Times,* 8 August 1963, p. 26, col. 5. Valuable studies of the long, tortuous, and multifaceted histories of African Americans and the white working class in the United States trying to earn a respected livelihood include David E. Bernstein, *Only One Place of Redress: African Americans, Labor Regulations and the Courts from Reconstruction to the New Deal* (Durham, N.C.: Duke University Press, 2001); Philip S. Foner, *Organized Labor and the Black Worker, 1619–1973* (New York: Praeger Publishers, 1974); Horowitz, *"Negro and White, Unite and Fight!"*; Bruce Nelson, *Divided We Stand: American Workers and the Struggle for Black Equality* (Princeton, N.J.: Princeton University Press, 2001); David R. Roediger, *The Wages of Whiteness: Race and the Making of the American Working Class* (London: Verso, 1991); Bracey, Meier, and Rudwick, *Black Workers and Organized Labor;* and Sugrue, "Affirmative Action from Below."

32. President's Committee on Equal Employment Opportunity, *The American Dream—Equal Opportunity* (Washington, D.C.: U.S. Government Printing Office, 1962), pp. 18–19. Benjamin W. Wolkinson, *Blacks, Unions, and the EEOC: A Study of Administrative Futility* (Lexington, Mass.: Lexington Books, 1973), pp. 9–33, 147nn3,4,8. See also Irwin Dubinsky, "Trade Union Discrimination in the Pittsburgh Construction Industry: How and Why It Operates," *Urban Affairs Quarterly* 6 (March 1971): 297–318; Louis L. Knowles and Kenneth Prewitt, eds., *Institutional Racism in America* (Englewood Cliffs, N.J.: Prentice-Hall, 1969), pp. 22–24, 118; and Norgren and Hill, *Toward Fair Employment,* pp. 18–19.

33. M. T. Puryear, "The Negro Worker: His Status, His Problems, and His Needs," background paper (1964), Part II, Series I, Box 12, pp. 5–6, NUL; "Apprenticeship—A Key to the Future," typescript draft for bro-

chure, 18 October 1966, pp. 2, 3–4, 11, Part III, Box 134, folder 4, NUL; "Labor Education Advancement Program" booklet (New York: National Urban League, 1967), unpaginated, Part III, Box 135, folder 9, NUL.

34. Herbert Hill, *Labor Union Control of Job Training: A Critical Analysis of Apprenticeship Outreach Programs and the Hometown Plans* (Washington, D.C.: Institute for Urban Affairs and Research, 1974), pp. 2–6, 26, 28–35.

35. Ibid., pp. 35–41, 59–65, 109.

36. F. Ray Marshall and Vernon M. Briggs Jr., *The Negro and Apprenticeship* (Baltimore: Johns Hopkins University Press, 1967), pp. iv, 5, 13, 24–25, 41, 45, 227, 232–233; W. Lloyd Warner and James C. Abegglen, *Big Business Leaders in America* (New York: Harper and Bros., 1955), pp. 226–228.

37. Samuel Krislov, *The Negro in Federal Employment: The Quest for Racial Opportunity* (Minneapolis: University of Minnesota Press, 1967) 92–93, 98, 148, quotation on p. 144; Robert Maranto and David Schultz, *A Short History of the United States Civil Service* (Lanham, Md.: University Press of America, 1991), pp. 95, 111.

38. Weiss, *National Urban League,* p. 261; Krislov, *The Negro in Federal Employment,* pp. 32–33, 91, 100; Maranto and Schultz, *Short History,* pp. 116–117; Roger Waldinger, *Still the Promised City? African-Americans and New Immigrants in Postindustrial New York* (Cambridge, Mass.: Harvard University Press, 1996), pp. 220–221; Brown et al., *Whitewashing Race,* pp. 73–74.

39. Waldinger, *Still the Promised City?* pp. 209–211, 217–219, 227, 229–231, 249, quotations on pp. 209 and 219; Dennis Clark, "The Expansion of the Public Sector and Irish Economic Development," in *Self-Help in Urban America: Patterns of Minority Business Enterprise,* ed. Scott Cummings (Port Washington, N.Y.: National University Publications, 1980), pp. 177–187.

40. Kenneth R. Mladenka, "Public Employee Unions, Reformism, and Black Employment in 1,200 American Cities," *Urban Affairs Quarterly* 26 (1991): 532–548; Waldinger, *Still the Promised City?* pp. 28, 230. David A. Thomas and John J. Gabarro, in *Breaking Through: The Making of Minority Executives in Corporate America* (Boston: Harvard Business School Press, 1999), develop what they call diversity processes, programs, and strategies.

41. U.S. Commission on Civil Rights, *The Economic Progress of Black Men in America* (Washington, D.C.: U.S. Commission on Civil Rights, 1986), Clearinghouse Publication 91, pp. 83–84; Lynn C. Burbridge, *The Glass Ceiling in Different Sectors of the Economy* (Washington, D.C.: U.S. Department of Labor, 1994), pp. iii–v, 70–73.

42. Kenneth R. Miller, "The American Negro in Industry," press release, National Association of Manufactures, New York, 5 June 1954, pp. 1, 7–9, HM&L.

43. "Planned Progress" and "Cheers for Three," pages from unspecified Avon publication (1969), folder: Policies/Minority Employment, 1968–1973, Box 110, Avon/HM&L; "John A. Ewald" [retirement announcement], *Avon Annual Report for the Year 1967* (New York: Avon Products, 1968), p. 16, HM&L.

44. Young and Silberman quoted in Ginzberg, *The Negro Challenge,* pp. 17–23, 31.

45. "Equal Employment Opportunity Affirmative Action Program of Sun Oil Company," internal document (undated; attached to memo of 12 May 1970); "Analysis of Minority Group Representation in Work Force as of June 30, 1970," internal report; "A Minority Upgrading Program," Personnel Services–Products Group, internal document (June 1970); all in Series 5, Box 473, folder: Minority Affairs, Sun/ HM&L. For typical criticisms of personnel testing from a civil rights perspective, see Ginzberg, *The Negro Challenge,* pp. 85, 94; and Knowles and Prewitt, *Institutional Racism,* p. 21. Although NUL programs trained people to take tests, its spokespersons often objected to tests' class and cultural biases. See, for instance, "Plans for Progress National College Relations Conference" Atlanta 11/1–4/65, Part III, Box 135, folder 8, NUL; "Integration in Industry," *Factory* (December 1964), reprinted by NUL, Part III, Box 254, folder 7, NUL.

46. "What's It Like to Be a Negro in Management," *Business Management* 29 (April 1966): 60–88.

47. Ibid., p. 62; Eli Ginzberg, "Spot and Encourage Initiative," *Nation's Business* 49 (April 1961): 74–78.

48. Brian J. O'Connell, *Blacks in White-Collar Jobs* (Montclair, N.J.: Allanheld, Osmun and Co., 1979), pp. 1–2, 8, 62; Mark McColloch, *White Collar Workers in Transition: The Boom Years, 1940–1970* (Westport, Conn.: Greenwood Press, 1983); Gelber, *Black Men and Businessmen,* pp. 130–134.

49. "The Unfinished Business of Negro Jobs," *Business Week,* 12 June 1965, pp. 82–92, 97–102, 105–106; Charles Marshall, "Open Doors Are Not Enough," in *Business and Social Progress: Views of Two Generations of Executives,* ed. Clarence C. Walton (New York: Praeger Publishers, 1970), pp. 35–37; Moreno, *From Direct Action to Affirmative Action,* pp. 145–146, 199–201, 251, chap. 9. For useful historically based analyses of the origin and impact of affirmative action policies in the public and the private sectors, see Hugh Davis Graham, *The Civil Rights Era: Origins and Development of National Policy* (New York: Oxford University Press, 1990), pp. 4, 6, 187–189, 471–472, 475–476; Moreno, *From Direct Action to Affirmative Action;* John David Skrentny, *The Ironies of Affirmative Action: Politics, Culture, and Justice in America* (Chicago: University of Chicago Press, 1996); and Sugrue, "Affirmative Action from Below."

50. George Schermer, *Employer's Guide to Equal Opportunity* (Washington, D.C.: Potomac Institute, 1966), pp. 23, 34, quotation on p. 23.

51. National Alliance of Businessmen (NAB), *First Annual Report* (Washington, D.C., 1968/1969), pp. 1, 4–5. President Lyndon Johnson forcefully applied his authority to urge business leaders' participation in NAB. Joseph A. Califano Jr., *The Triumph and Tragedy of Lyndon Johnson: The White House Years* (New York: Simon and Schuster, 1991), pp. 223–226. See also Fred Luthans and Richard M. Hodgetts, *Social Issues in Business: Poverty, Civil Rights, Ecology, and Consumerism* (New York: Macmillan Co., 1972), pp. 125–131.

52. NAB, *First Annual Report,* pp. 17–18. NAB literature and references to NAB occur frequently in the archived records of the firms I examined in files related to racial issues. NAB clearly helped those firms chart their courses. See especially Avon Products, Accession no. 2155; Charles B. McCoy Papers, Accession no. 1815; Sun Oil Co., Accession no. 1317; HM&L. Urban Research Corporation, *Training the Hardcore* (New York: General Learning Corporation, 1969), vol. 1, p. 17; vol. 9, pp. 21–23, 26, 32–33.

53. Schermer, *Employer's Guide,* pp. 2–3, 10–13; Robert L. Kahn et al., *Discrimination without Prejudice: A Study of Promotion Practices in Industry* (Ann Arbor: University of Michigan Institute for Social Research, 1964), p. 45. See also Gelber, *Black Men and Businessmen,* pp. 130–134, 138; Knowles and Prewitt, *Institutional Racism,* pp. 1, 4–7; Ginzberg, *The Negro Challenge,* p. 55; Gertrude Ezorsky, *Racism*

and Justice: The Case for Affirmative Action (Ithaca, N.Y.: Cornell University Press, 1991), pp. 9–14; and Robert P. Quinn, Joyce M. Tabor, and Laura K. Gordon, *The Decision to Discriminate: A Study of Executive Selection* (Ann Arbor: Institute for Social Research, 1968).

54. Schermer, *Employer's Guide*, pp. 10–13, 16, 19, 23, 29, 42–43.

55. Ibid., pp. 27, 34–36, 49–50.

56. Eleanor Roosevelt's press release, 16 August 1962, *AAUW Archives, 1881–1976* (New York: NYT Microfilming Corporation of America, 1980), Reel 121, Group 699. Graham, *The Civil Rights Era,* pp. 41–42; Moreno, *From Direct Action to Affirmative Action,* pp. 188–189; Skrentny, *The Ironies of Affirmative Action,* p. 7.

57. "Planned Progress," pages from unspecified Avon publication (1969), folder: Policies/Minority Employment, 1968–1973, Box 110, Avon/HM&L.

58. Nathan Glazer, *Affirmative Discrimination* (Cambridge, Mass.: Harvard University Press, 1975); Stephan Thernstrom and Abigail Thernstrom, *America in Black and White: One Nation, Indivisible* (New York: Simon and Schuster, 1997).

59. "What's It Like to Be a Negro in Management," p. 63; Thomas Sowell, *A Personal Odyssey* (New York: Free Press, 2000), pp. 163, 306; "Coming: Wide-Open Split among Negro Leaders."

60. Carter A. Daniel, *MBA: The First Century* (Lewisburg, Pa.: Bucknell University Press, 1998), pp. 185–186, 199–200.

61. Theresa A. Hammond, *A White-Collar Profession: African American Certified Public Accountants since 1921* (Chapel Hill: University of North Carolina Press, 2002), pp. 86–87; Gelber, *Black Men and Businessmen,* pp. 129–130, quotation on p. 130.

62. Personnel Department, "Procedure Bulletin no. 24 (revised)" memo, "Exempt Appraisal Program," 15 March 1969, pp. 1–2, Avon/HM&L.

63. George David and Glegg Watson document racial culture shock throughout their book *Black Life in Corporate America: Swimming in the Mainstream* (Garden City, N.Y.: Anchor Press/Doubleday, 1982), specifically referring to it on p. 43. See also Sharon M. Collins, *Black Corporate Executives: The Making and Breaking of a Black Middle Class* (Philadelphia: Temple University Press, 1997); Ulwyn L. J. Pierre, *The Myth of Black Corporate Mobility* (New York: Garland Publishing, 1998), chaps. 2, 6; and Schermer, *Employer's Guide,* pp. 45–53.

6. Strangers on the Ladder

1. Hugh Davis Graham, *The Civil Rights Era: Origins and Development of National Policy* (New York: Oxford University Press, 1990), pp. 414–415; Lois Kathryn Herr, *Women, Power, and AT&T: Winning Rights in the Workplace* (Boston: Northeastern University Press, 2003); Alice Kessler-Harris, *In Pursuit of Equity: Women, Men, and the Quest for Economic Citizenship in Twentieth-Century America* (New York: Oxford University Press, 2001), pp. 246–261, 266, 294. For an overview, see Sara Alpern, "In the Beginning: A History of Women in Management" in *Women in Management: Trends, Issues, and Challenges in Managerial Diversity,* ed. Ellen A. Fagenson (Newbury Park, Calif.: Sage Publications, 1993), pp. 19–51.

2. Susan B. Riley to Edith H. Sherrard, "Preliminary Thinking about Desegregation," memo, 24 September 1954, *AAUW Archives, 1881–1976* (New York: NYT Microfilming Corporation of America, 1980), Series V, Reel 116, Group 595. Riley was president of AAUW 1951–1955.

3. "What's It Like to Be a Negro in Management," *Business Management* 29 (April 1966): 60–88; Eli Ginzberg, ed., *The Negro Challenge to the Business Community* (New York: McGraw-Hill Book Co., 1964), p. 96.

4. "Management Meetings: Minority Employment and the Hardcore," agenda, 13 June 1968, folder: Policies/Minority Employment, 1968–1973, Series V, Box 110, Avon/HM&L.

5. D. D. Stone to Donald P. Jones, "Executive Compensation," memo, 24 September 1969, folder: Executive Compensation; "Issue: Need for Creating a New Position," presentation notes, ca. 1969, "Minority Affairs"; R. W. Donahue to Donald P. Jones, untitled memo, 19 June 1969, folder: Minority Affairs; all Series V, Box 473, Sun/HM&L. See also "The Unfinished Business of Negro Jobs," *Business Week,* 12 June 1965: 82–92, 97–102, 105–106.

6. Alice Kessler-Harris, *Out to Work: A History of Wage-Earning Women in the United States* (New York: Oxford University Press, 1982), pp. 274–279, 286; Kessler-Harris, *In Pursuit of Equity,* p. 18; Elaine Tyler May, "Pushing the Limits, 1940–1961," in *No Small Courage: A History of Women in the United States,* ed. Nancy F. Cott (New York: Oxford University Press, 2000), pp. 476–484.

7. Dorothy Sue Cobble, "Recapturing Working-Class Feminism: Union Women in the Postwar Era," in *Not June Cleaver: Women and Gender in Postwar America, 1945–1960,* ed. Joanne Meyerowitz (Philadelphia: Temple University Press, 1994), pp. 57–83; Kessler-Harris, *Out to Work,* pp. 295–299; Angel Kwolek-Folland, *Incorporating Women: A History of Women and Business in the United States* (New York: Twayne Publishers, 1998), pp. 153–158; May, "Pushing the Limits," pp. 491–500; Ruth Rosen, *The World Split Open: How the Modern Women's Movement Changed America* (New York: Penguin Books, 2000), chap. 1. George F. Davenel, "When Johnny Comes Marching Home Will You Go Marching Out?" *Independent Woman* 24 (July 1945): 182–183, 201.

8. This trend held for women in the labor force as a percentage both of the total workforce and of all women. Ben J. Wattenberg, ed., *The Statistical History of the United States* (New York: Basic Books, 1976), pp. 132–133.

9. C. C. Furnas, ed., *Research in Industry: Its Organization and Management* (New York: D. Van Nostrand Co., 1948), pp. 285–288.

10. Katharine Hamill, "Women as Bosses," *Fortune* 53 (June 1956): 108.

11. "Women in the Workforce: Where They Stand, What They Want," *Management Review* 59 (November 1970): 20–23; "Labor Letter," *Wall Street Journal* column (10 July 1979): 1. On "unintended bias" in managerial decisions, see also Benson Rosen and Thomas H. Jerdee, "Sex Stereotyping in the Executive Suite," *Harvard Business Review* 52 (March–April 1974): 45–58.

12. Alison J. Clarke, *Tupperware: The Promise of Plastic in 1950s America* (Washington, D.C.: Smithsonian Institution Press, 1999), p. 134; Jane R. Plitt, *Martha Matilda Harper and the American Dream* (Syracuse, N.Y.: Syracuse University Press, 2000), pp. 70–71.

13. Mary Kay Ash, *Mary Kay* (New York: Harper and Row, 1981), pp. 8–9, 26, 97–99.

14. Ibid., pp. 18–19, 24, 28–29, 34, 99–101; "Mary Kay Ash, Cosmetic Line Founder," obituary, *Denver Rocky Mountain News,* 23 November 2001; Ash, *Mary Kay on People Management* (New York: Warner Books, 1984), p. 175.

15. Plitt, *Martha Matilda Harper,* pp. 70–71, 84–85; Kathy Peiss, *Hope in a Jar: The Making of America's Beauty Culture* (New York: Metropolitan Books, 1998), pp. 79–80, 87–88, 92–94; Julie A. Willett, *Perma-*

nent Waves: The Making of the American Beauty Shop (New York: New York University Press, 2000), pp. 24–26.

16. For a recent summary, see William H. Chafe, "The Road to Equality, 1962–Today," in *No Small Courage*, ed. Cott, pp. 529–586. On working class women's activism, see Dorothy Sue Cobble, *The Other Women's Movement: Workplace Justice and Social Rights in Modern America* (Princeton: Princeton University Press, 2004); and Nancy F. Gabin, *Feminism in the Labor Movement: Women and the United Auto Workers, 1935–1975* (Ithaca, N.Y.: Cornell University Press, 1990).

17. Betty Friedan, *The Feminine Mystique* (New York: W. W. Norton and Co., 1963), pp. 315, 345–346.

18. Chafe, "Road to Equality," pp. 496–498; Cobble, "Recapturing Working-Class Feminism," p. 68; Kessler-Harris, *In Pursuit of Equity,* 5–6, 18, 204; Nancy MacLean, "The Hidden History of Affirmative Action: Working Women's Struggles in the 1970s and the Gender of Class," *Feminist Studies* 25 (1999): 48; Mabel Newcomer, *A Century of Higher Education for Women* (New York: Harper and Brothers, 1959), pp. 47, 248.

19. Daniel Horowitz, *Betty Friedan and the Making of "The Feminine Mystique": The American Left, the Cold War, and Modern Feminism* (Amherst: University of Massachusetts Press, 1998), p. 226; Lerner quoted on p. 213. Cobble, "Recapturing Working-Class Feminism," pp. 74–75, 82n78; Graham, *Civil Rights Era,* p. 137; Kessler-Harris, *In Pursuit of Equity,* pp. 205–208, 211–235; Gerda Lerner, *Fireweed: A Political Autobiography* (Philadelphia: Temple University Press, 2002); MacLean, "Hidden History," p. 48.

20. Friedan, *Feminine Mystique,* pp. 69–70, 74; Horowitz, *Betty Friedan,* pp. 1–3; Horowitz, "Rethinking Betty Friedan and *The Feminine Mystique:* Labor Union Radicalism and Feminism in Cold War America," *American Quarterly* 48 (1996): 1–42; Joanne Meyerowitz, "Beyond the Feminine Mystique: A Reassessment of Postwar Mass Culture, 1946–1958," *Journal of American History* 79 (1993): 1455–1482. See also Susan Lynn, "Gender and Progressive Politics: A Bridge to Social Activism of the 1960s," in *Not June Cleaver,* ed. Meyerowitz, pp. 103–127.

21. On the passage of the 1964 Civil Rights Act and early struggles to get EMOC attention for gender issues, see Graham, *Civil Rights Era,* pp. 12–13, 137–139; Kessler-Harris, *In Pursuit of Equity,* pp. 239–

245; Donald Allen Robinson, "Two Movements in Pursuit of Equal Employment Opportunity," *Signs* 4 (1979): 413–433, esp. 414–420; and Rosen, *The World Split Open,* pp. 71–72. *The American Dream— Equal Opportunity* (Washington, D.C.: U.S. Government Printing Office, 1962), the 1962 report on the Community Leaders' Conference, which women attended, sponsored by the President's Committee on Equal Employment Opportunity, addressed only class and race. On the development of feminist concerns and tactics, see Sara Evans, *Personal Politics: The Roots of Women's Liberation in the Civil Rights Movement and the New Left* (New York: Alfred A. Knopf, 1979); and Jo Freeman, *The Politics of Women's Liberation* (New York: David MacKay Co., 1975).

22. Cobble, "Recapturing Working-Class Feminism," pp. 58–63, 68; Gabin, *Feminism in the Labor Movement,* pp. 1, 77, 119–120, 128, 152, 189; MacLean, "Hidden History," pp. 47–53, quotation on p. 51.

23. Mariwyn D. Heath, *A History of the National Federation of Business and Professional Women's Clubs, Inc. (BPW/USA),* vol. 3 (Washington, D.C.: The Federation, 1994), pp. 5, 11–12; "National Business Woman," *National Business Woman* 35 (November 1956): 2, 38; "From Your Head," "To Your Toes," "Your Nylons," "And Your Wardrobe," *National Business Woman* 36 (January 1957): 3–9; *National Business Woman* 36 (July 1957).

24. Helen G. Hurd, "Leadership Problems of the White Collar Woman Worker," *Independent Woman* 35 (May 1956): 2–3; "Sharemanship: An Individual Responsibility," *National Business Woman* 42 (June 1963): 16–17.

25. Friedan, *Feminine Mystique,* pp. 19, 33, 315, 338, 364, 374.

26. Freeman, *Politics of Women's Liberation,* pp. 85–87, 93, 116–119, 125, 167; Aileen C. Hernandez and Letitia P. Sommers, *The First Five Years, 1966–1971* (Chicago: National Organization for Women, n.d.), pp. 1, 5, 10–11, 21; Rosen, *World Split Open.* For a leading participant's perspective that places NOW and the women's movement in political and business contexts, see Aileen C. Hernandez, *EEOC and the Women's Movement, 1965–1975* (Newark, N.J.: Rutgers University Law School, 1975).

27. Susan Davis, "Organizing from Within," *MS* 1 (August 1972): 92–99; Evans, *Personal Politics,* pp. 214–216; Freeman, *Politics of Women's Liberation,* pp. xi, 57–61, 105; Vivian Gornick, "Consciousness"

[1971], in *Radical Feminism: A Documentary Reader*, ed. Barbara Crow (New York: New York University Press, 2000), pp. 287–300, quotation on p. 295; Joan Robins, *Handbook of Women's Liberation* (North Hollywood, Calif.: NOW Library Press, 1970), pp. 6–11, 137–153, 170, quotations on pp. 10–11; Rosen, *World Split Open*, pp. 78, 110–115, 118, 196–200.

28. June Arnold, "Consciousness-Raising," in *Radical Feminism*, ed. Crow, pp. 282–285, quotation on p. 285; Gay Abarbanell and Harriet Perl, *Guidelines to Feminist Consciousness Raising* (Los Angeles: National Task Force on Consciousness Raising of the National Organization for Women, 1976), pp. 24, 32–33. See also Robins, *Handbook*, pp. 142–152; and Gornick, "Consciousness," pp. 287–300.

29. Abarbanell and Perl, *Guidelines*, pp. 47, 50–51.

30. Herb Goldberg, *The Hazards of Being Male: Surviving the Myth of Masculine Privilege* (Plainview, N.Y.: Nash Publishing Co., 1976), pp. 15–19, 96, 101–102, 135–136, 141–144. See also Karl Bednarik, *The Male in Crisis*, trans. Helen Sebba (New York: Alfred A. Knopf, 1970); Mike Bradley et al., *Unbecoming Men: A Men's Consciousness-Raising Group Writes on Oppression and Themselves* (Washington, N.J.: Times Change Press, 1971); Warren Farrell, *The Liberated Man: Beyond Masculinity: Freeing Men and Their Relationships with Women* (New York: Random House, 1974), esp. pp. 182–183; and Jack Nichols, *Men's Liberation: A New Definition of Masculinity* (New York: Penguin, 1975).

31. Caroline Bird, with Sara Welles Briller, *Born Female: The High Cost of Keeping Women Down* (New York: David McKay Co., 1968), pp. 9–10, 143, 189, 191; Robins, *Handbook*, pp. 85–96; Rosen, *World Split Open*, p. 196.

32. Wyndham Robertson, "The Ten Highest-Ranking Women in Big Business," *Fortune* 87 (April 1973): 81–89.

33. Bird, *Born Female*, pp. 104–10; Katharine Graham, *Personal History* (New York: Vintage Books, 1997), pp. 336, 339–340, 416–422, 429–430; Robertson, "The Ten Highest-Ranking Women," p. 83.

34. Carl N. Degler, "Revolution without Ideology: The Changing Place of Women in America," *Daedalus* 93 (1964): 653–670. This special issue on women featured a distinguished panel that included Erik Erikson and David Riesman.

35. Bird, *Born Female*; Freeman, *Politics of Women's Liberation*, p. 118;

Friedan, *Feminine Mystique,* pp. 19, 33, 338, 364, 374; Gornick, "Consciousness," p. 290; Carol Hanisch, "The Personal Is Political" [1970], in *Radical Feminism,* ed. Crow, pp. 113–116; C. Wright Mills, *The Sociological Imagination* (New York: Grove Press, 1961; first published 1959), pp. 3–10; Robins, *Handbook,* p. 138; Rosen, *World Split Open,* pp. 196–197; Kathie Sarachild, "A Program for Feminist Consciousness-Raising" [1968] in *Radical Feminism,* ed. Crow, pp. 273–276.

36. Herr, *Women, Power, and AT&T,* pp. xiii–xv, 1–15, 32. Through close documentation and interviews, Herr narrates the famous case, settled in January 1973, that the EEOC and NOW built. For studies of race and sex discriminatory practices and history at AT&T see Phyllis A. Wallace, ed., *Equal Employment Opportunity and the AT&T Case* (Cambridge, Mass.: MIT Press, 1976). For the case itself, see Marjorie A. Stockford, *The Bellwomen: The Story of the Landmark AT&T Sex Discrimination Case* (New Brunswick, N.J.: Rutgers University Press, 2004).

37. Interview with Herr and access to LKH, 11–12 November 2001. Saul Alinsky, *Rules for Radicals: A Pragmatic Primer for Realistic Radicals* (New York: Random House, 1971); Pamela Allen, *Free Space: A Perspective on the Small Group in Women's Liberation* (New York: Times Change Press, 1970); Robin Morgan, comp., *Sisterhood Is Powerful: An Anthology of Writings from the Women's Liberation Movement* (New York: Random House, 1970). Herr's copy of Bird was a 1971 edition from Pocket Books.

38. "Professional Women's Caucus Annual Meeting," press release, 8 October 1971, for meeting of 16 October 1971, LKH. Herr, *Women, Power, and AT&T,* pp. 90, 92; Horowitz, *Betty Friedan,* pp. 228–231.

39. Herr, "Corporate Feminism," typescript, ca. 1972, LKH; Herr, "External Realities: Feminists and the Corporation," typescript, 1972, pp. 17, 19, LKH; Herr, *Women, Power, and AT&T,* pp. 89–90; Alinsky, *Rules for Radicals,* p. 128.

40. Garda W. Bowman, N. Beatrice Worthy, and Stephen A. Greyser, "Are Women Executives People?" *Harvard Business Review* 43 (July–August 1965): 14–28, 164–168, quotation on p. 16; Herr, *Women, Power, and AT&T,* pp. 42, 119–121.

41. J. L. Moses et al., "The Utilization of Women in the Management of the Bell System," typescript, August 1970, pp. 9–11, 14–21, LKH.

42. Herr, *Women, Power, and AT&T,* esp. pp. 17–25, 106–113, 142–148, 158–162, quotations on pp. 162–163. See also Wallace, ed., *Equal Employment Opportunity and the AT&T Case;* and Stockford, *The Bellwomen.*

43. General Electric, *Women and Business: Agenda for the Seventies* (New York: General Electric, 1972), pp. 8, 28, 37–38, 58–60. For background on this report, see Herr, *Women, Power, and AT&T,* p. 72. "GE Reaches Accord with U.S. Settling Charges of Job Bias," *Wall Street Journal,* 16 June 1978. Eleanor Roosevelt, press release for President's Commission on the Status of Women, 16 August 1962, *AAUW Archives, 1881–1976* (New York: NYT Microfilming Corporation of America, 1980) Reel 121, Group 699.

44. *Avon Annual Report for the Year 1958,* pp. 3, 16; *Avon Annual Report for the Year 1959,* p. 14; *Avon Annual Report 1964,* pp. 7–9; *Avon Annual Report 1966,* pp. 8, 10; *Avon Annual Report 1967,* pp. 9, 13; (New York: Avon Products, 1959, 1960, 1965, 1967, 1968, respectively), HM&L. "Procedure Bulletin no. 24 (revised)," 15 March 1969; Series III, Box 5, Avon/HM&L.

45. "Procedure Bulletin no. 24 (revised)," 15 March 1969; "Non-Exempt Internal Promotion," 28 March 1969; "Guidelines for Conducting the Performance Appraisal Interview," 15 March 1969; Series III, Box 5. W. J. Williams, "Management Development," memo, 26 April 1969, Management Manual, vol. 2; "Procedure Bulletin no. 24 (revised)," "Management Appraisal Program," memo, 15 May 1971, p. 7; Series III, Box 7, Avon/HM&L. Series III of the Avon archives, HM&L, contains large numbers of documents on these subjects, with many iterations of these and other personnel issues.

46. "Organization Manual 1971," Series III, Box 5, Avon/HM&L.

47. "Managing a Woman Effectively" (1972), Series III, Box 110, Avon/HM&L.

48. *Avon Corporate Responsibilities: Today's Challenges* (New York: Avon Products, 1977), p. 2, Series III, Box 110, Avon/HM&L. Corporate social responsibility peaked as a publication topic in the 1970s. See Nels Gunderson, *Corporate Social Responsibility: A Review of the Literature* (Monticello, Ill.: Vance Bibliographies, 1986). M. Jane Kay, "Women in Management—Past, Present, Future," *NAM Reports,* 31 July 1972, photocopy, Series III, Box 129, Press Releases, Avon/

HM&L. *Avon Annual Report 1972*, p. 3; *Avon Annual Report 1973*, pp. 3–4 (New York: Avon Products 1973, 1974).

49. "Corporate Responsibility Plan 1973," quotation on p. 2; "Equal Opportunities in Employment," Procedure Bulletin no. 48, memo, 6 March 1973, Series III, Box 110, Avon/HM&L.

50. Francine E. Gordon, "Bringing Women into Management: The Role of the Senior Executive," in *Bringing Women into Management,* ed. Gordon Strober and Myra H. Strober (New York: McGraw-Hill Book Co., 1975), pp. 113–125.

51. Hurd, "Leadership Problems," pp. 2–3.

52. Margaret Cussler, *The Woman Executive* (New York: Harcourt, Brace and Co., 1958), pp. vii, xi, 3, 7, 13, 17–22.

53. Ibid., p. 21. Editors of *Fortune* magazine, *The Executive Life* (Garden City, N.Y.: Doubleday, 1956), pp. 69–73.

54. Hurd, "Leadership Problems," p. 3. Eli Ginzberg, "Challenge and Resolution," in *Corporate Lib: Women's Challenge to Management,* ed. Eli Ginzberg and Alice M. Yohalem (Baltimore: Johns Hopkins University Press, 1973), p. 144.

55. John N. Given, "Women in Executive Posts," *Office Executive* 35 (December 1960): 32–33.

56. Bowman, Worthy, and Greyser, "Are Women Executives People?" pp. 176, 178. See also Frances M. Fuller and Mary B. Batchelder, "Opportunities for Women at the Administrative Level," *Harvard Business Review* 31 (January–February 1953): 111–128; Hamill, "Women as Bosses"; Newcomer, *A Century of Higher Education for Women,* pp. 246–249.

57. Garda W. Bowman, "What Helps or Harms Promotability?" *Harvard Business Review* 42 (January–February 1964): 6–26, 184–196.

58. Louis L. Knowles and Kenneth Prewitt, eds., *Institutional Racism in America* (Englewood Cliffs, N.J.: Prentice-Hall, 1969); Bird, *Born Female,* pp. 52–58, 106–113, and passim.

7. Uncovering the Power of Pull

1. "Corporate Women," *Business Week,* 8 June 1992, pp. 74–83.

2. "Open Letter to an Employer," Box 478; H. R. Sharbaugh, "Educational Development Program," memo, 11 June 1970, folder "D to G,"

Box 469; H. R. Sharbaugh, "Exempt Job Opportunity Posting," memo and procedure statement, 16 November 1970, folder "Job Opportunity Listings," Box 470; "Issue: Need for Creating a New Position," presentation notes, ca. 1969, folder "Minority Affairs," Box 473; all Series V, Sun/HM&L. Unless otherwise noted, all Sun documents cited in this chapter are from Series V, Sun/HM&L.

3. J. H. Perrine, "Equal Employment Opportunity Affirmative Action" memo, 17 July 1970, folder "Minority Affairs," Box 473; Executive Committee Meeting minutes, 21 January 1975, 19 February 1975; Human Resources Task Force minutes, 30 January 1975, 6 February 1975, all in folder "Women's Awareness Seminars, 1975–6," Box 477.

4. Sun Oil Company, Products Group, "A Developmental Process for Individual Career Planning," March 1975, folder "Women's Awareness Seminars, 1975–6," Box 477. "Task Force—Upward Mobility of Women—Recommendations," Task Force memo to Products Group MDC, 18 July 1975; H. L. Kephart, "Upward Mobility Awareness Program," memo, 16 October 1975; folder "Women's Awareness Seminars, 1975–6," Box 477

5. Boyle/Kirkman Associates, Section 4, incomplete copy of report (October 1975), folder "Women's Awareness Seminars, 1975–6," Box 477.

6. Executive Committee Meeting, minutes, 26 March 1975, 23 July 1975; "Task Force—Upward Mobility of Women—Recommendations," Task Force memo to Products Group MDC, 18 July 1975; Deborah Correll McDonough to Ted Burtis, memo, 16 January 1976; all in folder "Women's Awareness Seminars, 1975–6," Box 477.

7. Barbara C. Harris to T. A. Burtis, memo, 31 May 1977, folder "Women's Alliance," Box 477.

8. Information Science Incorporated, *How to Eliminate Discriminatory Practices: A Guide to EEO Compliance* (New York: AMACOM, 1975), pp. 9–13, 23–25, 31–32.

9. R. F. Kress to T. A. Burtis, memo, 14 June 1977, 11 July 1977; Theodore A. Burtis, memo, 22 July 1977; R. B. Anderson to T. A. Burtis, memo, 25 August 1977, all in folder "Women's Alliance," Box 477; Ted Burtis, confidential memo, in "Sun Executive," no. 8 (23 August 1977), Box 479.

10. Betty W. McAllister to Delores Faircloth and Maureen Lontit, letter, 9 June 1978; "Sun women's organization notes from Marcus Hook," 14 November 1977; "Key Points—Phila. Meeting," 21 November 1977;

Maureen Cass, group letter, 28 December 1977; *Sun Women's Organization Newsletter* no. 2 (June 1978): 1; "Out to Lunch," *Reports* [newsletter of SWO of Philadelphia] 1, no. 1 (ca. August 1978); all in Box 478.

11. Marj H. Adler et al., Sun Women's Organization letter, 7 October 1977; "Key Points from Organizing Meeting," 11 November 1977; "Sun women's organization notes from Marcus Hook," 14 November 1977; "Key Points—Phila. Meeting," 21 November 1977; M[arjorie] H[.] A[dler], untitled typed document, 3 February 1978; *Sun Women's Organization Newsletter* no. 2 (June 1978): 1; "Suggested Agenda for the Future," *NOTES*, October 1978: 3; *Reports* 1, no. 1 (ca. August 1978); "RAP Sessions," *Reports* [no no.], 22 November 1978; all in Box 478.

12. "Sun Women's Council Questionnaire Results," 9 March 1979, Box 478; Shirley K. Evans to Sara Forster, memo, 12 December 1977, Box 478; Lena Sharpe, "Notes—Meeting of Sun Women's Organization," Radnor, 2 May 1978, Box 479.

13. *Sun Women's Organization Newsletter,* no. 1 (January 1978): 3; "Suggestions for Programs—Sun Women's Council," n.d., Box 478; Lena Sharpe, "Notes—Meeting of Sun Women's Organization," Radnor, 2 May 1978; *Reports* 1, no. 1 (ca. August 1978); list of questions attached to letter, Judith Ann Fritsch to Harry Levinson, 9 November 1981, Box 479. Regarding films, see flyers announcing showings of *Minorities in Organizations* (shown 29 October 1979 and 14 November 1979) and *What You Are Is Where You Were When* (shown 9 and 10 January 1979), both in Box 478; *Women in Management: Threat or Opportunity?* 25 June 1981, Box 479. Rosabeth Moss Kanter, *Men and Women of the Corporation* (New York: Basic Books, 1977); John T. Molloy, *The Woman's Dress for Success Book* (New York: Warner Books, 1978)—Molloy's first such book actually instructed men on grooming: *Dress for Success* (New York: P. H. Wyden, 1975); Betty Lehan Harragan, *Games Mother Never Taught You: Corporate Gamesmanship for Women* (New York: Warner Books, 1977), and "Career Advice: Dear Betty Harragan," *Working Woman* 10 (April 1985): 33, 36. Marilyn Moats Kennedy asserted that "people in the office isolate themselves from reality" by not acknowledging the importance of power politics; *Office Politics: Seizing Power, Wielding Clout* (Chicago: Follett Publishing Co., 1980), p. 17.

14. "The Courts Back Women on Job Equality," *Business Week,* 25 November 1972, pp. 44, 48, folder "Library Resources/Women 1972–1985," Box 129, Avon/HM&L. On tokenism, see George David and Glegg Watson, *Black Life in Corporate America: Swimming in the Mainstream* (Garden City, N.Y.: Anchor Press/Doubleday, 1982); Philip Moss and Chris Tilly, *Stories Employers Tell: Race, Skill, and Hiring in America* (New York: Russell Sage Foundation, 2001), esp. chap. 6; Marylin Bender, "Corporate Tokenism for Women?" *New York Times,* 20 February 1972; M. Barbara Boyle, "Equal Opportunity for Women Is Smart Business," *Harvard Business Review* 51 (May–June 1973): 85–95. "GE Reaches Accord with U.S. Settling Charges of Job Bias," *Wall Street Journal,* 16 June 1978. On the perceived slowness of movement up corporate ladders, see women's itemized questions to Harry Levinson, an expert on executive behavior, in list of questions attached to letter, Judith Ann Fritsch to Harry Levinson, 9 November 1981, Box 479.

15. Cynthia Fuchs Epstein, *Woman's Place: Options and Limits in Professional Careers* (Berkeley: University of California Press, 1970), pp. 1, 3, 11; Epstein, "Bringing Women In: Rewards, Punishments, and the Structure of Achievement," in *Women and Success: The Anatomy of Achievement,* ed. Ruth B. Kundsin (New York: William Morrow and Co., 1974), pp. 18–19 (originally published as *Successful Women in the Sciences: An Analysis of Determinants* by the New York Academy of Sciences, 1973). SWO book lists included those in *Sun Women's Organization Newsletter* no. 1 (January 1978): 3; and *NOTES* (August 1978) n.p., both in Box 478.

16. Epstein, *Woman's Place,* pp. 151–152, 166–188.

17. Charles D. Orth III and Frederic Jacobs, "Women in Management: Pattern for Change," *Harvard Business Review* 49 (July–August 1971): 139–147. Gail Sheehy, *Passages: Predictable Crises of Adult Life* (New York: P. Dutton and Co., 1974), pp. 109, 131–134, 224–225. For review excerpts, see *Book Review Digest* (New York: H. W. Wilson Co., 1976), p. 1096. For best-seller listings, see *World Almanac and Book of Facts* (New York: Newspaper Enterprise Association, 1977–1979), which took rankings from *Publishers Weekly; Passages* ranked second for nonfiction and fourth for paperbacks in 1976–1977 (see 1978, pp. 421–422).

18. Daniel J. Levinson et al., *The Seasons of a Man's Life* (New York: Alfred A. Knopf, 1978), front cover and pp. 97–101.

19. Margaret Hennig and Anne Jardim, *The Managerial Woman* (Garden City, N.Y.: Anchor Press/Doubleday, 1977), pp. 102, 115, 123, 126, 129–133, 150–153. See also Patricia Fanning, "Manager's Journal," *Wall Street Journal,* 3 April 1978.

20. Harragan, *Games,* pp. 380–381. Kanter, *Men and Women,* pp. 181–184.

21. For instance, William A. Gray and Marilynne Miles Gray, eds., *Mentoring: A Comprehensive Annotated Bibliography of Important References* (Vancouver: International Association for Mentoring, 1986), listed 789 references, with 129 from business alone, 95 mixed including business, 7 mixed without business, 7 from law, 58 from medicine, 395 from education, and 98 from "other" sources An earlier compilation had yielded a similar ratio, with 41 in business management, 34 in professional advancement, 124 in education, and 33 in "other": Ruth B. Noller and Barbara R. Frey, *Mentoring: An Annotated Bibliography* (Buffalo, N.Y.: Bearly Limited, 1983). Most references to "mentor" in the *New York Times* index prior to 1990 pertain to sports or political mentoring, not business.

22. Margaret V. Higginson and Thomas L. Quick, *The Ambitious Woman's Guide to a Successful Career* (New York: AMACOM, 1975), chap. 9; 2nd ed. (1980), chaps. 7 and 10, esp. pp. 125–129.

23. "Women Finally Get Mentors of Their Own," *Business Week,* 23 October 1978, pp. 74, 79–80. See also Georgia Dullea, "On Ladder to Top, Mentor Is Key Step," *New York Times,* 26 January 1981, Style (women's) section; Ruth Halcomb, "Mentors and the Successful Woman," *Across the Board* 17 (February 1980): 13–18. Eliza G. C. Collins and Patricia Scott, "Everyone Who Makes It Has a Mentor," *Harvard Business Review* 56 (July–August 1978): 89–101.

24. Gerard R. Roche, "Much Ado about Mentors," *Harvard Business Review* 57 (January–February 1979): 14–16, 20, 24, 26–28.

25. Bibliographers and others credited the ongoing "resurgence" of interest in mentoring to the influx of women and minorities into the workplace. Gray and Gray, *Mentoring,* p. 55. See also David Marshall Hunt and Carol Michael, "Mentorship: A Career Training and Development Tool," *Academy of Management Review* 8 (1983): 475–485; and Mi-

chael Zey, *The Mentor Connection* (Homewood: Dow Jones Irwin, 1984), p. 3. Sharan Merriam, "Mentors and Protégés: A Critical Review of the Literature," *Adult Education Quarterly* 33 (Spring 1983): 161–173; Ron Zemke, "Cooling Mentormania," *Training* 22 (August 1985): 49.

26. Kanter, *Men and Women*, pp. 181–184; Collins and Scott, "Everyone Who Makes It Has a Mentor." The Collins and Scott study was extensively quoted for years, for instance, in Nancy W. Collins, *Professional Women and Their Mentors* (Englewood Cliffs, N.J.: Prentice Hall, 1983), pp. 95–96, 99–100. Michael Fagan, "The Term *Mentor*: A Review of the Literature and a Pragmatic Suggestion," *International Journal of Mentoring* 2 (Winter 1988): 5–8. See also Agnes K. Missirian, *The Corporate Connection: Why Executive Women Need Mentors to Reach the Top* (Englewood Cliffs, N.J.: Prentice-Hall, 1982).

27. Jonathan P. Hicks, "A Black's Climb to Executive Suite," *New York Times*, 22 May 1987; Caitlin Deinard and Raymond A. Friedman, *Black Caucus Groups at Xerox Corporation (A)*, case study 9-491-047 (Boston: Harvard Business School Publishing Division, 1991); Elizabeth Lesly, "Sticking It Out at Xerox by Sticking Together," *Business Week*, 29 November 1993, p. 77; Lena Williams, "For the Black Professional, the Obstacles Remain," *New York Times*, 15 July 1987; "Xerox Faces New Bias Accusations," *Cincinnati Post Online Edition*, www.cincypost.com, publication 22 March 2002 (accessed 1 August 2003).

28. Rand quotation in Leon E. Wynter and Jolie Solomon, "The New Work Force: A New Push to Break the 'Glass Ceiling,'" *Wall Street Journal*, 15 November 1989; Deinard and Friedman, *Black Caucus Groups at Xerox*, pp. 2–10.

29. Wynter and Solomon, "The New Work Force"; Deinard and Friedman, *Black Caucus Groups at Xerox*, pp. 7–13; Lesly, "Sticking It Out."

30. Jo Freeman, *The Politics of Women's Liberation* (New York: David MacKay Co., 1975), pp. 48, 62–67, 125, 154, 167–168.

31. Kanter, *Men and Women*, pp. 49–67, 181–185, 282; Higginson and Quick, *Ambitious Woman's Guide* (1975), pp. 171–172, 184–185; (1980), pp. 121–125, 210–211, 224–226.

32. Hennig and Jardim, *Managerial Woman*, pp. xii–xvi, 123.

33. Ibid., pp. 161–172.

34. Marcille Gray Williams, *The New Executive Woman* (Radnor, Pa.:

Chilton Book Co., 1977), pp. ix–x, 221–224, chap. 4; Letty Cottin Pogrebin, *Getting Yours: How to Make the System Work for the Working Woman* (New York: David McKay Co., 1975), pp. 3–8, quotations on pp. 6–7.

35. Mary Scott Welch, "How Women Just Like You Are Getting Better Jobs," *Redbook: The Magazine for Young Women,* September 1977, pp. 121, 176–188.

36. V. Dallas Merrell, *Huddling: The Informal Way to Management Success* (New York: AMACOM, 1979). Geraldine R. Eidson, "Threshold to New Horizons," *National Business Woman,* March 1978: 2, 11–13; in Chronological Files, 1978–79, Chandler/HM&L. Jessica Lipnack and Jeffrey Stamps, *Networking: The First Report and Directory* (Garden City, N.Y.: Doubleday and Co., 1982), pp. 1–6; Lipnack and Stamps, *The Networking Book: People Connecting with People* (New York: Routledge and Kegan Paul, 1986), pp. 1–2; Marilyn Ferguson, *The Aquarian Conspiracy: Personal and Social Transformation in the 1980s* (New York: St. Martin's Press, 1987; first published 1980), pp. 62–63, 112, 213–221.

37. Like "mentoring," which entered business and popular lexicons from education, arts, and the social sciences, "networking" entered primarily from anthropology and sociology. Its long use in transportation and communication systems, and its business uses in nonpersonnel contexts, gave it a certain cachet. See J. Clyde Mitchell, "Social Networks," *Annual Review of Anthropology* 3 (1974): 279–299. Regarding current usage, see *Brewer's Dictionary of Twentieth-Century Phrase and Fable,* 1st U.S. ed. (Boston: Houghton Mifflin Co., 1992). John Ayto uses U.S. examples in *Twentieth Century Words* (Oxford: Oxford University Press, 1999), p. 489; Sara Tulloch uses British examples: *Oxford Dictionary of New Words* (Oxford: Oxford University Press, 1991), p. 211; Robert K. Barnhart, Sol Steinmetz, with Clarence L. Barnhart, *Third Barnhart Dictionary of New English* (New York: H. W. Wilson Co., 1990), p. 339. Quotation from N. H. Mager and S. K. Mager, *Prentice-Hall Encyclopedia Dictionary of English Usage* (Englewood Cliffs, N.J.: Prentice-Hall, 1993), p. 252.

38. *Business Periodicals Index* vols. 23–34, 46 (New York: H. W. Wilson Co., 1981–1992, 2004). Some of the earlier books to appear on networking serve as good evidence of its gendered origin—for example, Mary Scott Welch, *Networking: The Great New Way for Women to*

Get Ahead (New York: Harcourt Brace Jovanovich, 1980); and Barbara B. Stern, *Is Networking for You? A Working Woman's Alternative to the Old Boy System* (Englewood Cliffs, N.J.: Prentice-Hall, 1981).

39. Sun Women's Organization, "Proposal for a New Cooperation on the Advancement of Women at Sun," 19 May 1980, pp. 1–2, Box 479.

40. F. J. Roethlisberger and William J. Dickson, *Management and the Worker* (Cambridge, Mass.: Harvard University Press, 1939), p. 354; Nancy J. Weiss, *The National Urban League, 1910–1940* (New York: Oxford University Press, 1974), p. 260; Caroline Bird, *Born Female: The High Cost of Keeping Women Down* (New York: David McKay Co., 1968), pp. 52–59; St. Clair Drake and Horace Cayton, *Black Metropolis: A Study of Negro Life in a Northern City,* quoted by Harold M. Baron in Louis L. Knowles and Kenneth Prewitt, eds., *Institutional Racism in America* (Englewood Cliffs, N.J.: Prentice-Hall, 1969), p. 134. Susan Fraker, "Why Women Aren't Getting to the Top," *Fortune,* 16 April 1984. pp. 40–45. See also Mary Fainsod Katzenstein, "Feminism within American Institutions: Unobtrusive Mobilization in the 1980s," *Signs* 16 (1990): 27–54.

41. Fraker, "Why Women Aren't Getting to the Top"; Margaret Price, "Women Reaching for the Top," *Industrial Week,* 16 May 1983, pp. 38–42.

42. Carol Hymowitz and Timothy D. Schellhardt, "The Glass Ceiling," *Wall Street Journal,* 24 March 1986.

43. Maureen Dowd, "Women in New York Politics Find Fast Track Has Slowed," *New York Times,* 12 August 1986; Jonathan Hicks, "Blacks in Business Get a Tantalizing Glimpse of the Top," *New York Times,* 7 August 1988. *Business Periodicals Index,* vols. 33–34 (1990–1992); the 1992–1993 edition, vol. 35, listed twenty articles under the heading, and new pieces continued to be listed throughout the decade. *New York Times* data from electronic searches on Lexis-Nexis Academic Universe (16 August 2001).

44. Ann M. Morrison et al., *Breaking the Glass Ceiling: Can Women Reach the Top of America's Largest Corporations?* (Reading, Mass.: Addison-Wesley Publishing Co., 1987), pp. 13–14, 24–25, 126. A second, slightly expanded, edition followed in 1992.

45. Susan B. Garland and Lisa Driscoll, "Can the Feds Bust Through the 'Glass Ceiling'?" *Business Week,* 29 April 1991, p. 33; U.S. Department of Labor, *A Report on the Glass Ceiling Initiative* (Wash-

ington, D.C.: U.S. Department of Labor, 1991), pp. 1–5 ; "Glass Ceiling Commission," http://www.ilr.cornell.edu/library/e_archive/gov_ reports/GlassCeiling (accessed 9 July 2001); Federal Glass Ceiling Commission, *Good for Business: Making Full Use of the Nation's Human Capital* (Washington, D.C.: U.S. Department of Labor, 1995), Dole quoted on p. iii.

46. *Report on the Glass Ceiling Initiative,* pp. 13–24. See also Sharon M. Collins, *Black Corporate Executives: The Making and Breaking of a Black Middle Class* (Philadelphia: Temple University Press, 1997), pp. 29–43.

47. Susan B. Garland, "Throwing Stones at the 'Glass Ceiling,'" *Business Week,* 19 August 1991, p. 29.

48. David Braddock and Lynn Bachelder, *The Glass Ceiling and Persons with Disabilities* (Chicago: Institute on Disability and Human Development, University of Illinois at Chicago, 1994), pp. 2, 12–13, 16–17, 23–28. See also Ruth O'Brien, *Crippled Justice: The History of Modern Disability Policy in the Workplace* (Chicago: University of Chicago Press, 2001); Angela D. Johnson, "They Had No Idea What to Say to Me," *DiversityInc* 2 (October–November 2003): 57–61.

49. Glass Ceiling Commission, *Good for Business,* pp. 26–36.

50. Ibid.

51. Carol Hymowitz, "Taking a Chance: Many Blacks Jump Off the Corporate Ladder to Be Entrepreneurs," *Wall Street Journal,* 2 August 1984; Hicks, "A Black's Climb"; Lesly, "Sticking It Out"; and Williams, "For the Black Professional."

52. Hymowitz and Schellhardt, "The Glass Ceiling"; Steven P. Galante, "Venturing Out on Their Own," *Wall Street Journal,* 24 March 1986; Robin Pogrebin, "Ways to Rise Above the 'Glass Ceiling,'" *New York Times,* 14 August 1988; Susan B. Garland, "How to Keep Women Managers on the Corporate Ladder," *Business Week,* 2 September 1991, p. 64; Fraker, "Why Women Aren't Getting to the Top"; Catalyst, *Women Entrepreneurs: Why Companies Lose Female Talent and What They Can Do About It* (New York: Catalyst, 1998), esp. pp. 13–19. On women's moves to entrepreneurship, see Debra Michals, "Beyond 'Pin Money': The Rise of Women's Small Business Ownership, 1945–1980" (Ph.D. diss., New York University, 2002).

53. John P. Fernandez, *Racism and Sexism in Corporate Life: Changing Values in American Business* (Lexington, Mass.: D. C. Heath and Co.,

1981), pp. xxi, 64, 293–294, 296, 298; Ellen J. Wagner, *Sexual Harassment in the Workplace* (New York: AMACOM, 1991), pp. 12–13. See also Lin Farley, *Sexual Shakedown: The Sexual Harassment of Women on the Job* (New York: McGraw-Hill Book Co., 1978), esp. chap. 3. For a detailed exposé of harassment as a means of driving women from the workplace even when they were profit makers, see Susan Antilla, *Tales from the Boom-Boom Room: Women vs. Wall Street* (Princeton, N.J.: Bloomberg Press, 2002).

54. Angel Kwolek-Folland, *Engendering Business: Men and Women in the Corporate Office, 1870–1930* (Baltimore: Johns Hopkins University Press, 1994), esp. pp. 165–168.

55. Catherine A. MacKinnon, *Sexual Harassment of Working Women: A Case of Sex Discrimination* (New Haven: Yale University Press, 1979), pp. 47–55, quotation on p. 55; Gordon Allport, *The Nature of Prejudice* (Garden City, N.Y.: Doubleday Anchor Books, 1958; first ed. 1954), pp. 14–15, 33–35, 41–43, 48–59; Kanter, *Men and Women,* pp. 223–237.

56. Higginson and Quick, *Ambitious Woman's Guide* (1975), pp. 147–149, 158–160; (1980), pp. 129–137.

57. *Business Periodicals Index* 21 (1978–1979); 22 (1979–1980): 1492.

58. For feminist advice, see, for example, Farley, *Sexual Shakedown,* esp. chap. 5; Ruth Halcomb, *Women Making It: Patterns and Profiles of Success* (New York: Ballantine Books, 1979), pp. 47–48; Harragan, *Games,* p. 319; Higginson and Quick, *Ambitious Woman's Guide* (1980), pp. 129–134. "Can't You Take a Joke?" *National Business Woman* 65 (June–July 1984): 17.

59. Linda K. Kerber and Jane Sherron De Hart, eds., *Women's America: Refocusing the Past* (New York: Oxford University Press, 1995), pp. 601–603; Barbara Lindemann and David D. Kadue, *Primer on Sexual Harassment* (Washington, D.C.: Bureau of National Affairs, 1992) pp. 1–5, 38–46; Susan Gluck Mezey, *In Pursuit of Equity: Women, Public Policy, and the Federal Courts* (New York: St. Martin's Press, 1992), pp. 166–179; Wagner, *Sexual Harassment,* pp. 17–19. For more extensive discussions, see Martha Chamallas, "Writing about Sexual Harassment: A Guide to the Literature," *UCLA Women's Law Journal* 4 (Fall 1993): 37–58; Farley, *Sexual Shakedown;* MacKinnon, *Sexual Harassment;* and Deborah L. Rhode, *Justice and Gender: Sex Discrim-*

ination and the Law (Cambridge, Mass.: Harvard University Press, 1989), pp. 230–236.

60. Editorial, "Pull Down the Pinups, Raze the Glass Ceiling," *Business Week,* 18 March 1991, p. 140.

61. Collins, *Black Corporate Executives,* esp. chap. 8; James E. Ellis, "The Black Middle Class," *Business Week,* 14 March 1988, p. 62; Ulwyn L. J. Pierre, *The Myth of Black Corporate Mobility* (New York: Garland Publishing, 1998). In 1996, Texaco agreed to the largest racial discrimination settlement to date, $140 million in a federal lawsuit. Kurt Eichenwald, "Texaco to Make Record Payout in Bias Lawsuit," *New York Times,* 16 November 1996. Antilla, *Tales from the Boom-Boom Room; Good for Business,* pp. 26–36, quotation on p. 36.

62. Oren Arnold, *The Golden Strand: An Informal History of the Rotary Club of Chicago* (Chicago: Quadrangle Books, 1966), illustration opp. p. 153.

63. Lawrence Otis Graham, *Member of the Club: Reflections on Life in a Racially Polarized World* (New York: HarperCollins, 1995), pp. xiv–xvi, chap. 1. *New York* magazine first published Graham's story as a cover article, "Invisible Man," in 1992. For earlier practices of discrimination in private clubs, see James M. Mayo, *The American Country Club* (New Brunswick, N.J.: Rutgers University Press, 1998), pp. 19, 192–193.

64. Scott quoted in Rhode, *Justice and Gender,* p. 404n2. Gwendolyn M. Parker, *Trespassing: My Sojourn in the Halls of Privilege* (Boston: Houghton Mifflin Co., 1997), pp. 154–157.

65. Kanter, *Men and Women,* pp. 226–227, 266–267.

66. "Private Clubs and the Racial Issue," *U.S. News and World Report,* 29 January 1962, pp. 45–46; "Bias by Clubs Attacked by Carolina Legislators," *New York Times,* 13 March 1987; "Pressing Country Clubs to Accept Blacks," *New York Times,* 3 February 1991; Mayo, *American Country Club,* pp. 176–177, 194, 197. Oscar Suris, "GM's Smith, Losh Quit Exclusive Club as Black Official Is Denied Membership," *Wall Street Journal,* 21 October 1994.

67. Lynette Holloway, "What? No Husband?" *New York Times,* 16 August 1993; Marcia Chambers, "Seeking Fairness on the Fairways," *New York Times,* 28 March 1997. David Rynecki, "Golf and Power: Inside the Secret Refuge of the Business Elite," *Fortune* 147 (14 April

2003): 164–174. See also Martha Burk, *Cult of Power: Sex Discrimination in Corporate America and What Can Be Done about It* (New York: Scribner, 2005). As chair of the National Council of Women's Organizations, Burk challenged sex discrimination at the Augusta National Golf Club, emphasizing the handicap it imposes on women for success in business and other arenas.

68. Ruth Bader Ginsburg, "Women as Full Members of the Club: An Evolving American Ideal," *Human Rights* 6 (1977): 1–21; "Public Controversy over Private Clubs," *National Business Woman* 65 (June–July 1984): 12–13; Sonia L. Nazario, "Gentlemen of the Club," *Wall Street Journal*, 24 March 1986; Deborah L. Rhode, "Private Clubs and Public Values," *Stanford Lawyer* 22 (1987): 14–22; Rhode, *Justice and Gender*, pp. 279–285.

69. Cynthia A. Leiferman, "Private Clubs: A Sanctuary for Discrimination?" *Baylor Law Review* 40 (Winter 1988): 71–112; Mezey, *In Pursuit of Equality*, pp. 200–204; Rhode, *Justice and Gender*, pp. 279–282; Phillip S. Dingle, "Controversy at the Club," *Florida Bar Journal* 64 (1990): 10–15.

70. Sue Avery, "High Court Says Rotary Can't Exclude Women: A Matter of Survival, Not Rights," *Los Angeles Times*, 5 May 1987; David G. Savage, "High Court Says Rotary Can't Exclude Women: Upholds California Law Curbing Sex Bias," *Los Angeles Times*, 5 May 1987; Stuart Taylor Jr., "High Court Rules that Rotary Clubs Must Admit Women," *New York Times*, 5 May 1987; Taylor, "Justices Back New York Law Ending Sex Bias by Big Clubs," *New York Times*, 21 June 1988. Bruce Geelhoed, *The Rotary Club of Indianapolis, 1913–1998: A Club, a Community, and a Century* (Carmel, Ind.: Guild Press of Indiana, 2000), pp. ix, 169–177.

8. Social Tools for Self-Help

1. My ranking of book titles is based on an electronic library catalog subject search on 10 March 2003 of the Baker Library at Harvard Business School, the New York Public Research Libraries, and the Library of Congress. For examples of books from this period, see Kathleen Kelley Reardon, *The Secret Handshake: Mastering the Politics of the Business Inner Circle* (New York: Currency/Doubleday, 2000); and Wayne Baker, *Achieving Success through Social Capital: Tapping the Hidden*

Resources in Your Personal and Business Networks (San Francisco: Jossey-Bass/Wiley, 2000).

2. Adam Bellow, "In Praise of Nepotism," *Atlantic Monthly,* July–August 2003, pp. 98–105. For evidence of decreasing U.S. socioeconomic mobility, see Alan B. Krueger, "The Apple Falls Close to the Tree, Even in the Land of Opportunity," *New York Times,* 14 November 2002. Recent studies show that people who endorse meritocracy support affirmative action to the degree that they perceive ongoing discrimination. Faye J. Crosby, *Affirmative Action Is Dead; Long Live Affirmative Action* (New Haven: Yale University Press, 2004), pp. 232–233. For arguments on behalf of affirmative action, see Barbara R. Bergman, *In Defense of Affirmative Action* (New York: HarperCollins Publishers, 1996); Michael K. Brown et al., *Whitewashing Race: The Myth of a Color-Blind Society* (Berkeley: University of California Press, 2003); Gertrude Ezorsky, *Racism and Justice: The Case for Affirmative Action* (Ithaca, N.Y.: Cornell University Press, 1991).

3. Gail Sheehy, *Passages: Predictable Crises of Adult Life* (New York: P. Dutton and Co., 1974), p. 227. Each of the following authors also noted the newness of the term "networking" and women's growing awareness of this ancient practice: Carol Kleiman, *Women's Networks: The Complete Guide to Getting a Better Job, Advancing Your Career, and Feeling Great as a Woman through Networking* (New York: Lippincott and Crowell, 1980), p. xiii; Mary Scott Welch, *Networking: The Great New Way for Women to Get Ahead* (New York: Harcourt Brace Jovanovich, 1980), p. 5; Barbara B. Stern, *Is Networking for You? A Working Woman's Alternative to the Old Boy System* (Englewood Cliffs, N.J.: Prentice-Hall, 1981), p. 2; Dawn-Marie Driscoll and Carol R. Goldberg, *Members of the Club: The Coming of Age of Executive Women* (New York: Free Press/Macmillan, 1993), pp. 5–7.

4. Carol Hymowitz, "Sisterhood, Inc.," *Wall Street Journal,* 31 August 1979; Meg Cox, "Manager's Journal: Courses for Women," *Wall Street Journal,* 1 October 1979.

5. Jeffrey Goldberg, "D.C. Women Overcome Barriers: An 'Old Girls' Network' Aids Female Entrepreneurs," *Washington Post,* 11 July 1988; Camille Lavington with Stephanie Losee, *You've Only Got Three Seconds: How to Make the Right Impression in Your Business and Social Life* (New York: Main Street Books/Doubleday, 1997), pp. xvi, 12–14, 190–199; Jane White, *A Few Good Women: Breaking*

the Barriers to Top Management (Englewood Cliffs, N.J.: Prentice Hall, 1992).

6. Driscoll and Goldberg, *Members of the Club,* pp. xii–xv. Carter A. Daniel, *MBA: The First Century* (Lewisburg, Pa.: Bucknell University Press, 1998), pp. 198, 260. "The Voice of *Working Women* Speaks for You," *National Business Woman* 67 (June–July 1986): 23; *Women's Enterprise,* online version, http://womens-enterprise.com (accessed 22 May 2000); Committee of 200, www.c200.org (accessed 26 May 2000); "Welcome to the LPGA Golf Clinics for Women," www.jbcgolf .com and www.lpga.com/news/index.cfm?cont_id=17526 (accessed 10 August 2003). Myra Marx Ferree and Patricia Yancey Martin, eds., *Feminist Organizations: Harvest of the New Women's Movement* (Philadelphia: Temple University Press, 1995). For a sampling of articles, see Cynthia Davis, "Advancement by Association," *National Business Woman* 67 (June–July 1986): 18–19; and Jennifer Casper, "For Women Entrepreneurs, It's Networking That Works: Local Groups Provide Expertise, Friendship," *Washington Post,* 18 June 1990.

7. Lois Kathryn Herr, *Women, Power, and AT&T: Winning Rights in the Workplace* (Boston: Northeastern University Press, 2003), pp. 158–159; Herr, "Mentoring Circles—The First Year," typescript for presentation, 9 July 1991, LKH; Herr, "Guidelines for Participants in Mentoring," typewritten handout, 1 October 1991, LKH; Herr, "Mentoring Circles," typescript for presentation, 29 May 2001, LKH; Kathy E. Kram, *Mentoring at Work* (Lanham, Md.: University Press of America, 1988).

8. Catalyst, www.catalystwomen.org (accessed 26 May 2000). Examples of Catalyst's Glass Ceiling Commission publications include *Cracking the Glass Ceiling: Strategies for Success* (1994); *Women in Corporate Leadership: Progress and Prospects* (1996); *Women of Color in Corporate Management: Dynamics of Career Advancement* (1998); *Women of Color in Corporate Management: Opportunities and Barriers* (1999); *Creating Women's Networks: A How-To Guide for Women and Companies* (1999); *Women of Color in Corporate Management: Three Years Later* (2002); all (New York: Catalyst).

9. Dagmar McGill et al., "Empowering Women: Achieving Change through Advocacy Networks" (1983), accession 89-289; Sarah Harder, "Advocacy Networks: New Strength for the Women's Move-

ment," reprinted from *Graduate Woman*, November–December 1981: 19–22; Peg Downey, "Organizational Networking: The Power of Co-operation," February 1983; all in vertical files, AAUW Archive.

10. *Fellows Network: A Newsletter for Fellowship and Grant Recipients* 1 (Summer 1983), AAUW Educational Foundation; "Take Time for Net-working," *Leader in Action* 1 (Spring 1982): 10; annual programs for 25–29 June 1983, 13–14 July 1985, 22–25 June 1991, 22–27 June 1995; all in vertical files, AAUW Archive.

11. Elizabeth Lesly and Maria Mallory, "Inside the Black Business Net-work," *Business Week*, 29 November 1993, pp. 70–72, 77, 80–81, Savage quotation on p. 72. Sheryl Hilliard, "Smashing the Glass Ceil-ing," *Black Enterprise* 21 (August 1990): 99–108, Thomas quotation on p. 108. For case studies from many ethnicities, see John Sibley But-ler, *Entrepreneurship and Self-Help among Black Americans: A Re-consideration of Race and Economics* (Albany: State University of New York, 1991); Scott Cummings, ed., *Self-Help in Urban America: Patterns of Minority Business Enterprise* (Port Washington, N.Y.: Na-tional University Publications, 1980). For analysis augmented by mul-tiple autobiographies of successful native-born males from several non-majority ethnicities, see Donna E. Thompson and Nancy DiTomaso, eds., *Ensuring Minority Success in Corporate Management* (New York: Plenum Press, 1988). Almost all of the essays include social capital as a factor in each writer's explanations of success and failure.

12. Earl G. Graves, "Remembering Leaders and Mentors," *Black Enter-prise* 16 (January 1986): 9; Graves, *How to Succeed in Business with-out Being White* (New York: HarperBusiness, 1997), pp. 31–34, 39–58, 113; Donette Dunbar, "Twenty Years of Making Contacts," *Black Enterprise* 21 (August 1990): 31; Lesly and Mallory, "Inside the Black Business Network," p. 80.

13. Raymond A. Friedman and Donna Carter, *African American Network Groups: Their Impact and Effectiveness* (Washington, D.C.: Executive Leadership Council, 1993), pp. 1–3. Friedman and Caitlin Deinard, *Black Caucus Groups at Xerox Corporation (A),* (Boston: Harvard Business School, 1991); Leon E. Wynter and Jolie Solomon, "The New Work Force: A New Push to Break the 'Glass Ceiling,'" *Wall Street Journal*, 15 November 1989. Jonathan P. Hicks, "A Black's Climb to the Executive Suite," *New York Times*, 22 May 1987. See also David A. Thomas and John J. Gabarro, *Breaking Through: The Making of*

Minority Executives in Corporate America (Boston: Harvard Business School Press, 1999), pp. 2, 57; Graves, *How to Succeed in Business without Being White,* pp. 56, 256.

14. Friedman and Carter, *African American Network Groups,* pp. 1, 6–14; Rosabeth Moss Kanter and Barry A. Stein, *A Tale of "O": On Being Different,* VHS video (Cambridge, Mass.: Goodmeasure, 1979); Catalyst, *Cracking the Glass Ceiling,* p. 50; George Davis and Glegg Watson, *Black Life in Corporate America: Swimming in the Mainstream* (Garden City, N.Y.: Anchor Press/Doubleday, 1982), pp. 4–5.

15. Lawrence Otis Graham, *Our Kind of People: Inside America's Black Upper Class* (New York: HarperCollins Publishers, 1999), pp. 14, 84–85, 102–108, 125.

16. Ibid., pp. 14–15, 127–129, 148–150. Thomas W. Dortch Jr., *The Miracles of Mentoring: How to Encourage and Lead Future Generations* (New York: Broadway Books/Random House, 2000).

17. Dunbar, "Twenty Years of Making Contacts"; National Minority Supplier Development Council, www.nmsdcus.org (accessed 28 June 2000). Daniel, *MBA,* p. 186; www.nbmba.org (accessed 23 August 2003). Crawford B. Bunkley, *The African American Network* (New York: Penguin Books, 1996).

18. Kris Hudson, "Area Indian Professionals Form TiE," *Rocky Mountain News,* 14 October 2000; www.tie.org (accessed 3 September 2003).

19. GlobalMecca.com, www.globalmecca.com/mentor.html (accessed 19 December 1999; site not operative by 23 August 2003).

20. Ann E. Tanneyhill, "The Elk—the Masons—the Shrine," memo to Vernon E. Jordan Jr., 24 January 1973; "Cultivation of Women's Clubs," confidential memo to Jordan, 28 November 1973; both Part III, box 306, folder 11, NUL.

21. *"All We Need Is a Helping Hand": A Look at the Urban League's OJT Program in Akron, Ohio* (New York: National Urban League, 1972), pp. 7, 11–23, 30; Part III, box 281, folder 11, NUL.

22. David R. Crain and W. W. Charters, *Personal Leadership in Industry* (New York: McGraw-Hill Book Co., 1925), chaps. 4 and 15, quotations on pp. 210, 212. General Electric's Management Leadership Program included some class time but emphasized individualized "personal apprenticeships." A. V. Feigenbaum and H. W. Tulloch, "Management Apprenticeships," in M. Joseph Dooher and Vivienne Marquis, eds., *The Development of Executive Talent: A Handbook of*

Management Development Techniques and Case Studies (New York: American Management Association, 1952), pp. 100–108, quotations on p. 100.

23. Anne Jardim and Margaret Hennig, "The Last Barrier," *Working Woman* 15 (November 1990): 130–134, 164; Basia Hellwig, "The Breakthrough Generation: Seventy-Three Women Ready to Run Corporate America," *Working Woman* 10 (April 1985): 98–101, 146–150; Federal Glass Ceiling Commission, *Good for Business: Making Full Use of the Nation's Human Capital* (Washington, D.C.: U.S. Department of Labor, 1995), p. 8.

24. For an example of standard recommendations for formalization, see Charles A. Durakis, "Making the New Executive a Team Member," *Personnel* 62 (October 1985): 58–60. David Clutterbuck, "How Much Does Career Success Depend on a Helping Hand from Above?" *International Management* 37 (April 1982): 17–19. Charles D. Orth III and Frederic Jacobs, "Women in Management: Pattern for Change," *Harvard Business Review* 49 (July–August 1971): 139–147.

25. Rosabeth Moss Kanter, *Men and Women of the Corporation* (New York: Basic Books, 1977), pp. 267–281.

26. Thompson and DiTomaso, *Ensuring Minority Success,* pp. 19, 347–355, 364–365, 375–377. See also Catalyst, *Successful Initiatives for Breaking the Glass Ceiling to Upward Mobility for Minorities and Women* (New York: Catalyst, 1993), pp. 15–26.

27. Graham and his informants also advised "the minority job hunter" to join and be active in minority business groups and conferences. Lawrence Otis Graham, *The Best Companies for Minorities* (New York: Plume Books/Penguin Group, 1993), pp. xvii–xxii, xxv, xxvii, xxx–xxxi, 424–427, 431–437.

28. Glass Ceiling Commission, *Good for Business,* pp. 38–56, quotations on pp. 46, 54; U.S. Department of Labor, *The Glass Ceiling Initiative: Are There Cracks in the Ceiling?* (Washington, D.C.: U.S. Government Printing Office, 1997), pp. 14–18. Michael Roper points out that in Britain, too, "mentoring has become an issue in attempts to redress [gender] inequalities." *Masculinity and the British Organization Man since 1945* (Oxford: Oxford University Press, 1994), p. 99.

29. Carol Hymowitz, "Tradition-Bound Alcoa Develops Training to Challenge Concern's Old-Boy Networks," *Wall Street Journal,* 15 November 1983; C. Stone Brown, "Affirmative Action and Beyond,"

DiversityInc 2 (October–November 2003): 67–68. On diversity management, see the journal *DiversityInc,* founded in 2002; the affiliated Web site, www.diversityinc.com, was launched in 1998. Erin Kelly and Frank Dobbin, "How Affirmative Action Became Diversity Management: Employer Response to Antidiscrimination Law, 1961–1996," *American Behavioral Scientist* 41 (1998): 960–984; American Institute for Managing Diversity, www.aimd.org/.

30. Kram, *Mentoring at Work,* pp. 4, 194–200. See also Murray H. Reich, "Executive Views from Both Sides of Mentoring," *Personnel* 62 (March 1985): 42–46; "Mentoring Process Works Best When It Is Kept Informal, Finds Study," *Management Review* 73 (June 1984): 55; Margo Murray, *Beyond the Myths and Magic of Mentoring: How to Facilitate an Effective Mentoring Process* (San Francisco: Jossey-Bass, 1st ed. 1991, rev. ed. 2001). For examples of praise for the impact of mentoring, see Dortch, *The Miracles of Mentoring;* Marc Freedman, *The Kindness of Strangers: Adult Mentors, Urban Youth, and the New Voluntarism* (San Francisco: Jossey-Bass, 1993; and Jack Cavanaugh, "Help for Students: Business Mentors," *New York Times,* 18 December 1988.

31. Cynthia DeReimer, "Mentors: What They Can (and Can't) Do," *Essence* 11 (December 1980): 34, 39, 42; Ruth B. Noller and Barbara R. Frey, *Mentoring: An Annotated Bibliography* (Buffalo, N.Y.: Bearly Limited, 1983), p. 2. On problems related to mentoring relationships, see Leslie Aldridge Westoff, "Mentor or Lover?" *Working Woman* 11 (October 1986): 116–119; Reich, "Executive Views"; Peter Kizilos, "Take My Mentor, Please!" *Training* 27 (April 1990): 49–55; Thomas F. O'Boyle, "Mentor-Protégé Ties Can Be Strained," *New York Times,* 12 June 1990; and Selwyn Feinstein, "Women and Minority Workers in Business Find a Mentor Can Be a Rare Commodity," *Wall Street Journal,* 10 November 1987. On the limitations that women begin to discern in synthetic networking, see Meg Cox, "Clearer Connections: The Nebulous 'Networks' of the '70s Give Way to Pragmatic Business Contacts," *Wall Street Journal,* 24 March 1986; "Networking: Getting Past the Clichés," *National Business Woman* 62 (January–February 1981): 12–13.

32. Marc Freedman and Rachel Baker, *Workplace Mentoring for Youth: Context, Issues, Strategies* (Washington, D.C.: Academy for Educa-

tional Development, 1995), pp. 7–12; Friedman and Carter, *African American Network Groups,* p. 4; Herminia Ibarra, "Personal Networks of Women and Minorities in Management: A Conceptual Framework," *Academy of Management Review* 18 (January 1993): 56–87. Alvin N. Puryear and Charles A. West, *Black Enterprise, Inc.: Case Studies of a New Experiment in Black Business Development* (Garden City, N.Y.: Anchor Books, 1973), pp. 44–45, 401–402.

33. David A. Thomas reviewed many studies in "The Impact of Race on Managers' Experiences of Developmental Relationships (Mentoring and Sponsorship): An Intra-Organizational Study," *Journal of Organizational Behavior* 11 (1990): 479–492. See also Kram, *Mentoring at Work,* p. 199; Barbara Ettorre, "Breaking the Glass, or Just Window Dressing?" *Management Review* 81 (March 1992): 16–22.

34. Michael Fagan, "The Term *Mentor:* A Review of the Literature and a Pragmatic Suggestion," *International Journal of Mentoring* 2 (Winter 1988): 4–8; Freedman and Baker, *Workplace Mentoring,* pp. 7–8; Sharan Merriam, "Mentors and Protégés: A Critical Review of the Literature," *Adult Education Quarterly* 33 (Spring 1983): 161–173. William A. Gray, "Formalized Mentoring," *Canadian Public Administration* 29 (Winter 1986): 636–638; Westoff, "Mentor or Lover?"; Kizilos, "Take My Mentor, Please!" p. 55; Kram, *Mentoring at Work,* pp. 160–167; Karen Matthes, "Corporate Mentoring: Beyond the Blind Date," *HR Focus* 68 (November 1991): 23; Murray, *Beyond the Myths and Magic* (2001 ed.), pp. 191–198; Ronald J. Burke and Carol A. McKeen, "Developing Formal Mentoring Programs in Organizations," *Business Quarterly* 53 (Winter 1989): 76–79; Thompson and DiTomaso, *Ensuring Minority Success,* p. 367.

35. Thomas and Gabarro, *Breaking Through,* pp. 214, 230. See also Gary R. Schornack, "Mentorship Theory and Current Practice: A Study of Executives in the Greater Denver Region," *International Business and Economics Research Journal* 1 (December 2002): 15–25. Kram, *Mentoring at Work,* pp. 173–186. Florence M. Stone, *Coaching, Counseling, and Mentoring: How to Choose and Use the Right Technique to Boost Employee Performance* (New York: AMACOM, 1999), pp. 160–162.

36. Kanter, *Men and Women of the Corporation,* p. 280; Herr, *Women, Power, and AT&T,* pp. 158–159; Herr, "Mentoring Circles—The First

Year"; Herr, "Guidelines for Participants in Mentoring"; Herr, "Mentoring Circles"; overhead slides for "Welcome to the Association of Management Women" Mentoring Circle Program (ca. 1991), LKH.

37. Bill Sharp, *How to Be Black and Get a Job in the Advertising Agency Business Anyway* (Bethesda, Md.: Bill Sharp, 1969), p. 41; Davis and Watson, *Black Life in Corporate America,* pp. 2–3, 86.

38. The study usually gave separate data for African-American, Hispanic, and Asian-American women. Catalyst, *Women of Color in Corporate Management: Dynamics of Career Advancement* (New York: Catalyst, 1998), quotations on pp. 9, 11. See also Ibarra, "Personal Networks." Those whom some accuse of holding their jobs as affirmative-action beneficiaries, such as the African-American woman quoted here, began their careers believing in the ideals of meritocracy. Another corporate feminist, although grown cynical about office politics and social capital dynamics, dedicated her 1980 book "To meritocrats, both male and female." Helen J. McLane, *Selecting, Developing, and Retaining Women Executives: A Corporate Strategy for the Eighties* (New York: Van Nostrand Reinhold Co., 1980), p. v.

39. Lavington with Losee, *You've Only Got Three Seconds,* p. xiii; Carroll D. Murphy, "The Man for the Job," in [n.a.,] *Handling Men* (Chicago: A. W. Shaw Company, 1917), pp. 31–32.

40. Claude M. Steele, "Thin Ice: 'Stereotype Threat' and Black College Students," *Atlantic,* August 1999, pp. 44–54; Laurie A. Rudman and Peter Glick, "Prescriptive Gender Stereotypes and Backlash toward Agentic Women," *Journal of Social Issues* 57 (2001): 743–762; Monica Biernat and Melvin Manis, "Shifting Standards and Stereotype-Based Judgment," *Journal of Personality and Social Psychology* 66 (1994): 5–20; Biernat, "Gender and Height: Developmental Patterns in Knowledge and Use of an Accurate Stereotype," *Sex Roles* 29 (1993): 691–713.

41. Harvard School of Public Health, "National Mentoring Month," www.hsph.harvard.edu/chc/mentoringmonth (accessed 28 January 2002). Freedman, *Kindness of Strangers,* pp. 3–7, 34–38. See also Jean Rhodes, "Finding the Right Mentors," *New York Times on the Web,* www.nytimes.com/2001/04/02/opinion/02Rhod.html (accessed 2 April 2001).

42. Flyer in author's possession, National Coalition of Employers, "Networking Job Fair," Denver, Colo., 14 October 1999.

43. Henry Etzkowitz, Carol Kemelgor, and Brian Uzzi, *Athena Unbound:*

The Advancement of Women in Science and Technology (New York: Cambridge University Press, 2000), esp. pp. 115–130; Steven Shapin, *A Social History of Truth: Civility and Science in Seventeenth-Century England* (Chicago: University of Chicago Press, 1994). Stereotypes that work against women in science reemerged as a high-profile issue in January 2005. One consequence has been a resurgence of institutionalized efforts to reduce "push" discrimination and to synthesize pull on women's behalf. Sara Rimer, "For Women in Sciences, Slow Progress in Academia," *New York Times*, 15 April 2005.

44. Roland Owens, "A Black Scientist Shares His Keys to Success," *Science: Next Wave,* http://nextwave.sciencemag.org/cgi/content/full/2001/02/28/13 (accessed 20 August 2003); Brigid Schulte, "One Doctor Tries to Change the Establishment from the Inside," *Detroit Free Press,* 4 August 1998; Roland Owens, e-mail message to author, 19 August 2003; Carla Garnett, "Black Scientists Association Marks Tenth Anniversary," http://www.nih.gov/nihrecord/08_31_2004/story 01.htm (accessed 11 October 2004). See also National Academy of Sciences, *Adviser, Teacher, Role Model, Friend: On Being a Mentor to Students in Science and Engineering* (Washington, D.C.: National Academy Press, 1997).

45. A venerable example is the Nancy Lyman Roelker Mentorship Award, established by the American Historical Assocation in 1991 because "mentoring is as important to the discipline of history as fine scholarship and good teaching." http://www.historians.org/prizes/awarded/RoelkerWinner.htm (accessed 7 May 2005). A search on Google.com (7 May 2005) for "mentor" and "award" produced 5 million links.

46. American Academy of Management, http://aom.pace.edu/meetings/2002 (accessed 4 December 2001). See also Wayne E. Baker, *Networking Smart: How to Build Relationships for Personal and Organizational Success* (New York: McGraw-Hill, 1994); Baker, *Achieving Success;* Chip R. Bell, *Managers as Mentors: Building Partnerships for Learning* (San Francisco: Berrett-Koehler Publishers, 1996). A business book club ranked *Networking Smart* among the top thirty business books of 1994.

47. Max Messmer, "Mentoring: Building Your Company's Intellectual Capital," *HR Focus* 75 (September 1998): S11–S12. See also D. Jack Hensler, "Mentoring at the Management Level," *Industrial Management* 36 (November–December 1994): 20–21. Stone, *Coaching, Coun-*

seling, and Mentoring, p. 159. The survey results are in Schornack, "Mentorship Theory and Current Practice." William M. Mulkeley and Wailin Wong, "Six Degrees of Exploitation? New Programs Help Companies 'Mine' Worker Relationships for Business Prospects," *Wall Street Journal Online,* http://online.usj.com (accessed 4 August 2003).

48. Sherwood Ross, "Schmoozers Thrive as Workplace Barriers Fall," Reuters online, americaonline.com (accessed 31 August 2000).

49. Richard Wiseman, *The Luck Factor: Changing Your Luck, Changing Your Life* (New York: Miramax Books, 2003). "Managing Your Business: Even Top Executives Can Use Guidance from Mentors," *St. Petersburg Times,* 14 July 2003. See also Deborah Gibbons and Paul Olk, "Individual and Structural Origins of Friendship and Social Position among Professionals," *Journal of Personality and Social Psychology* 84 (2003): 340–351.

50. Kathleen Kelley Reardon, a management professor, exposed the "politics of the business inner circle" by which "political savvy" trumps technical competence for success. Her criteria for entry into the "exclusive club" do not mention race (neither does the index to her book), although the constraints of gender on success do merit a section, and she hedges that gatekeepers do favor their "own kind." Reardon, *Secret Handshake,* pp. vii, xv, 1, 173, 190–192, 196, 251. See also Susan L. Abrams, *The New Success Rules for Women* (Roseville, Calif.: Prima Publishing, 2000), chap. 7. The book jacket blurbs for Chip R. Bell's 1996 book, *Managers as Mentors,* describe the volume as an essential guide for managers to use in developing fundamental skills on which their own and their firms' successes could depend. Bell sums up mentoring as a "two-way relationship" that should teach "through consultation and affection," and that the practice involves building kinlike ties with high degrees of trust. Throughout, he assumes that the social distances between people can be readily shortened. More to the point, Bell rules out a pair of "leadership challenges[:] . . . the poor performer and . . . protégés with special mentoring needs"—what he calls "diversity situations." Falling back on the old notion that only those with obvious potential are appropriate candidates for mentors, Bell rejects the use of mentoring for "correction" or to "*fix* a performance problem or a discrepancy." He relegates the use of mentoring as an "affirmative action tool for remedying disparities in opportunity for the disadvantaged or for groups such as ethnic minorities who are underrepre-

sented" into the general category of "special mentoring programs." Integrating strangers is not part of Bell's mission for "the actual process of effective mentoring." Instead, his amused nostalgia for old-boy privilege contrasts with his disdain for affirmative action efforts that use mentoring to break through glass ceilings. These "politically correct" efforts, he asserts, must be "scraped away" for one to see the true core of mentoring. Bell, *Managers as Mentors,* book jacket, pp. x–xi, xiv, xvii, 6, 19. Two books by Wayne E. Baker, a business school professor of organizational behavior, bracket the ongoing dismissal of social capital's history. Baker's *Networking Smart: How to Build Relationships for Personal and Organizational Success* (1994) was a best seller among business titles. A full chapter proposed "managing diversity" as a "powerful competitive force," describing diversity in terms of ethnicity and gender. In contrast, his later book, *Achieving Success through Social Capital: Tapping the Hidden Resources in Your Personal and Business Networks* (2000), included only a sampling of women's and minority males' experiences, and no indication of the role they played in uncovering social capital. The index in Baker's earlier book contained references to ten pages on the glass ceiling and methods of eliminating it, while the index in the later book contained no such references. Baker began his 1994 chapter on diversity with a discussion of the African-American caucuses at Xerox, and he included several other references to their importance as early models of best practices. The later book has no chapter on diversity, and only two paragraphs on the Xerox caucuses. By 2000, Baker was defining diversity as the variety of "external ties" by which individuals can measure their social capital. In keeping with the times, his "practical, step-by-step guide to assessing your social capital, building your social capital, and using your social capital" divorced social capital from its history. Baker, *Networking Smart,* pp. 146–162, 364; Baker, *Achieving Success,* pp. xiii–xvi, 3–4, 39–40, 80, 91, 119–120, 123–124.

51. For instance, the American Management Association's 2003 guide, *Cracking the Corporate Code,* aims to eliminate "the demons of race and gender," but at the same time intends to be useful to all ambitious people, alerting them to "unwritten rules." Price M. Cobbs and Judith L. Turnock, *Cracking the Corporate Code: The Revealing Success Stories of Thirty-Two African-American Executives* (New York: AMACOM, 2003), pp. ix, xi, chap. 4. Earl Graves's 1997 advice in

How to Succeed in Business without Being White could just as easily be included in a book entitled simply *How to Succeed in Business.* Robert L. Crandall, "Foreword," in Graves, *How to Succeed in Business without Being White,* p. xviii.

52. As an example of ongoing concerns, see Glenn C. Loury, "Discrimination in the Post–Civil Rights Era: Beyond Market Interactions," *Journal of Economic Perspectives* 12 (Spring 1998): 117–126.

Index